# MIDNIGHTER

## ASSASSIN8

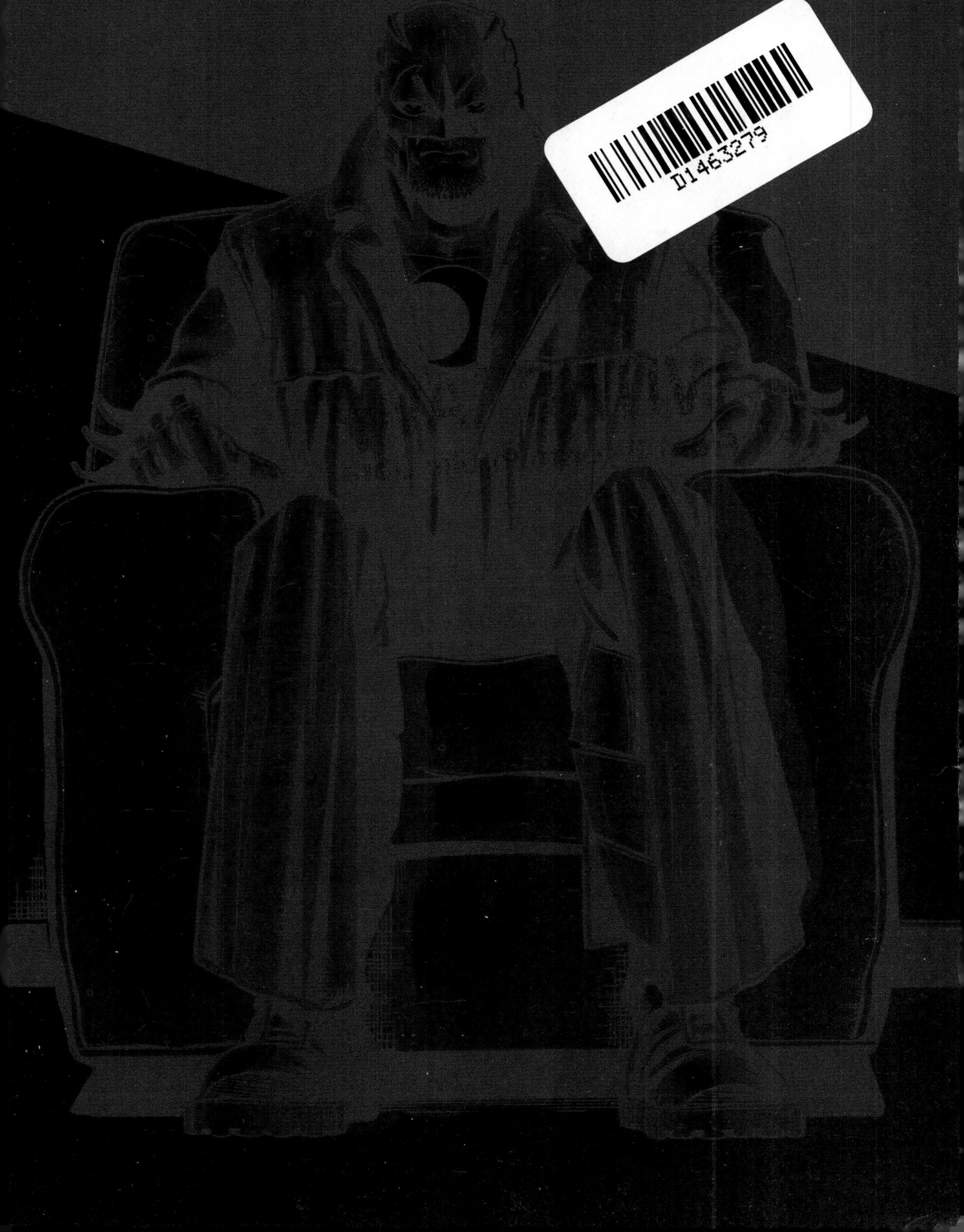

## ASSASSIN8

**Writer: Keith Giffen**
**Artists: Lee Garbett and Rick Burchett**
Colorists: Gabe Eltaeb and WildStorm FX
Letterers: Steve Wands with Sal Cipriano (#18)

## ORDINARY PEOPLE

**Writer: Christos Gage**
**Artist: John Paul Leon**
Colorists: Randy Mayor and Jonny Rench
Letterer: Phil Balsman

## THE HERCULES VIRUS

**Writers: Jimmy Palmiotti and Justin Gray**
**Artist: Brian Stelfreeze**
Colorist: Randy Mayor
Letterer: Phil Balsman

Collected Edition Cover and Original Series Covers (#16-20)
by Lee Garbett, Trevor Scott & Randy Mayor
Original Series Covers (#8-9)
by Chris Sprouse and Karl Story
with Randy Mayor

Jim Lee, Editorial Director
Scott Peterson and Scott Dunbier, Editors–Original Series
Scott Peterson, Editor–Collected Edition
Kristy Quinn, Assistant Editor
Ed Roeder, Art Director
Paul Levitz, President & Publisher
Georg Brewer, VP–Design & DC Direct Creative
Richard Bruning, Senior VP–Creative Director
Patrick Caldon, Executive VP–Finance & Operations
Chris Caramalis, VP–Finance
John Cunningham, VP–Marketing
Terri Cunningham, VP–Managing Editor
Amy Genkins, Senior VP–Business & Legal Affairs
Alison Gill, VP–Manufacturing
David Hyde, VP–Publicity
Hank Kanalz, VP–General Manager, WildStorm
Gregory Noveck, Senior VP–Creative Affairs
Sue Pohja, VP–Book Trade Sales
Steve Rotterdam, Senior VP–Sales & Marketing
Cheryl Rubin, Senior VP–Brand Management
Alysse Soll, VP–Advertising & Custom Publishing
Jeff Trojan, VP–Business Development, DC Direct
Bob Wayne, VP–Sales

978-1-4012-2001-3

SFI CERTIFIED SOURCING
FIBER USED IN THIS PRODUCT LINE MEETS THE SOURCING REQUIREMENTS OF THE SFI PROGRAM
WWW.SFIPROGRAM.ORG
PWC-SFICOC-260

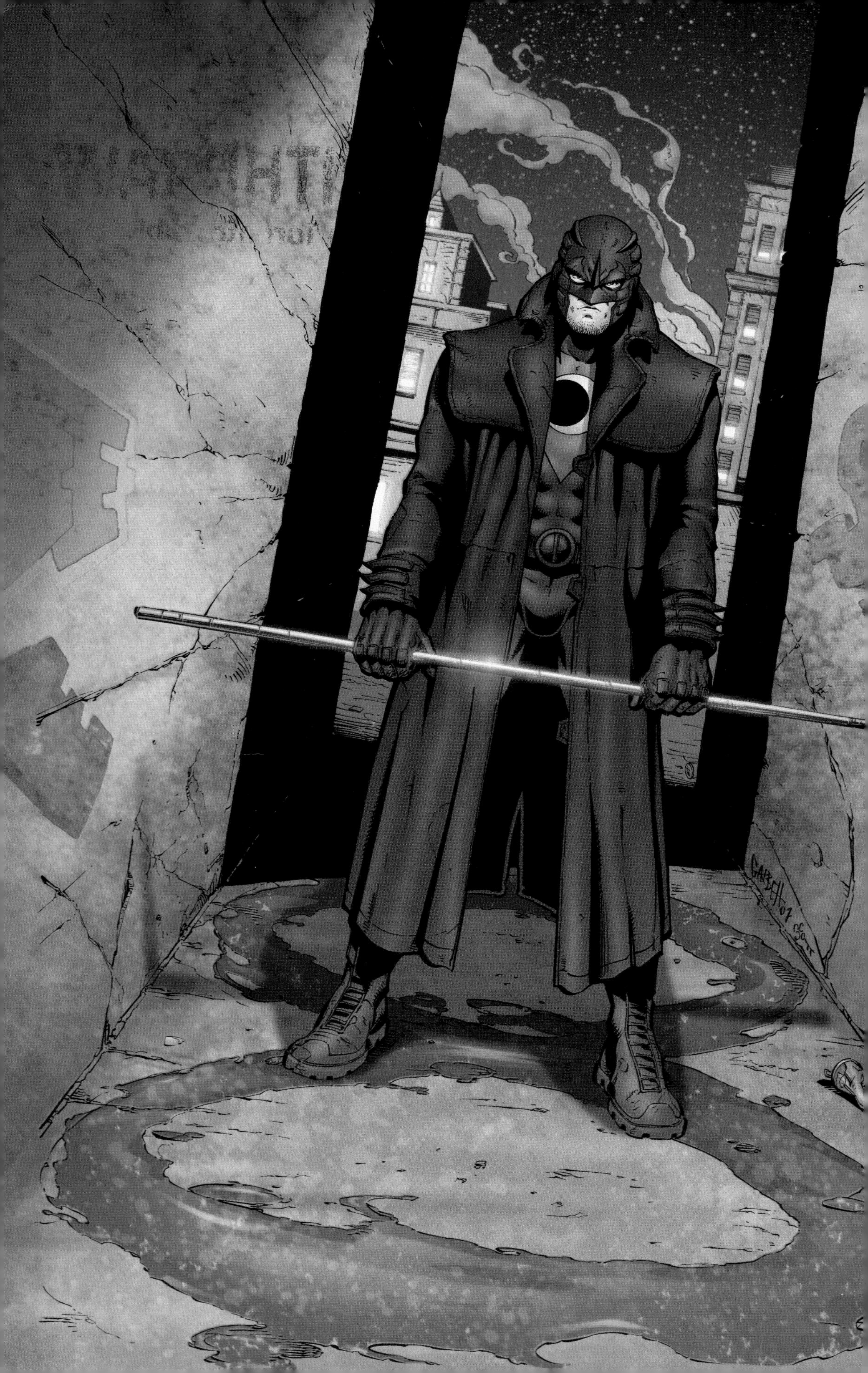

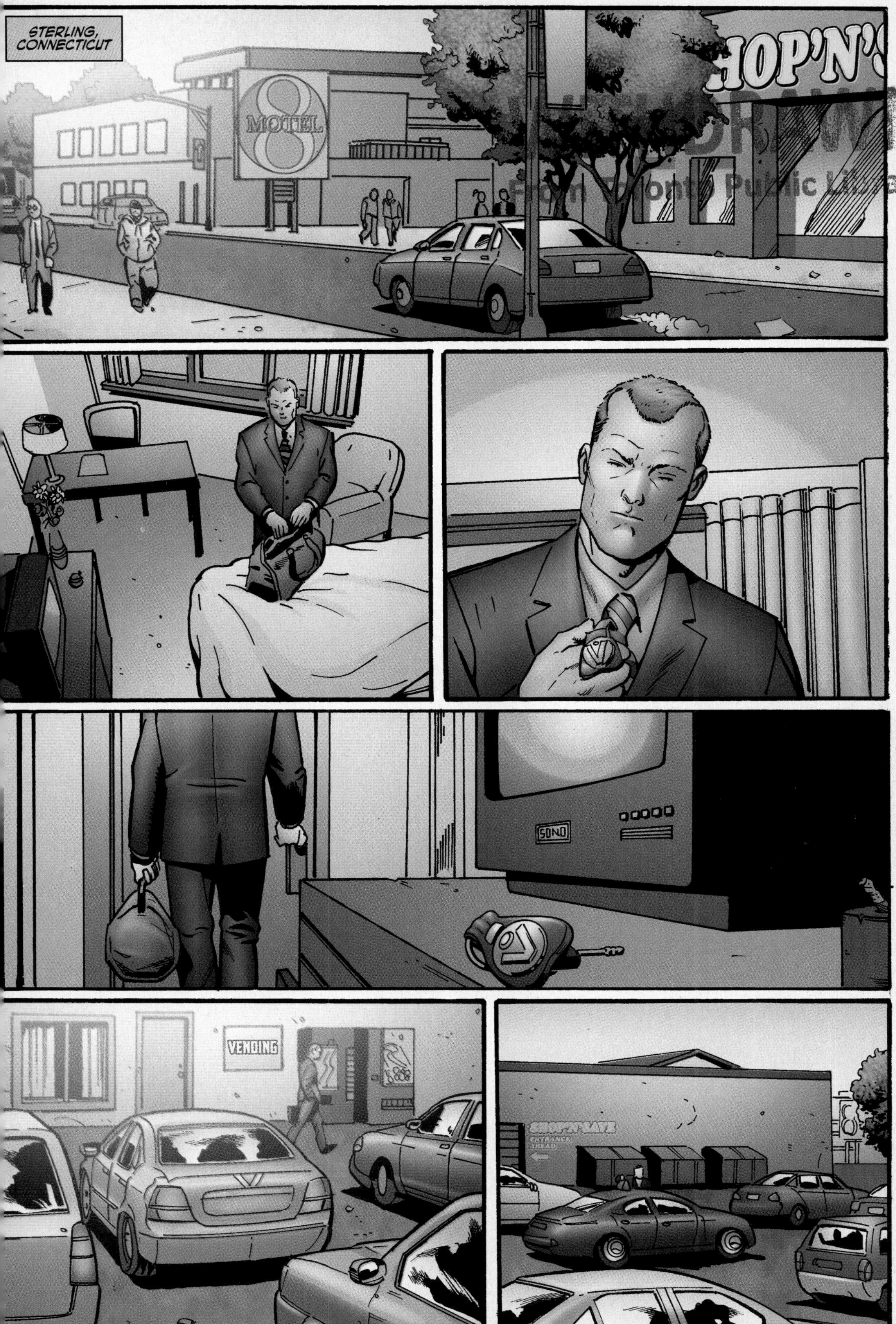
STERLING, CONNECTICUT
MOTEL
HOP'N'S
SONO
VENDING
SHOP'N'SAVE
ENTRANCE AHEAD

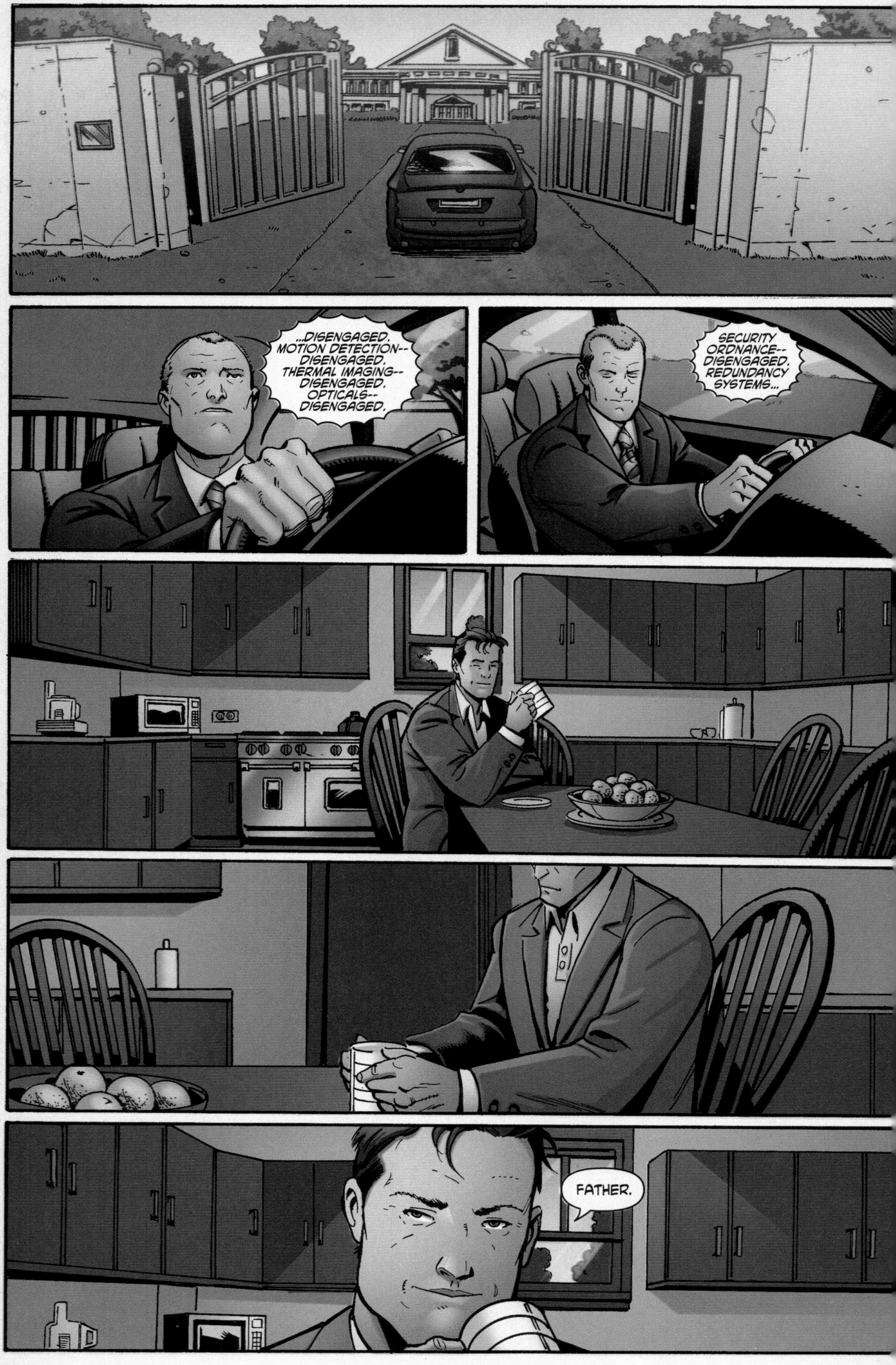
...DISENGAGED. MOTION DETECTION-- DISENGAGED. THERMAL IMAGING-- DISENGAGED. OPTICALS-- DISENGAGED.
SECURITY ORDNANCE-- DISENGAGED. REDUNDANCY SYSTEMS...
FATHER.

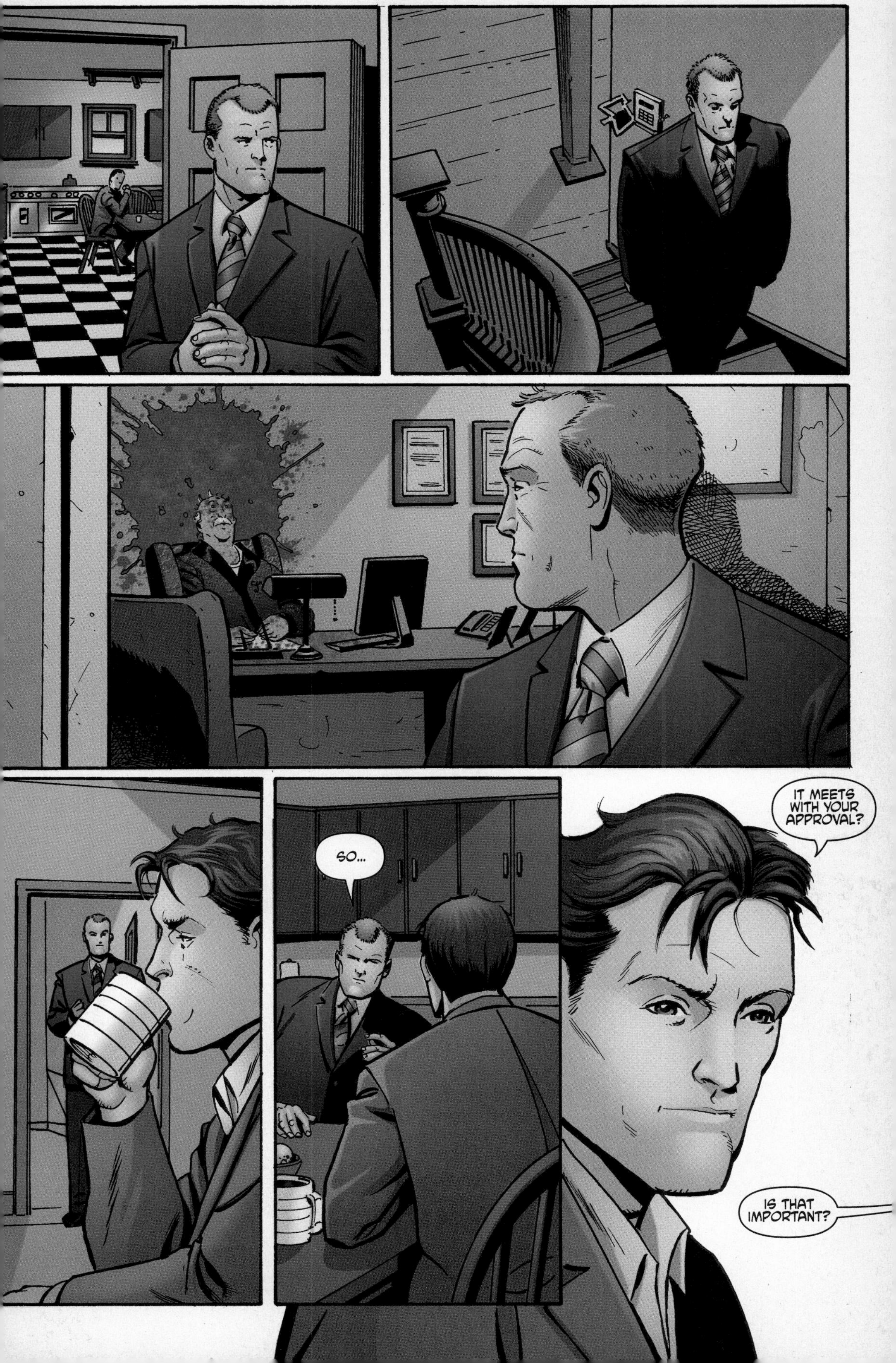
SO...
IT MEETS WITH YOUR APPROVAL?
IS THAT IMPORTANT?

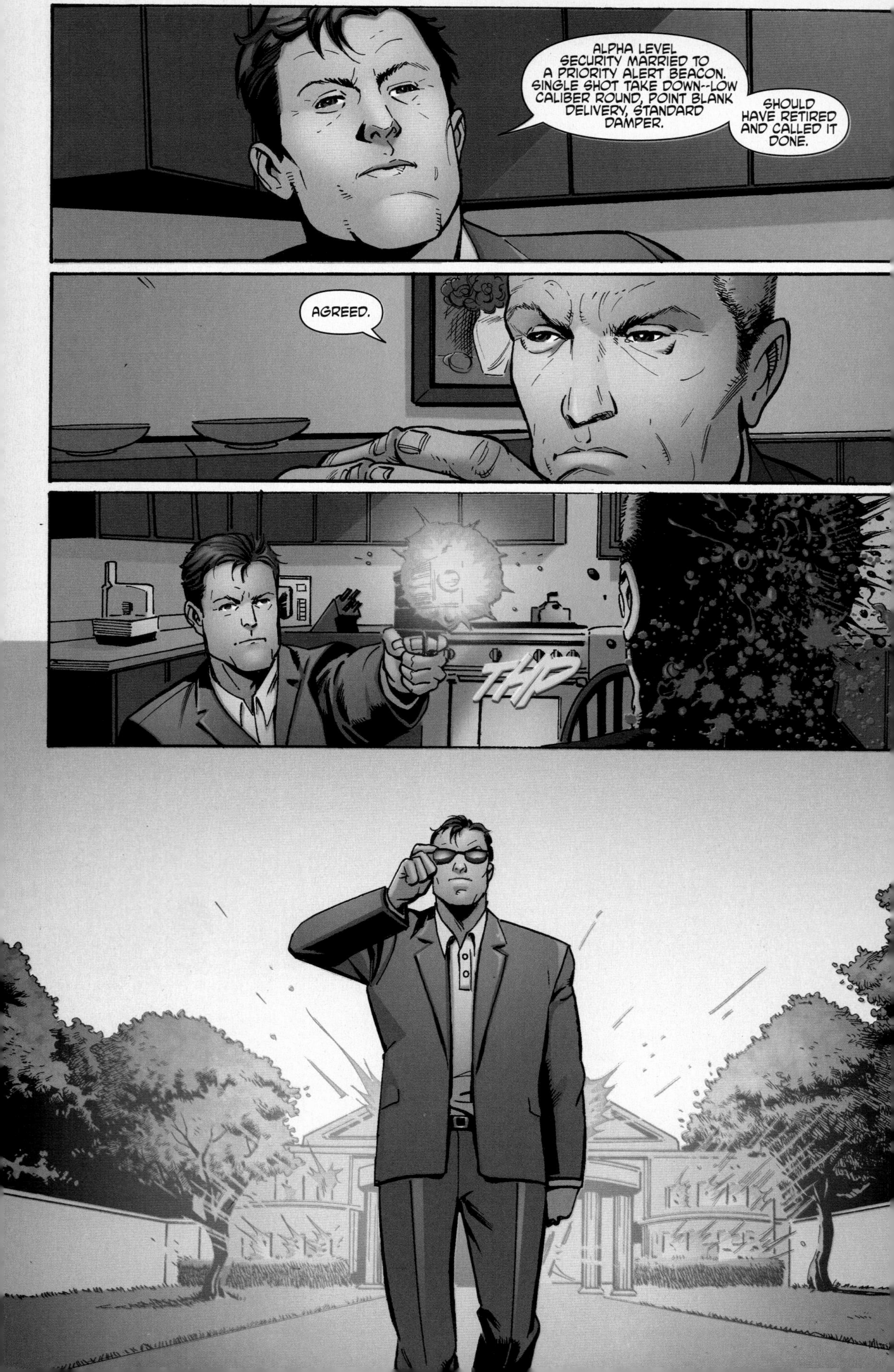
ALPHA LEVEL SECURITY MARRIED TO A PRIORITY ALERT BEACON. SINGLE SHOT TAKE DOWN--LOW CALIBER ROUND, POINT BLANK DELIVERY, STANDARD DAMPER.
SHOULD HAVE RETIRED AND CALLED IT DONE.
AGREED.
THP

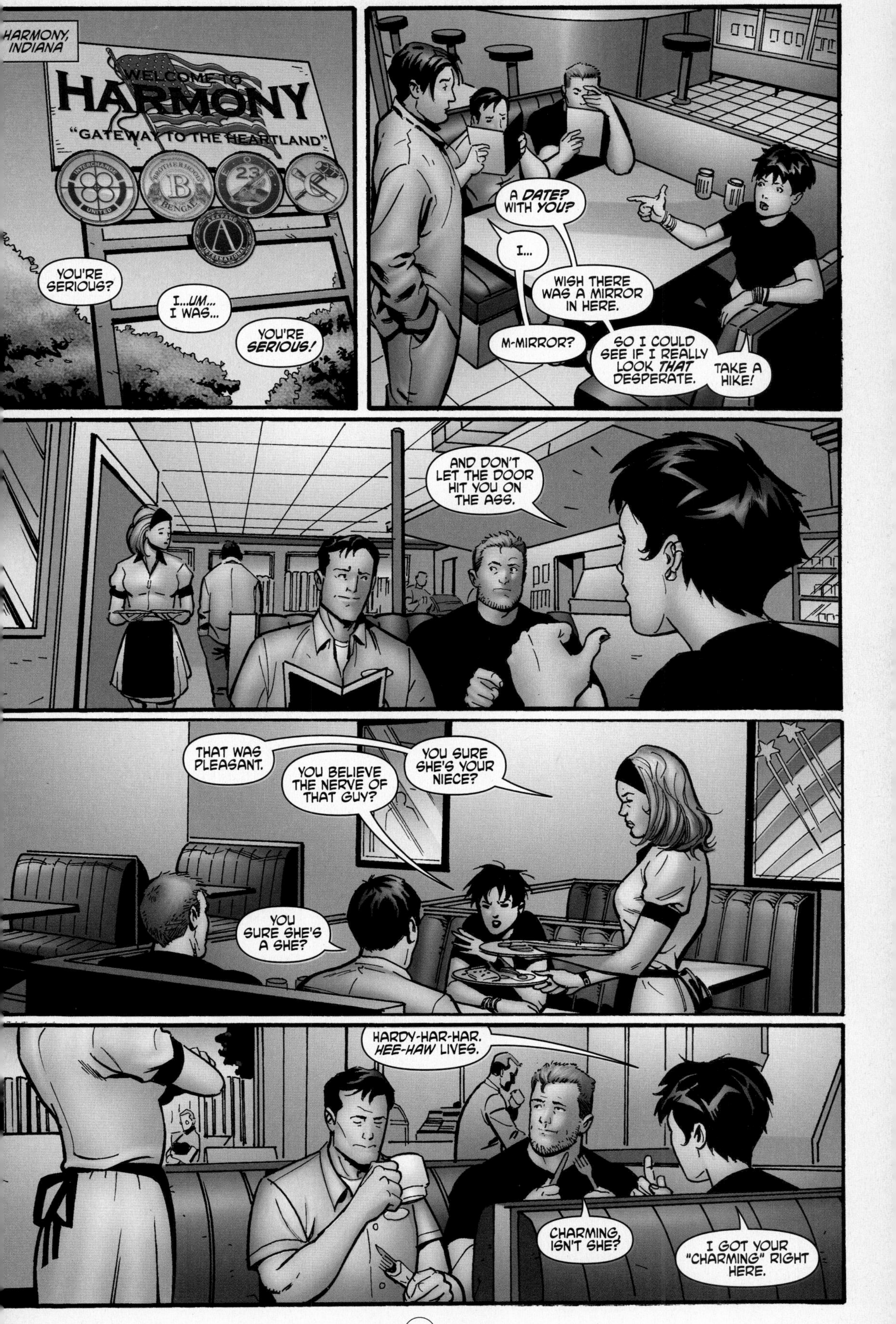
HARMONY, INDIANA
WELCOME TO
HARMONY
"GATEWAY TO THE HEARTLAND"
YOU'RE SERIOUS?
I...*UM*... I WAS...
YOU'RE *SERIOUS!*
A *DATE?* WITH *YOU?*
I...
WISH THERE WAS A MIRROR IN HERE.
M-MIRROR?
SO I COULD SEE IF I REALLY LOOK *THAT* DESPERATE.
TAKE A HIKE!
AND DON'T LET THE DOOR HIT YOU ON THE ASS.
THAT WAS PLEASANT.
YOU SURE SHE'S YOUR NIECE?
YOU BELIEVE THE NERVE OF THAT GUY?
YOU SURE SHE'S A SHE?
HARDY-HAR-HAR. *HEE-HAW* LIVES.
CHARMING, ISN'T SHE?
I GOT YOUR "CHARMING" RIGHT HERE.

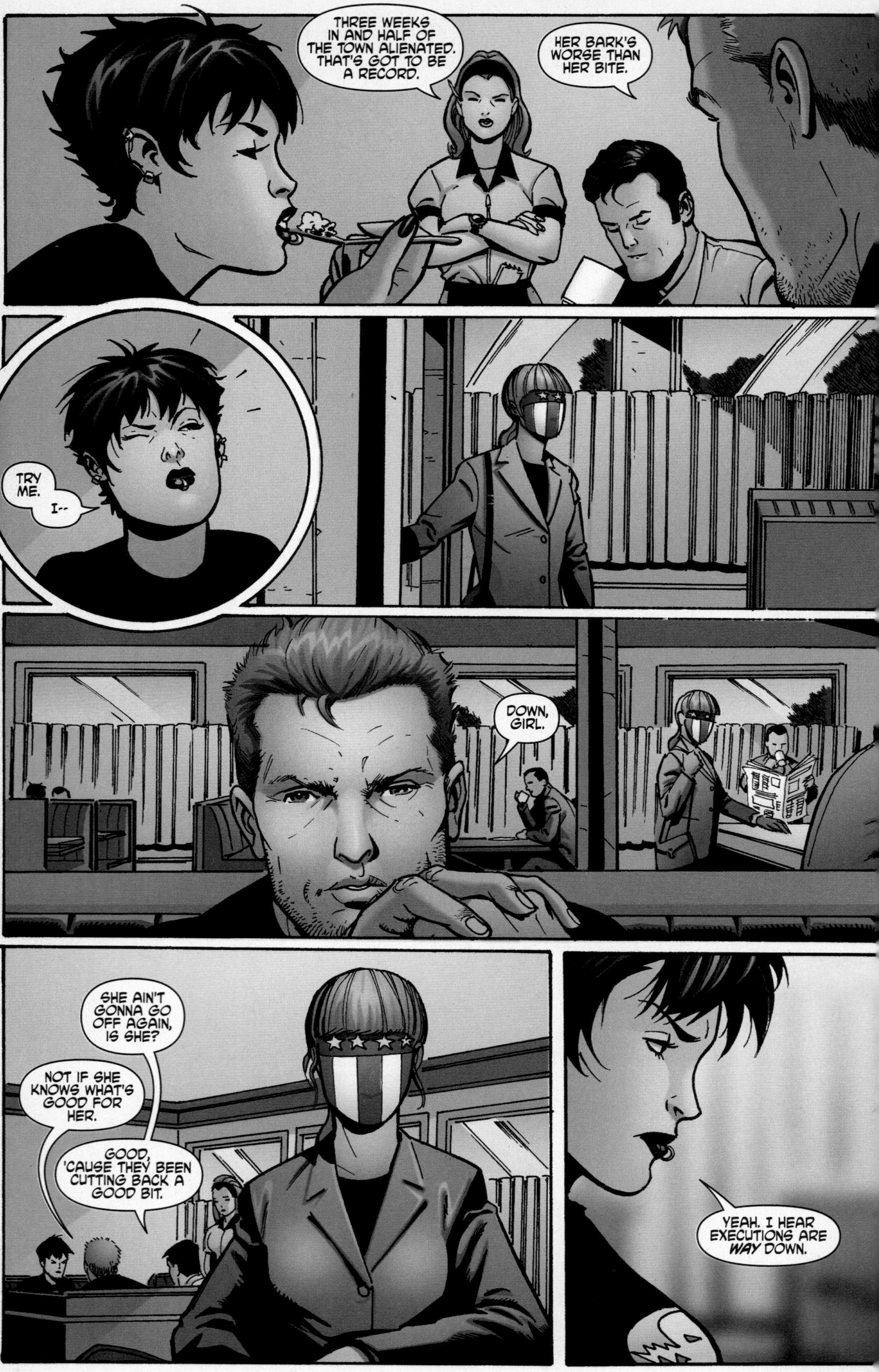
THREE WEEKS IN AND HALF OF THE TOWN ALIENATED. THAT'S GOT TO BE A RECORD.
HER BARK'S WORSE THAN HER BITE.
TRY ME.
I--
DOWN, GIRL.
SHE AIN'T GONNA GO OFF AGAIN, IS SHE?
NOT IF SHE KNOWS WHAT'S GOOD FOR HER.
GOOD, 'CAUSE THEY BEEN CUTTING BACK A GOOD BIT.
YEAH. I HEAR EXECUTIONS ARE *WAY* DOWN.

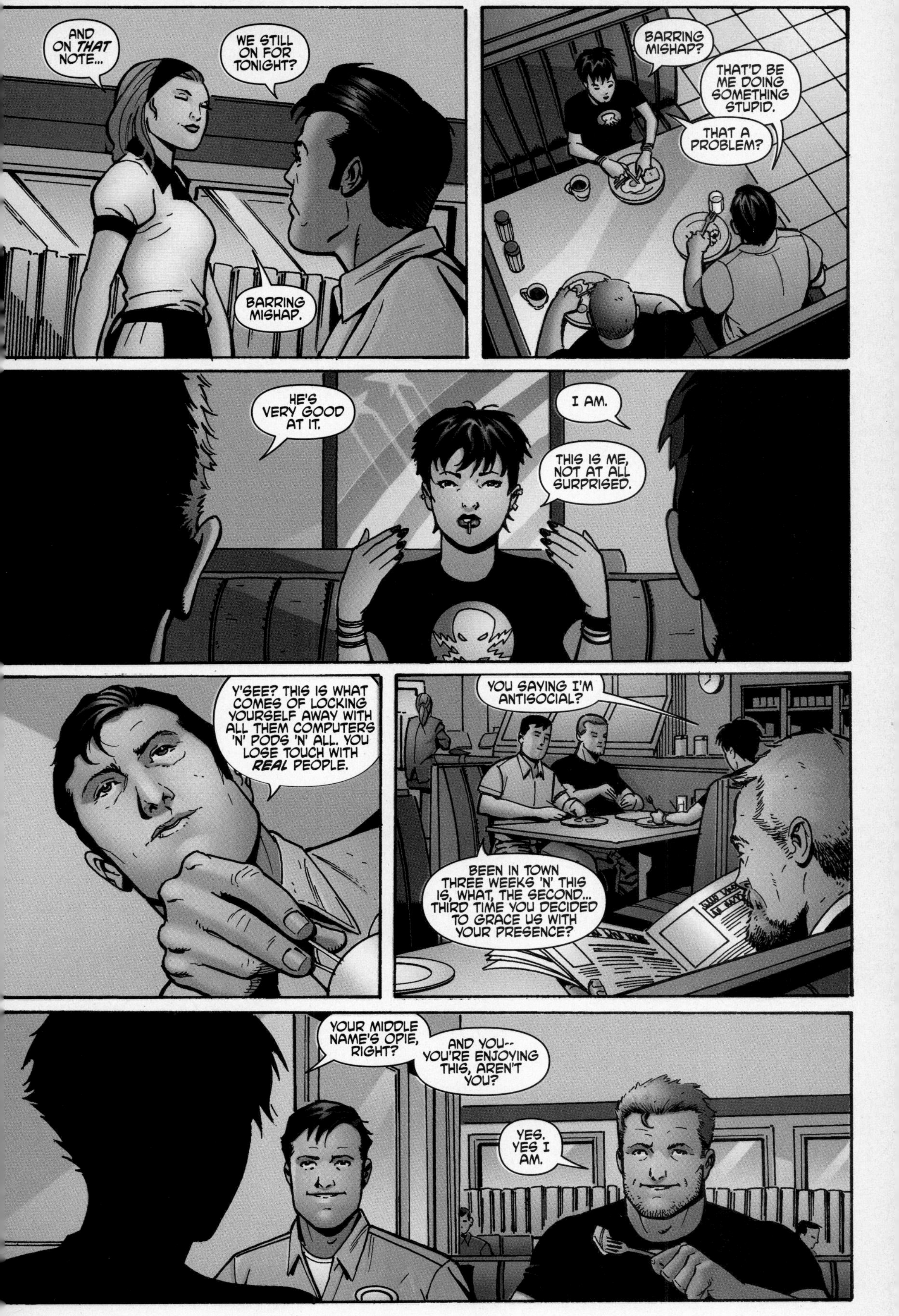
AND ON *THAT* NOTE...
WE STILL ON FOR TONIGHT?
BARRING MISHAP.
BARRING MISHAP?
THAT'D BE ME DOING SOMETHING STUPID.
THAT A PROBLEM?
HE'S VERY GOOD AT IT.
I AM.
THIS IS ME, NOT AT ALL SURPRISED.
Y'SEE? THIS IS WHAT COMES OF LOCKING YOURSELF AWAY WITH ALL THEM COMPUTERS 'N' PODS 'N' ALL. YOU LOSE TOUCH WITH *REAL* PEOPLE.
YOU SAYING I'M ANTISOCIAL?
BEEN IN TOWN THREE WEEKS 'N' THIS IS, WHAT, THE SECOND... THIRD TIME YOU DECIDED TO GRACE US WITH YOUR PRESENCE?
YOUR MIDDLE NAME'S OPIE, RIGHT?
AND YOU-- YOU'RE ENJOYING THIS, AREN'T YOU?
YES. YES I AM.

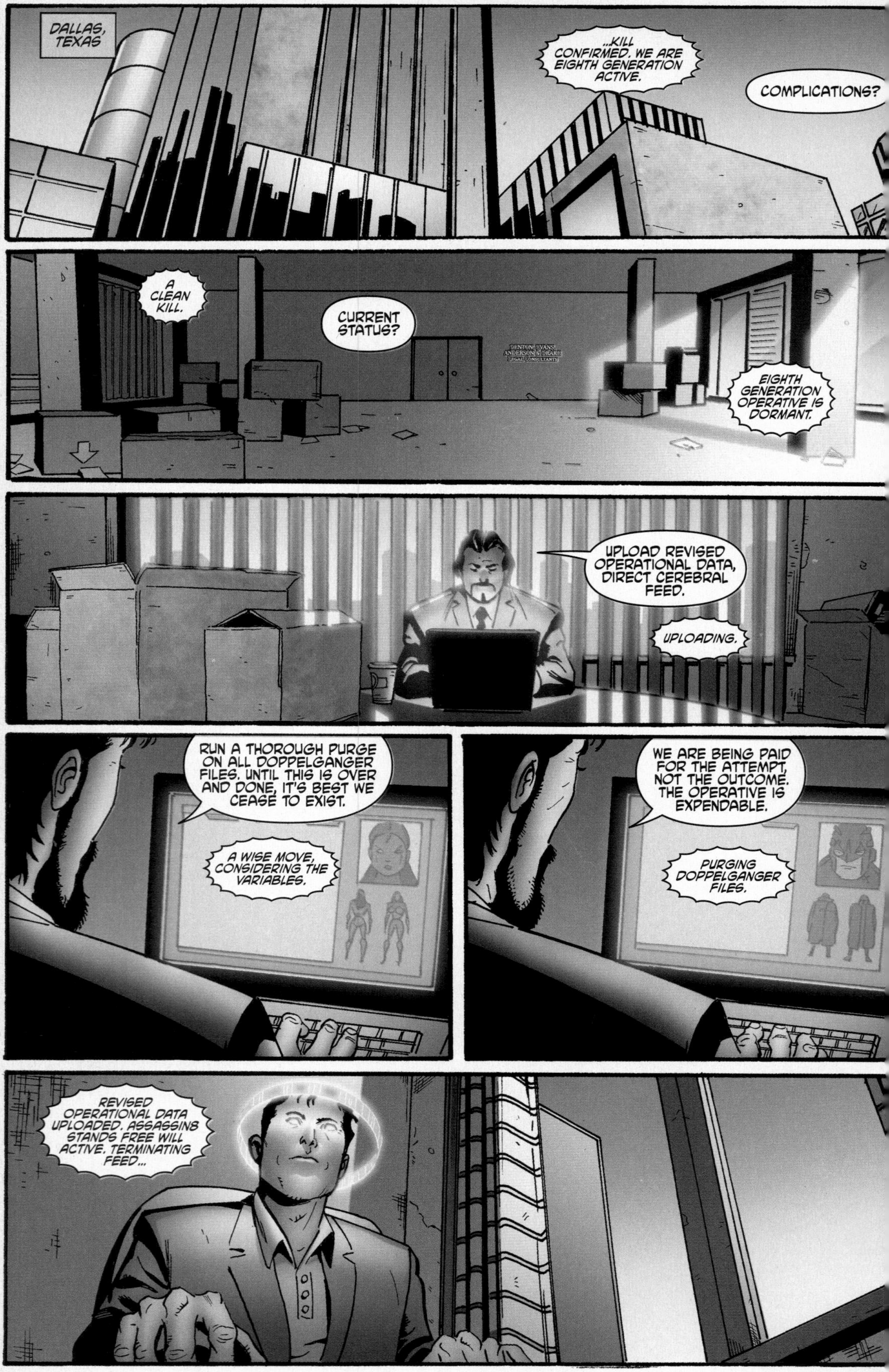
DALLAS, TEXAS
...KILL CONFIRMED. WE ARE EIGHTH GENERATION ACTIVE.
COMPLICATIONS?
A CLEAN KILL.
CURRENT STATUS?
DENTON EVANS ANDERSON & DRAKE LEGAL CONSULTANTS
EIGHTH GENERATION OPERATIVE IS DORMANT.
UPLOAD REVISED OPERATIONAL DATA, DIRECT CEREBRAL FEED.
UPLOADING.
RUN A THOROUGH PURGE ON ALL DOPPELGANGER FILES. UNTIL THIS IS OVER AND DONE, IT'S BEST WE CEASE TO EXIST.
A WISE MOVE, CONSIDERING THE VARIABLES.
WE ARE BEING PAID FOR THE ATTEMPT, NOT THE OUTCOME. THE OPERATIVE IS EXPENDABLE.
PURGING DOPPELGANGER FILES.
REVISED OPERATIONAL DATA UPLOADED. ASSASSIN8 STANDS FREE WILL ACTIVE. TERMINATING FEED...

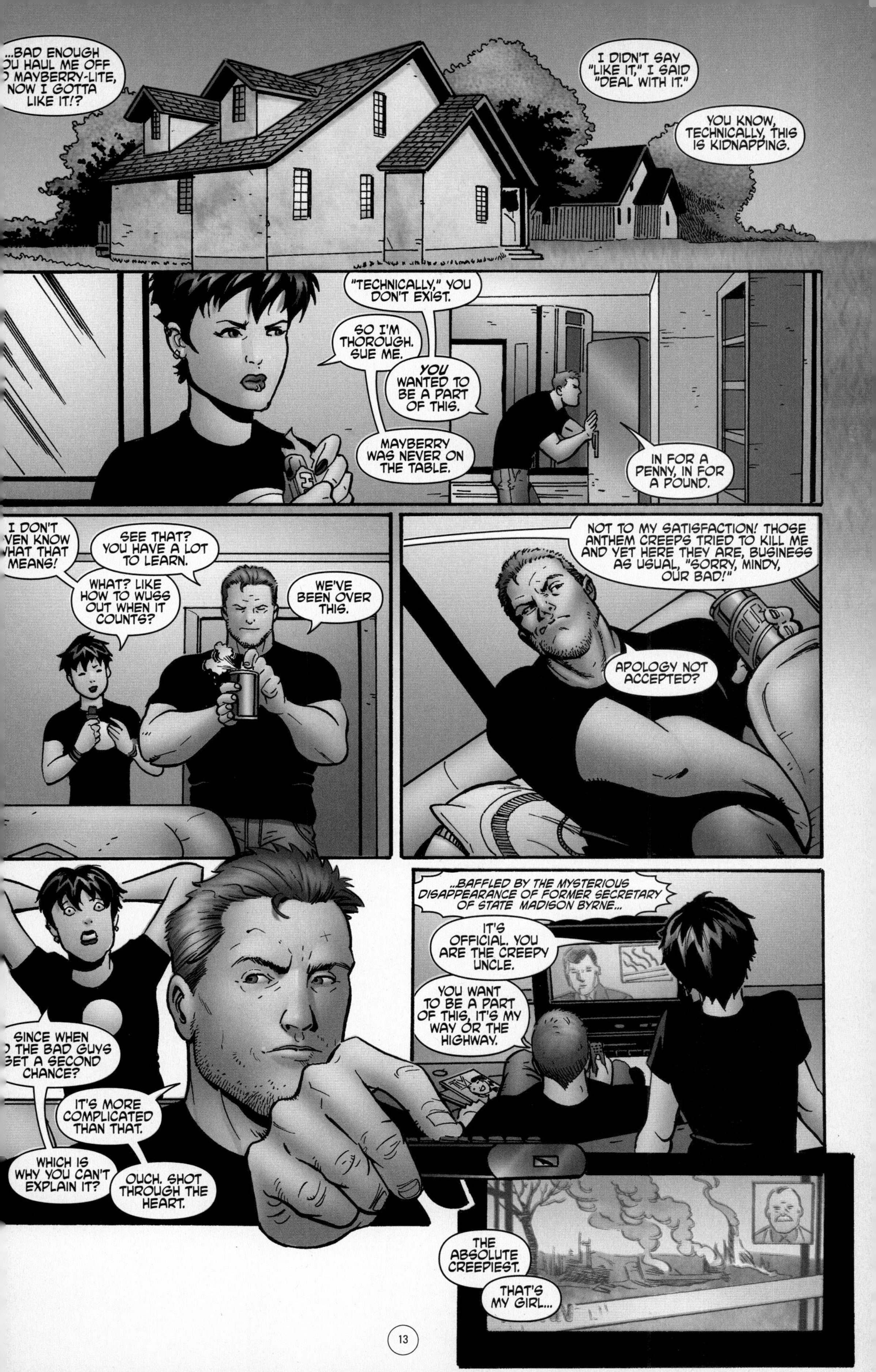
...BAD ENOUGH YOU HAUL ME OFF TO MAYBERRY-LITE, NOW I GOTTA LIKE IT!?
I DIDN'T SAY "LIKE IT," I SAID "DEAL WITH IT."
YOU KNOW, TECHNICALLY, THIS IS KIDNAPPING.
"TECHNICALLY," YOU DON'T EXIST.
SO I'M THOROUGH. SUE ME.
YOU WANTED TO BE A PART OF THIS.
MAYBERRY WAS NEVER ON THE TABLE.
IN FOR A PENNY, IN FOR A POUND.
I DON'T EVEN KNOW WHAT THAT MEANS!
SEE THAT? YOU HAVE A LOT TO LEARN.
WHAT? LIKE HOW TO WUSS OUT WHEN IT COUNTS?
WE'VE BEEN OVER THIS.
NOT TO MY SATISFACTION! THOSE ANTHEM CREEPS TRIED TO KILL ME AND YET HERE THEY ARE, BUSINESS AS USUAL, "SORRY, MINDY, OUR BAD!"
APOLOGY NOT ACCEPTED?
SINCE WHEN DO THE BAD GUYS GET A SECOND CHANCE?
IT'S MORE COMPLICATED THAN THAT.
WHICH IS WHY YOU CAN'T EXPLAIN IT?
OUCH. SHOT THROUGH THE HEART.
...BAFFLED BY THE MYSTERIOUS DISAPPEARANCE OF FORMER SECRETARY OF STATE MADISON BYRNE...
IT'S OFFICIAL. YOU ARE THE CREEPY UNCLE.
YOU WANT TO BE A PART OF THIS, IT'S MY WAY OR THE HIGHWAY.
THE ABSOLUTE CREEPIEST.
THAT'S MY GIRL...

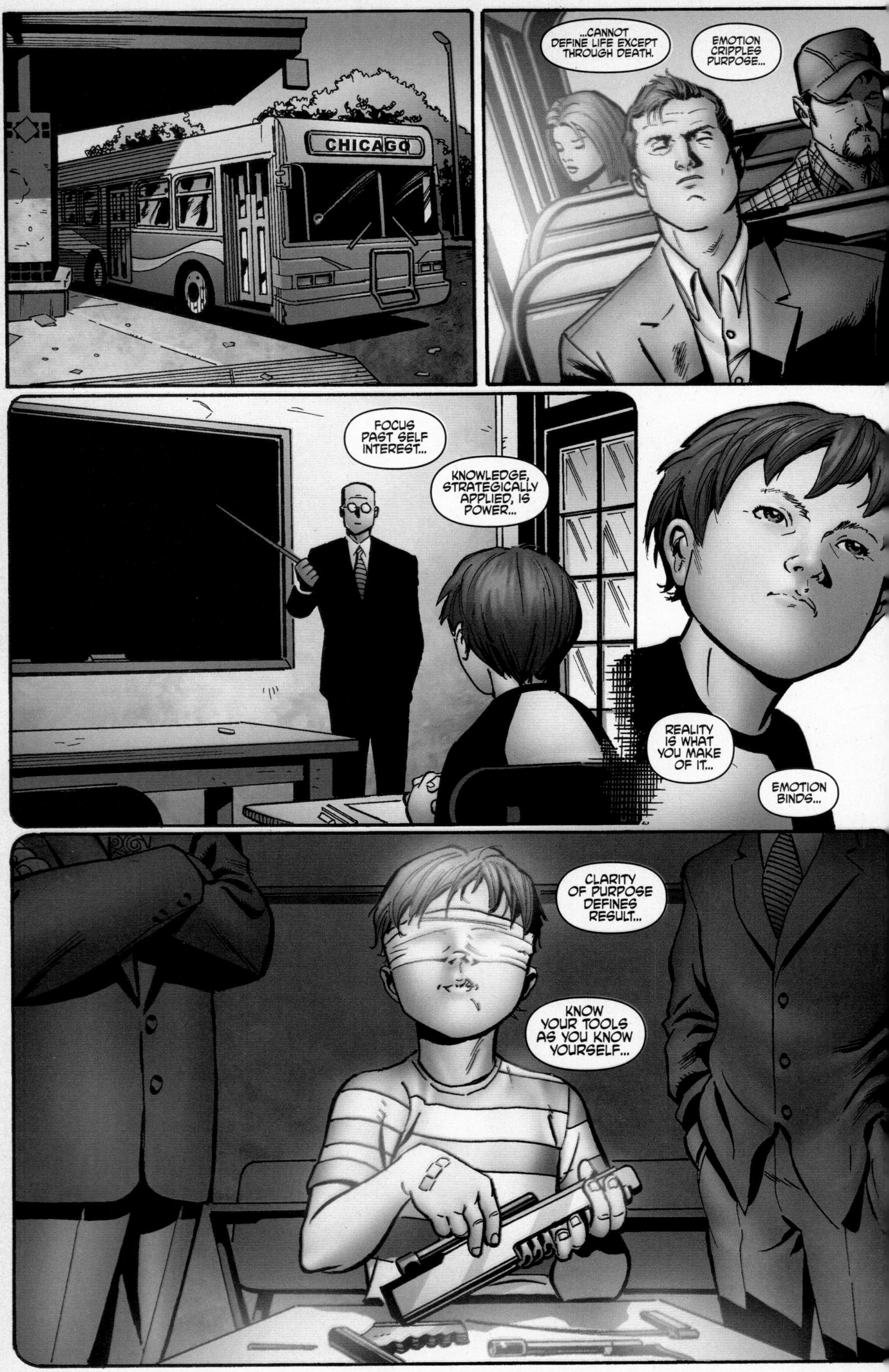
CHICAGO
...CANNOT DEFINE LIFE EXCEPT THROUGH DEATH.
EMOTION CRIPPLES PURPOSE...
FOCUS PAST SELF INTEREST...
KNOWLEDGE, STRATEGICALLY APPLIED, IS POWER...
REALITY IS WHAT YOU MAKE OF IT...
EMOTION BINDS...
CLARITY OF PURPOSE DEFINES RESULT...
KNOW YOUR TOOLS AS YOU KNOW YOURSELF...

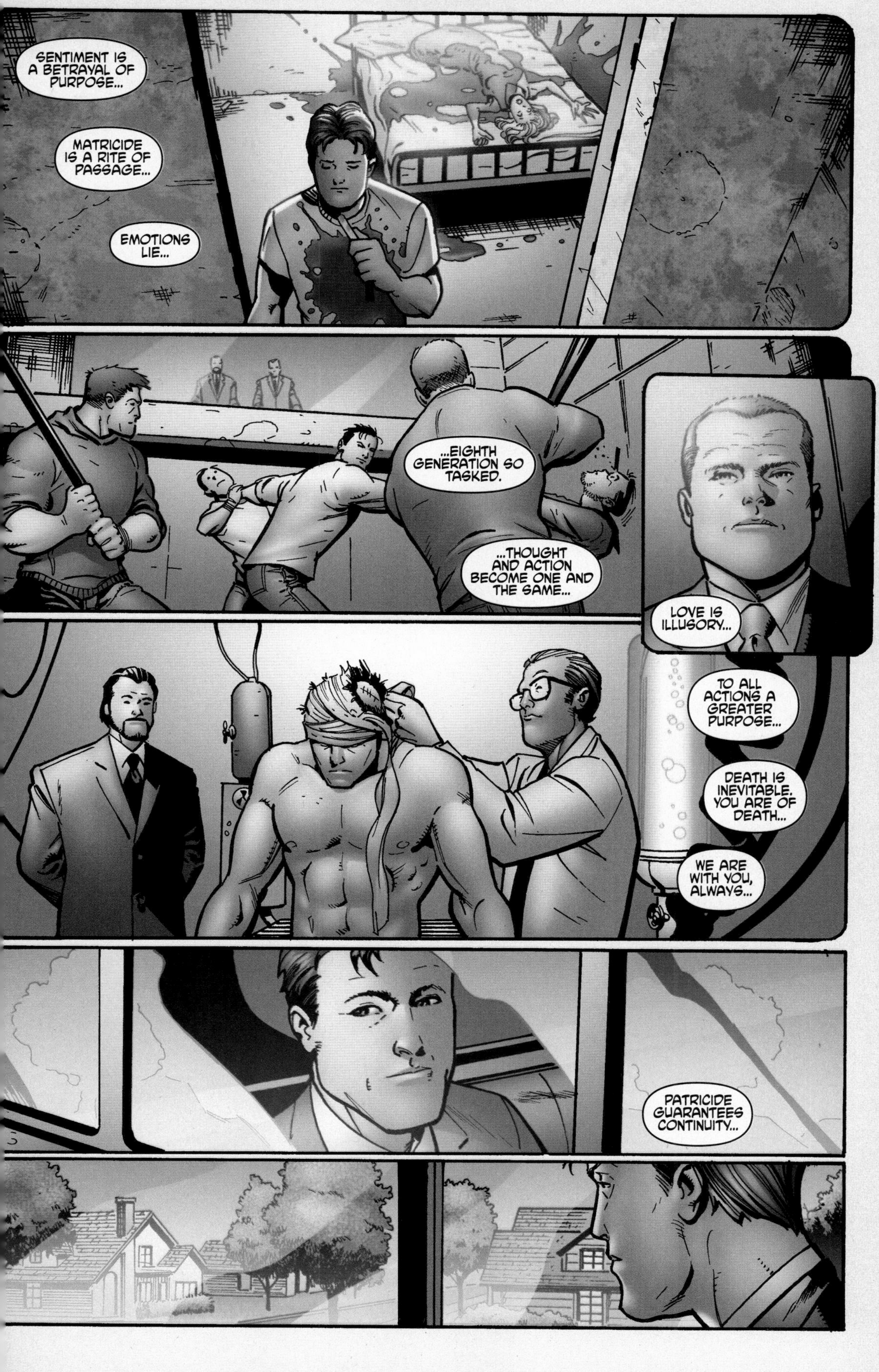
SENTIMENT IS A BETRAYAL OF PURPOSE...
MATRICIDE IS A RITE OF PASSAGE...
EMOTIONS LIE...
...EIGHTH GENERATION SO TASKED.
...THOUGHT AND ACTION BECOME ONE AND THE SAME...
LOVE IS ILLUSORY...
TO ALL ACTIONS A GREATER PURPOSE...
DEATH IS INEVITABLE. YOU ARE OF DEATH...
WE ARE WITH YOU, ALWAYS...
PATRICIDE GUARANTEES CONTINUITY...

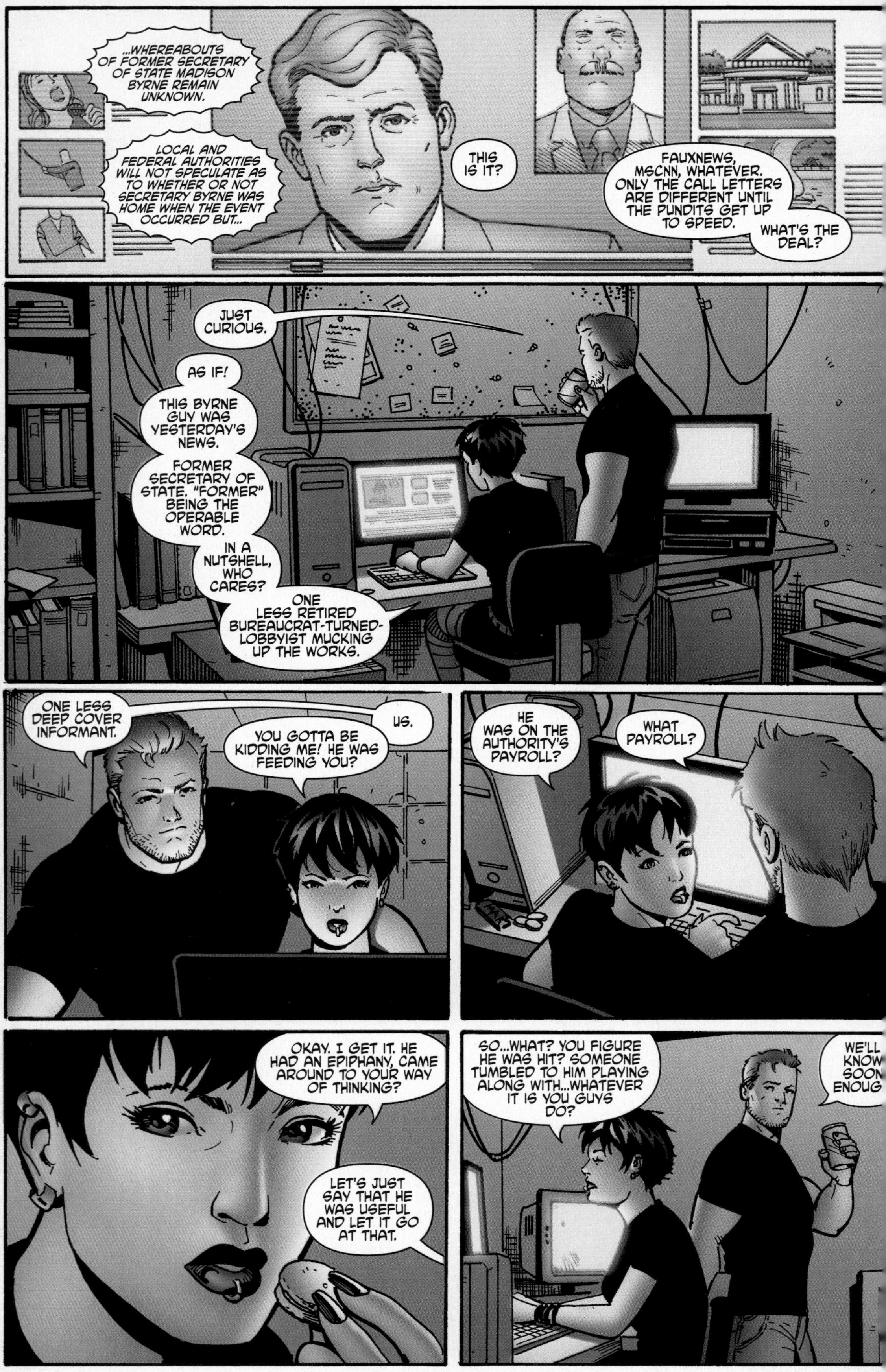
...WHEREABOUTS OF FORMER SECRETARY OF STATE MADISON BYRNE REMAIN UNKNOWN.
LOCAL AND FEDERAL AUTHORITIES WILL NOT SPECULATE AS TO WHETHER OR NOT SECRETARY BYRNE WAS HOME WHEN THE EVENT OCCURRED BUT...
THIS IS IT?
FAUXNEWS, MSCNN, WHATEVER. ONLY THE CALL LETTERS ARE DIFFERENT UNTIL THE PUNDITS GET UP TO SPEED.
WHAT'S THE DEAL?
JUST CURIOUS.
AS IF!
THIS BYRNE GUY WAS YESTERDAY'S NEWS.
FORMER SECRETARY OF STATE. "FORMER" BEING THE OPERABLE WORD.
IN A NUTSHELL, WHO CARES?
ONE LESS RETIRED BUREAUCRAT-TURNED-LOBBYIST MUCKING UP THE WORKS.
ONE LESS DEEP COVER INFORMANT.
US.
YOU GOTTA BE KIDDING ME! HE WAS FEEDING YOU?
HE WAS ON THE AUTHORITY'S PAYROLL?
WHAT PAYROLL?
OKAY. I GET IT. HE HAD AN EPIPHANY, CAME AROUND TO YOUR WAY OF THINKING?
LET'S JUST SAY THAT HE WAS USEFUL AND LET IT GO AT THAT.
SO...WHAT? YOU FIGURE HE WAS HIT? SOMEONE TUMBLED TO HIM PLAYING ALONG WITH...WHATEVER IT IS YOU GUYS DO?
WE'LL KNOW SOON ENOUG

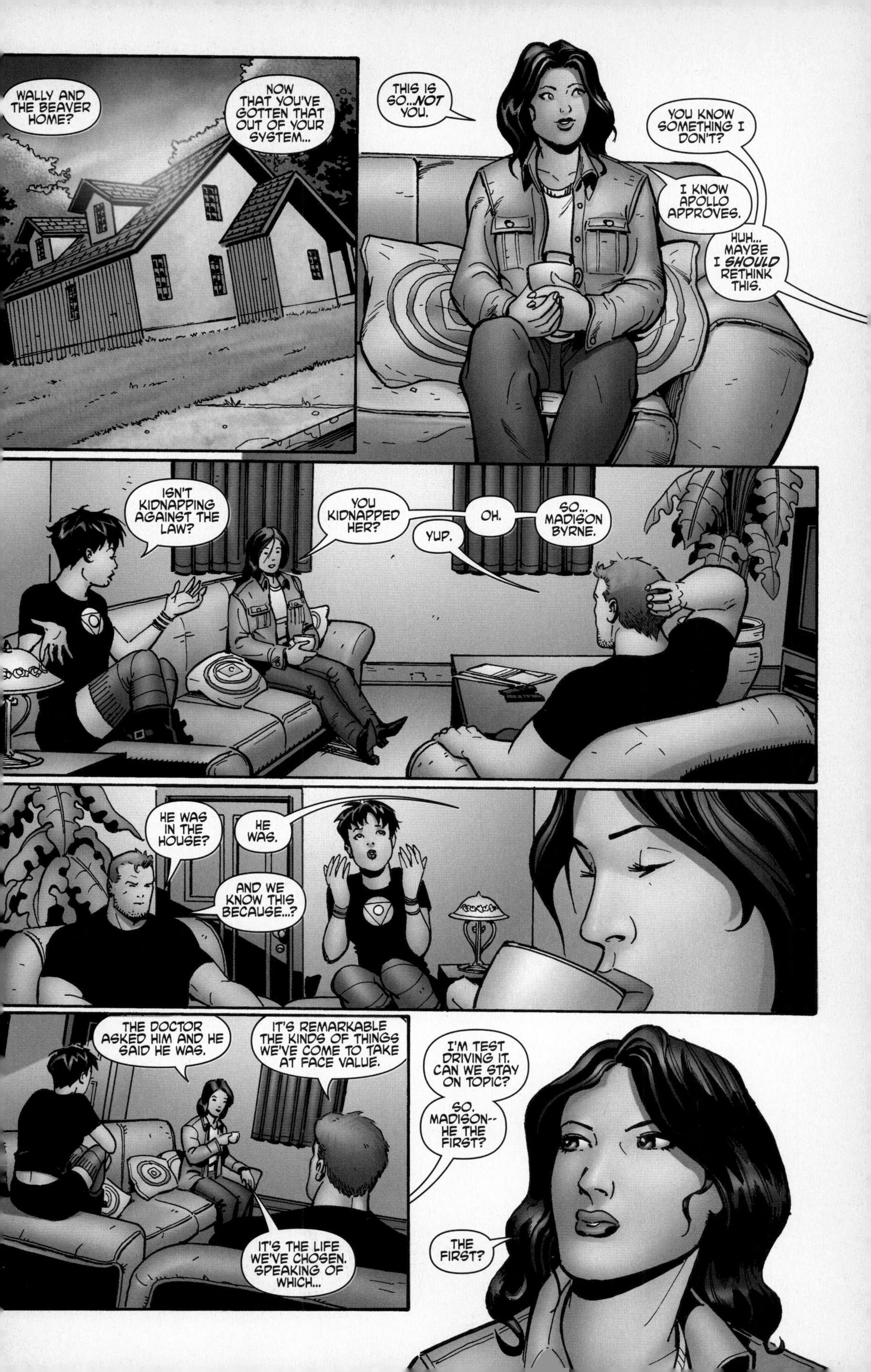
WALLY AND THE BEAVER HOME?
NOW THAT YOU'VE GOTTEN THAT OUT OF YOUR SYSTEM...
THIS IS SO...NOT YOU.
YOU KNOW SOMETHING I DON'T?
I KNOW APOLLO APPROVES.
HUH... MAYBE I SHOULD RETHINK THIS.
ISN'T KIDNAPPING AGAINST THE LAW?
YOU KIDNAPPED HER?
YUP.
OH.
SO... MADISON BYRNE.
HE WAS IN THE HOUSE?
HE WAS.
AND WE KNOW THIS BECAUSE...?
THE DOCTOR ASKED HIM AND HE SAID HE WAS.
IT'S REMARKABLE THE KINDS OF THINGS WE'VE COME TO TAKE AT FACE VALUE.
IT'S THE LIFE WE'VE CHOSEN. SPEAKING OF WHICH...
I'M TEST DRIVING IT. CAN WE STAY ON TOPIC?
SO. MADISON-- HE THE FIRST?
THE FIRST?

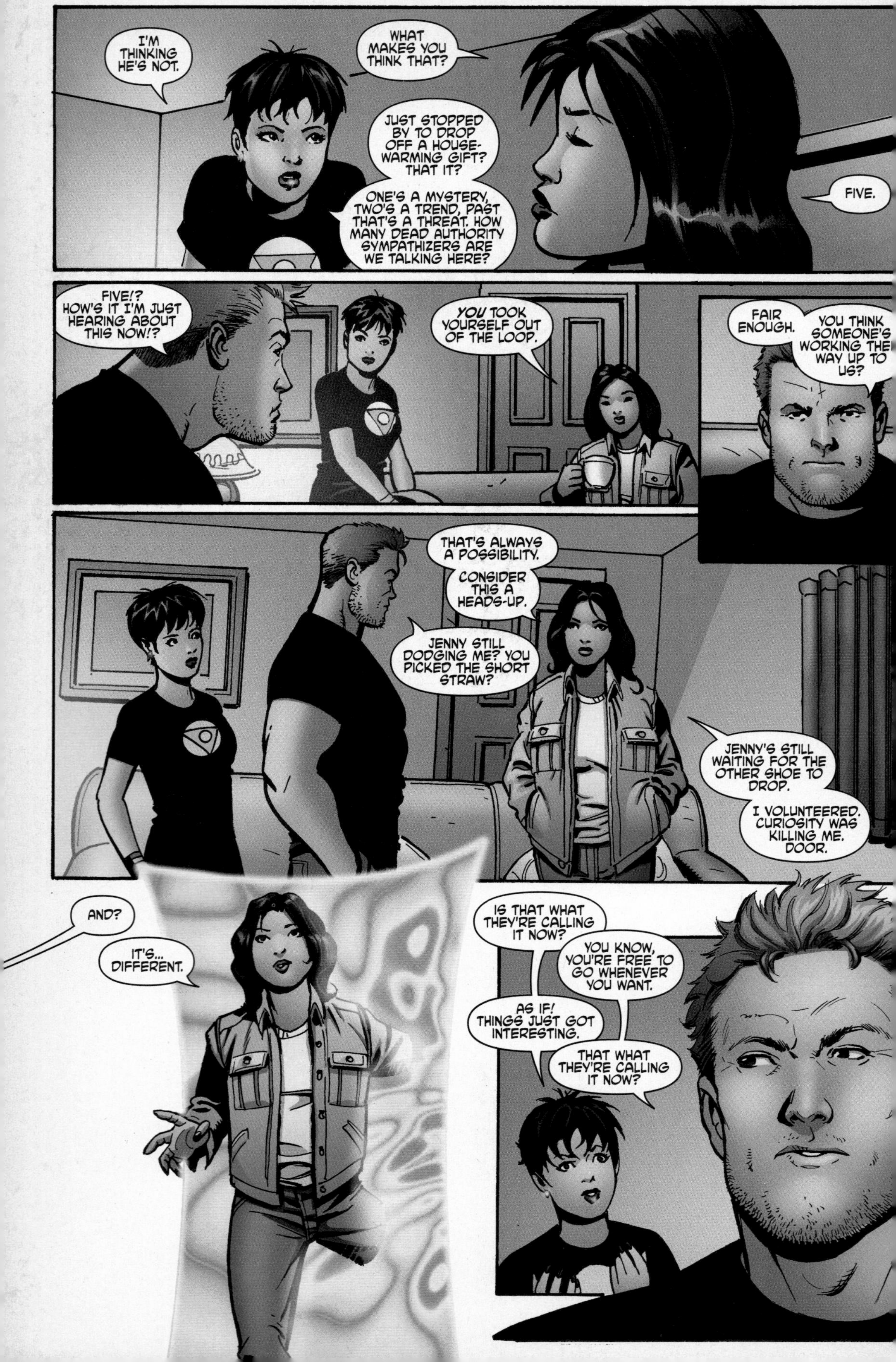
I'M THINKING HE'S NOT.
WHAT MAKES YOU THINK THAT?
JUST STOPPED BY TO DROP OFF A HOUSE-WARMING GIFT? THAT IT?
ONE'S A MYSTERY, TWO'S A TREND, PAST THAT'S A THREAT. HOW MANY DEAD AUTHORITY SYMPATHIZERS ARE WE TALKING HERE?
FIVE.
FIVE!? HOW'S IT I'M JUST HEARING ABOUT THIS NOW!?
YOU TOOK YOURSELF OUT OF THE LOOP.
FAIR ENOUGH.
YOU THINK SOMEONE'S WORKING THE WAY UP TO US?
THAT'S ALWAYS A POSSIBILITY.
CONSIDER THIS A HEADS-UP.
JENNY STILL DODGING ME? YOU PICKED THE SHORT STRAW?
JENNY'S STILL WAITING FOR THE OTHER SHOE TO DROP.
I VOLUNTEERED. CURIOSITY WAS KILLING ME. DOOR.
AND?
IT'S... DIFFERENT.
IS THAT WHAT THEY'RE CALLING IT NOW?
YOU KNOW, YOU'RE FREE TO GO WHENEVER YOU WANT.
AS IF! THINGS JUST GOT INTERESTING.
THAT WHAT THEY'RE CALLING IT NOW?

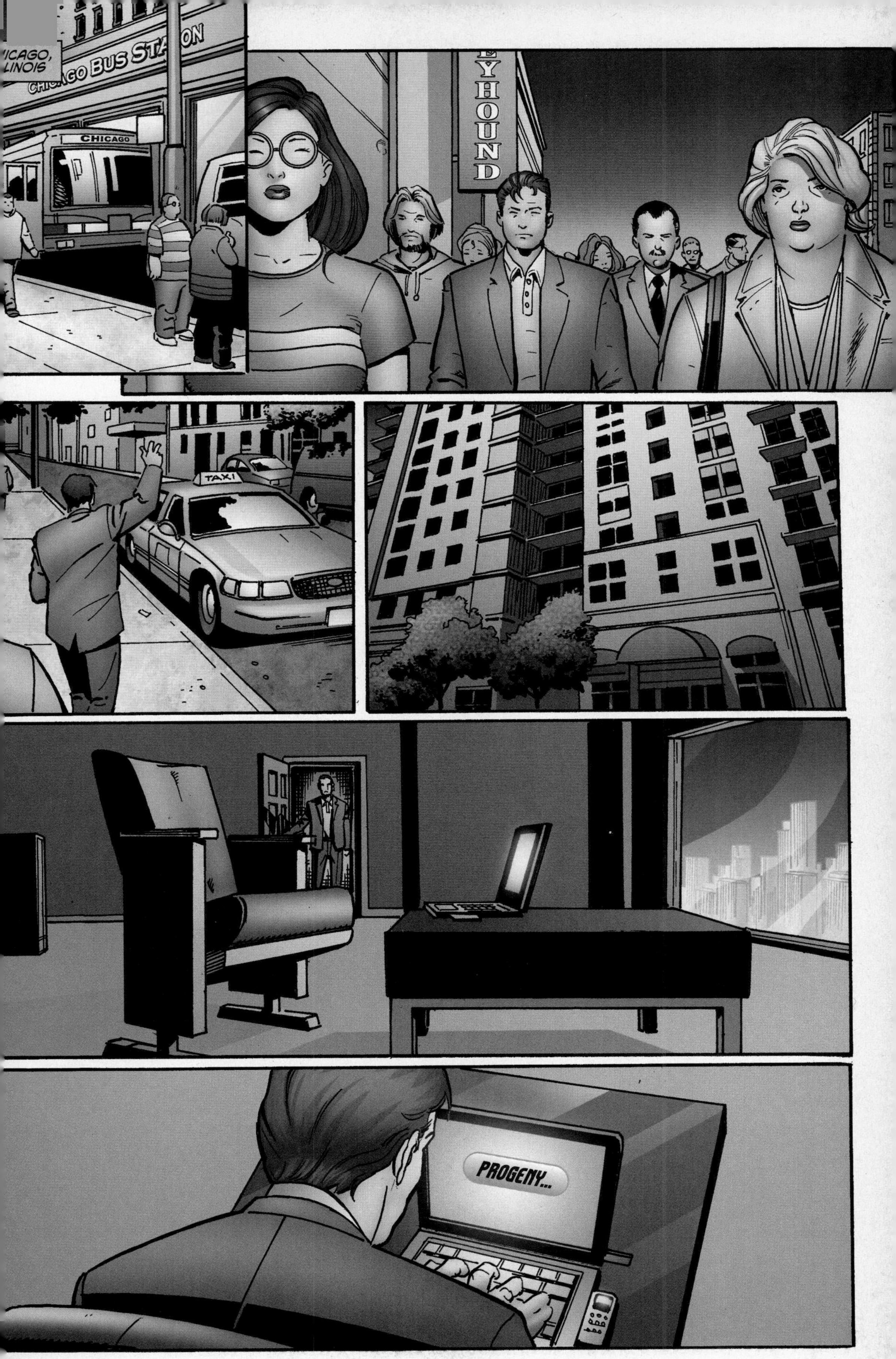
CHICAGO, ILLINOIS
CHICAGO BUS STATION
CHICAGO
GREYHOUND
TAXI
PROGENY...

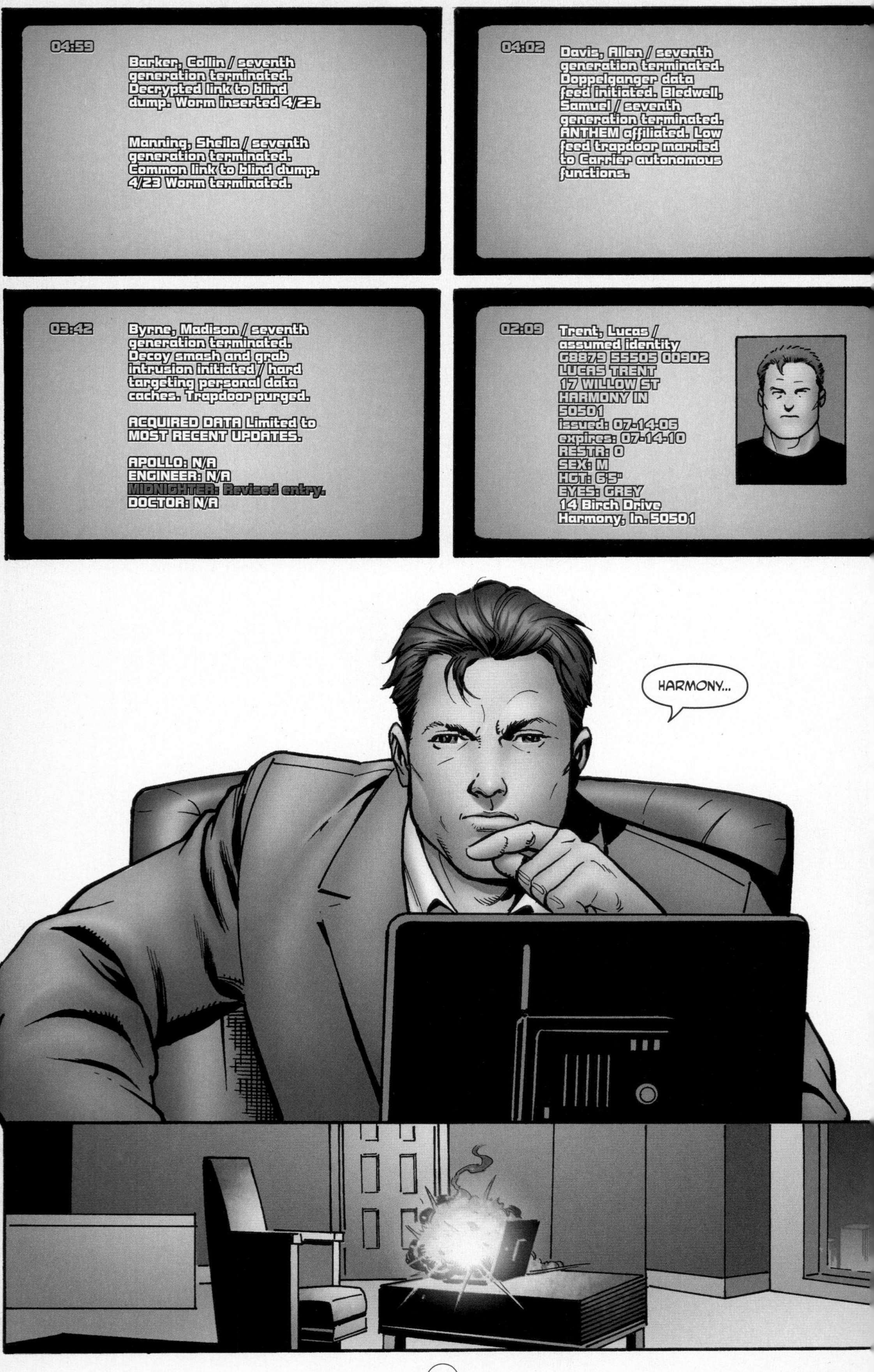
04:59
Barker, Collin / seventh generation terminated. Decrypted link to blind dump. Worm inserted 4/23.
Manning, Sheila / seventh generation terminated. Common link to blind dump. 4/23 Worm terminated.
04:02
Davis, Allen / seventh generation terminated. Doppelganger data feed initiated. Bledwell, Samuel / seventh generation terminated. ANTHEM affiliated. Low feed trapdoor married to Carrier autonomous functions.
03:42
Byrne, Madison / seventh generation terminated. Decoy smash and grab intrusion initiated / hard targeting personal data caches. Trapdoor purged.
ACQUIRED DATA Limited to MOST RECENT UPDATES.
APOLLO: N/A
ENGINEER: N/A
MIDNIGHTER: Revised entry.
DOCTOR: N/A
02:09
Trent, Lucas / assumed identity
G8879 55505 00902
LUCAS TRENT
17 WILLOW ST
HARMONY IN
50501
issued: 07-14-06
expires: 07-14-10
RESTR: 0
SEX: M
HGT: 6'5"
EYES: GREY
14 Birch Drive
Harmony, In. 50501
HARMONY...

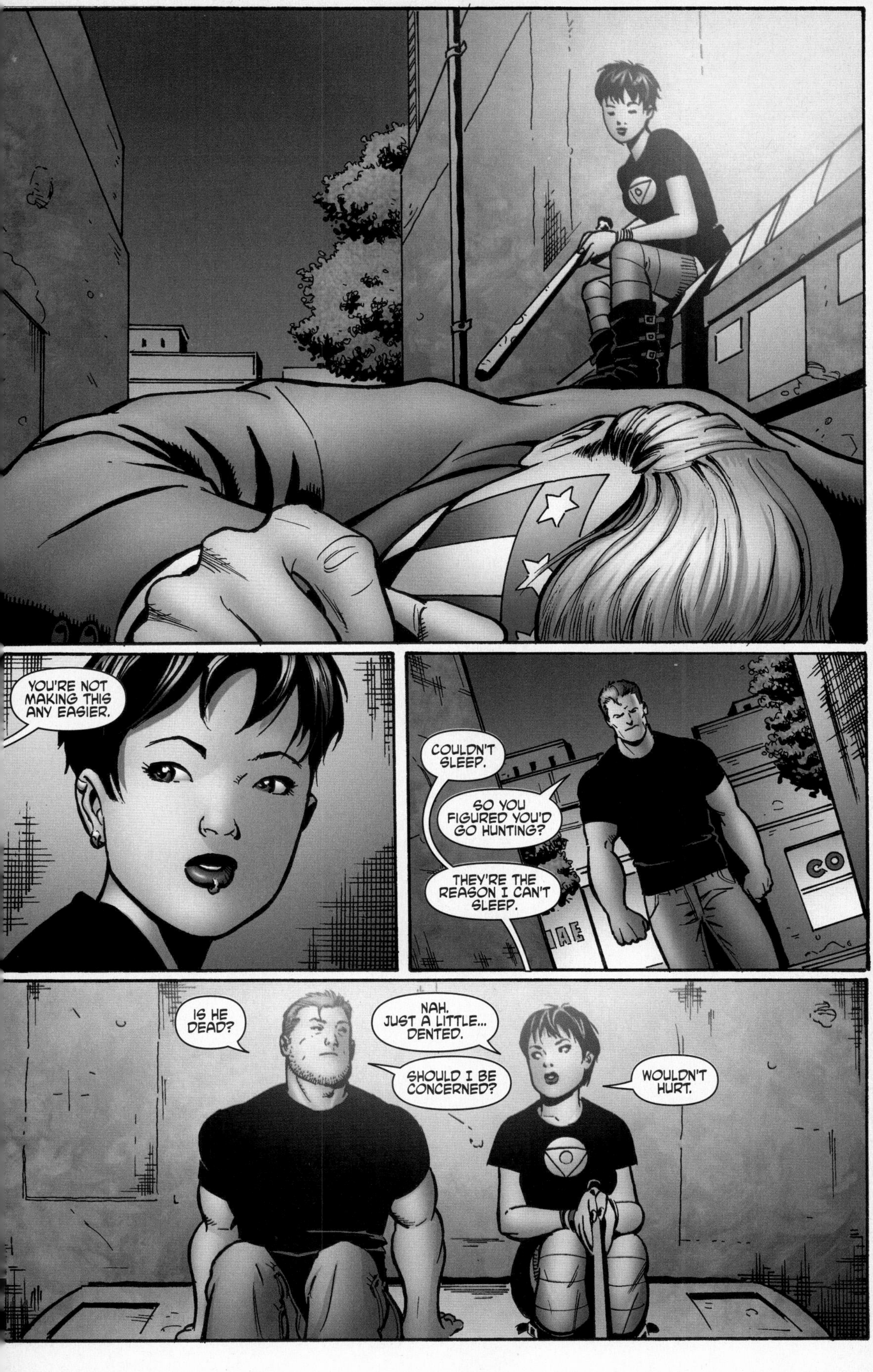
YOU'RE NOT MAKING THIS ANY EASIER.
COULDN'T SLEEP.
SO YOU FIGURED YOU'D GO HUNTING?
THEY'RE THE REASON I CAN'T SLEEP.
CO
IS HE DEAD?
NAH. JUST A LITTLE... DENTED.
SHOULD I BE CONCERNED?
WOULDN'T HURT.

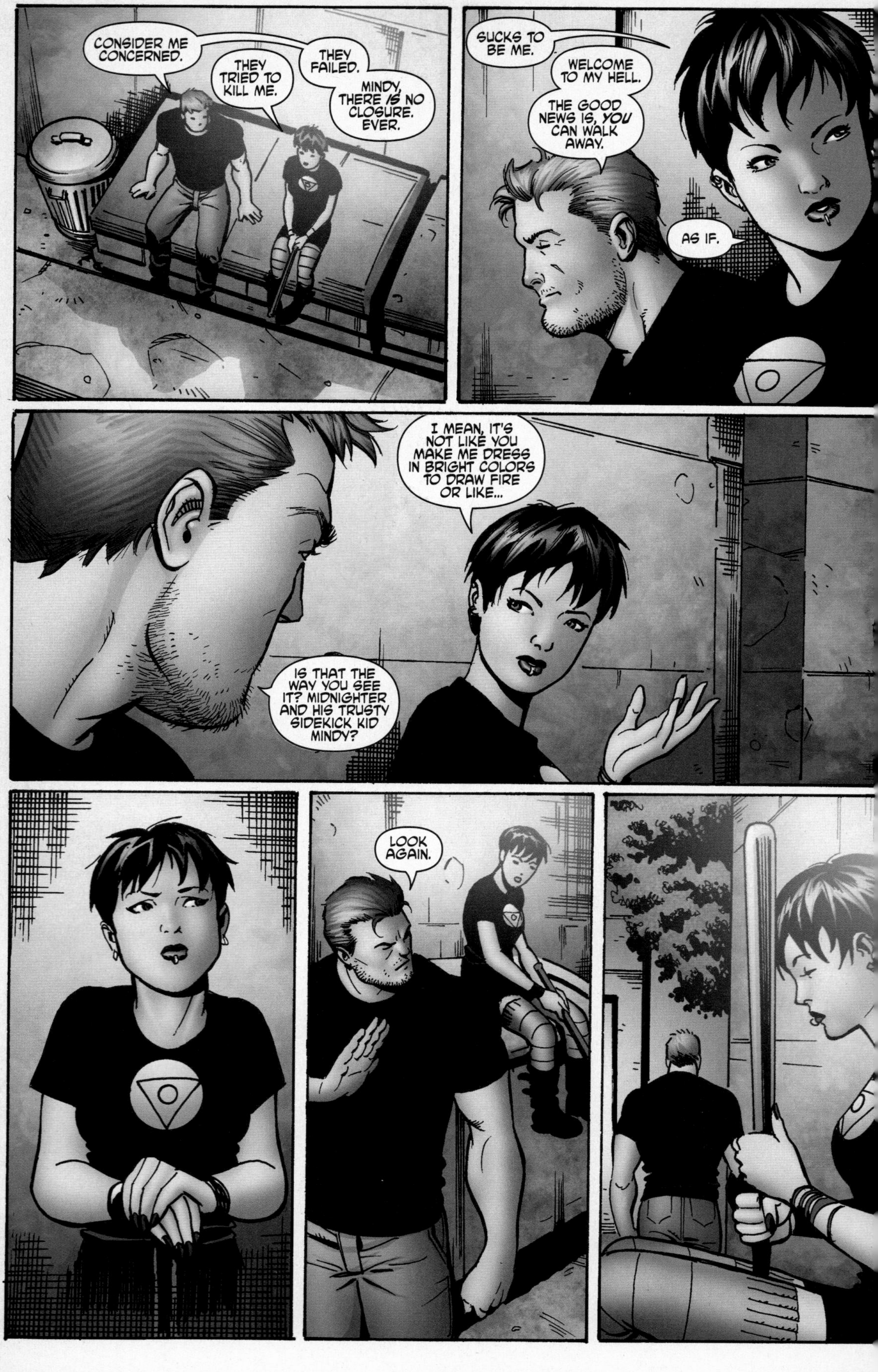
CONSIDER ME CONCERNED.
THEY TRIED TO KILL ME.
THEY FAILED.
MINDY, THERE IS NO CLOSURE. EVER.
SUCKS TO BE ME.
WELCOME TO MY HELL.
THE GOOD NEWS IS, YOU CAN WALK AWAY.
AS IF.
I MEAN, IT'S NOT LIKE YOU MAKE ME DRESS IN BRIGHT COLORS TO DRAW FIRE OR LIKE...
IS THAT THE WAY YOU SEE IT? MIDNIGHTER AND HIS TRUSTY SIDEKICK KID MINDY?
LOOK AGAIN.

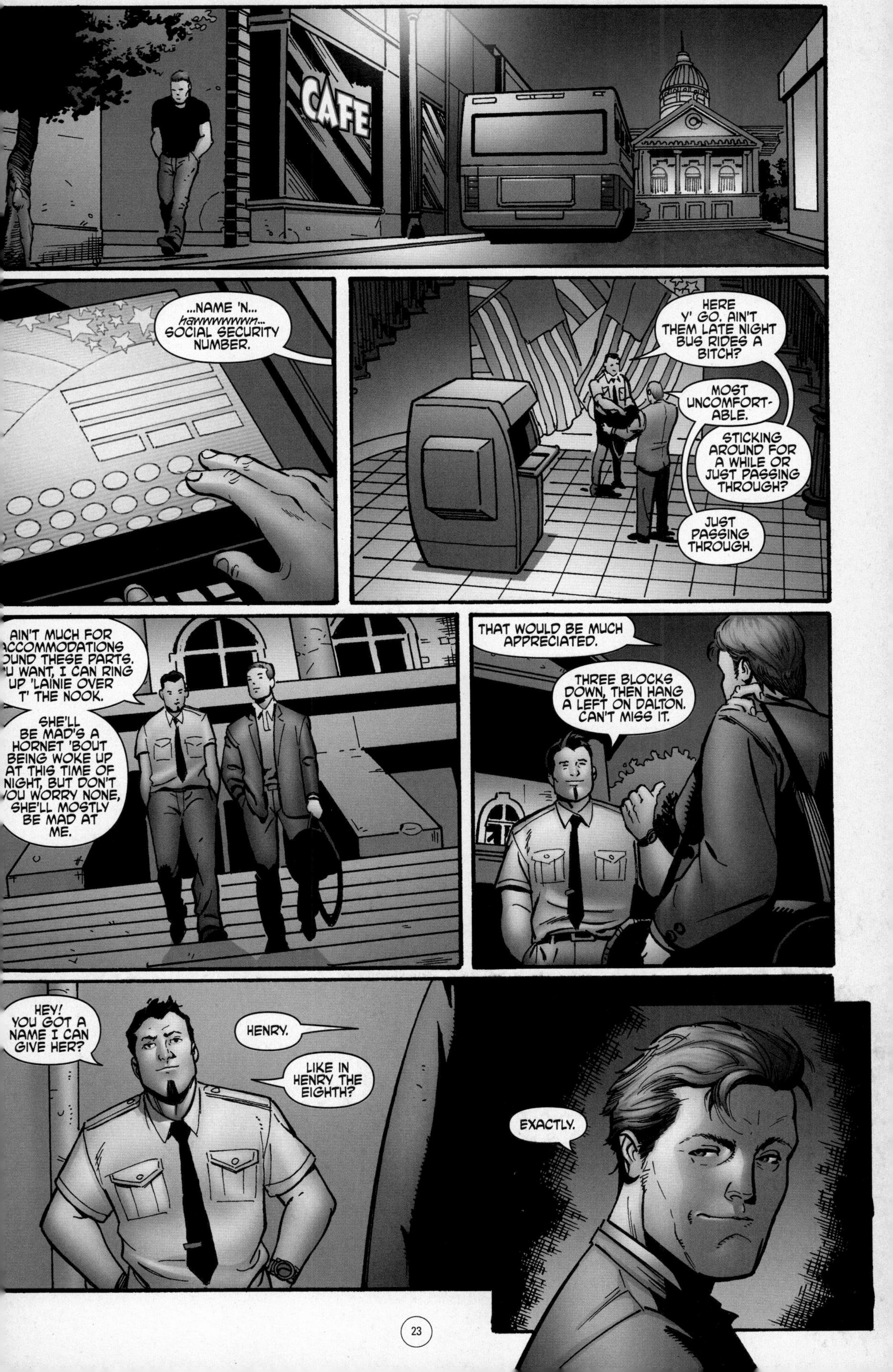
CAFE
...NAME 'N... hawwwwwwn... SOCIAL SECURITY NUMBER.
HERE Y' GO. AIN'T THEM LATE NIGHT BUS RIDES A BITCH?
MOST UNCOMFORT-ABLE.
STICKING AROUND FOR A WHILE OR JUST PASSING THROUGH?
JUST PASSING THROUGH.
AIN'T MUCH FOR ACCOMMODATIONS OUND THESE PARTS. U WANT, I CAN RING UP 'LAINIE OVER T' THE NOOK.
SHE'LL BE MAD'S A HORNET 'BOUT BEING WOKE UP AT THIS TIME OF NIGHT, BUT DON'T YOU WORRY NONE, SHE'LL MOSTLY BE MAD AT ME.
THAT WOULD BE MUCH APPRECIATED.
THREE BLOCKS DOWN, THEN HANG A LEFT ON DALTON. CAN'T MISS IT.
HEY! YOU GOT A NAME I CAN GIVE HER?
HENRY.
LIKE IN HENRY THE EIGHTH?
EXACTLY.

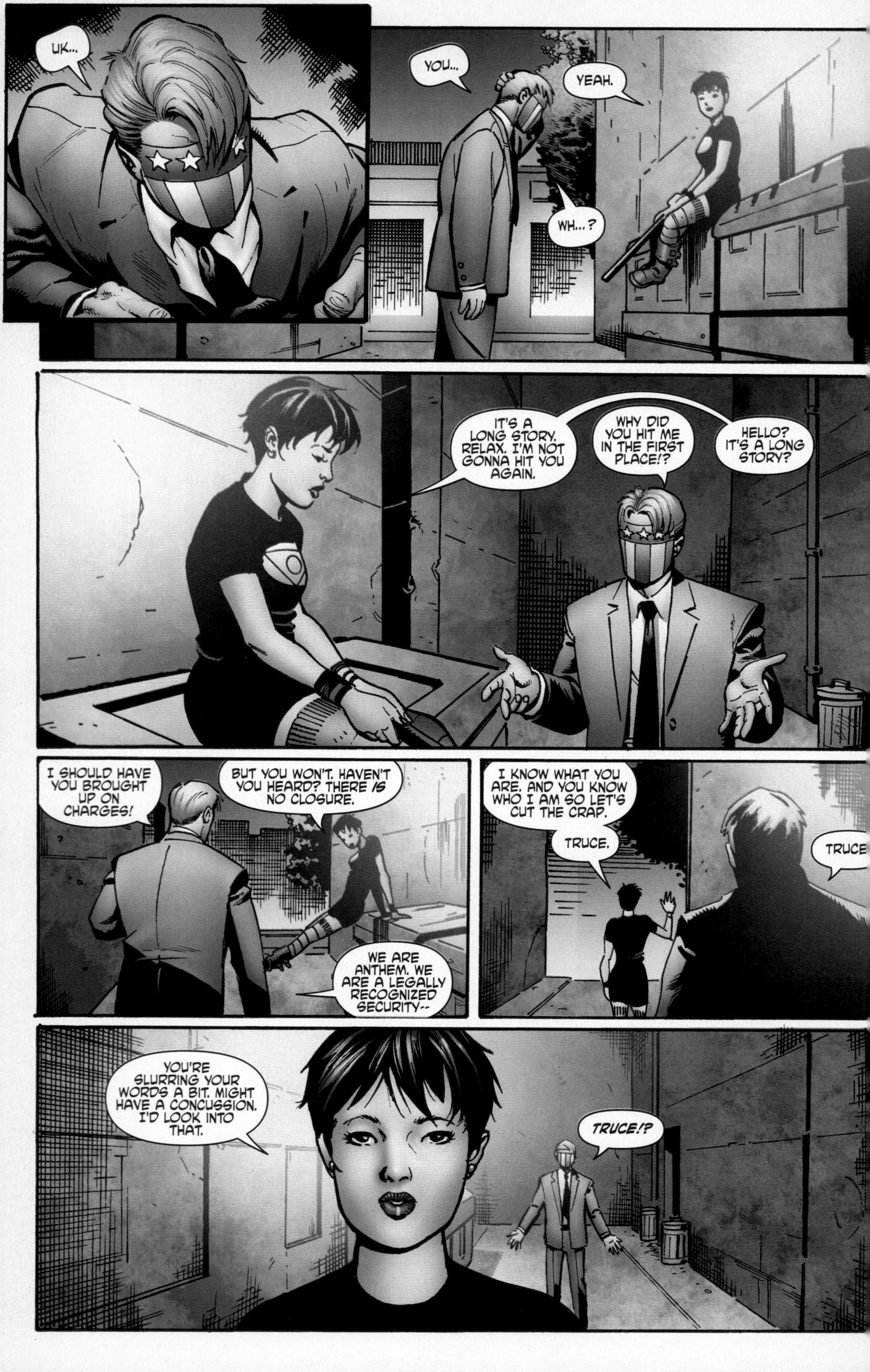
UK...
YOU...
YEAH.
WH...?
IT'S A LONG STORY. RELAX. I'M NOT GONNA HIT YOU AGAIN.
WHY DID YOU HIT ME IN THE FIRST PLACE!?
HELLO? IT'S A LONG STORY?
I SHOULD HAVE YOU BROUGHT UP ON CHARGES!
BUT YOU WON'T. HAVEN'T YOU HEARD? THERE *IS* NO CLOSURE.
WE ARE ANTHEM. WE ARE A LEGALLY RECOGNIZED SECURITY--
I KNOW WHAT YOU ARE. AND YOU KNOW WHO I AM SO LET'S CUT THE CRAP.
TRUCE.
TRUCE
YOU'RE SLURRING YOUR WORDS A BIT. MIGHT HAVE A CONCUSSION. I'D LOOK INTO THAT.
*TRUCE!?*

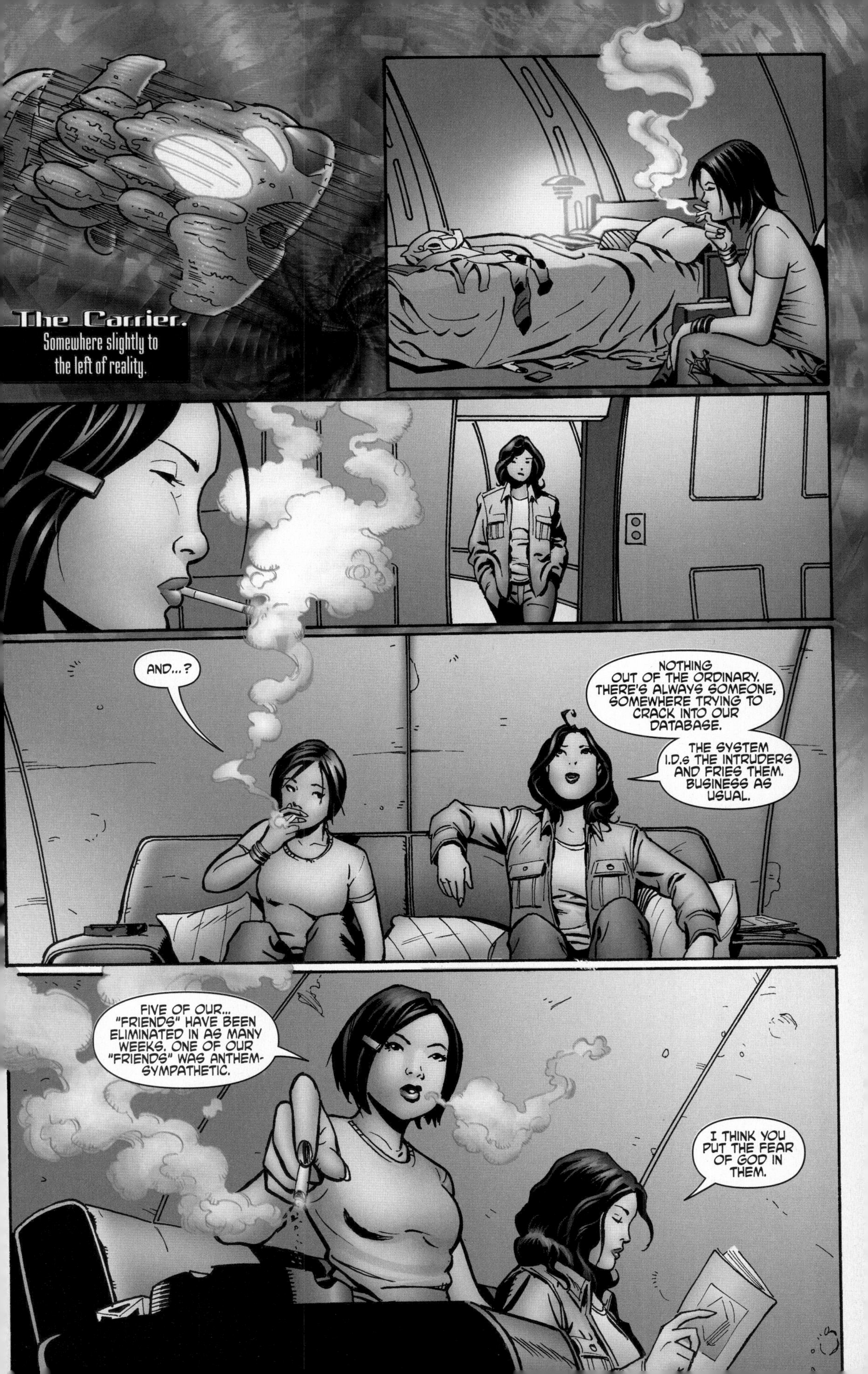
The Carrier.
Somewhere slightly to the left of reality.
AND...?
NOTHING OUT OF THE ORDINARY. THERE'S ALWAYS SOMEONE, SOMEWHERE TRYING TO CRACK INTO OUR DATABASE.
THE SYSTEM I.D.s THE INTRUDERS AND FRIES THEM. BUSINESS AS USUAL.
FIVE OF OUR... "FRIENDS" HAVE BEEN ELIMINATED IN AS MANY WEEKS. ONE OF OUR "FRIENDS" WAS ANTHEM-SYMPATHETIC.
I THINK YOU PUT THE FEAR OF GOD IN THEM.

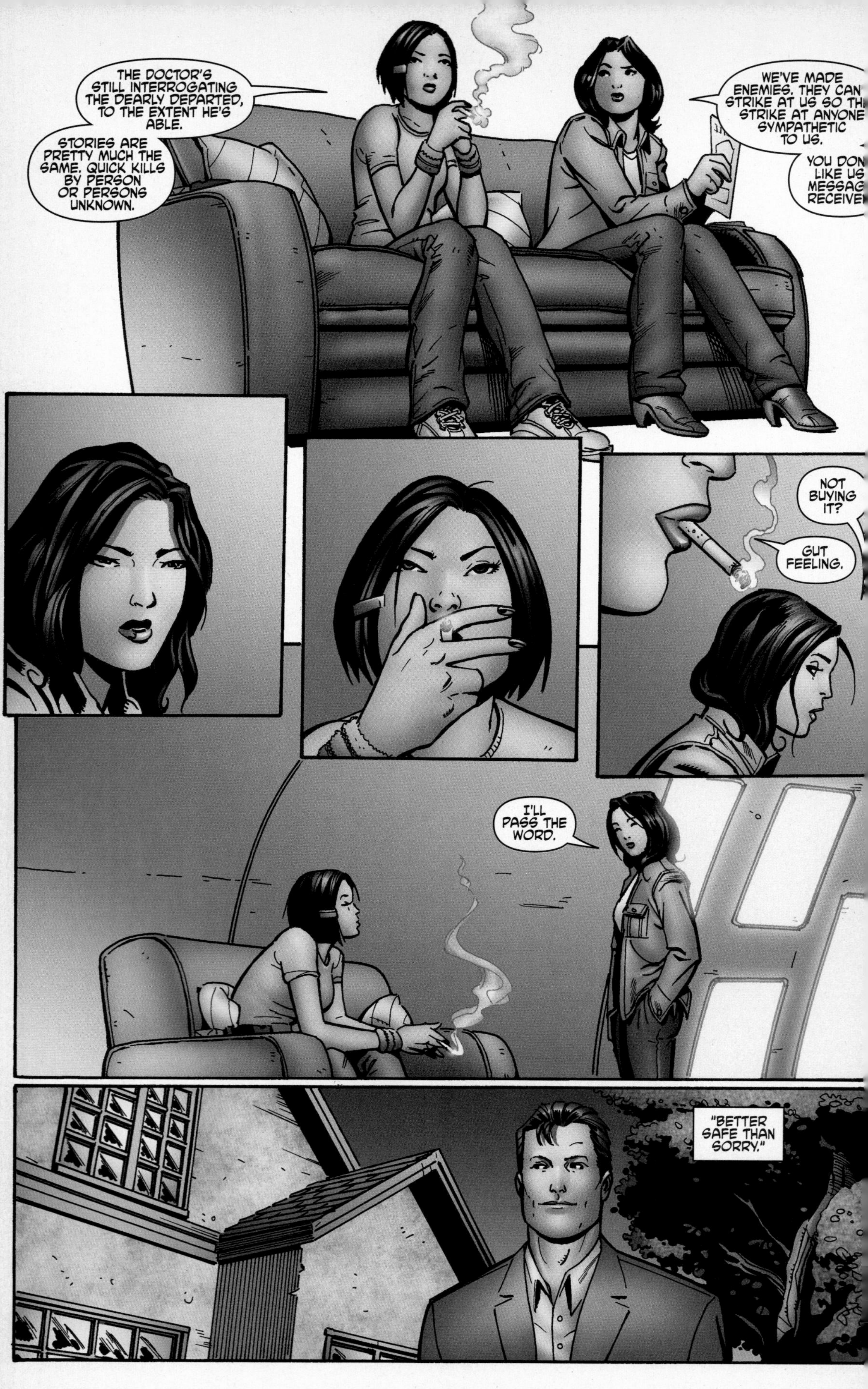
THE DOCTOR'S STILL INTERROGATING THE DEARLY DEPARTED, TO THE EXTENT HE'S ABLE.
STORIES ARE PRETTY MUCH THE SAME. QUICK KILLS BY PERSON OR PERSONS UNKNOWN.
WE'VE MADE ENEMIES. THEY CAN'T STRIKE AT US SO THEY STRIKE AT ANYONE SYMPATHETIC TO US.
YOU DON'T LIKE US, MESSAGE RECEIVED.
NOT BUYING IT?
GUT FEELING.
I'LL PASS THE WORD.
"BETTER SAFE THAN SORRY."

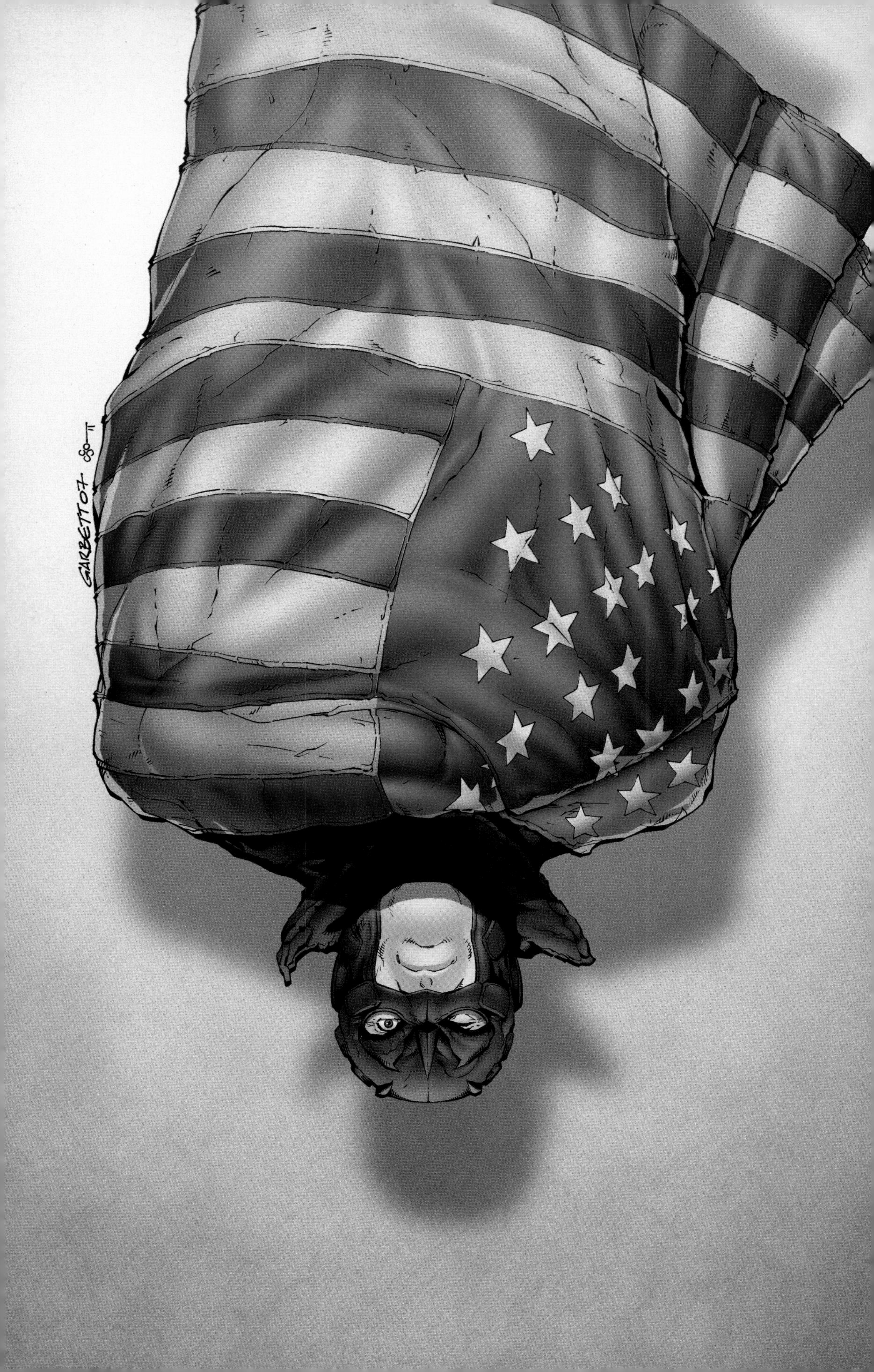
GARBETT07

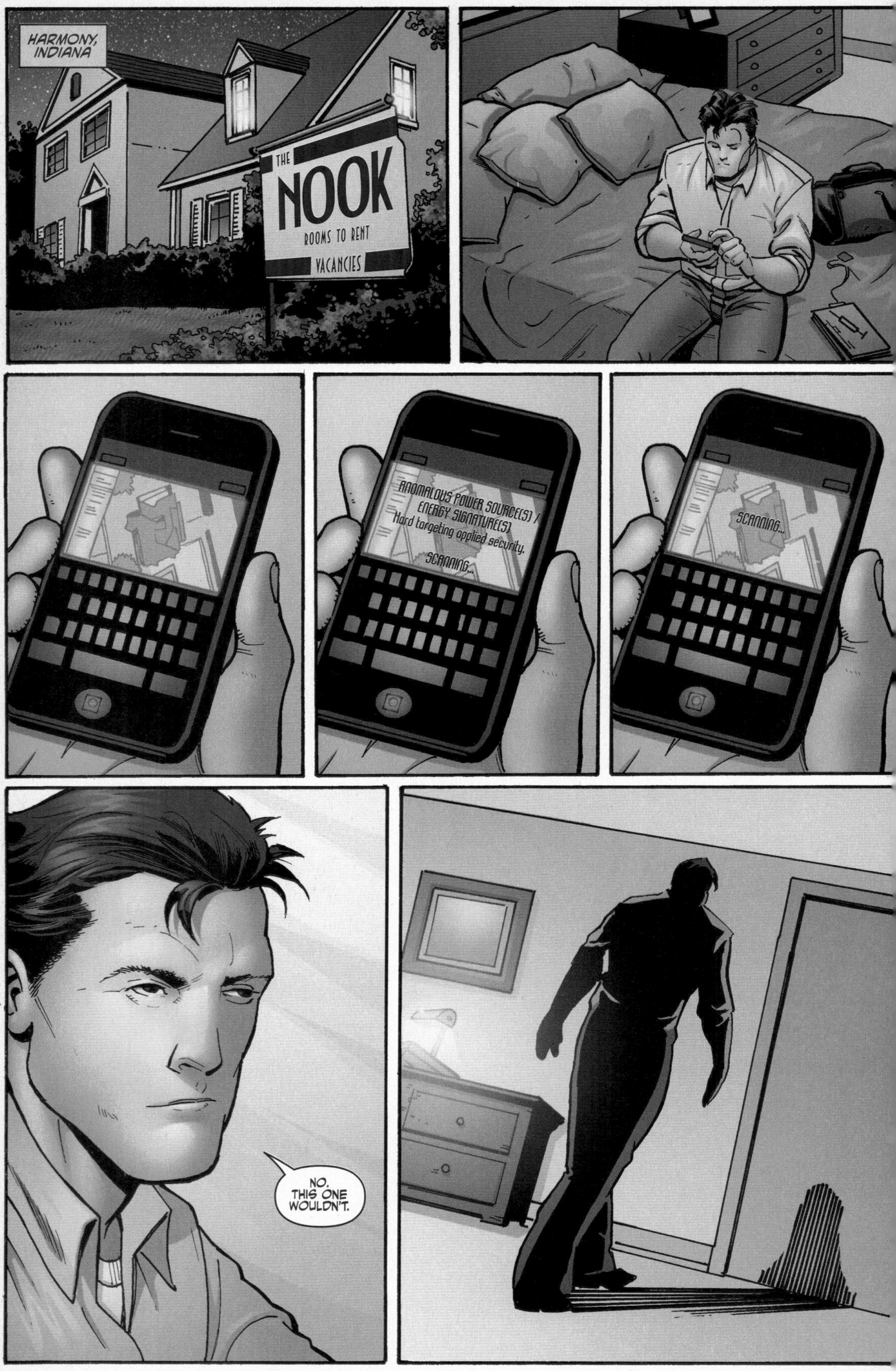
HARMONY, INDIANA
THE NOOK
ROOMS TO RENT
VACANCIES
ANOMALOUS POWER SOURCE(S) / ENERGY SIGNATURE(S)
Hard targeting applied security.
SCANNING...
SCANNING...
NO. THIS ONE WOULDN'T.

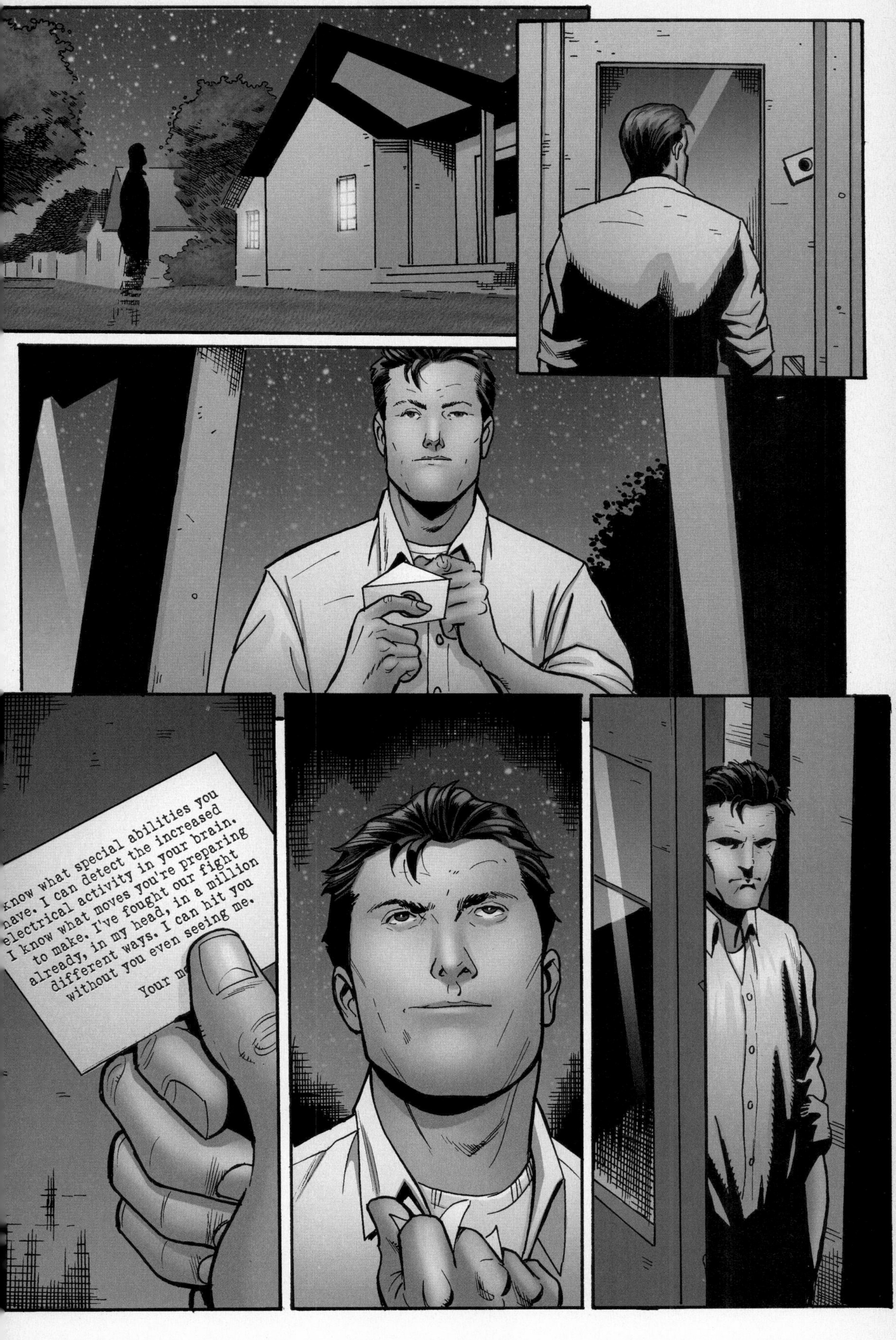

know what special abilities you
have. I can detect the increased
electrical activity in your brain.
I know what moves you're preparing
to make. I've fought our fight
already, in my head, in a million
different ways. I can hit you
without you even seeing me.
Your

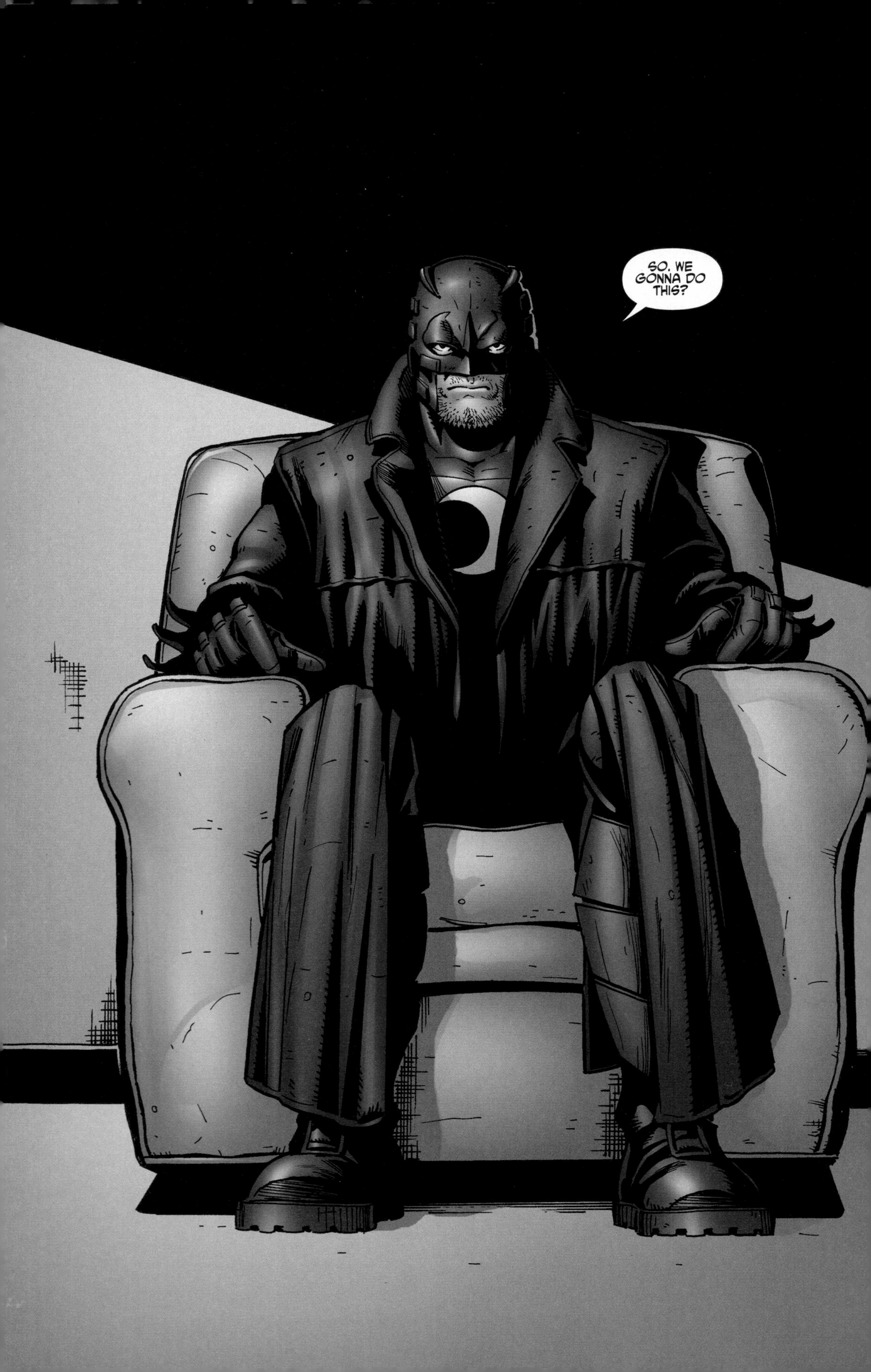
SO, WE GONNA DO THIS?

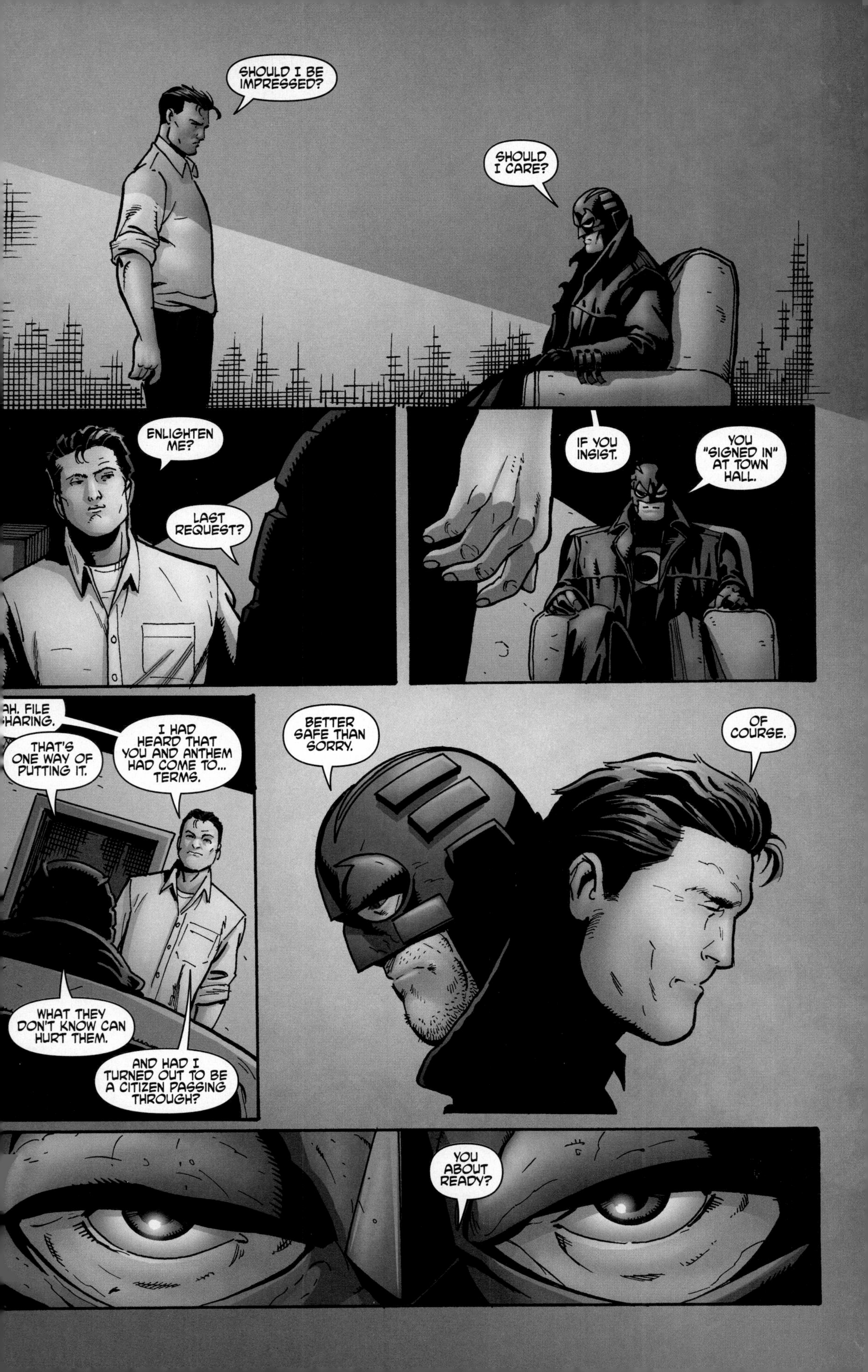
SHOULD I BE IMPRESSED?
SHOULD I CARE?
ENLIGHTEN ME?
LAST REQUEST?
IF YOU INSIST.
YOU "SIGNED IN" AT TOWN HALL.
AH. FILE SHARING.
I HAD HEARD THAT YOU AND ANTHEM HAD COME TO... TERMS.
THAT'S ONE WAY OF PUTTING IT.
WHAT THEY DON'T KNOW CAN HURT THEM.
AND HAD I TURNED OUT TO BE A CITIZEN PASSING THROUGH?
BETTER SAFE THAN SORRY.
OF COURSE.
YOU ABOUT READY?

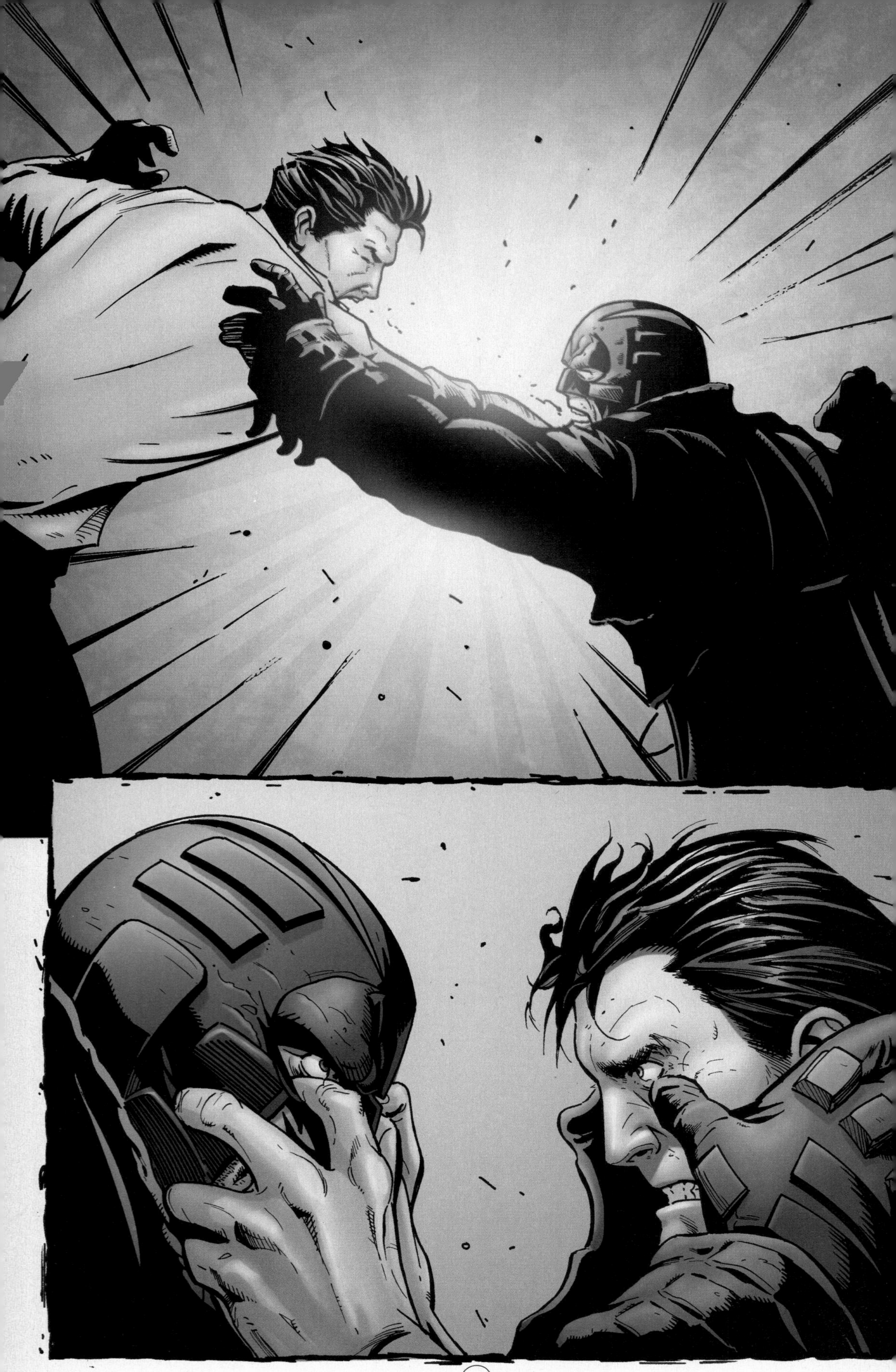

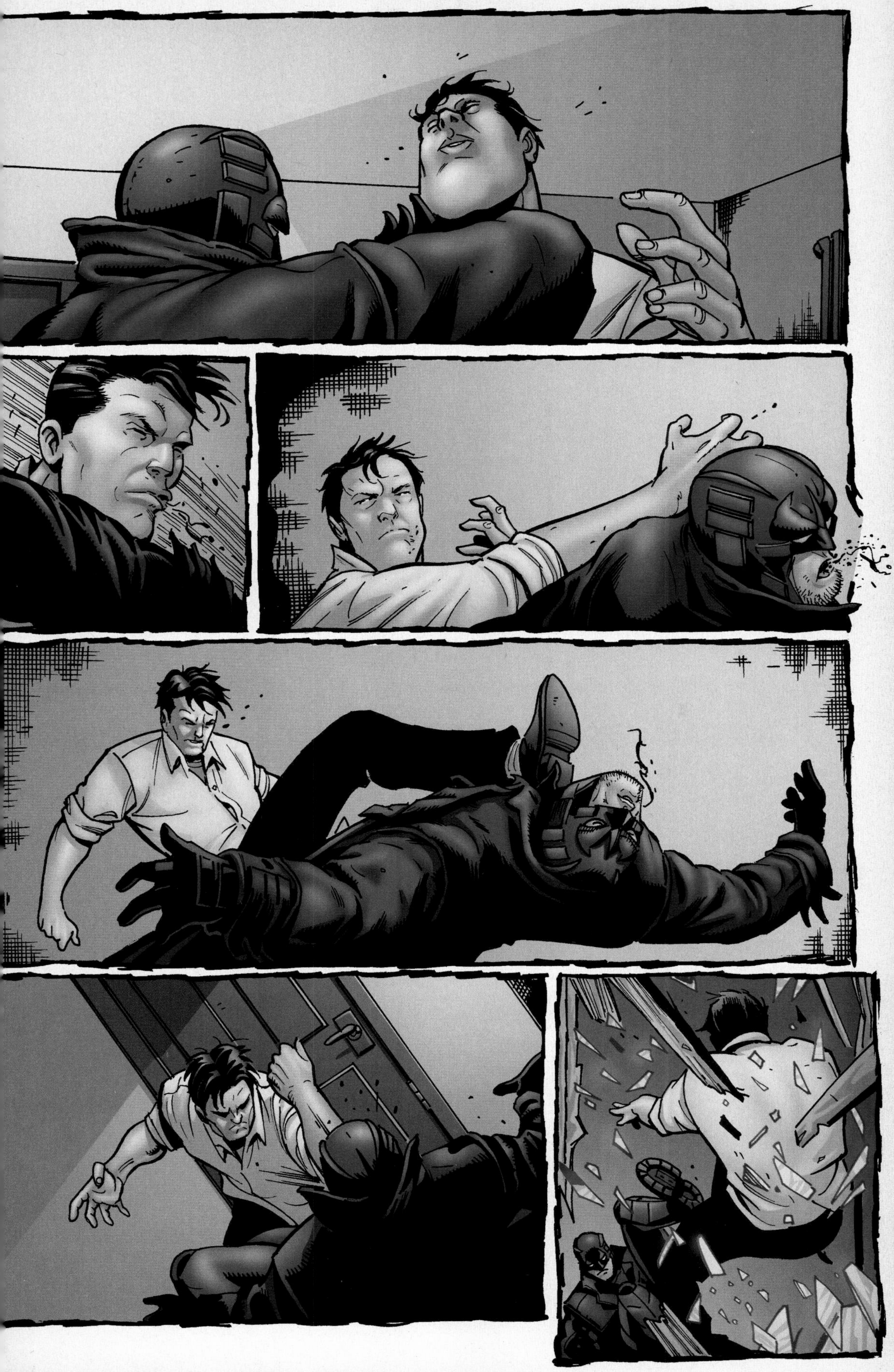

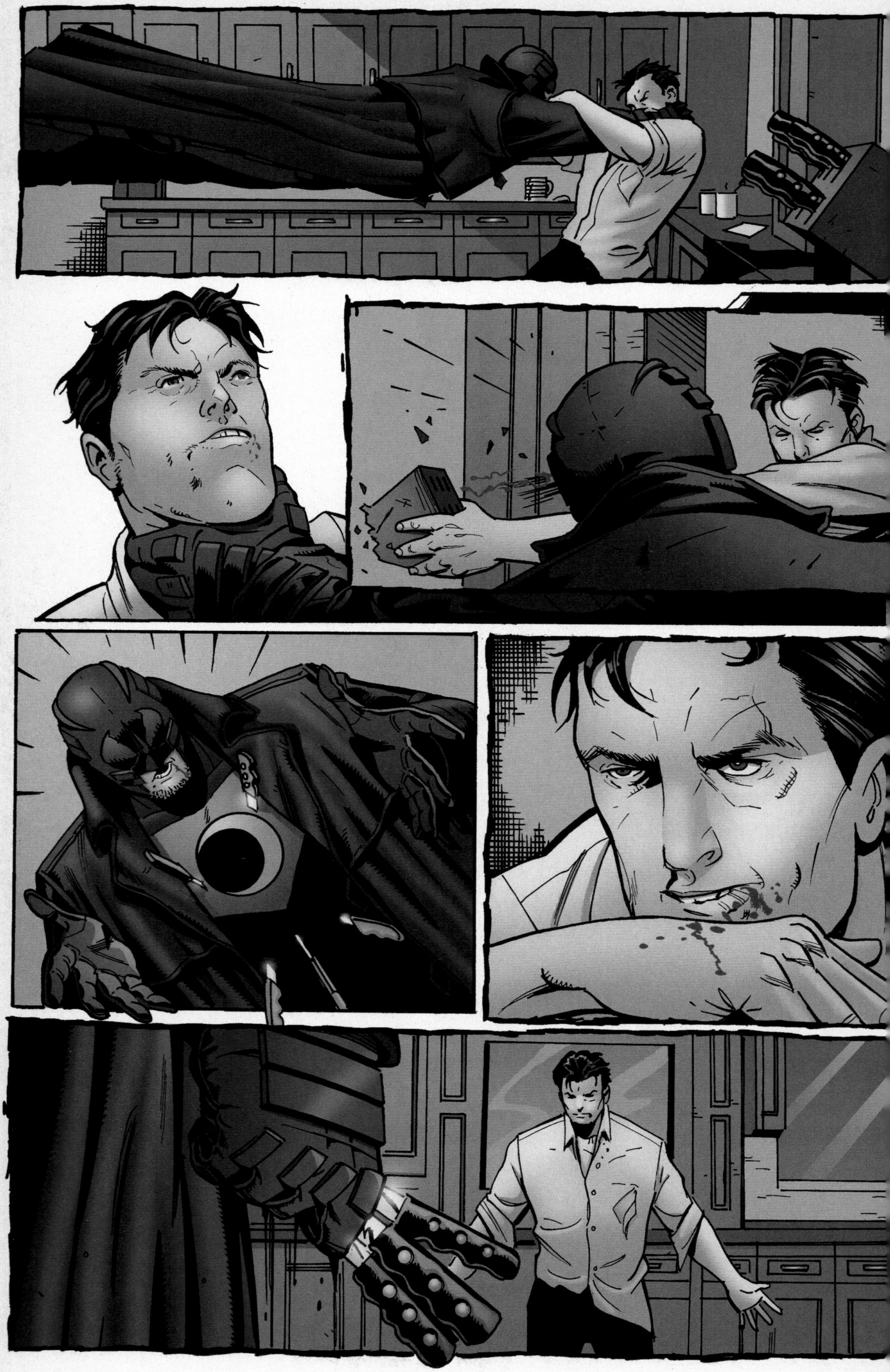

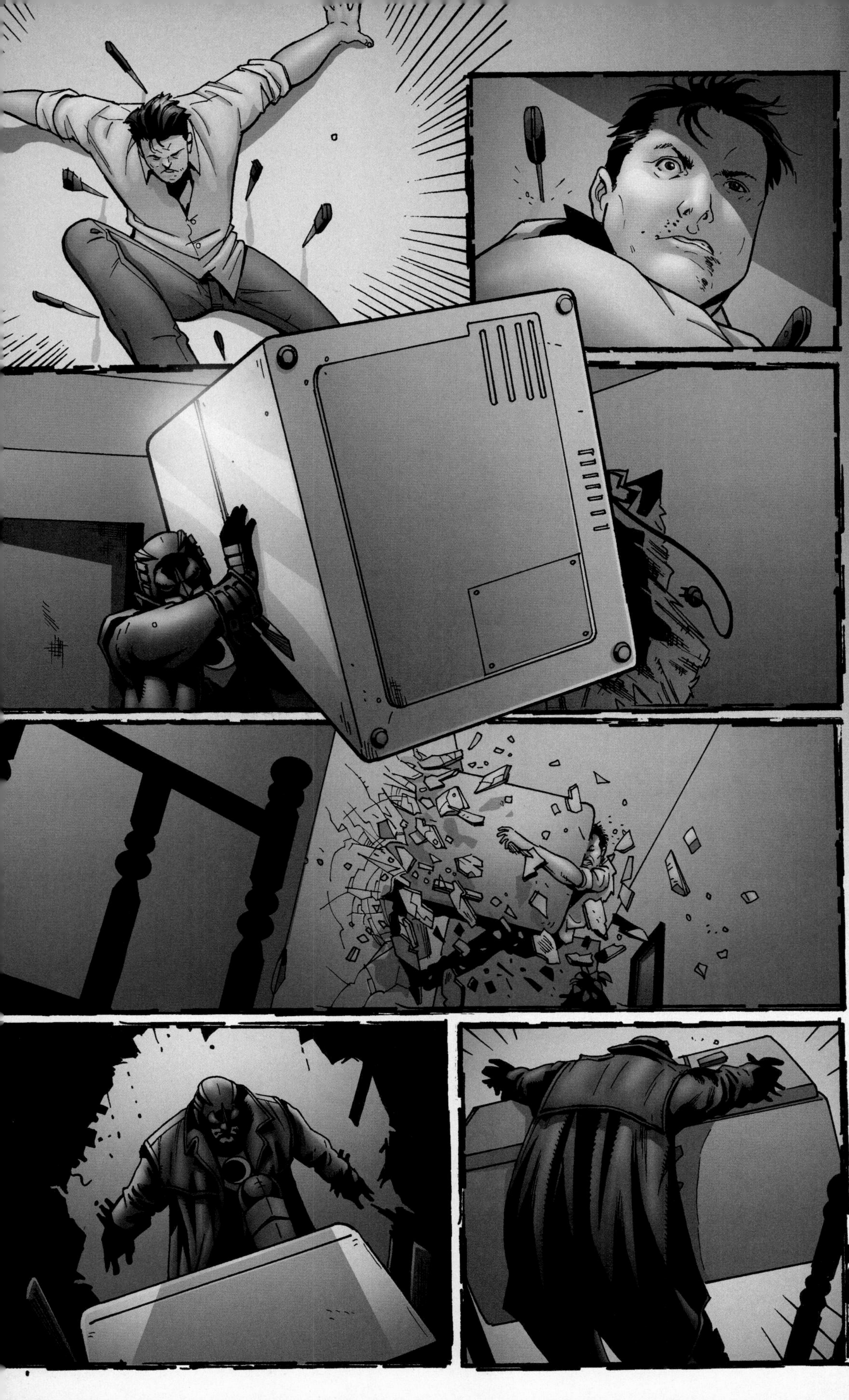

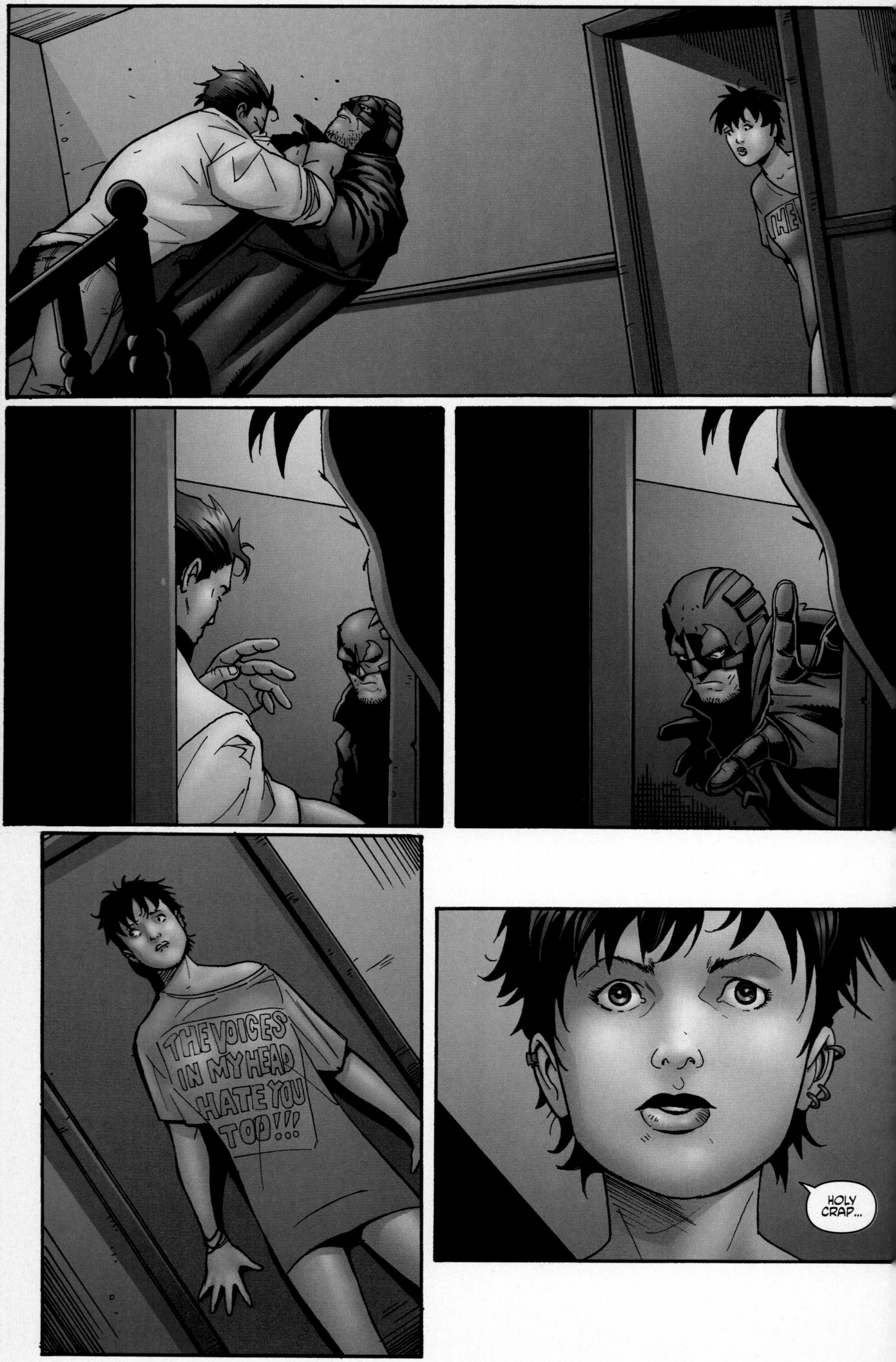
THE
THE VOICES IN MY HEAD HATE YOU TOO!!!
HOLY CRAP...

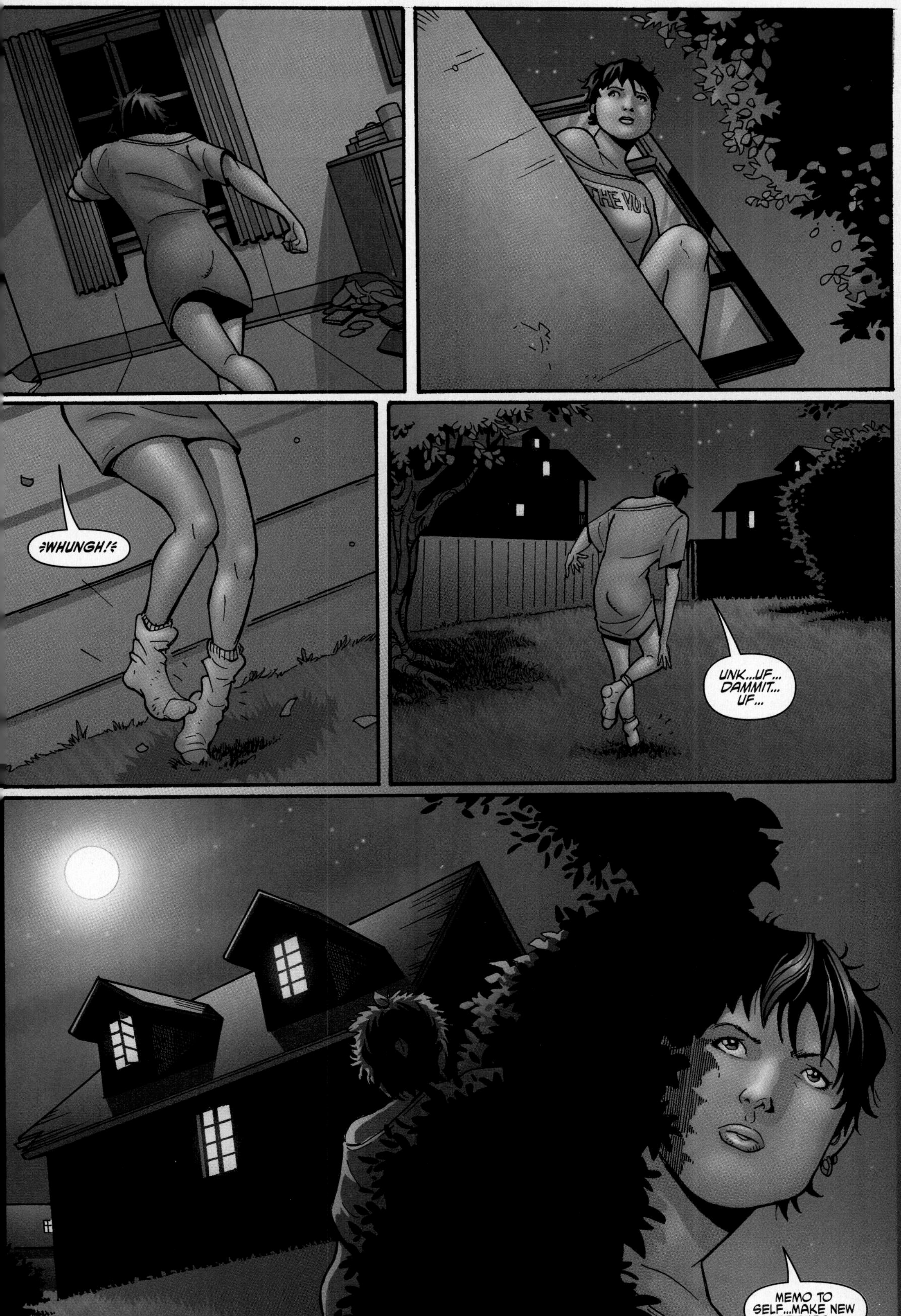
THE VO
WHUNGH!
UNK...UF... DAMMIT... UF...
MEMO TO SELF...MAKE NEW FRIENDS.

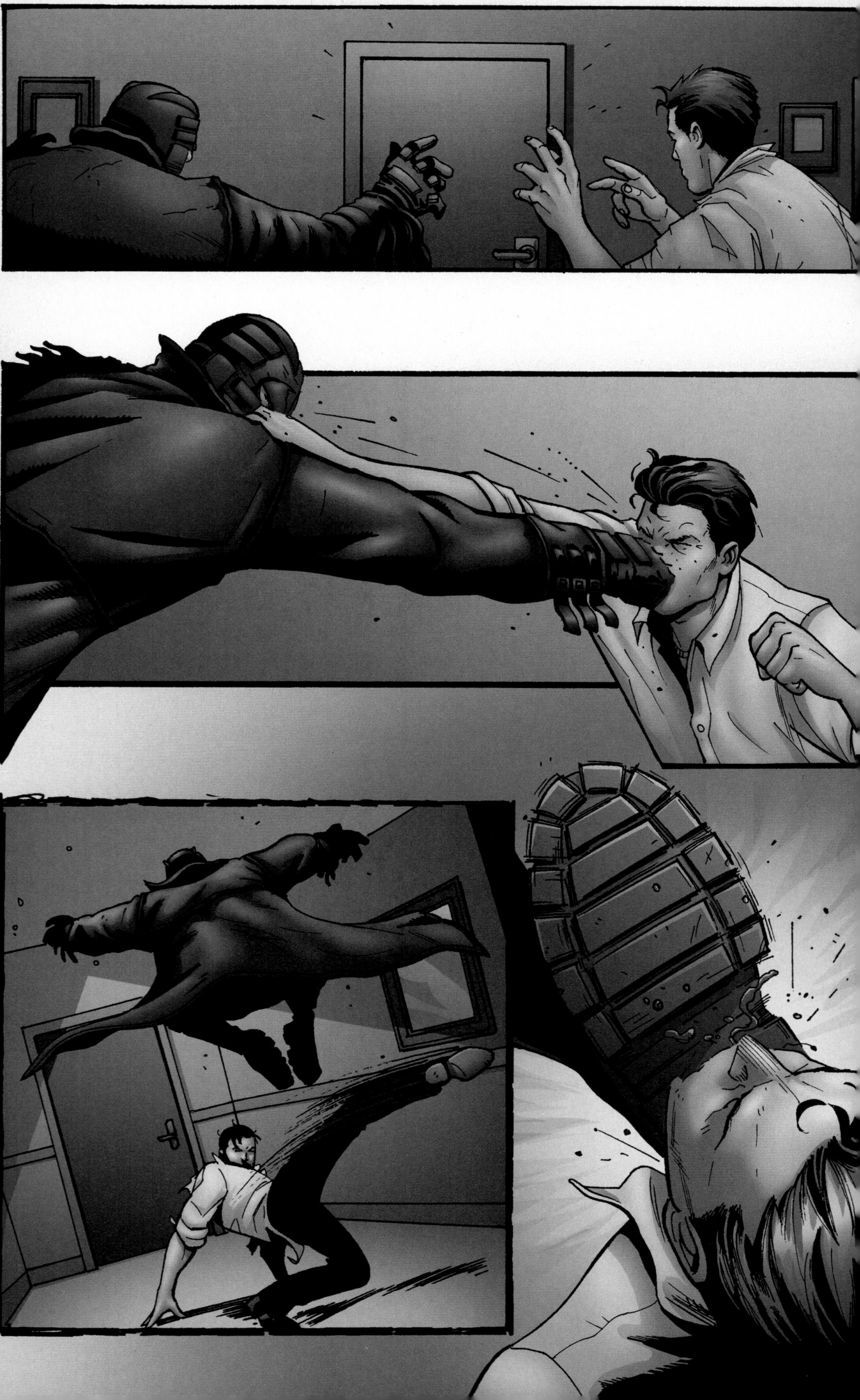

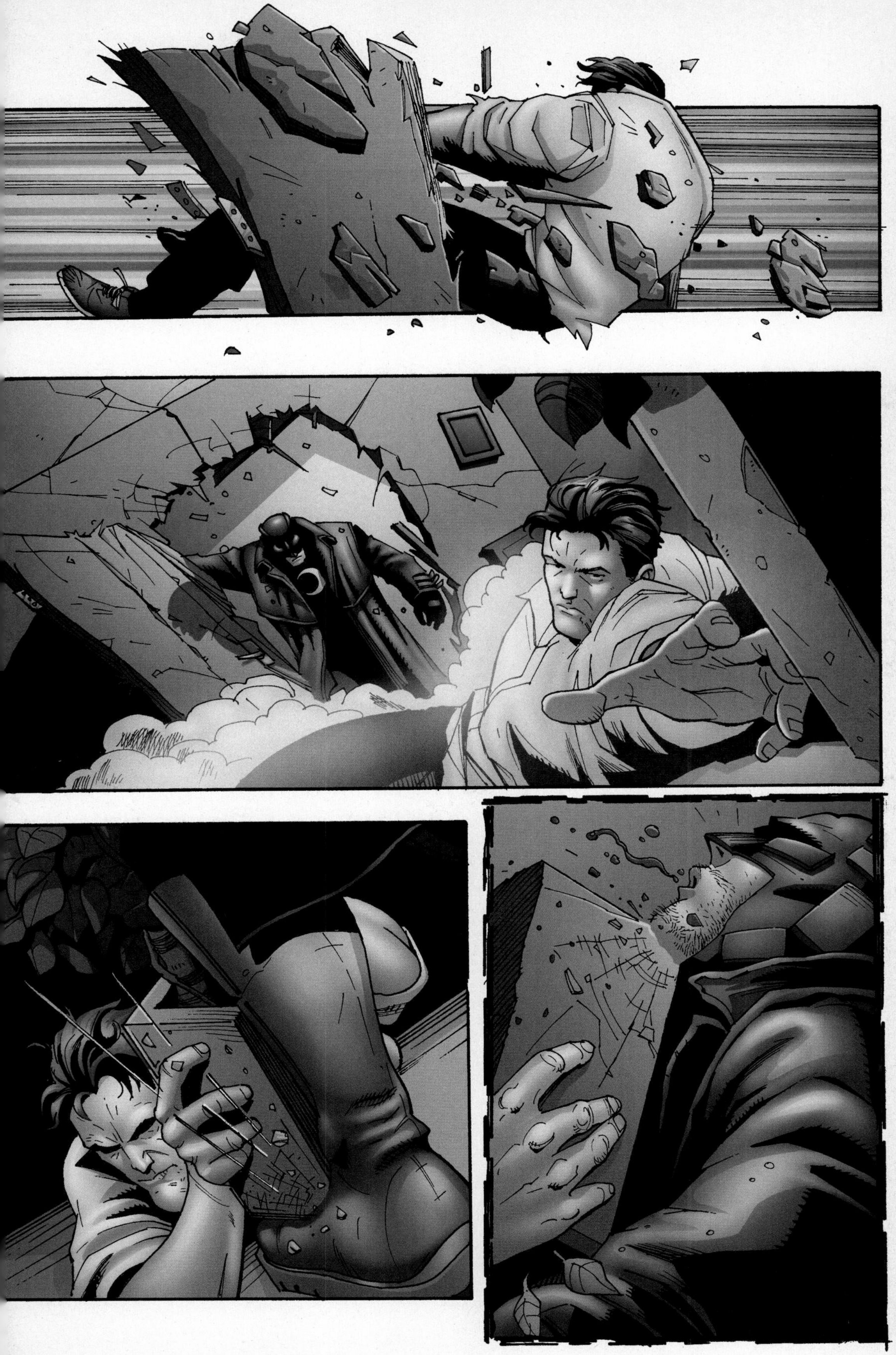

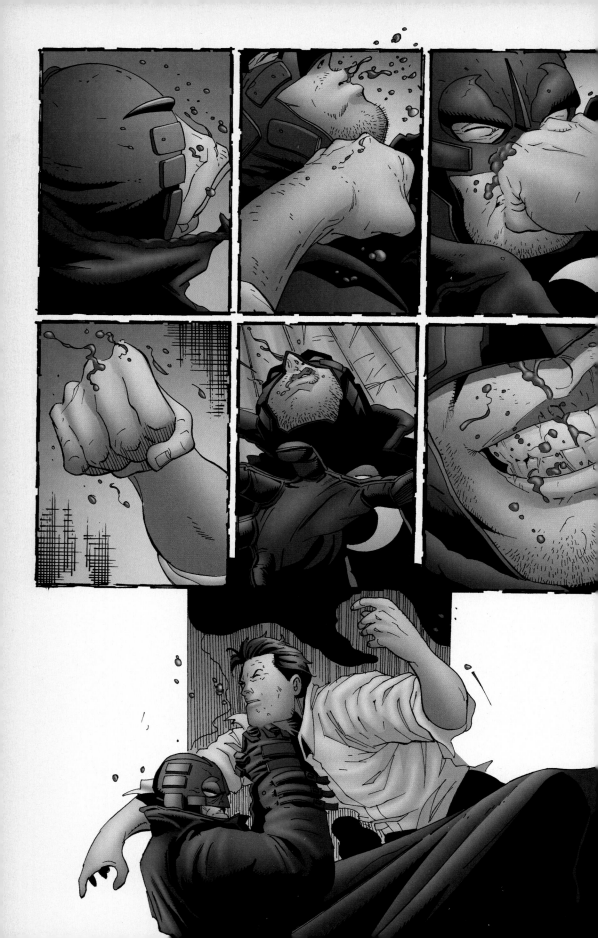

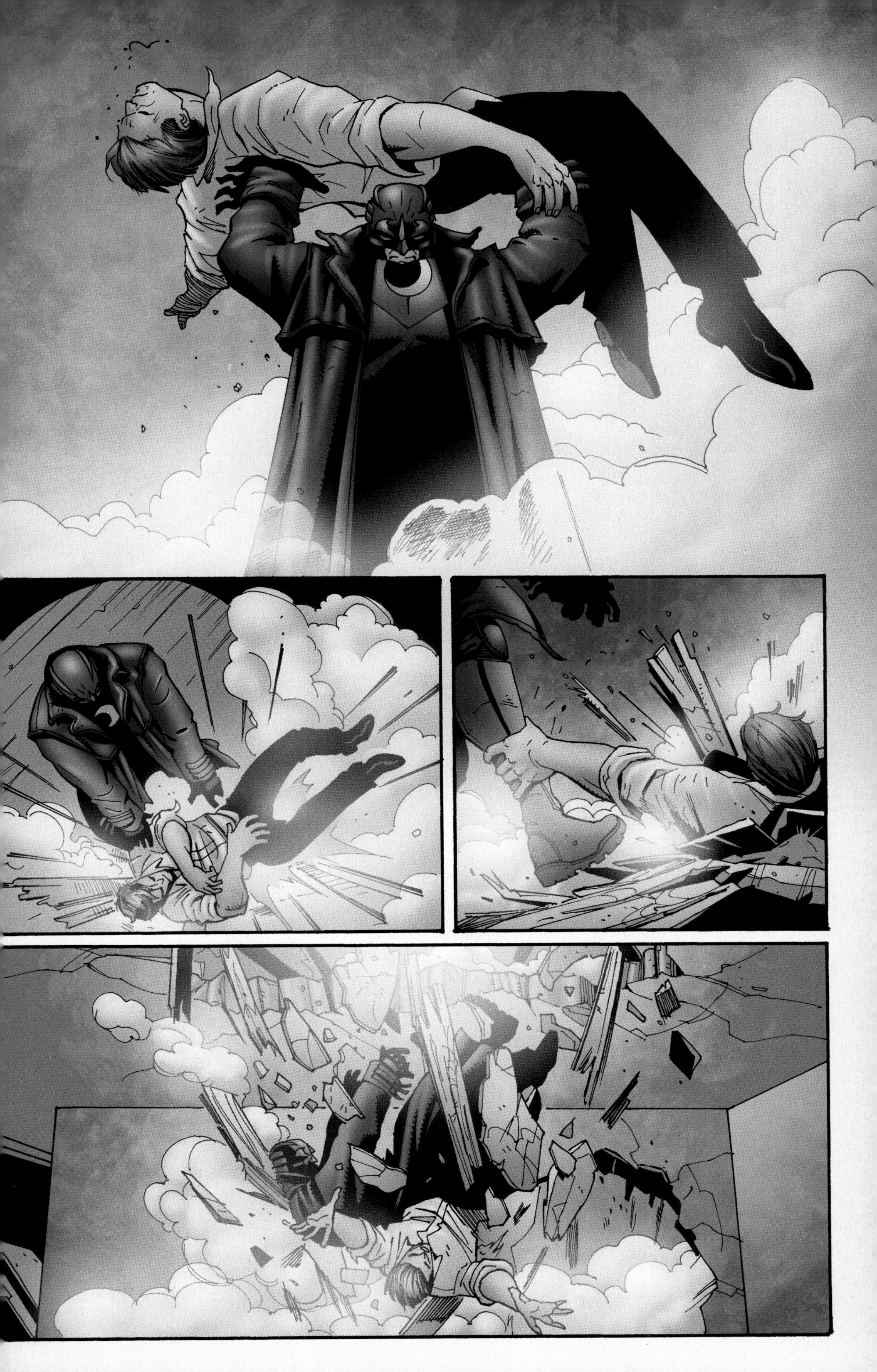

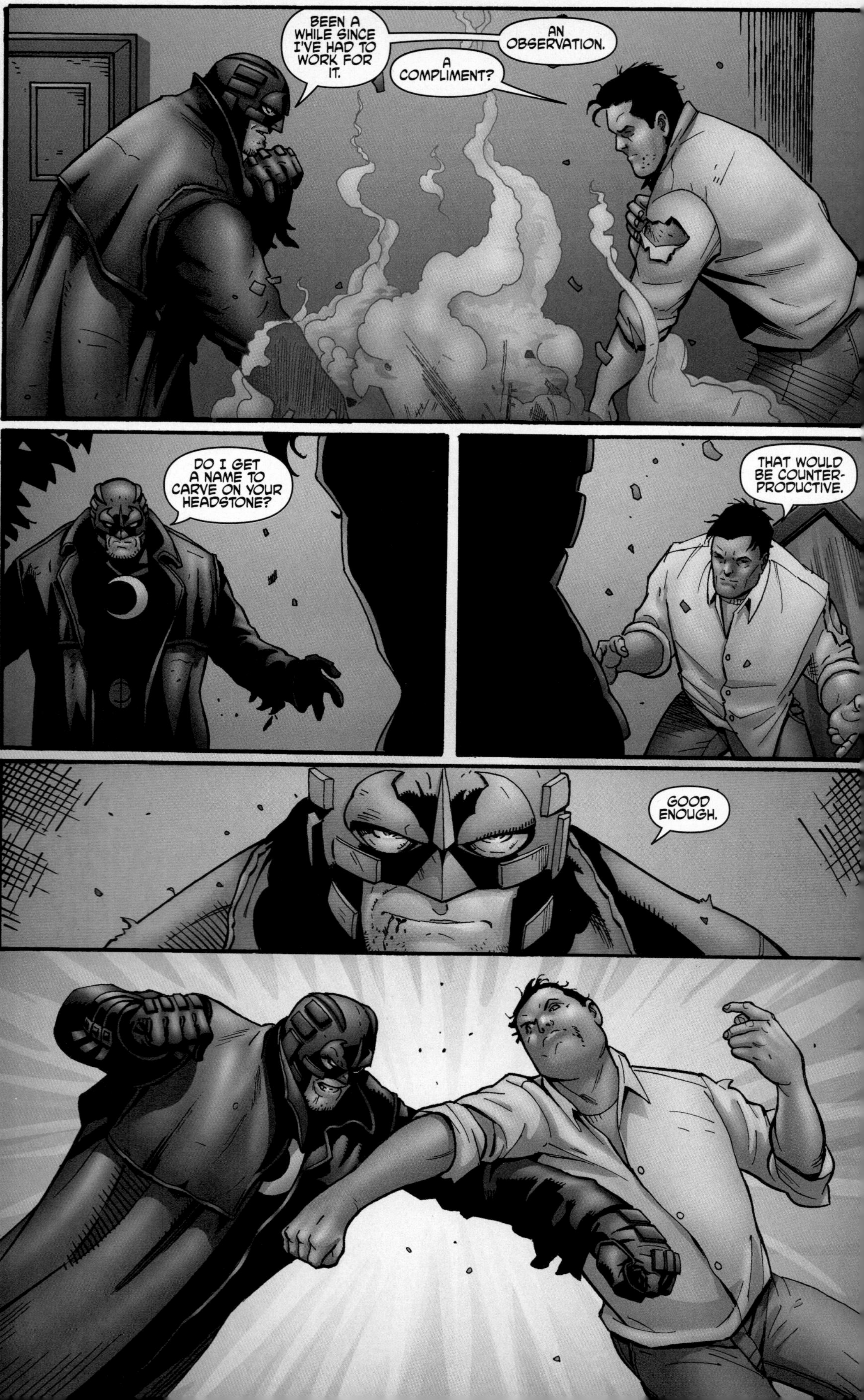
BEEN A WHILE SINCE I'VE HAD TO WORK FOR IT.
A COMPLIMENT?
AN OBSERVATION.
DO I GET A NAME TO CARVE ON YOUR HEADSTONE?
THAT WOULD BE COUNTER-PRODUCTIVE.
GOOD ENOUGH.

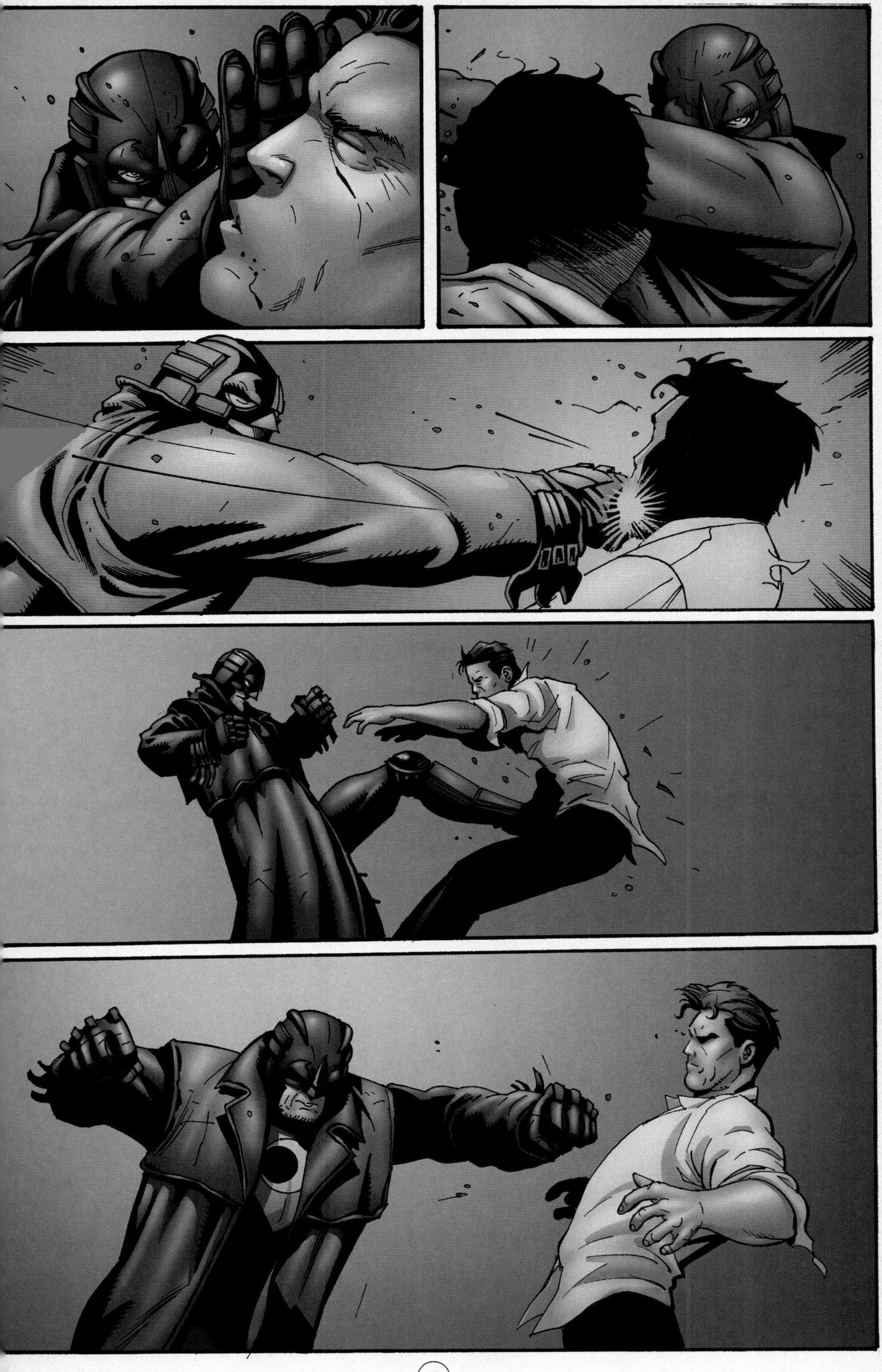

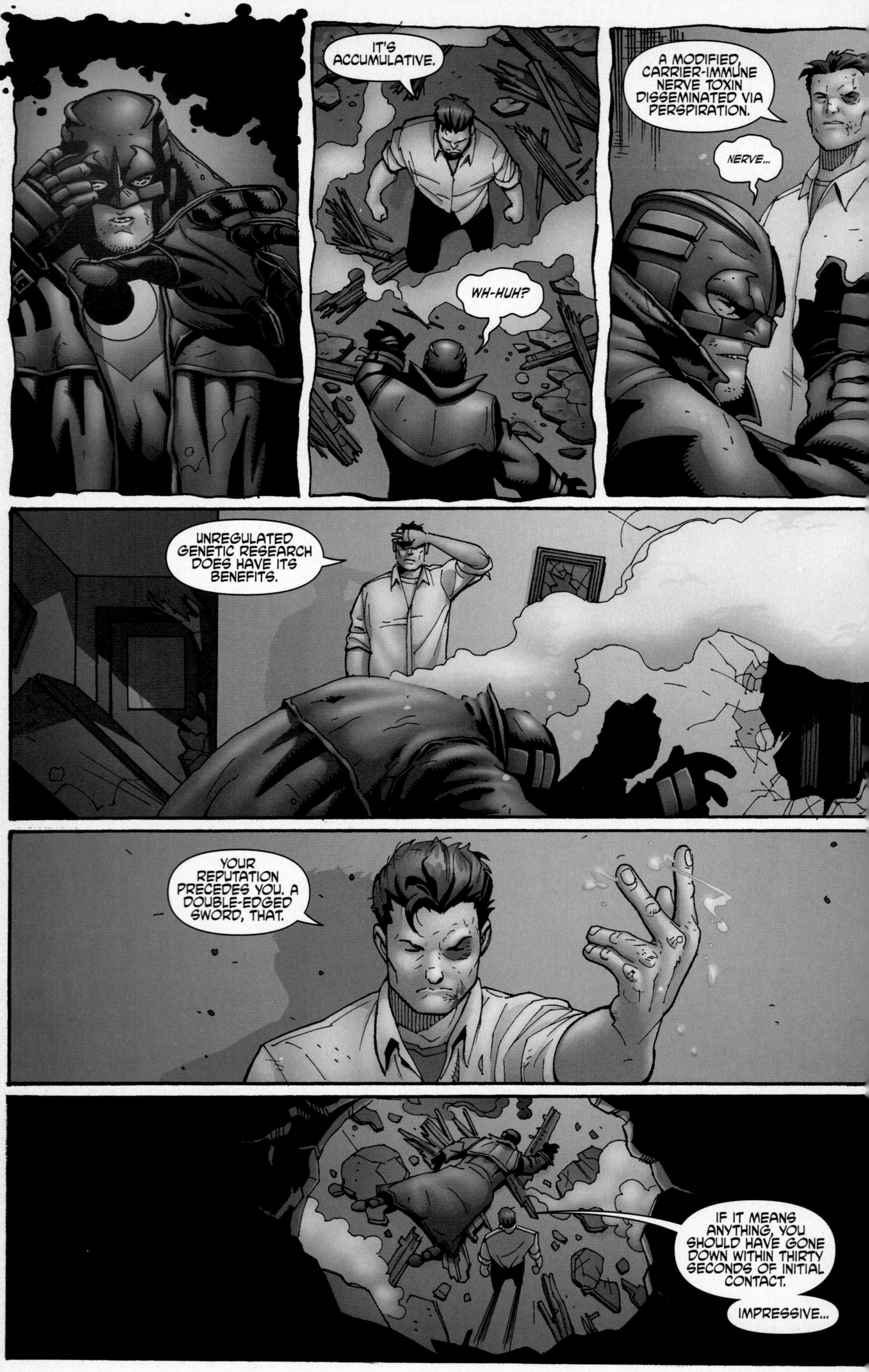
IT'S ACCUMULATIVE.
WH-HUH?
A MODIFIED, CARRIER-IMMUNE NERVE TOXIN DISSEMINATED VIA PERSPIRATION.
NERVE...
UNREGULATED GENETIC RESEARCH DOES HAVE ITS BENEFITS.
YOUR REPUTATION PRECEDES YOU. A DOUBLE-EDGED SWORD, THAT.
IF IT MEANS ANYTHING, YOU SHOULD HAVE GONE DOWN WITHIN THIRTY SECONDS OF INITIAL CONTACT.
IMPRESSIVE...

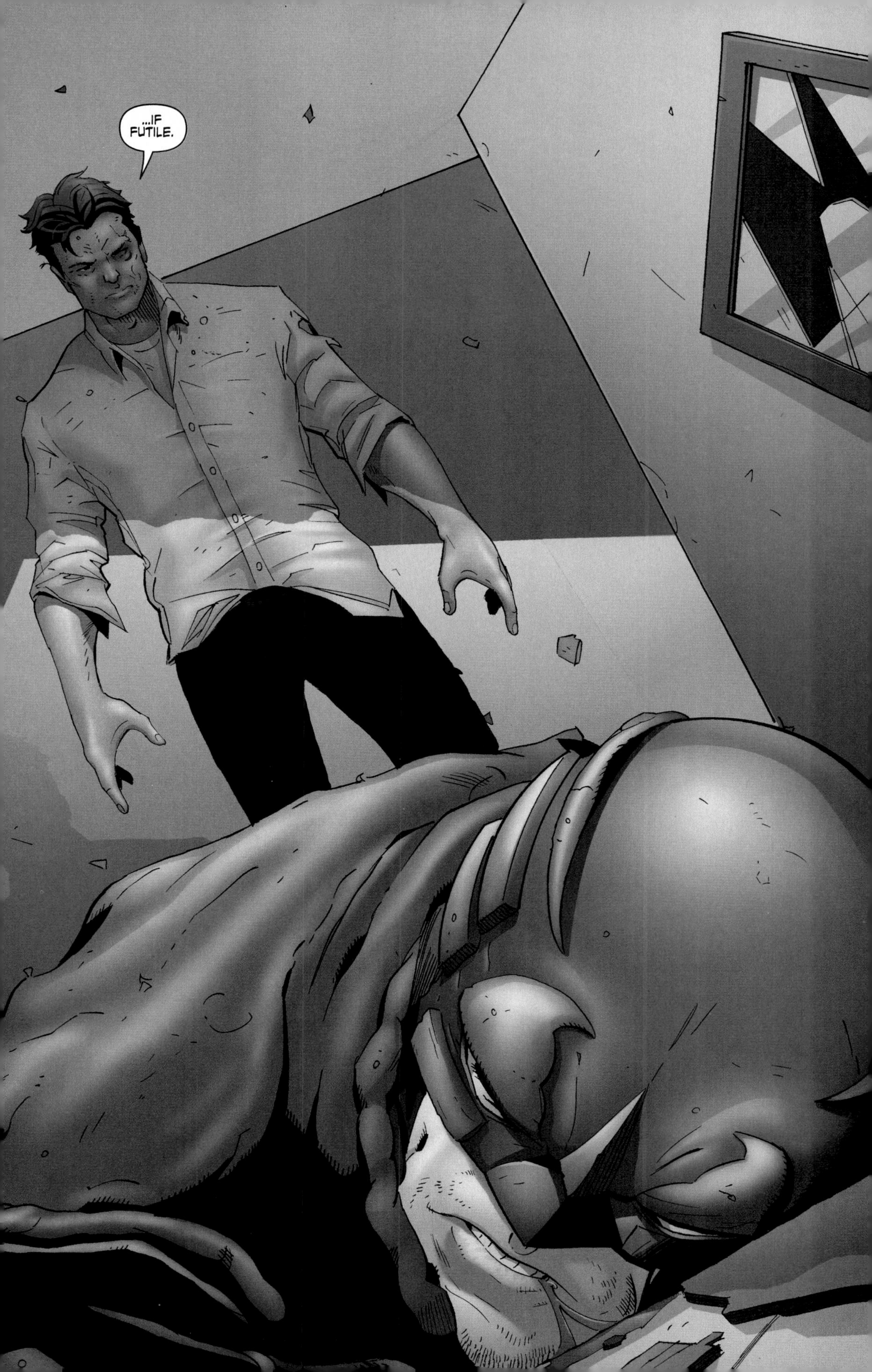
...IF FUTILE.

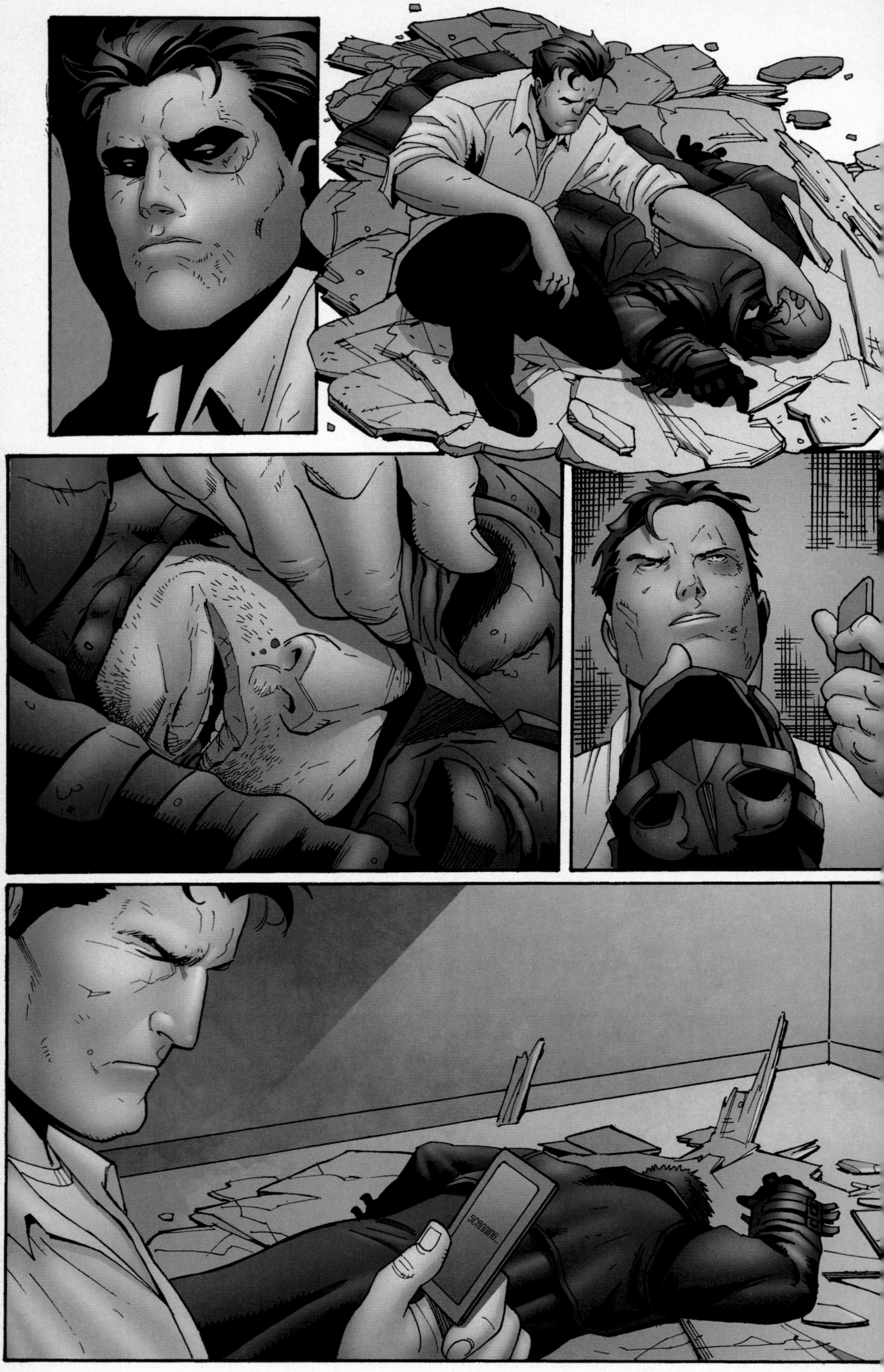
SCANNING...

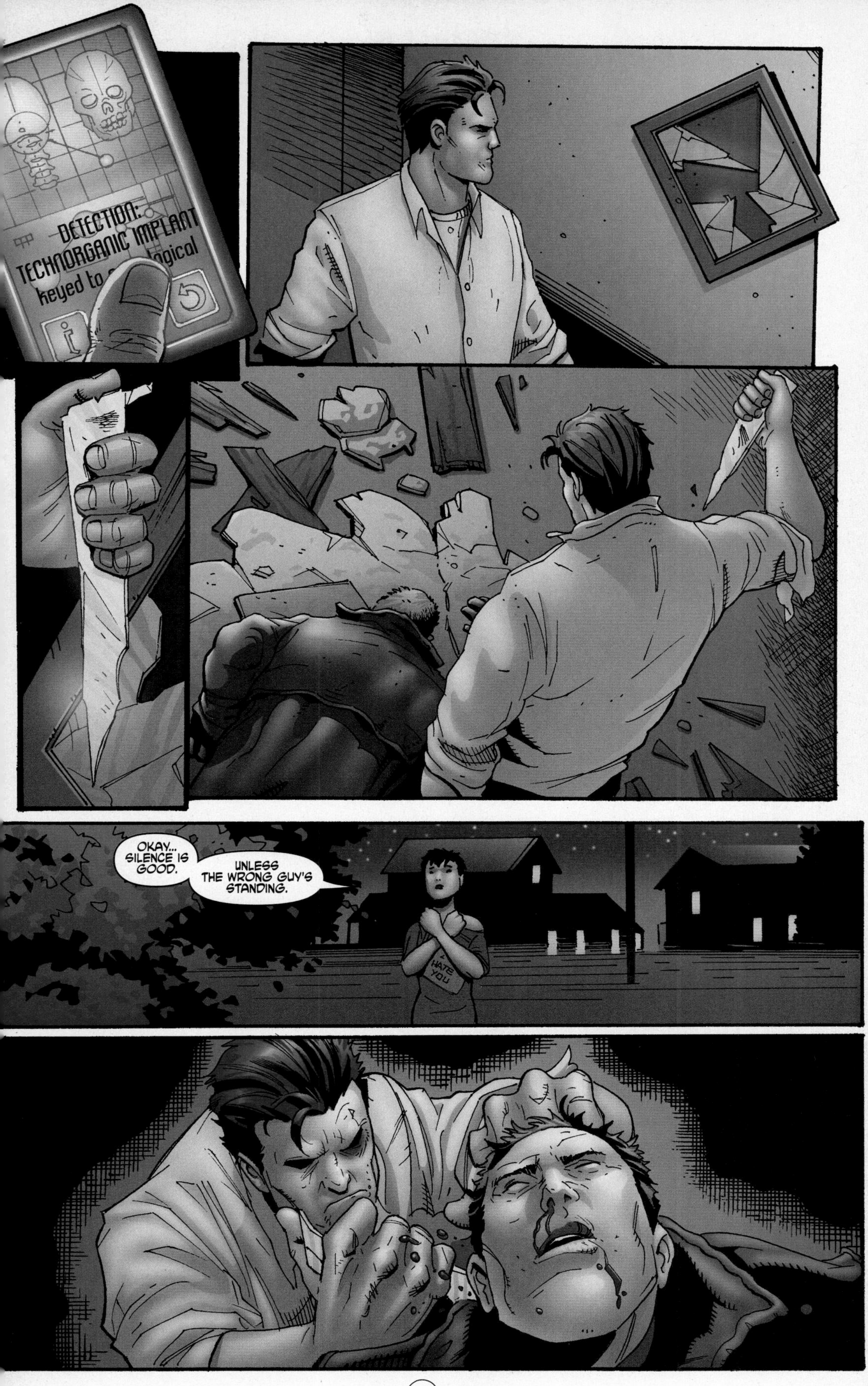
DETECTION:
TECHNORGANIC IMPLANT
OKAY... SILENCE IS GOOD.
UNLESS THE WRONG GUY'S STANDING.
I HATE YOU

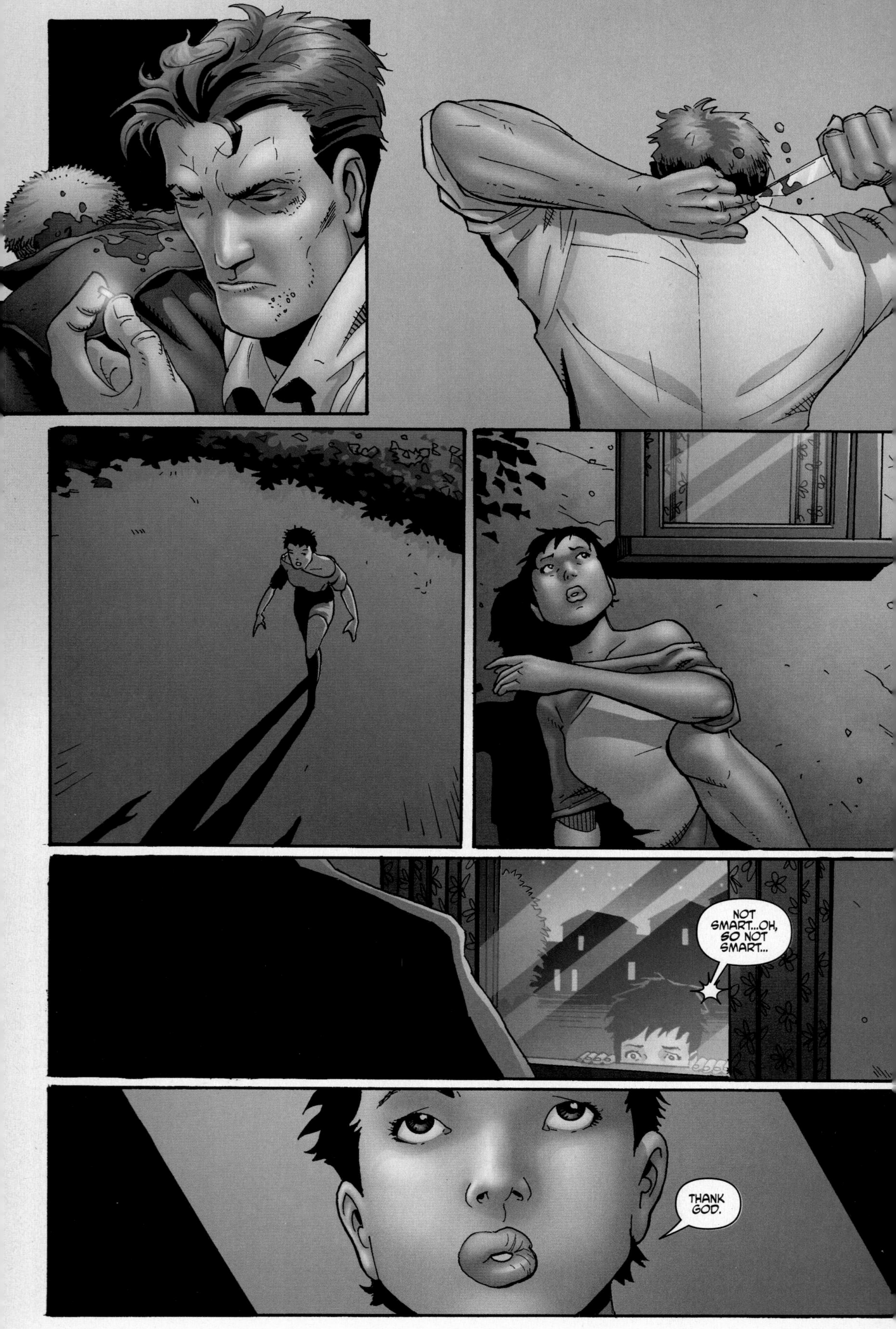
NOT SMART...OH, SO NOT SMART...
THANK GOD.

HEY! NEXT TIME A LITTLE WARNING...

...OKAY?... UM...

DOOR.

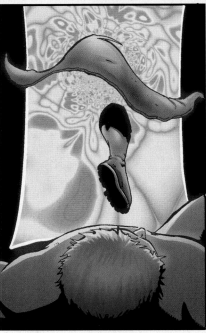

THAT CAN'T BE GOOD.

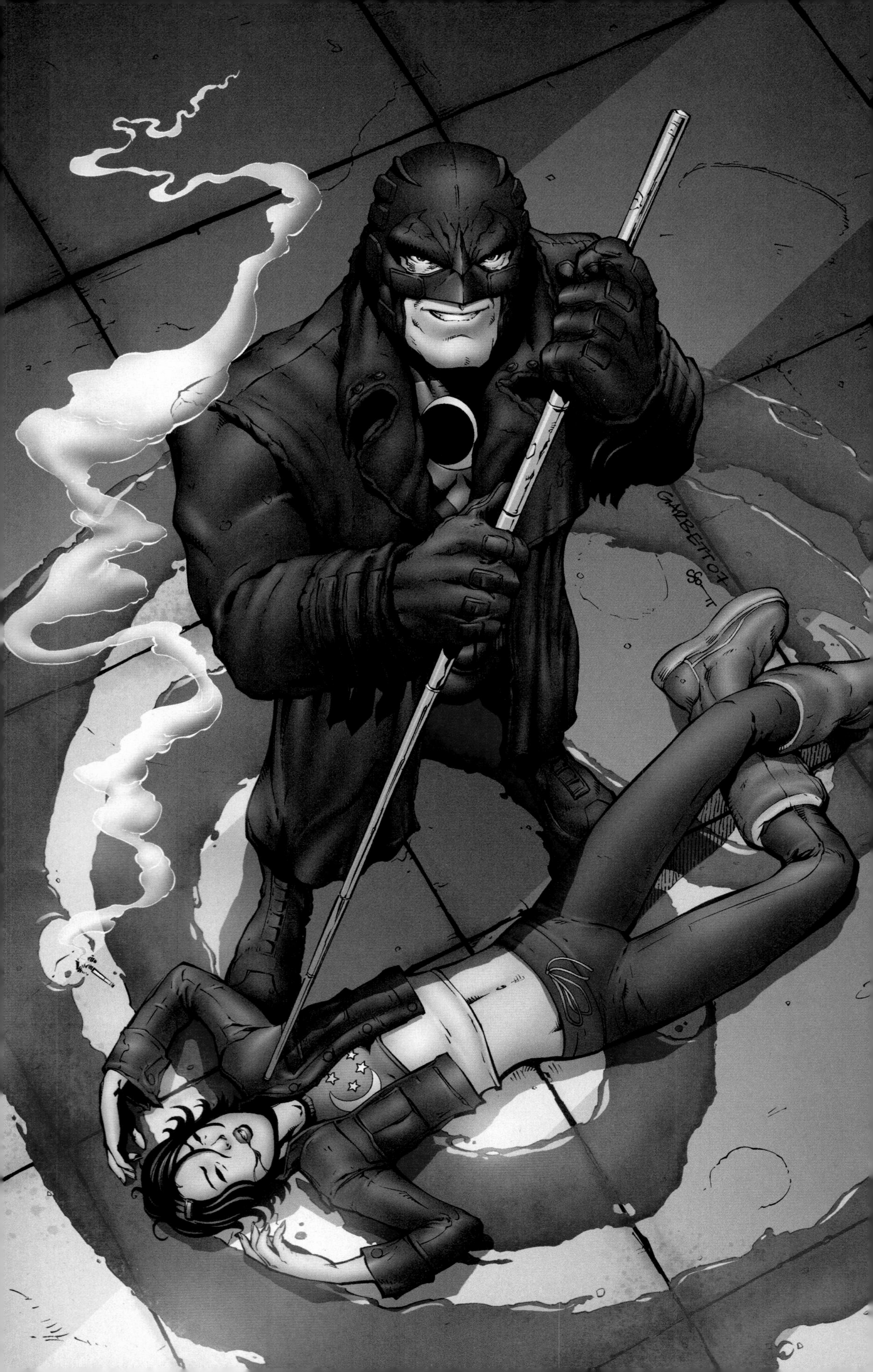
GARBETT07

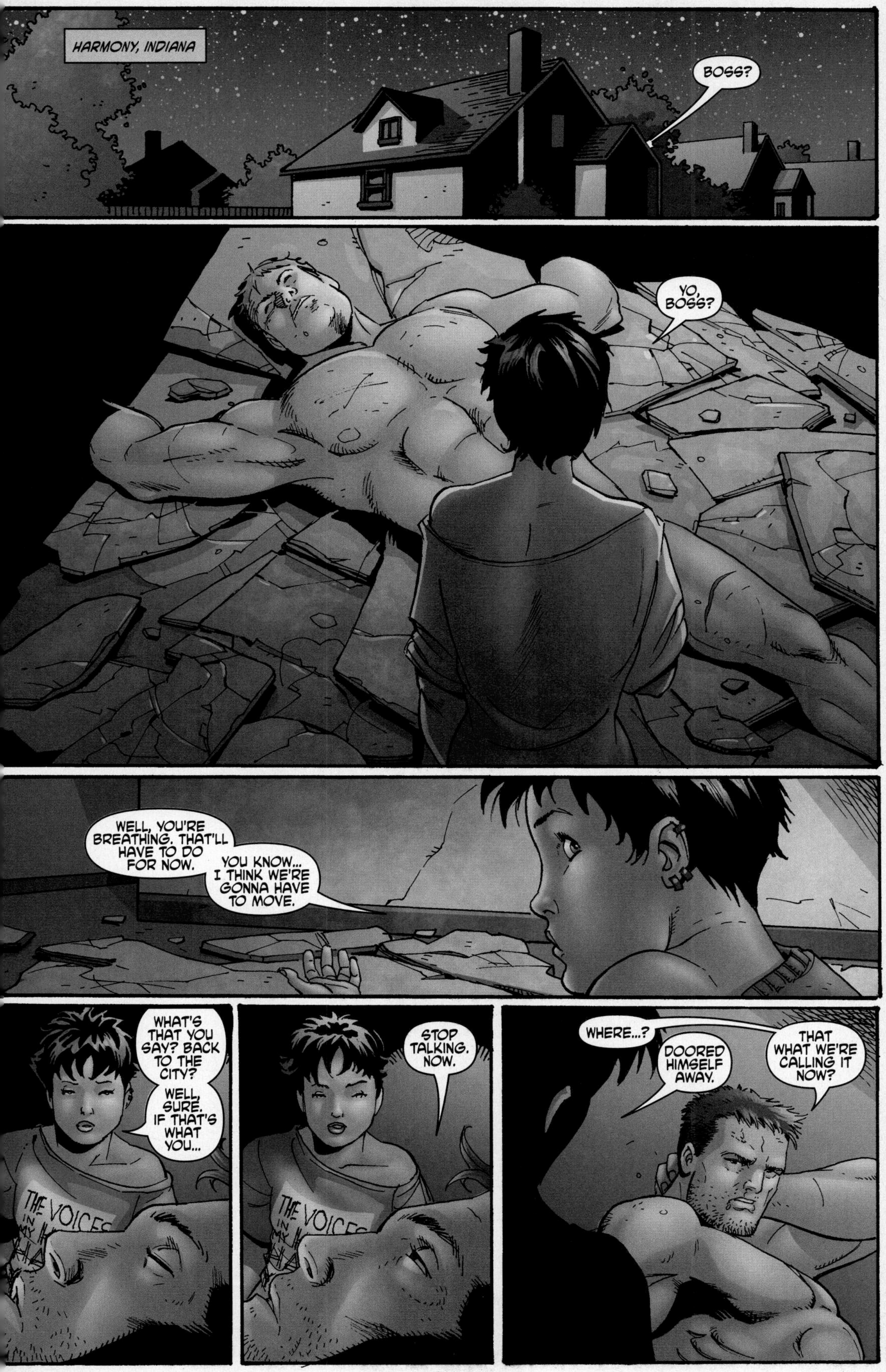
HARMONY, INDIANA
BOSS?
YO, BOSS?
WELL, YOU'RE BREATHING. THAT'LL HAVE TO DO FOR NOW.
YOU KNOW... I THINK WE'RE GONNA HAVE TO MOVE.
WHAT'S THAT YOU SAY? BACK TO THE CITY?
WELL, SURE. IF THAT'S WHAT YOU...
THE VOICES IN MY
STOP TALKING. NOW.
WHERE...?
DOORED HIMSELF AWAY.
THAT WHAT WE'RE CALLING IT NOW?

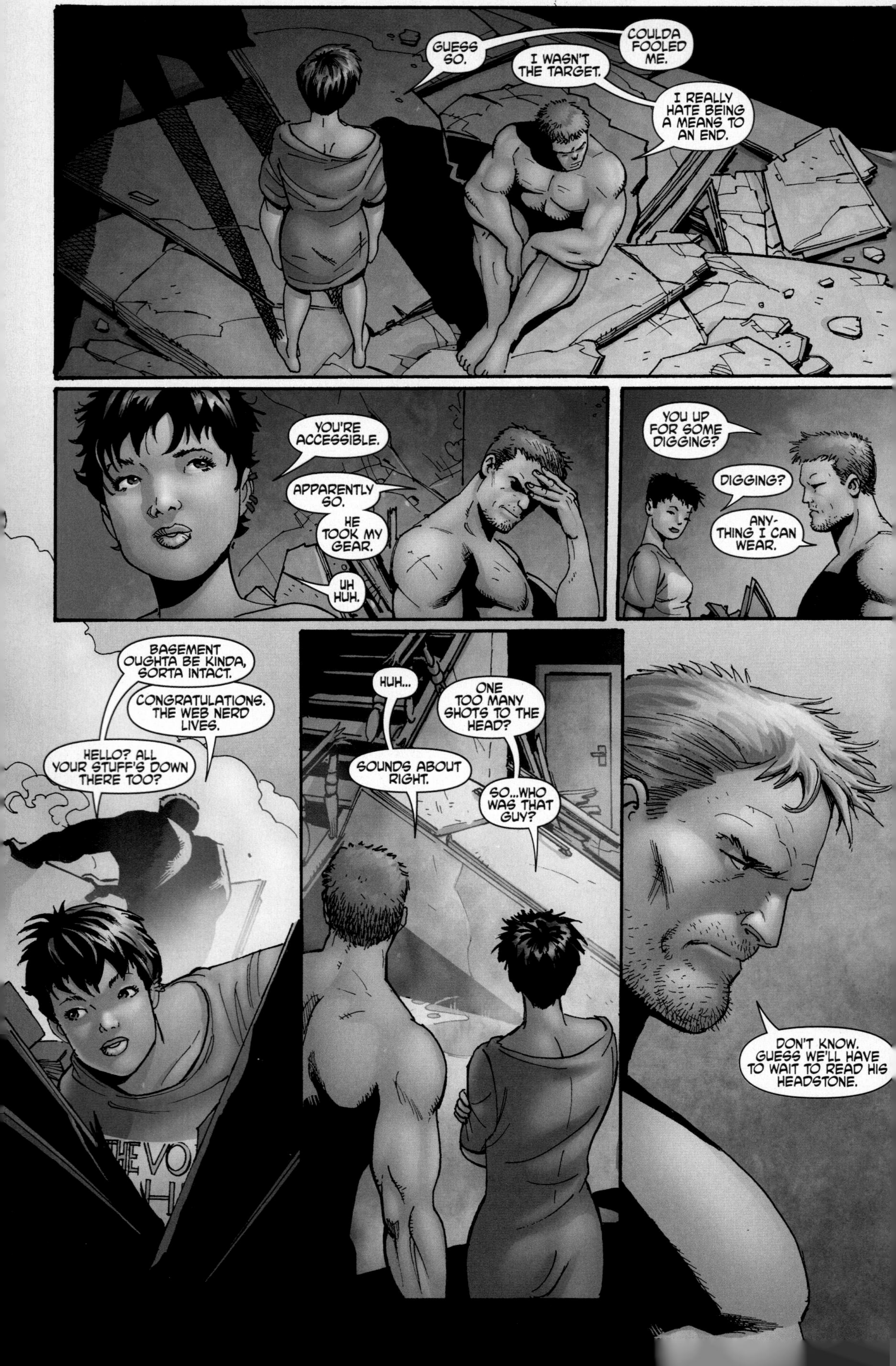
GUESS SO.
COULDA FOOLED ME.
I WASN'T THE TARGET.
I REALLY HATE BEING A MEANS TO AN END.
YOU'RE ACCESSIBLE.
APPARENTLY SO.
HE TOOK MY GEAR.
UH HUH.
YOU UP FOR SOME DIGGING?
DIGGING?
ANY-THING I CAN WEAR.
BASEMENT OUGHTA BE KINDA, SORTA INTACT.
CONGRATULATIONS. THE WEB NERD LIVES.
HELLO? ALL YOUR STUFF'S DOWN THERE TOO?
HUH...
ONE TOO MANY SHOTS TO THE HEAD?
SOUNDS ABOUT RIGHT.
SO...WHO WAS THAT GUY?
DON'T KNOW. GUESS WE'LL HAVE TO WAIT TO READ HIS HEADSTONE.

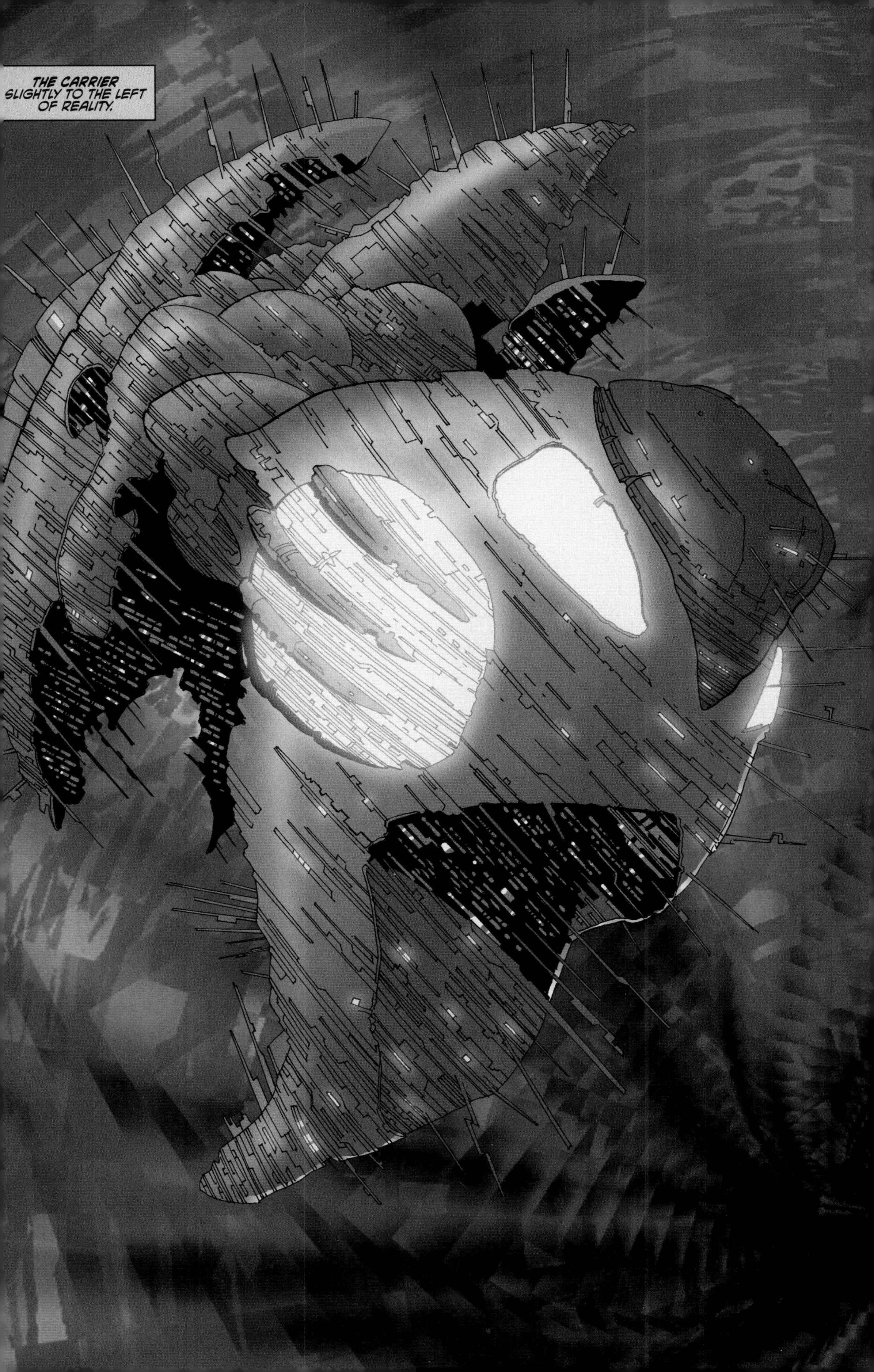
THE CARRIER SLIGHTLY TO THE LEFT OF REALITY.

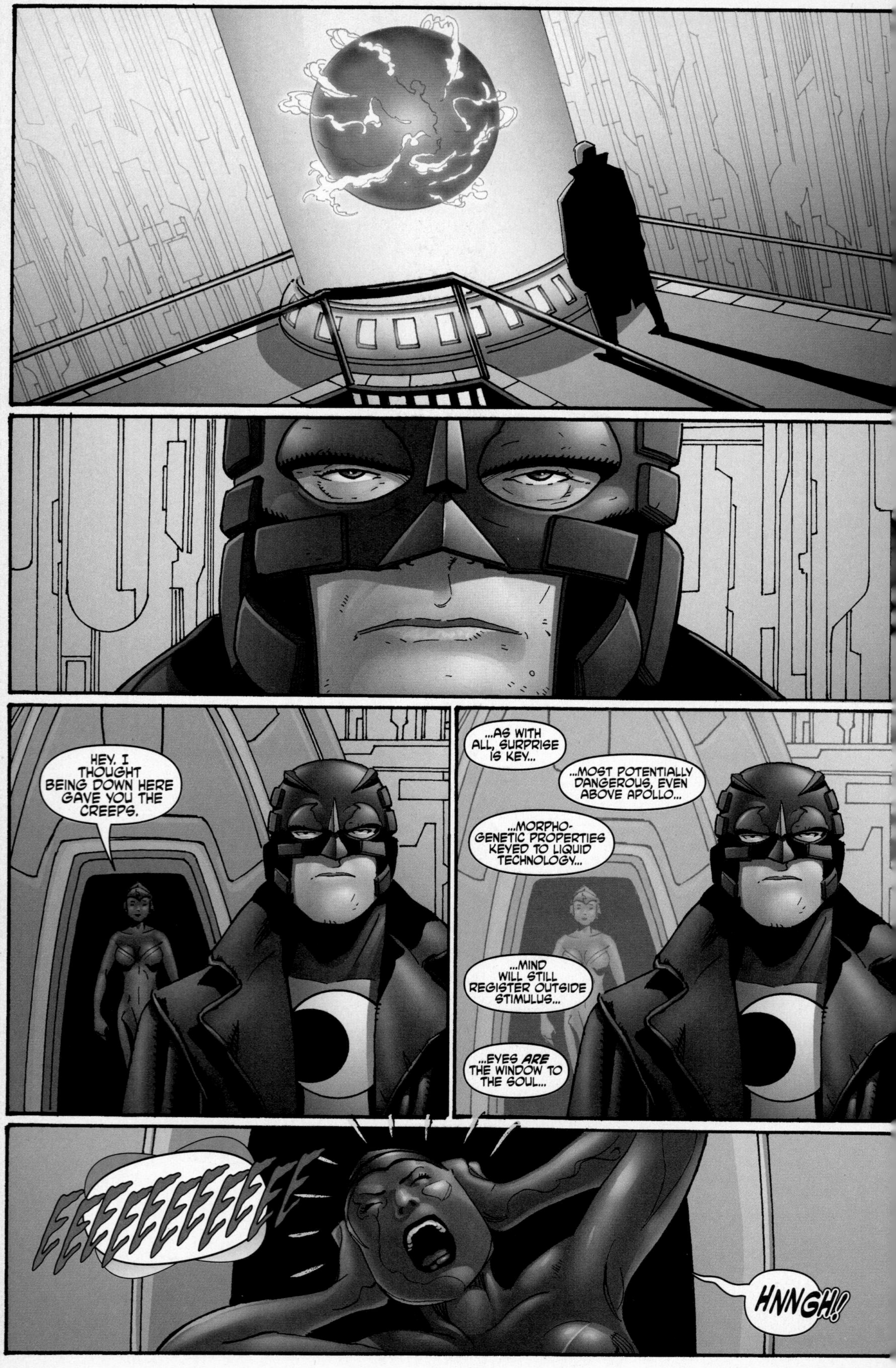
HEY. I THOUGHT BEING DOWN HERE GAVE YOU THE CREEPS.
...AS WITH ALL, SURPRISE IS KEY...
...MOST POTENTIALLY DANGEROUS, EVEN ABOVE APOLLO...
...MORPHO-GENETIC PROPERTIES KEYED TO LIQUID TECHNOLOGY...
...MIND WILL STILL REGISTER OUTSIDE STIMULUS...
...EYES *ARE* THE WINDOW TO THE SOUL...
EEEEEEEEEEEE
HNNGH!

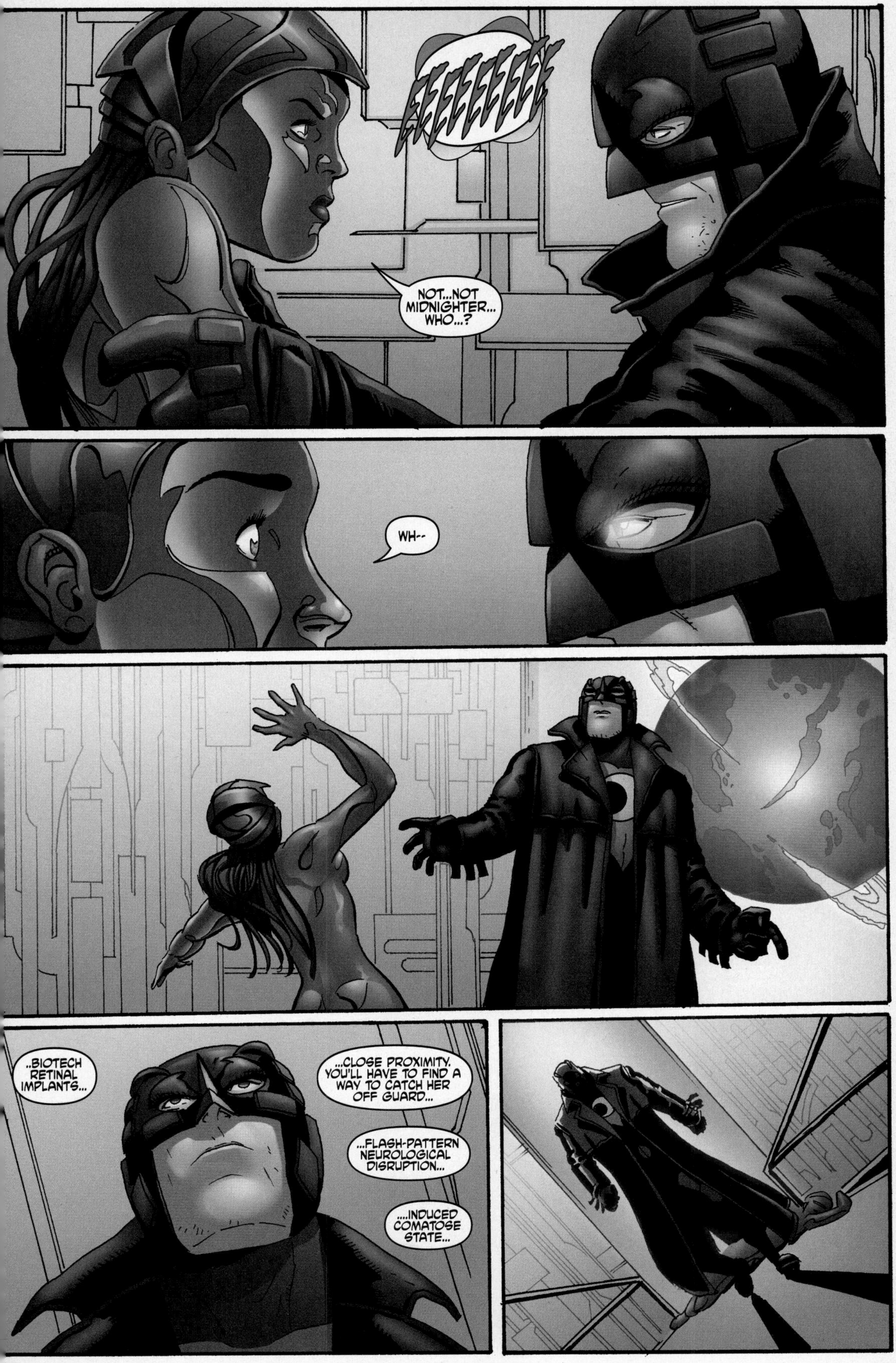
EEEEEEEEE
NOT...NOT MIDNIGHTER... WHO...?
WH--
..BIOTECH RETINAL IMPLANTS...
...CLOSE PROXIMITY. YOU'LL HAVE TO FIND A WAY TO CATCH HER OFF GUARD...
...FLASH-PATTERN NEUROLOGICAL DISRUPTION...
....INDUCED COMATOSE STATE...

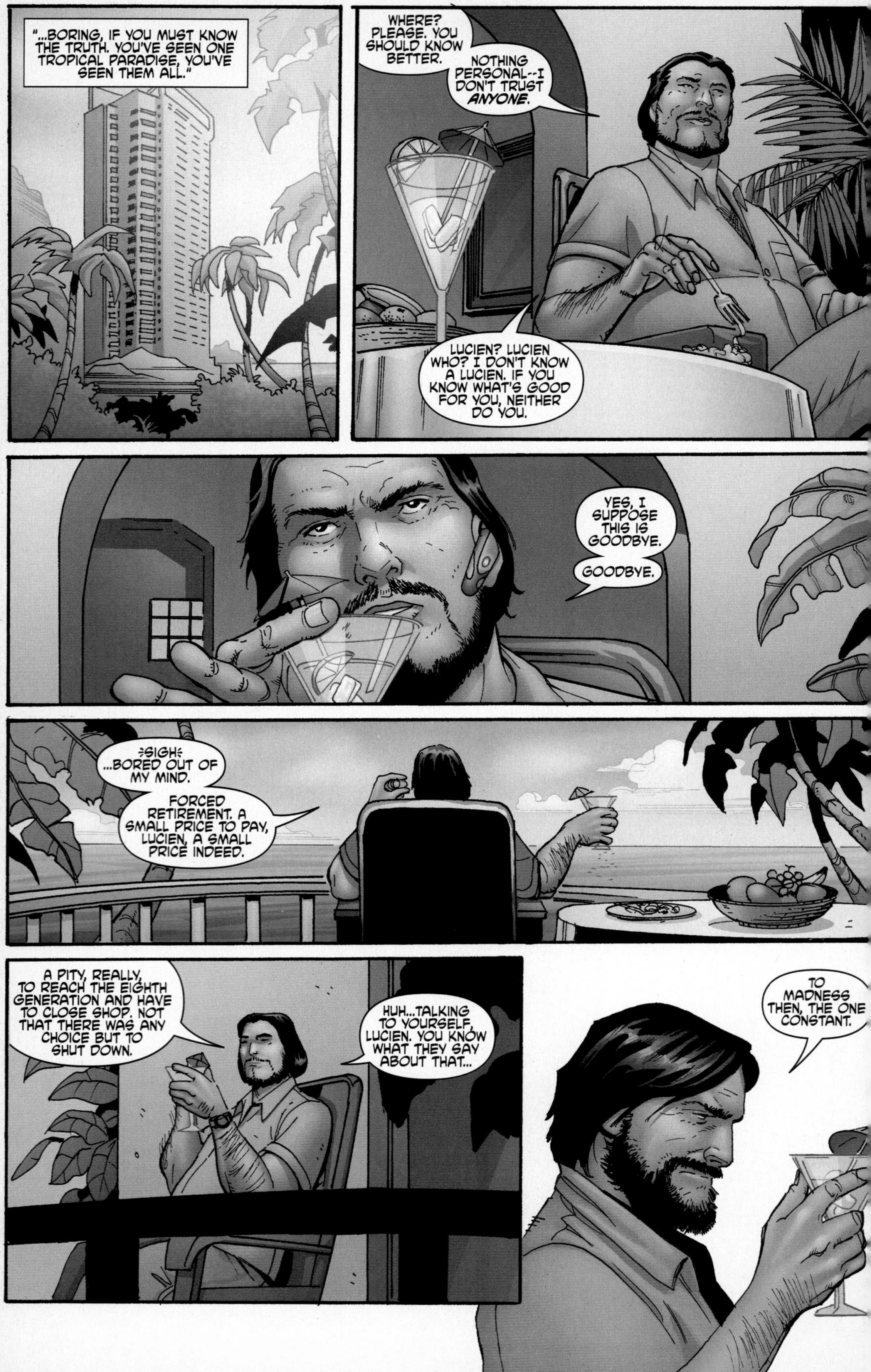
"...BORING, IF YOU MUST KNOW THE TRUTH. YOU'VE SEEN ONE TROPICAL PARADISE, YOU'VE SEEN THEM ALL."
WHERE? PLEASE. YOU SHOULD KNOW BETTER.
NOTHING PERSONAL--I DON'T TRUST ANYONE.
LUCIEN? LUCIEN WHO? I DON'T KNOW A LUCIEN. IF YOU KNOW WHAT'S GOOD FOR YOU, NEITHER DO YOU.
YES, I SUPPOSE THIS IS GOODBYE.
GOODBYE.
SIGH
...BORED OUT OF MY MIND.
FORCED RETIREMENT. A SMALL PRICE TO PAY, LUCIEN, A SMALL PRICE INDEED.
A PITY, REALLY, TO REACH THE EIGHTH GENERATION AND HAVE TO CLOSE SHOP. NOT THAT THERE WAS ANY CHOICE BUT TO SHUT DOWN.
HUH...TALKING TO YOURSELF, LUCIEN. YOU KNOW WHAT THEY SAY ABOUT THAT...
TO MADNESS THEN, THE ONE CONSTANT.

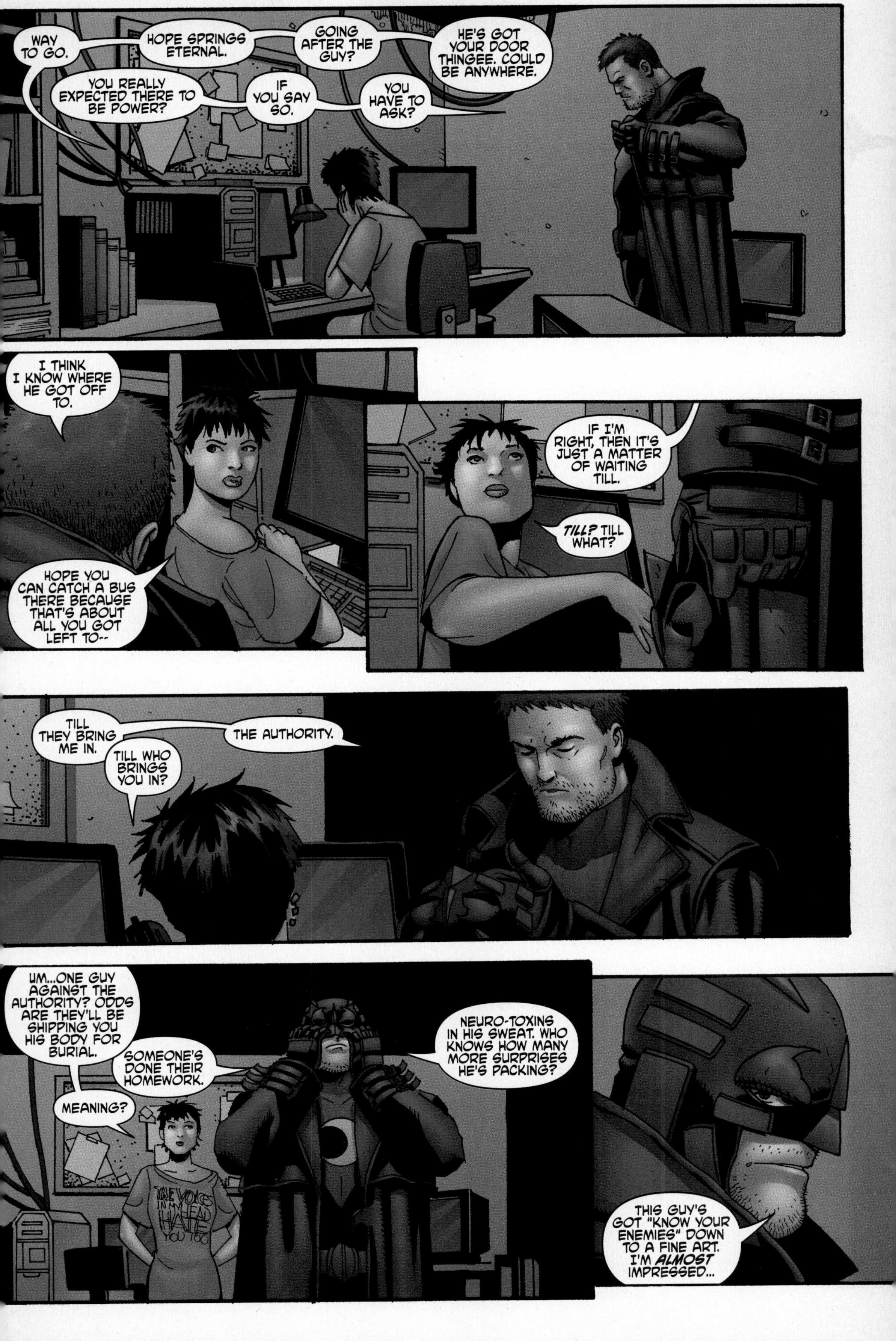
WAY TO GO.
YOU REALLY EXPECTED THERE TO BE POWER?
HOPE SPRINGS ETERNAL.
IF YOU SAY SO.
GOING AFTER THE GUY?
YOU HAVE TO ASK?
HE'S GOT YOUR DOOR THINGEE. COULD BE ANYWHERE.
I THINK I KNOW WHERE HE GOT OFF TO.
HOPE YOU CAN CATCH A BUS THERE BECAUSE THAT'S ABOUT ALL YOU GOT LEFT TO--
IF I'M RIGHT, THEN IT'S JUST A MATTER OF WAITING TILL.
*TILL?* TILL WHAT?
TILL THEY BRING ME IN.
TILL WHO BRINGS YOU IN?
THE AUTHORITY.
UM...ONE GUY AGAINST THE AUTHORITY? ODDS ARE THEY'LL BE SHIPPING YOU HIS BODY FOR BURIAL.
SOMEONE'S DONE THEIR HOMEWORK.
MEANING?
NEURO-TOXINS IN HIS SWEAT. WHO KNOWS HOW MANY MORE SURPRISES HE'S PACKING?
THE VOICES IN MY HEAD HATE YOU TOO
THIS GUY'S GOT "KNOW YOUR ENEMIES" DOWN TO A FINE ART. I'M *ALMOST* IMPRESSED...

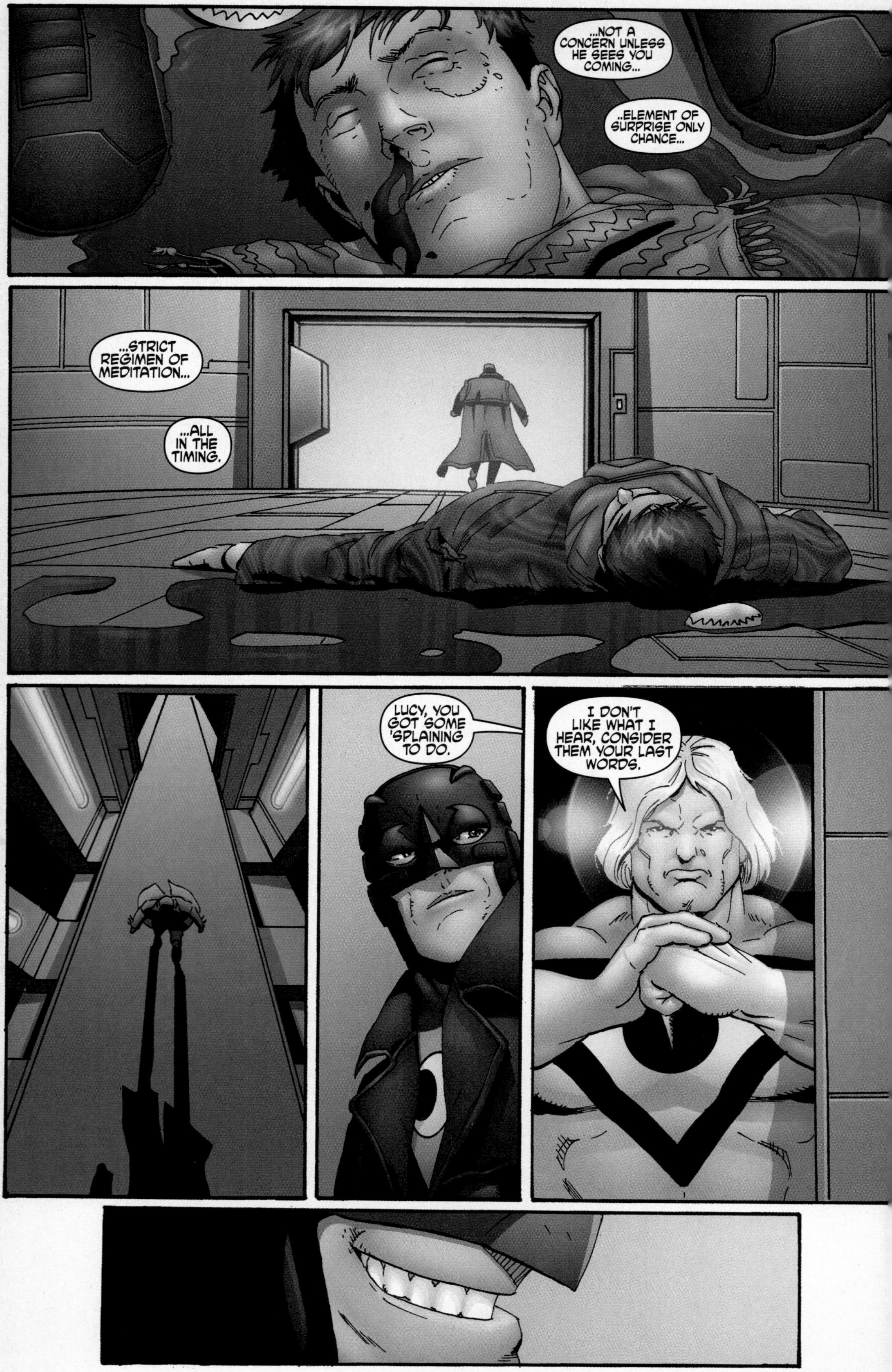
...NOT A CONCERN UNLESS HE SEES YOU COMING...
..ELEMENT OF SURPRISE ONLY CHANCE...
...STRICT REGIMEN OF MEDITATION...
...ALL IN THE TIMING.
LUCY, YOU GOT SOME 'SPLAINING TO DO.
I DON'T LIKE WHAT I HEAR, CONSIDER THEM YOUR LAST WORDS.

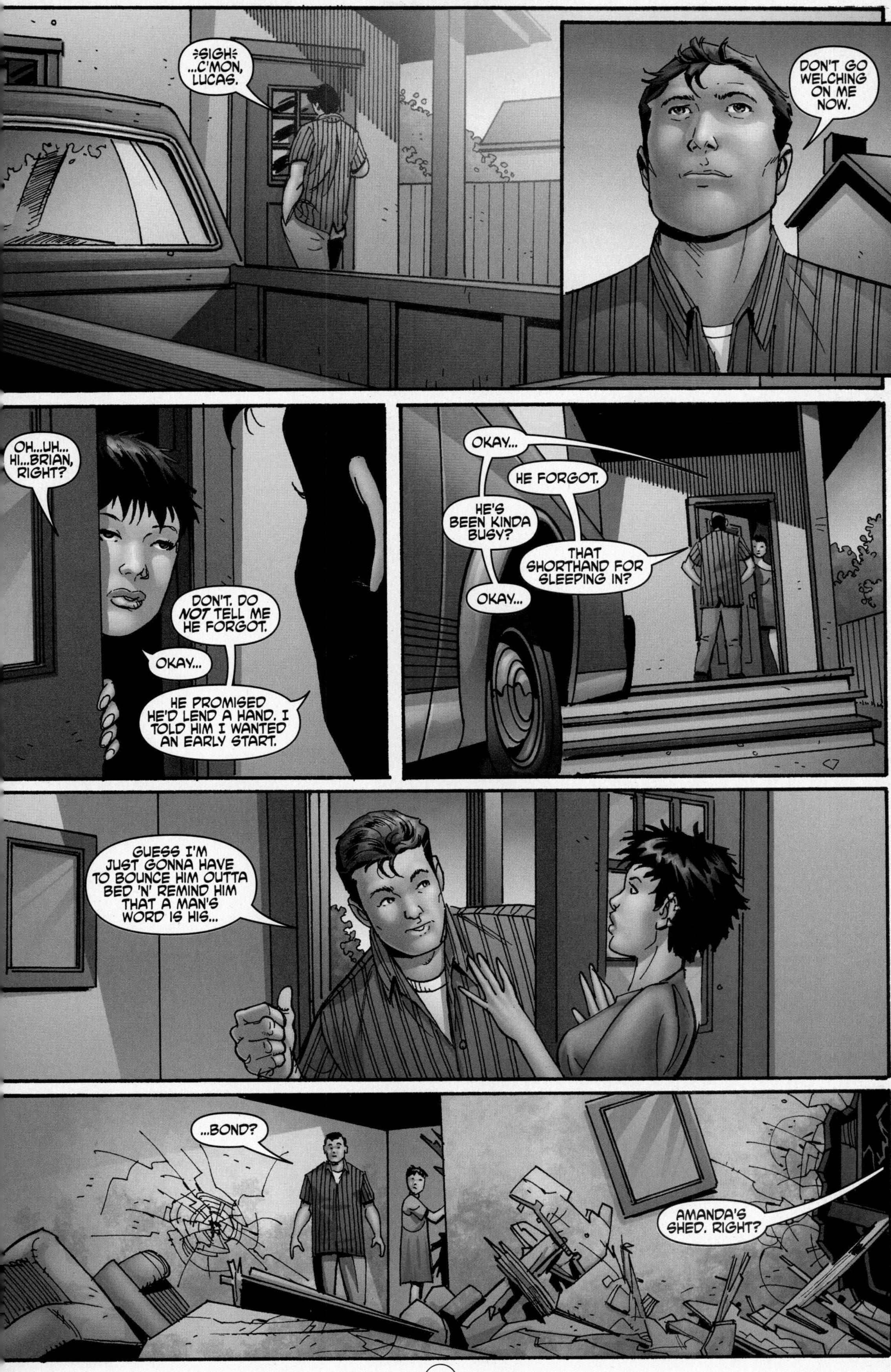

⇎SIGH⇎ ...C'MON, LUCAS.
DON'T GO WELCHING ON ME NOW.
OH...UH... HI...BRIAN, RIGHT?
DON'T. DO *NOT* TELL ME HE FORGOT.
OKAY...
HE PROMISED HE'D LEND A HAND. I TOLD HIM I WANTED AN EARLY START.
OKAY...
HE FORGOT.
HE'S BEEN KINDA BUSY?
THAT SHORTHAND FOR SLEEPING IN?
OKAY...
GUESS I'M JUST GONNA HAVE TO BOUNCE HIM OUTTA BED 'N' REMIND HIM THAT A MAN'S WORD IS HIS...
...BOND?
AMANDA'S SHED. RIGHT?

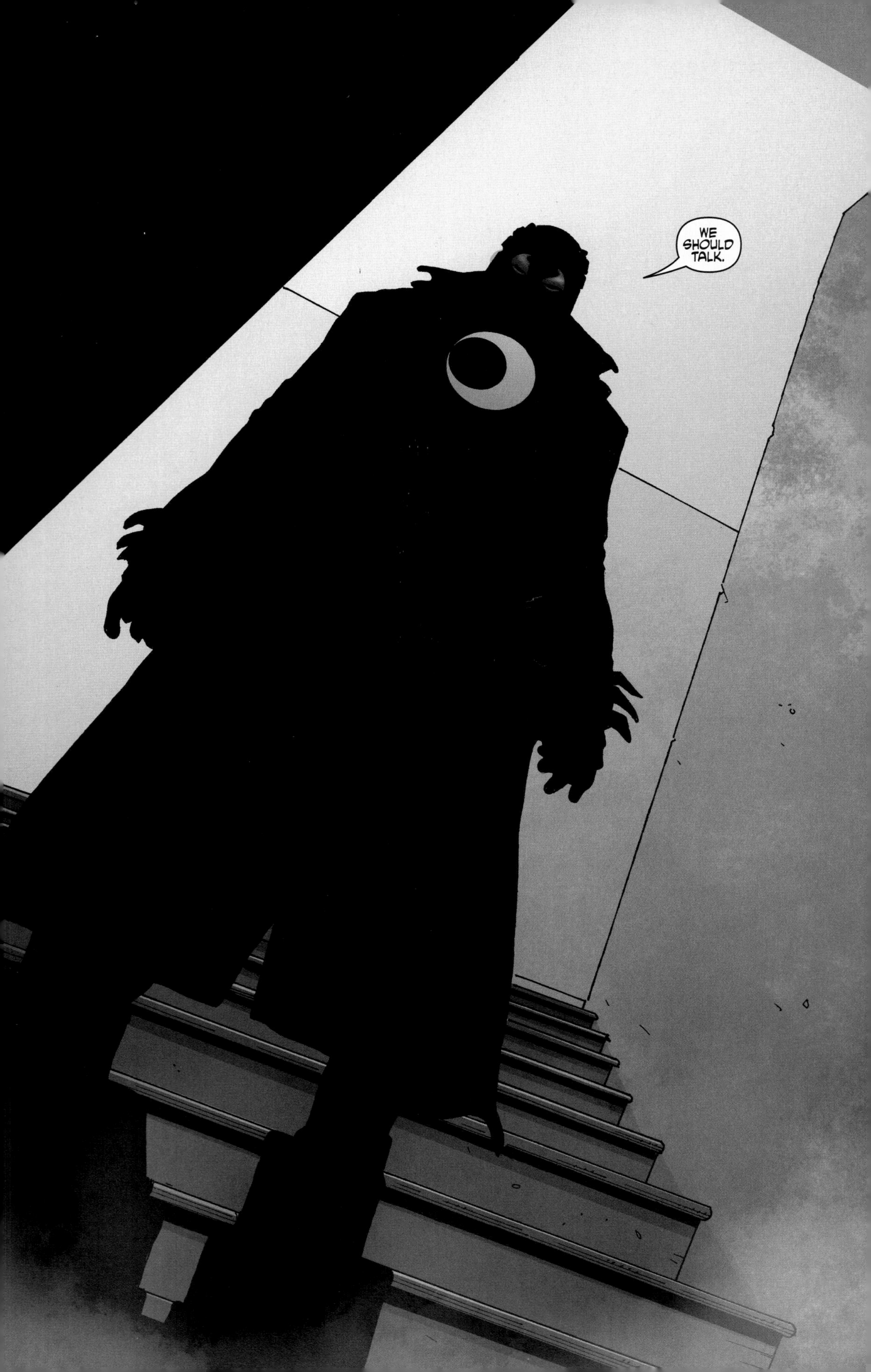
WE SHOULD TALK.

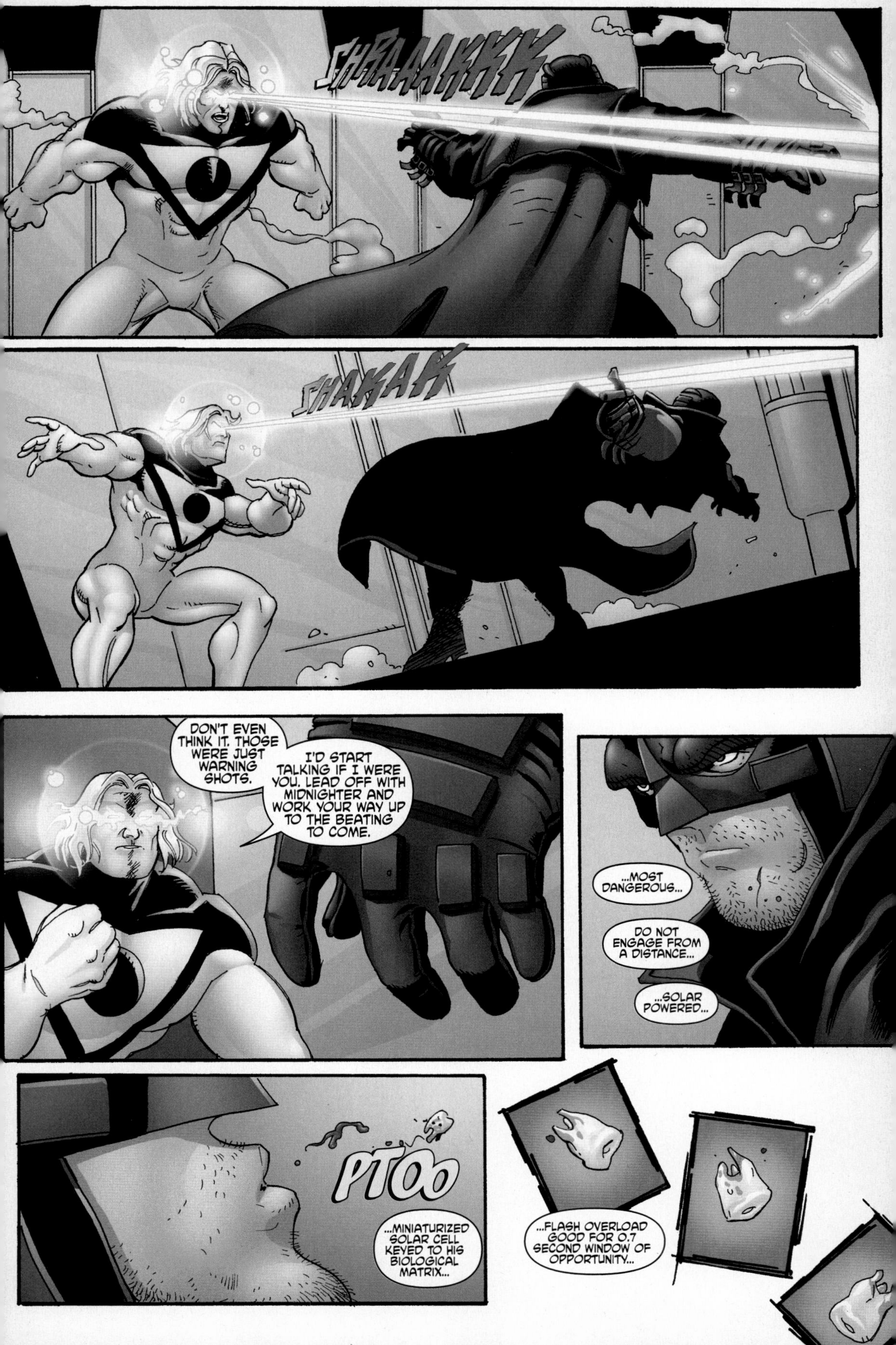
SHRAAAKKKK
SHAKAK
DON'T EVEN THINK IT. THOSE WERE JUST WARNING SHOTS.
I'D START TALKING IF I WERE YOU. LEAD OFF WITH MIDNIGHTER AND WORK YOUR WAY UP TO THE BEATING TO COME.
...MOST DANGEROUS...
DO NOT ENGAGE FROM A DISTANCE...
...SOLAR POWERED...
PTOo
...MINIATURIZED SOLAR CELL KEYED TO HIS BIOLOGICAL MATRIX...
...FLASH OVERLOAD GOOD FOR 0.7 SECOND WINDOW OF OPPORTUNITY...

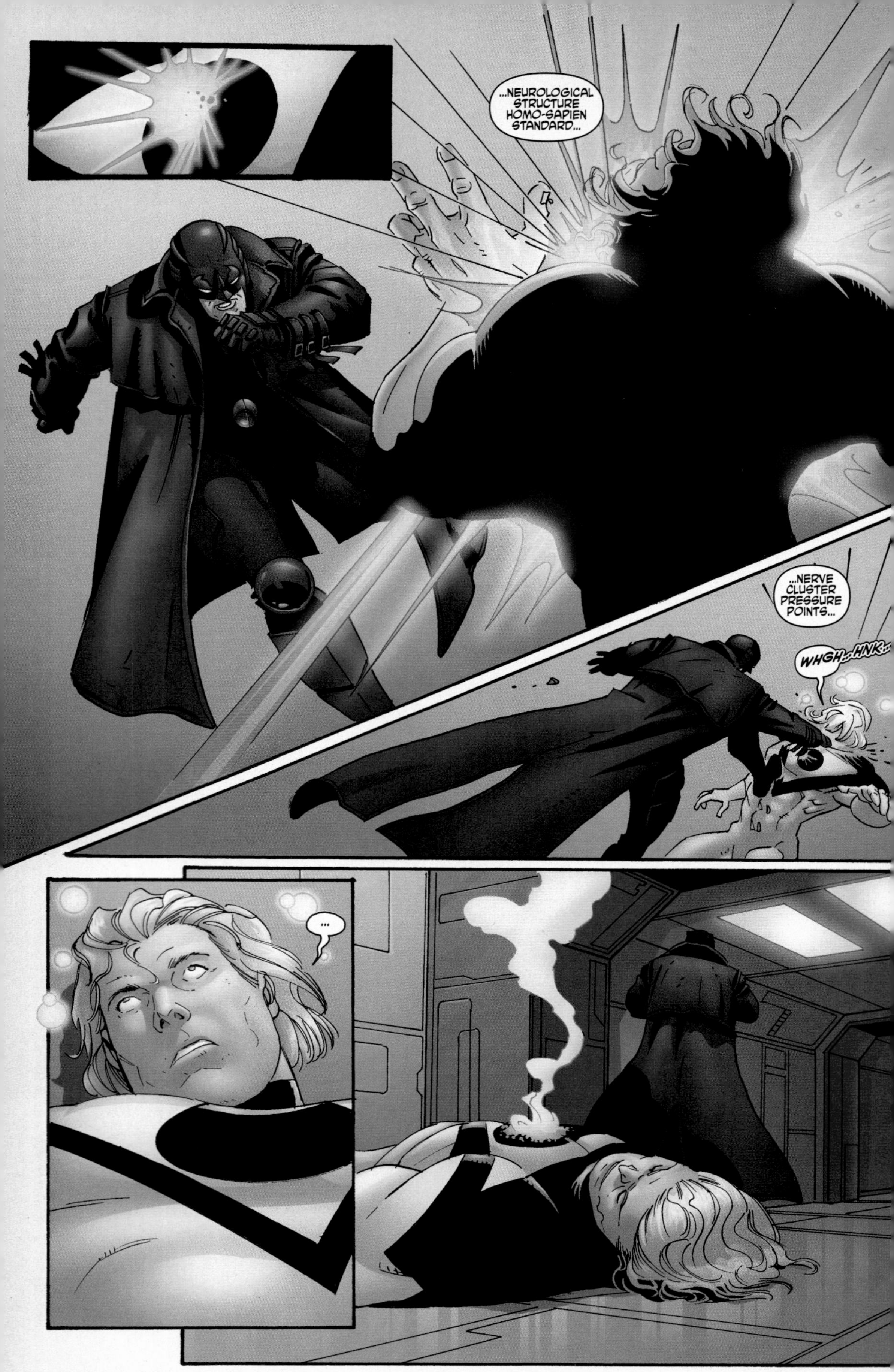
...NEUROLOGICAL STRUCTURE HOMO-SAPIEN STANDARD...
...NERVE CLUSTER PRESSURE POINTS...
WHGH...HNK...
...

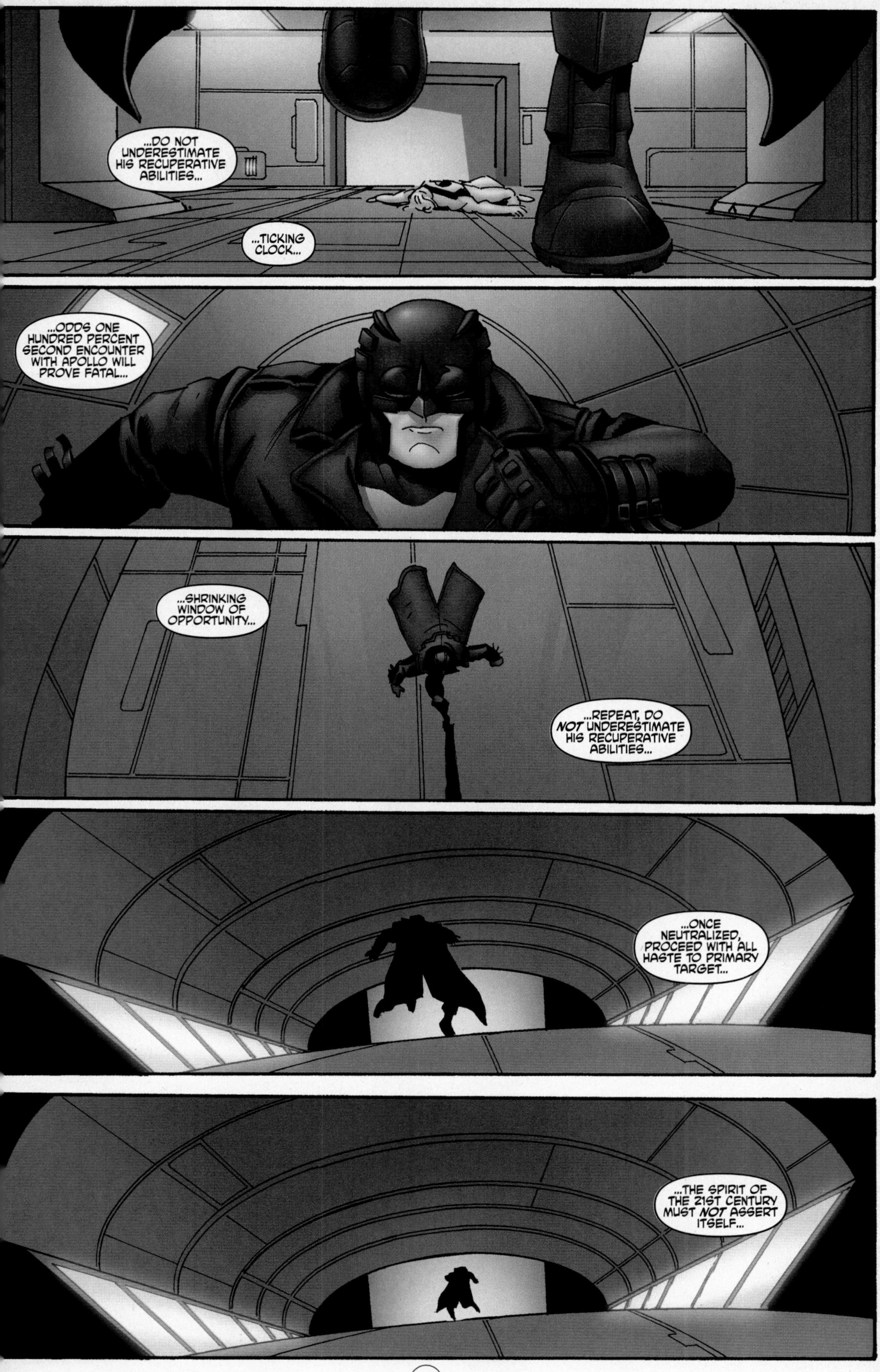
...DO NOT UNDERESTIMATE HIS RECUPERATIVE ABILITIES...
...TICKING CLOCK...
...ODDS ONE HUNDRED PERCENT SECOND ENCOUNTER WITH APOLLO WILL PROVE FATAL...
...SHRINKING WINDOW OF OPPORTUNITY...
...REPEAT, DO *NOT* UNDERESTIMATE HIS RECUPERATIVE ABILITIES...
...ONCE NEUTRALIZED, PROCEED WITH ALL HASTE TO PRIMARY TARGET...
...THE SPIRIT OF THE 21ST CENTURY MUST *NOT* ASSERT ITSELF...

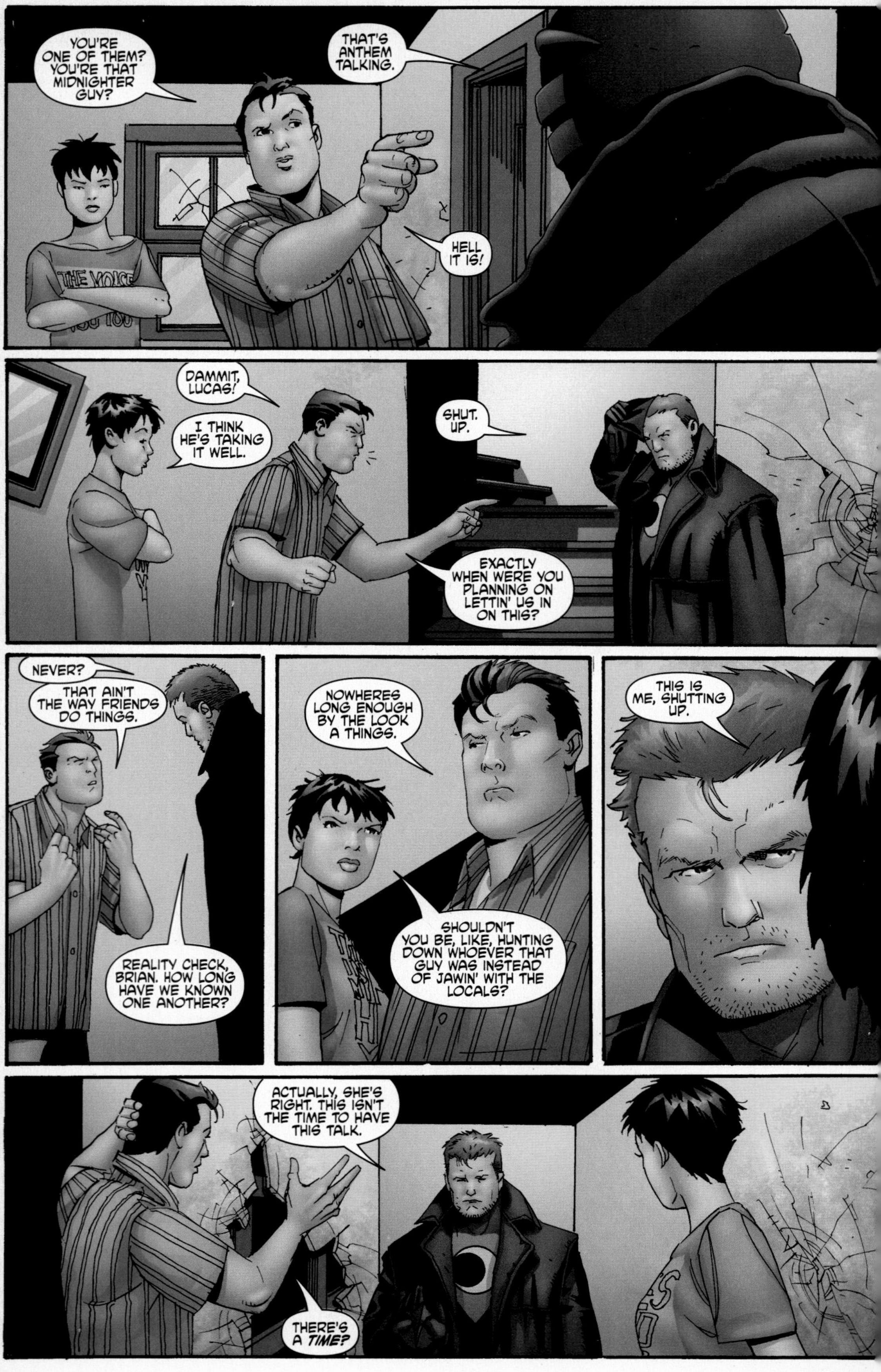
YOU'RE ONE OF THEM? YOU'RE THAT MIDNIGHTER GUY?
THAT'S ANTHEM TALKING.
HELL IT IS!
DAMMIT, LUCAS!
I THINK HE'S TAKING IT WELL.
SHUT. UP.
EXACTLY WHEN WERE YOU PLANNING ON LETTIN' US IN ON THIS?
NEVER?
THAT AIN'T THE WAY FRIENDS DO THINGS.
REALITY CHECK, BRIAN. HOW LONG HAVE WE KNOWN ONE ANOTHER?
NOWHERES LONG ENOUGH BY THE LOOK A THINGS.
SHOULDN'T YOU BE, LIKE, HUNTING DOWN WHOEVER THAT GUY WAS INSTEAD OF JAWIN' WITH THE LOCALS?
THIS IS ME, SHUTTING UP.
ACTUALLY, SHE'S RIGHT. THIS ISN'T THE TIME TO HAVE THIS TALK.
THERE'S A *TIME*?

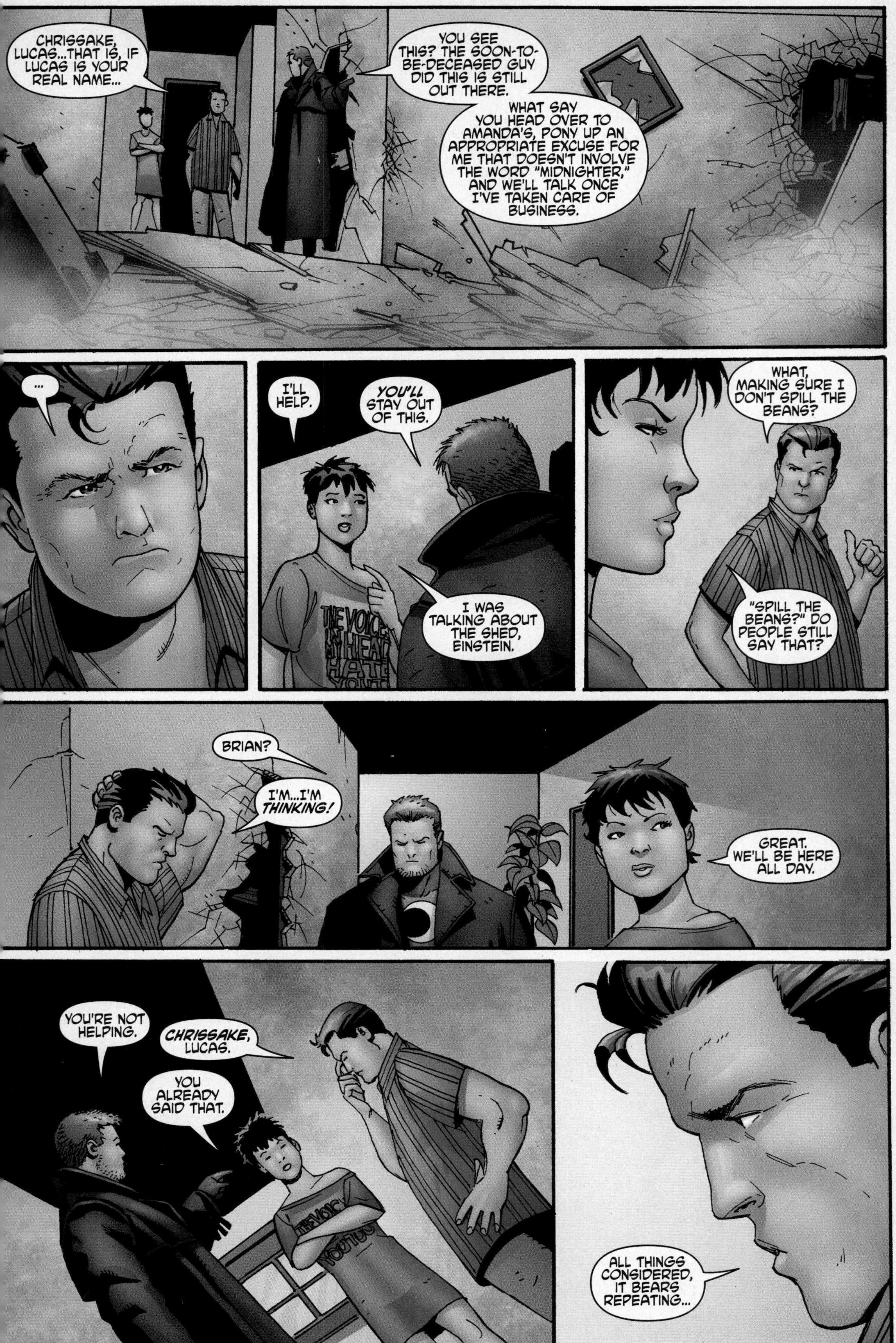
CHRISSAKE, LUCAS...THAT IS, IF LUCAS IS YOUR REAL NAME...
YOU SEE THIS? THE SOON-TO-BE-DECEASED GUY DID THIS IS STILL OUT THERE.
WHAT SAY YOU HEAD OVER TO AMANDA'S, PONY UP AN APPROPRIATE EXCUSE FOR ME THAT DOESN'T INVOLVE THE WORD "MIDNIGHTER," AND WE'LL TALK ONCE I'VE TAKEN CARE OF BUSINESS.
...
I'LL HELP.
*YOU'LL* STAY OUT OF THIS.
I WAS TALKING ABOUT THE SHED, EINSTEIN.
WHAT, MAKING SURE I DON'T SPILL THE BEANS?
"SPILL THE BEANS?" DO PEOPLE STILL SAY THAT?
BRIAN?
I'M...I'M *THINKING!*
GREAT. WE'LL BE HERE ALL DAY.
YOU'RE NOT HELPING.
*CHRISSAKE,* LUCAS.
YOU ALREADY SAID THAT.
ALL THINGS CONSIDERED, IT BEARS REPEATING...

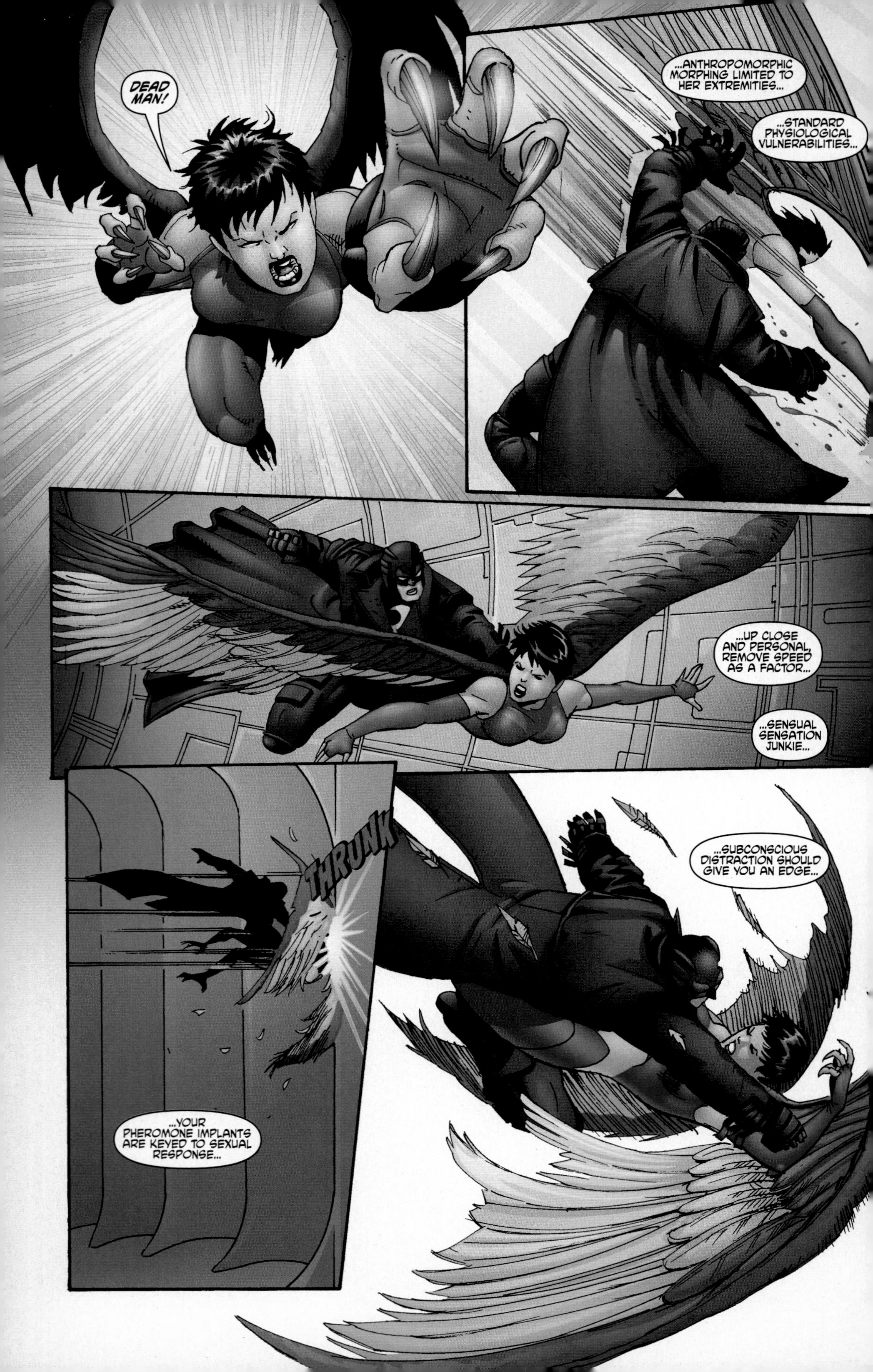

DEAD MAN!
...ANTHROPOMORPHIC MORPHING LIMITED TO HER EXTREMITIES...
...STANDARD PHYSIOLOGICAL VULNERABILITIES...
...UP CLOSE AND PERSONAL, REMOVE SPEED AS A FACTOR...
...SENSUAL SENSATION JUNKIE...
THRUNK
...YOUR PHEROMONE IMPLANTS ARE KEYED TO SEXUAL RESPONSE...
...SUBCONSCIOUS DISTRACTION SHOULD GIVE YOU AN EDGE...

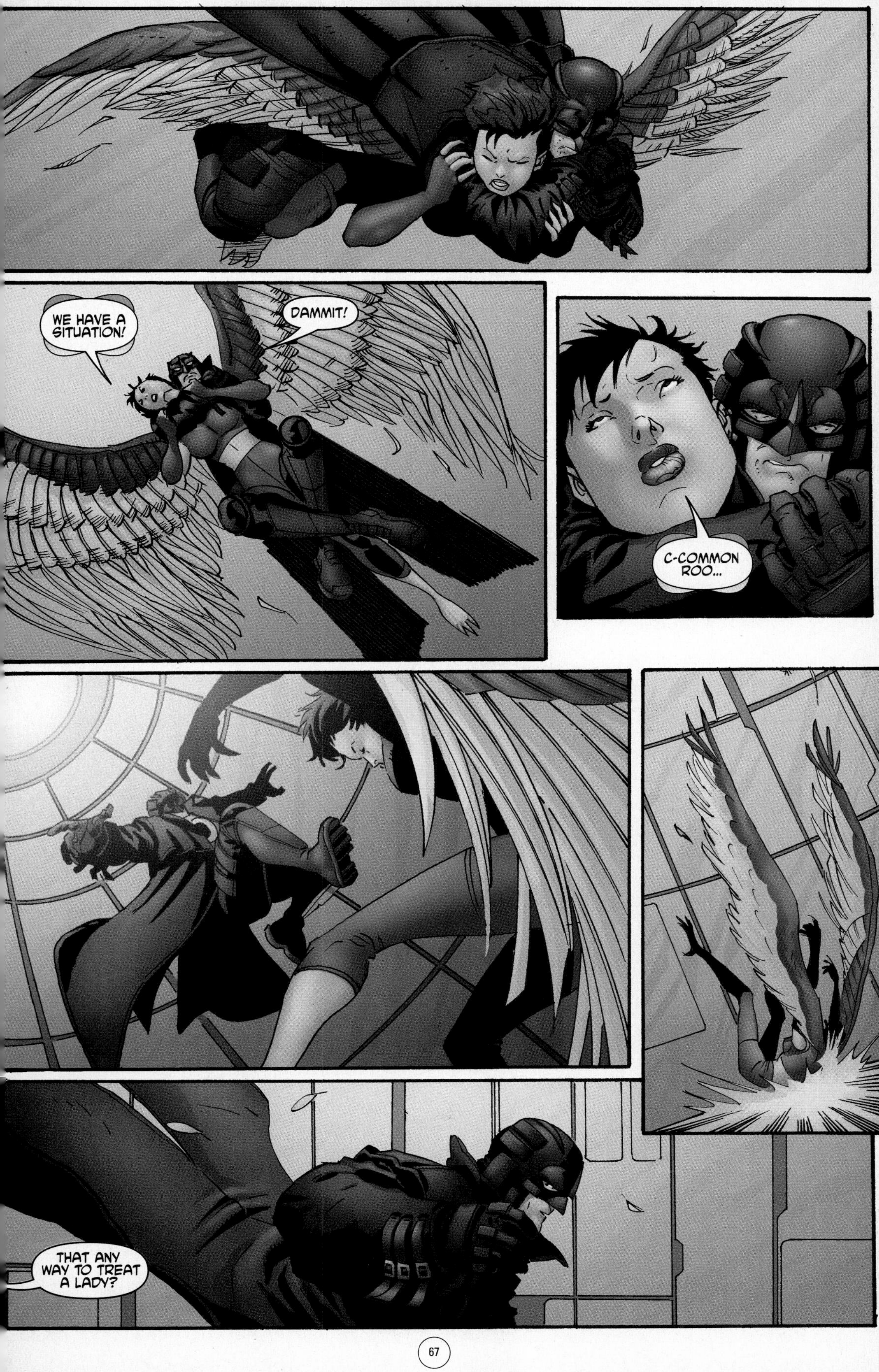
WE HAVE A SITUATION!
DAMMIT!
C-COMMON ROO...
THAT ANY WAY TO TREAT A LADY?

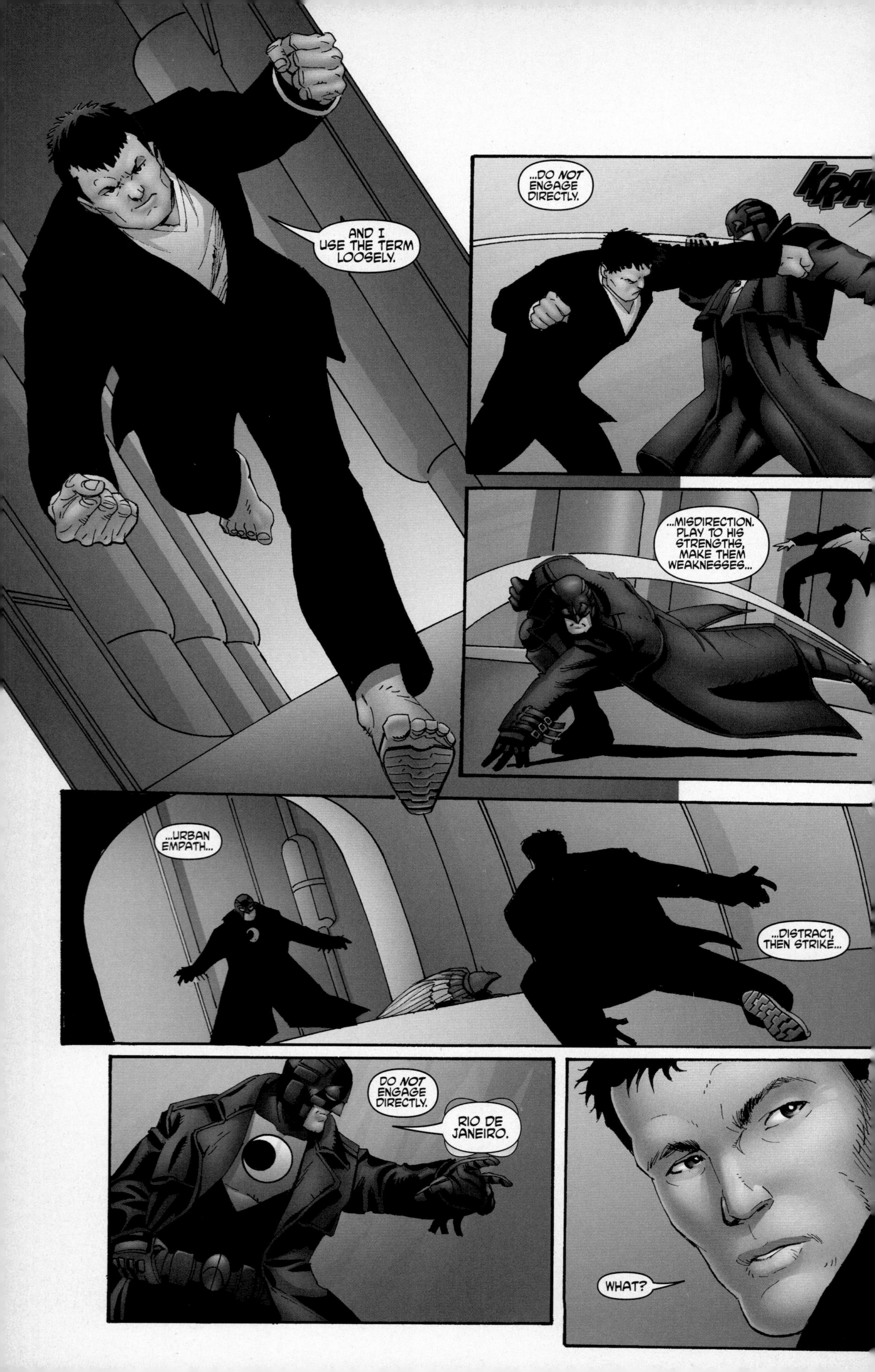

AND I USE THE TERM LOOSELY.
...DO NOT ENGAGE DIRECTLY.
KRAA
...MISDIRECTION. PLAY TO HIS STRENGTHS, MAKE THEM WEAKNESSES...
...URBAN EMPATH...
...DISTRACT, THEN STRIKE...
DO NOT ENGAGE DIRECTLY.
RIO DE JANEIRO.
WHAT?

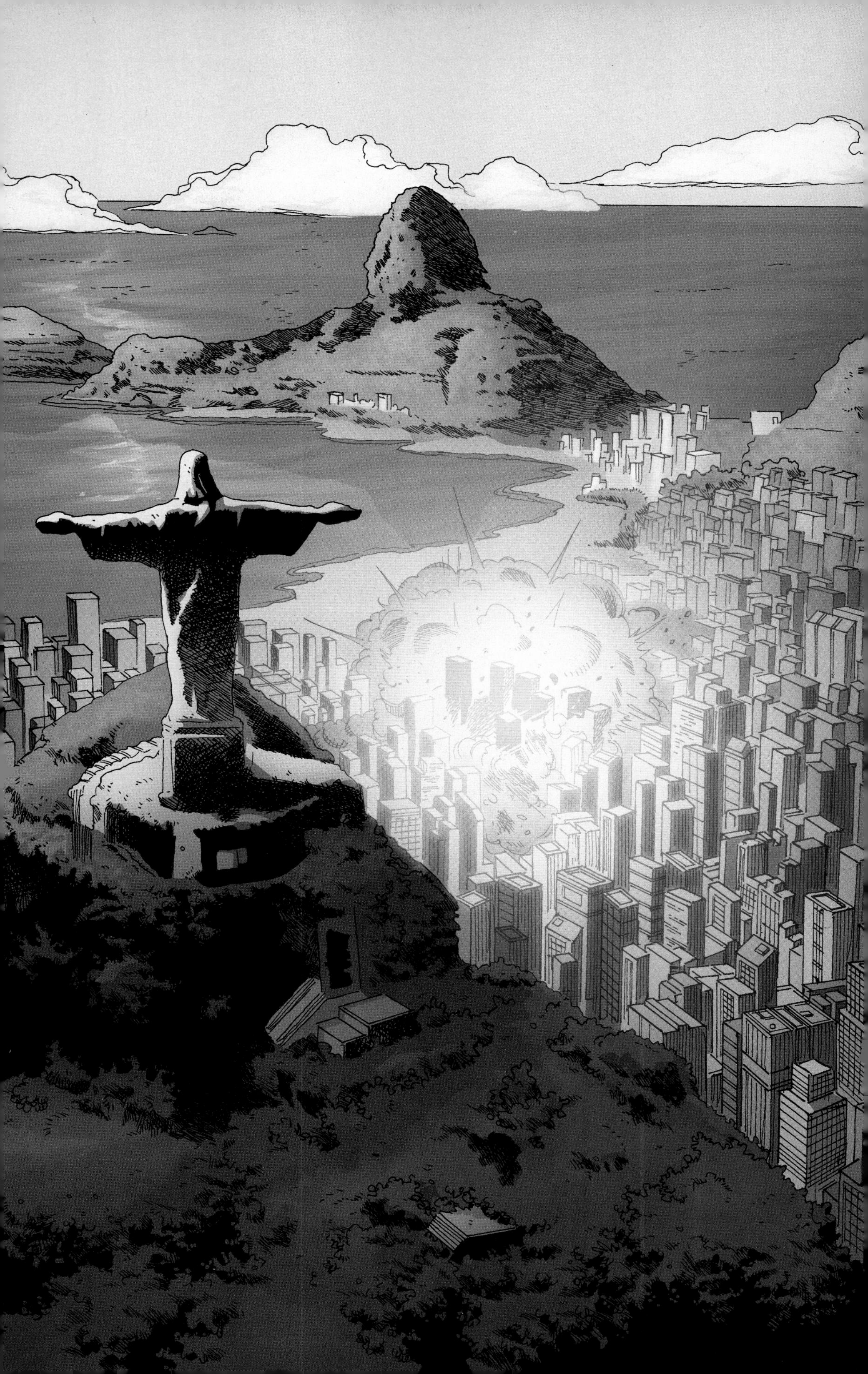

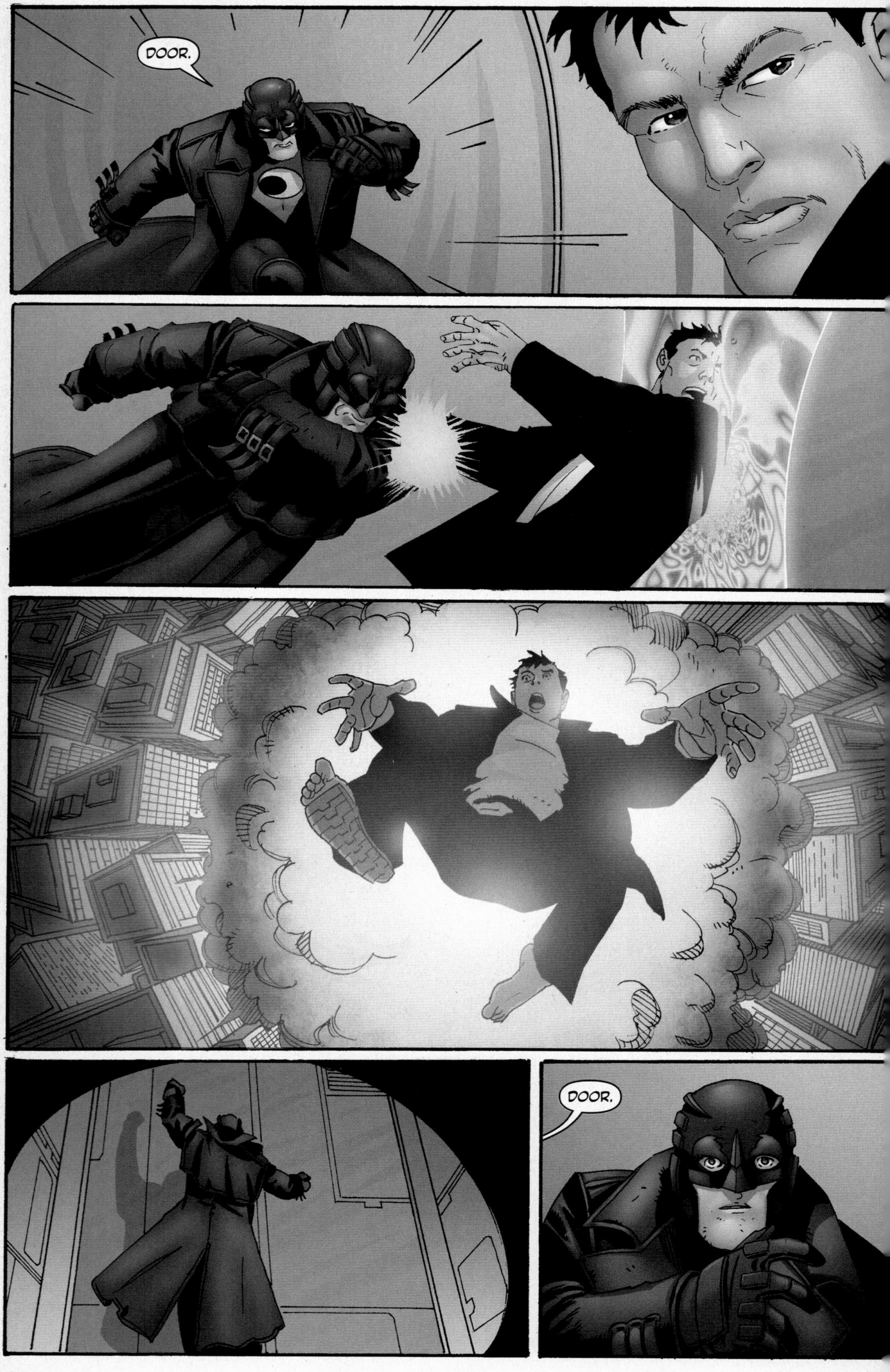
DOOR.
DOOR.

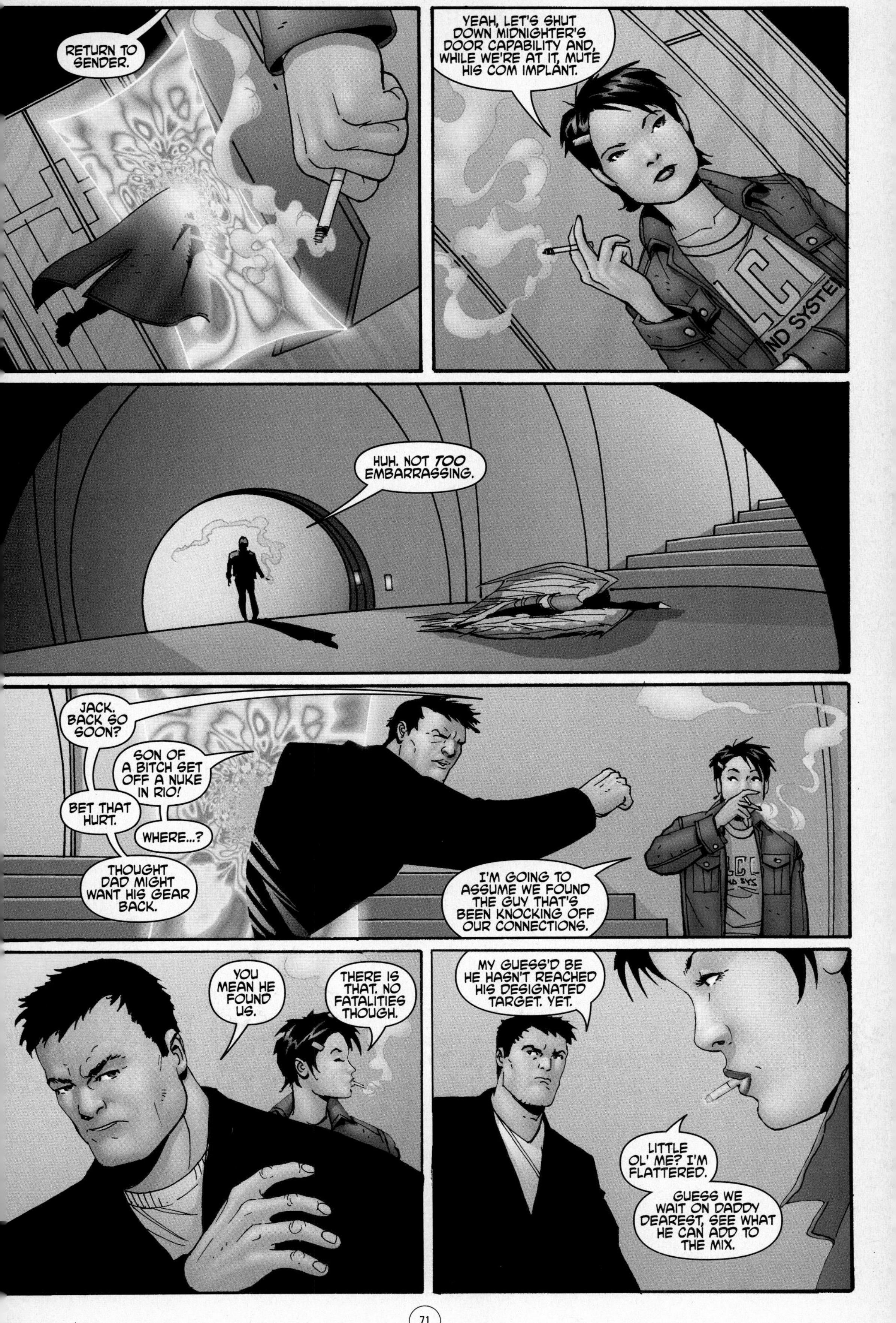
RETURN TO SENDER.
YEAH, LET'S SHUT DOWN MIDNIGHTER'S DOOR CAPABILITY AND, WHILE WE'RE AT IT, MUTE HIS COM IMPLANT.
HUH. NOT *TOO* EMBARRASSING.
JACK. BACK SO SOON?
SON OF A BITCH SET OFF A NUKE IN RIO!
BET THAT HURT.
WHERE...?
THOUGHT DAD MIGHT WANT HIS GEAR BACK.
I'M GOING TO ASSUME WE FOUND THE GUY THAT'S BEEN KNOCKING OFF OUR CONNECTIONS.
YOU MEAN HE FOUND US.
THERE IS THAT. NO FATALITIES THOUGH.
MY GUESS'D BE HE HASN'T REACHED HIS DESIGNATED TARGET. YET.
LITTLE OL' ME? I'M FLATTERED.
GUESS WE WAIT ON DADDY DEAREST, SEE WHAT HE CAN ADD TO THE MIX.

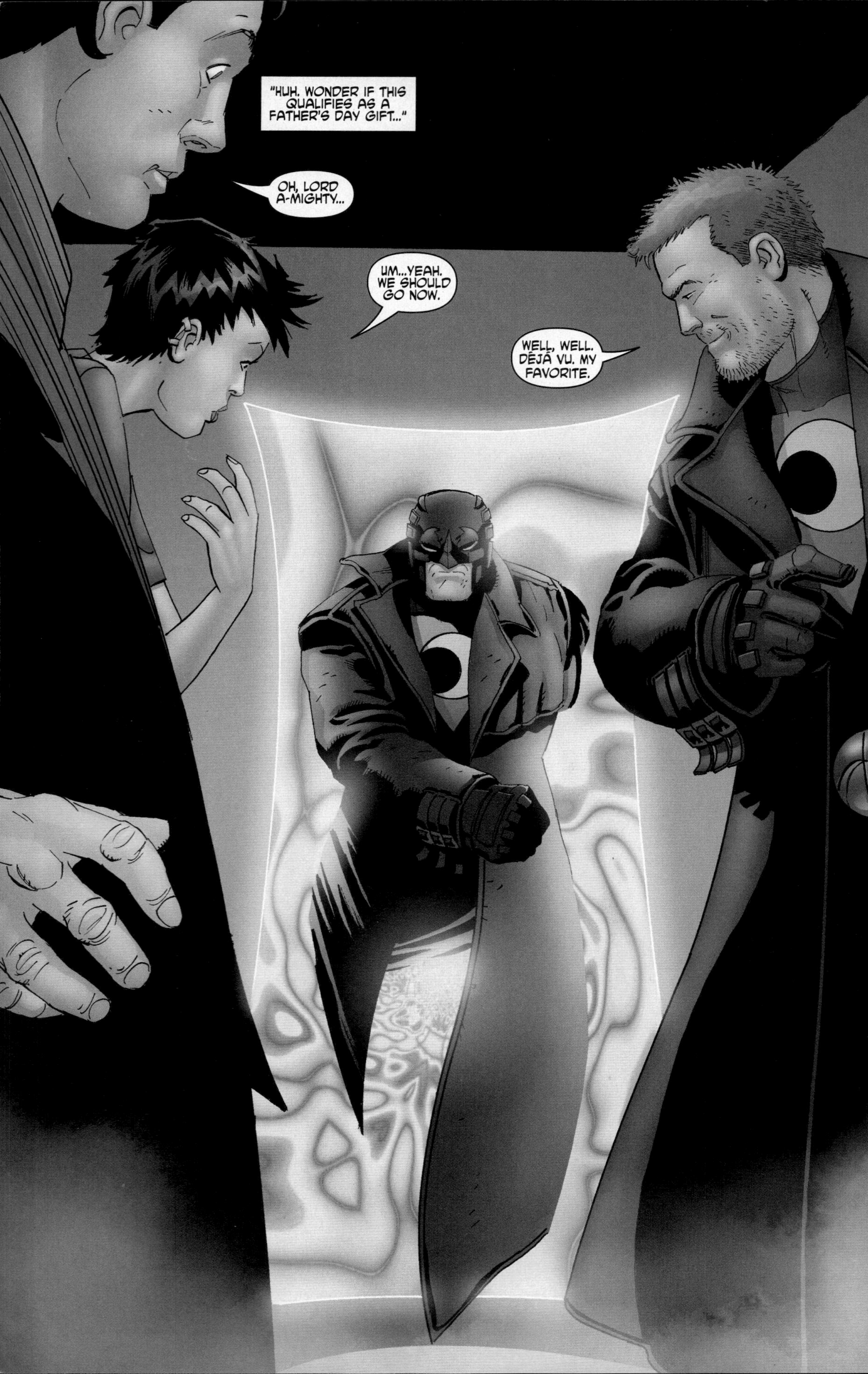
"HUH. WONDER IF THIS QUALIFIES AS A FATHER'S DAY GIFT..."
OH, LORD A-MIGHTY...
UM...YEAH. WE SHOULD GO NOW.
WELL, WELL. DÉJÀ VU. MY FAVORITE.

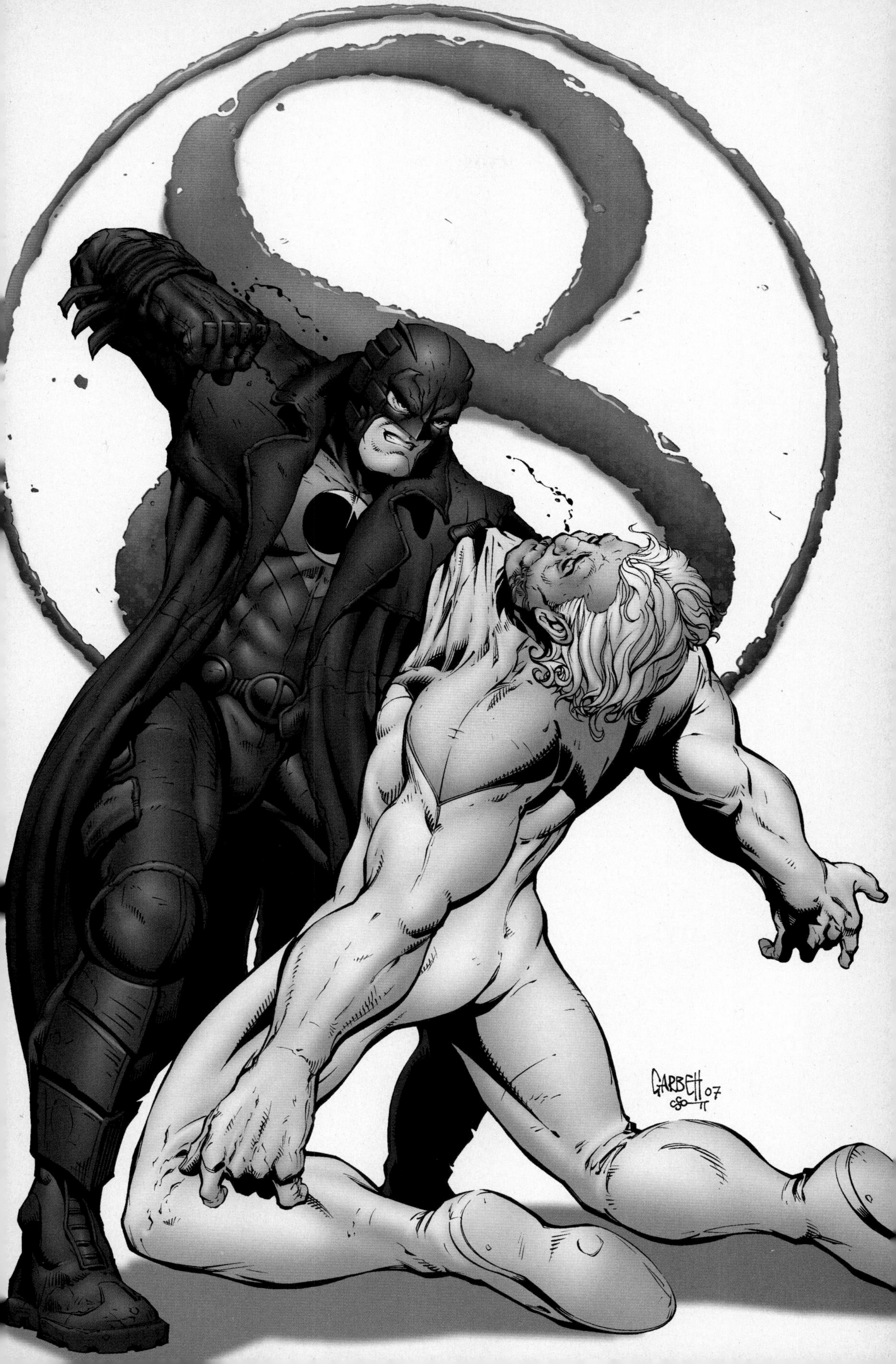
GARBETT 07

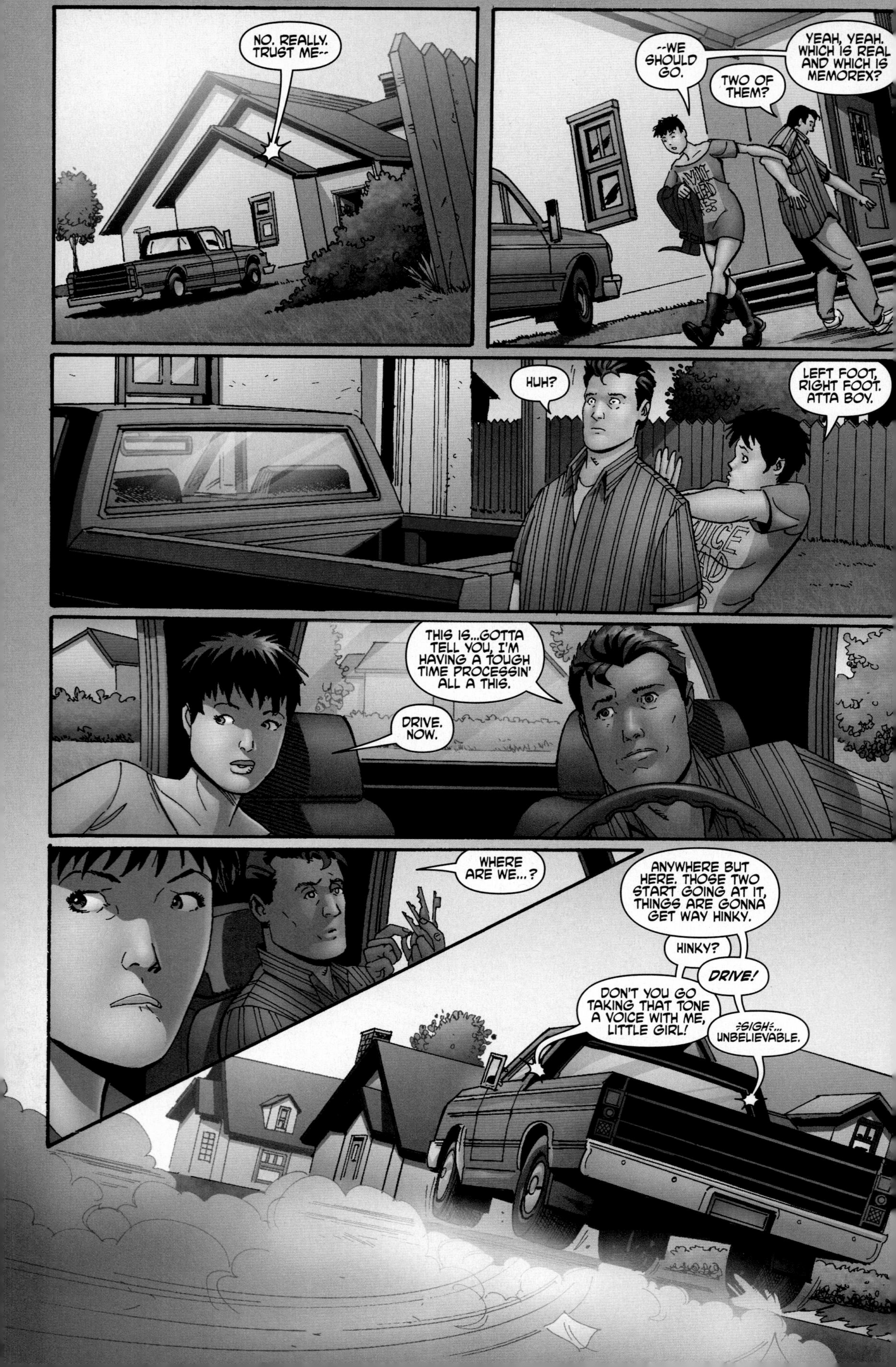
NO. REALLY. TRUST ME--
--WE SHOULD GO.
TWO OF THEM?
YEAH, YEAH. WHICH IS REAL AND WHICH IS MEMOREX?
HUH?
LEFT FOOT, RIGHT FOOT. ATTA BOY.
THIS IS...GOTTA TELL YOU, I'M HAVING A TOUGH TIME PROCESSIN' ALL A THIS.
DRIVE. NOW.
WHERE ARE WE...?
ANYWHERE BUT HERE. THOSE TWO START GOING AT IT, THINGS ARE GONNA GET WAY HINKY.
HINKY?
DRIVE!
DON'T YOU GO TAKING THAT TONE A VOICE WITH ME, LITTLE GIRL!
SIGH... UNBELIEVABLE.

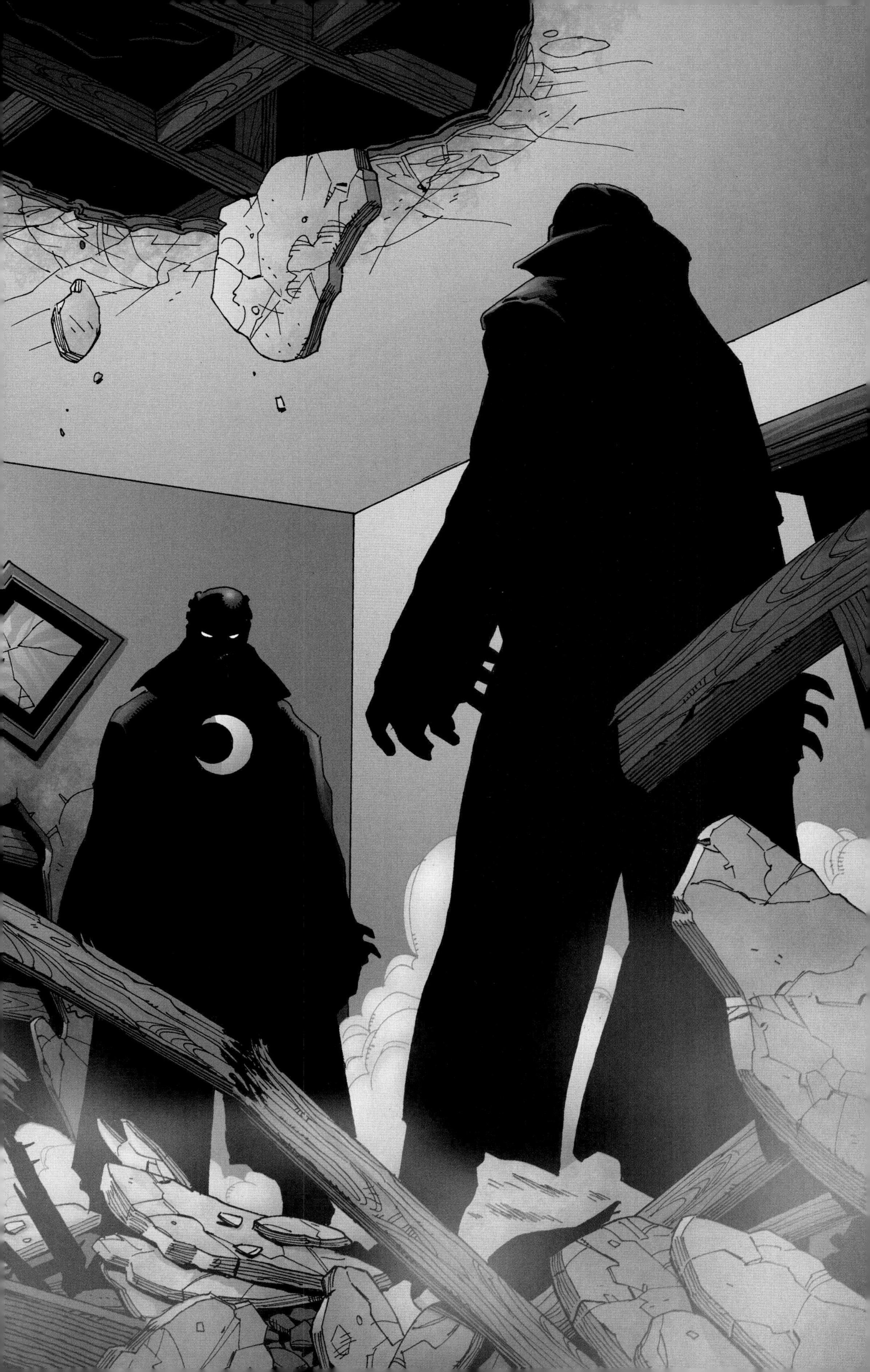

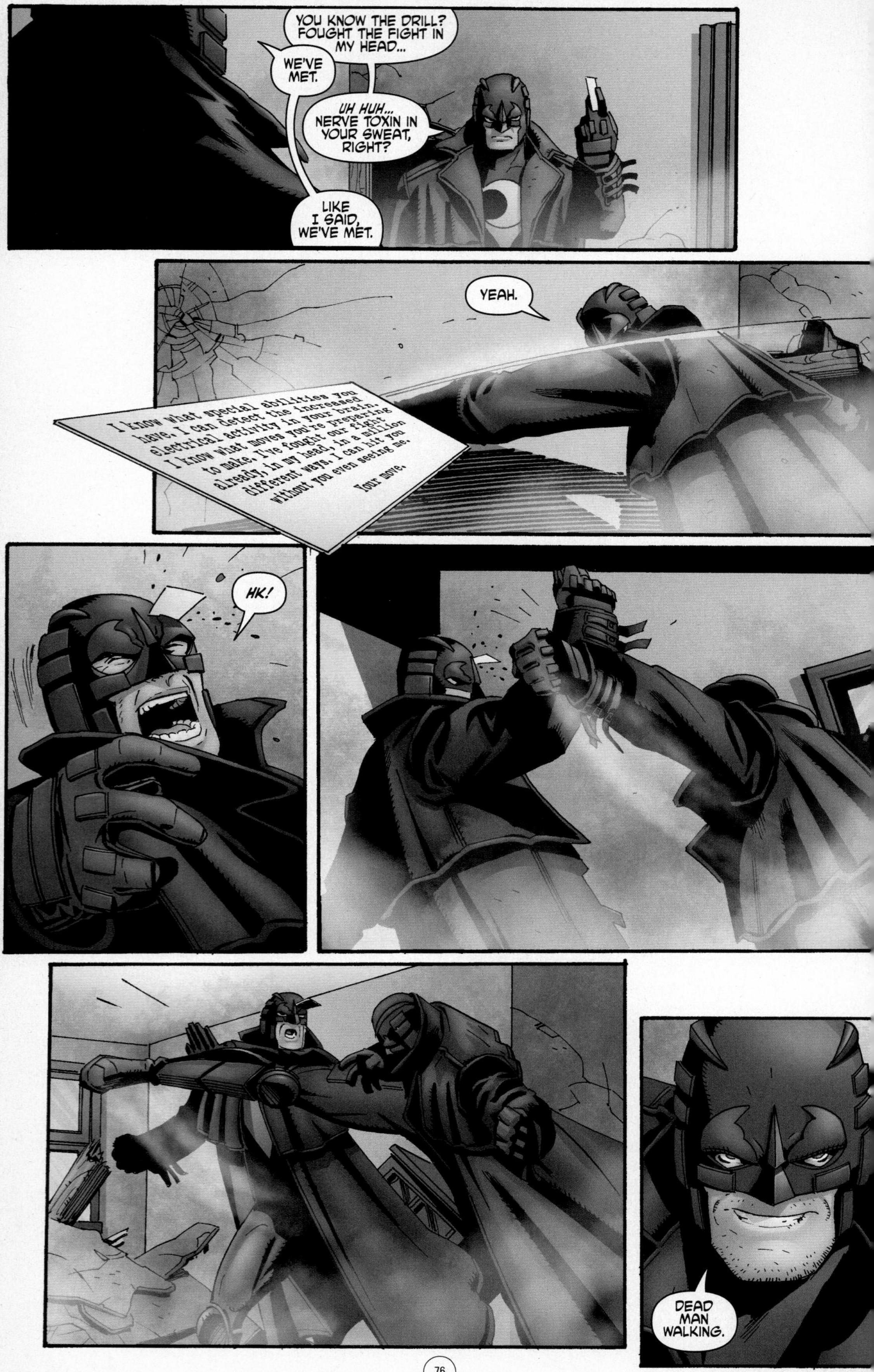
YOU KNOW THE DRILL? FOUGHT THE FIGHT IN MY HEAD...
WE'VE MET.
UH HUH... NERVE TOXIN IN YOUR SWEAT, RIGHT?
LIKE I SAID, WE'VE MET.
YEAH.
I know what special abilities you have. I can detect the increased electrical activity in your brain. I know what moves you're preparing to make. I've fought our fight already, in my head, in a million different ways. I can hit you without you even seeing me.
Your move.
HK!
DEAD MAN WALKING.

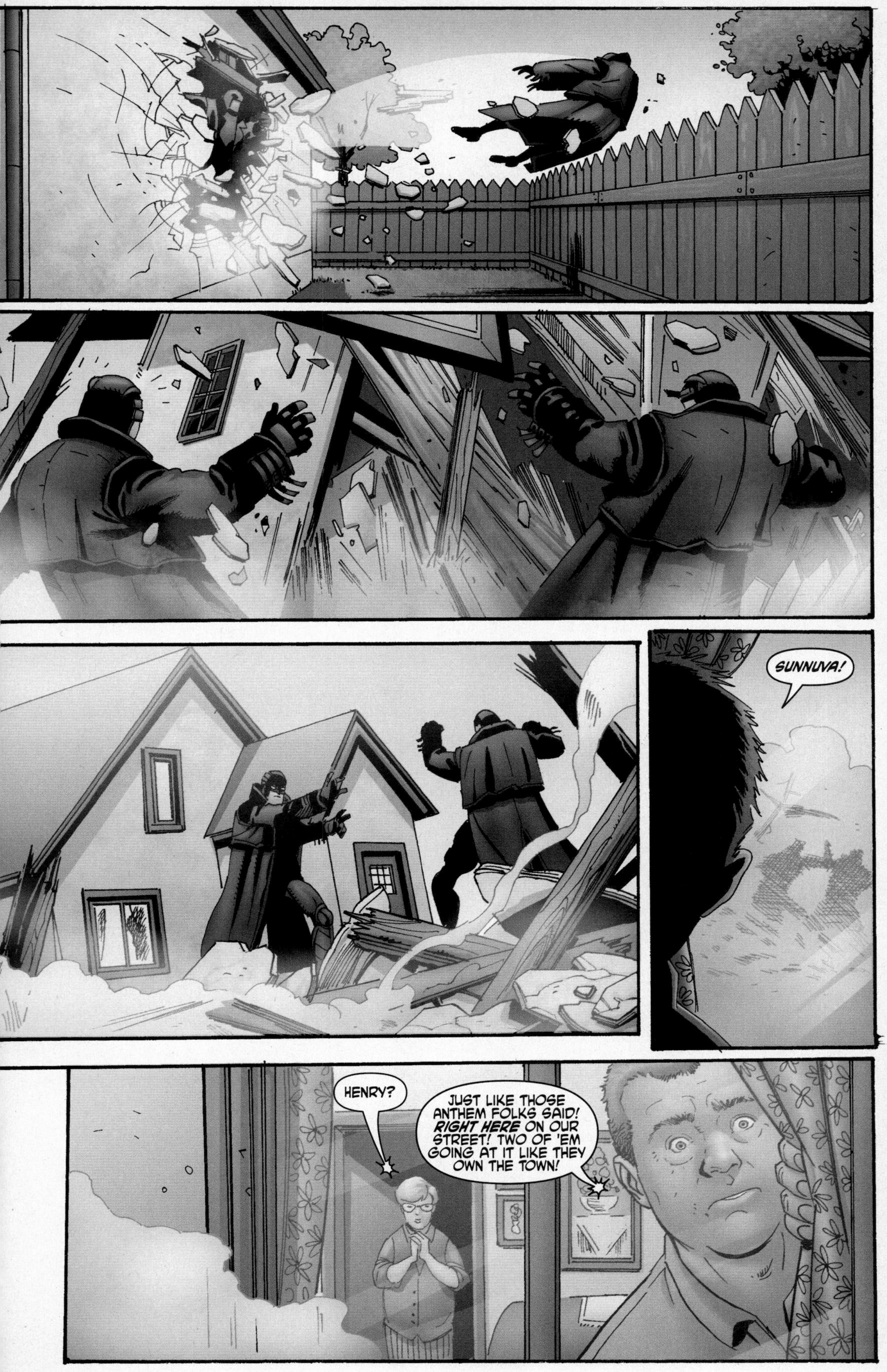
SUNNUVA!
HENRY?
JUST LIKE THOSE ANTHEM FOLKS SAID! RIGHT HERE ON OUR STREET! TWO OF 'EM GOING AT IT LIKE THEY OWN THE TOWN!

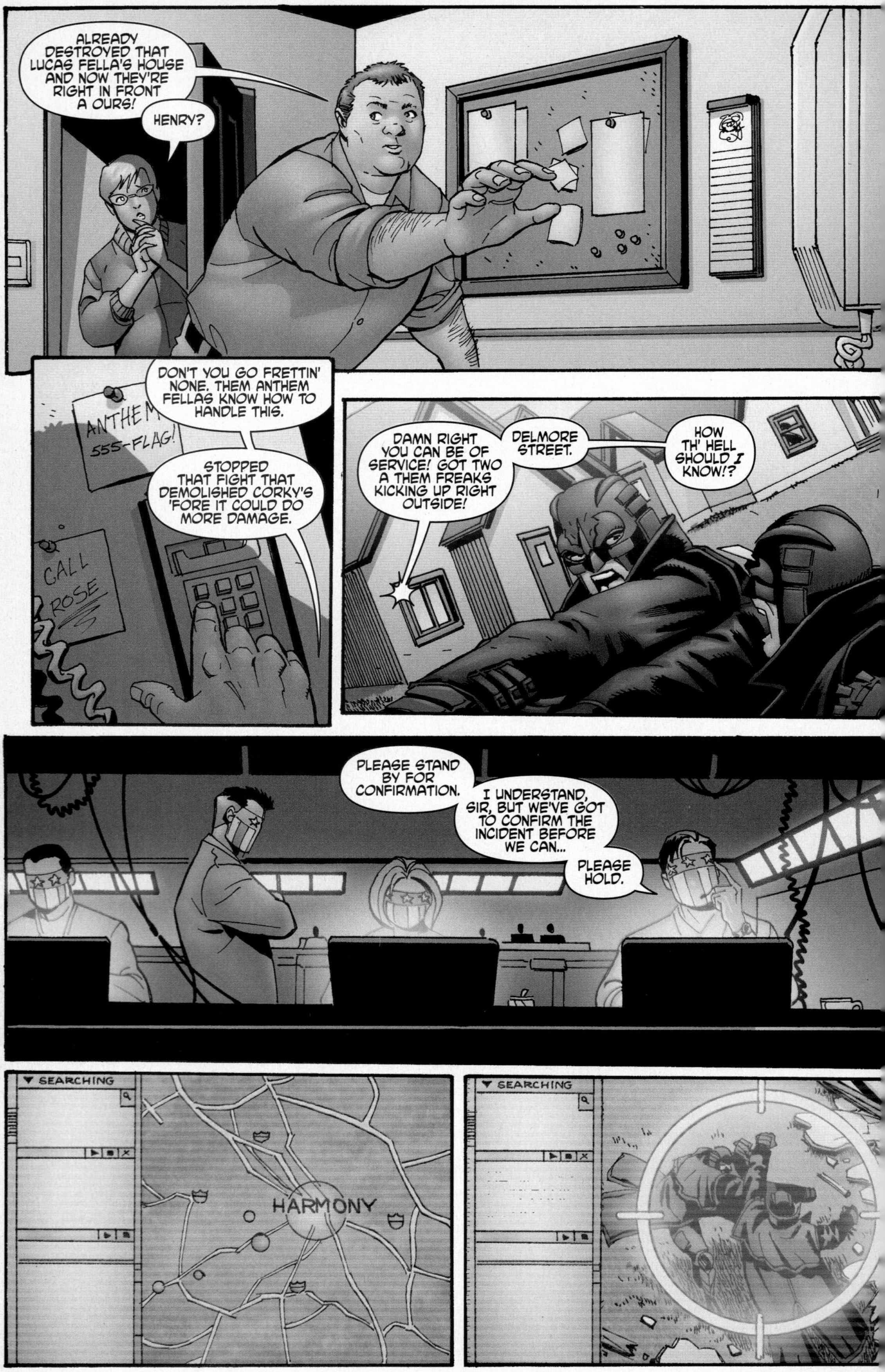
ALREADY DESTROYED THAT LUCAS FELLA'S HOUSE AND NOW THEY'RE RIGHT IN FRONT A OURS!
HENRY?
DON'T YOU GO FRETTIN' NONE. THEM ANTHEM FELLAS KNOW HOW TO HANDLE THIS.
STOPPED THAT FIGHT THAT DEMOLISHED CORKY'S 'FORE IT COULD DO MORE DAMAGE.
555-FLAG!
CALL ROSE
DAMN RIGHT YOU CAN BE OF SERVICE! GOT TWO A THEM FREAKS KICKING UP RIGHT OUTSIDE!
DELMORE STREET.
HOW TH' HELL SHOULD I KNOW!?
PLEASE STAND BY FOR CONFIRMATION.
I UNDERSTAND, SIR, BUT WE'VE GOT TO CONFIRM THE INCIDENT BEFORE WE CAN...
PLEASE HOLD.
▼ SEARCHING
HARMONY
▼ SEARCHING

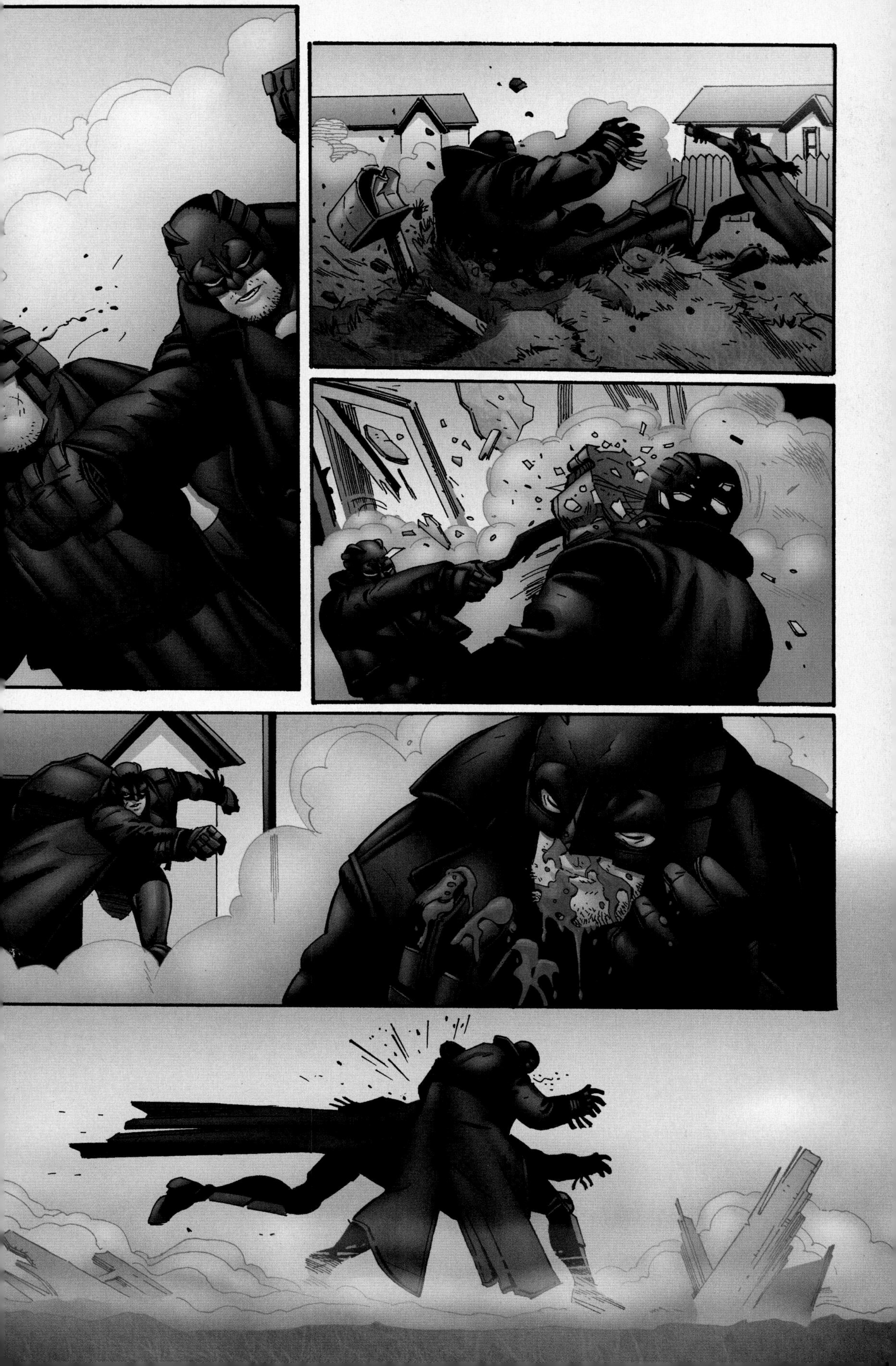

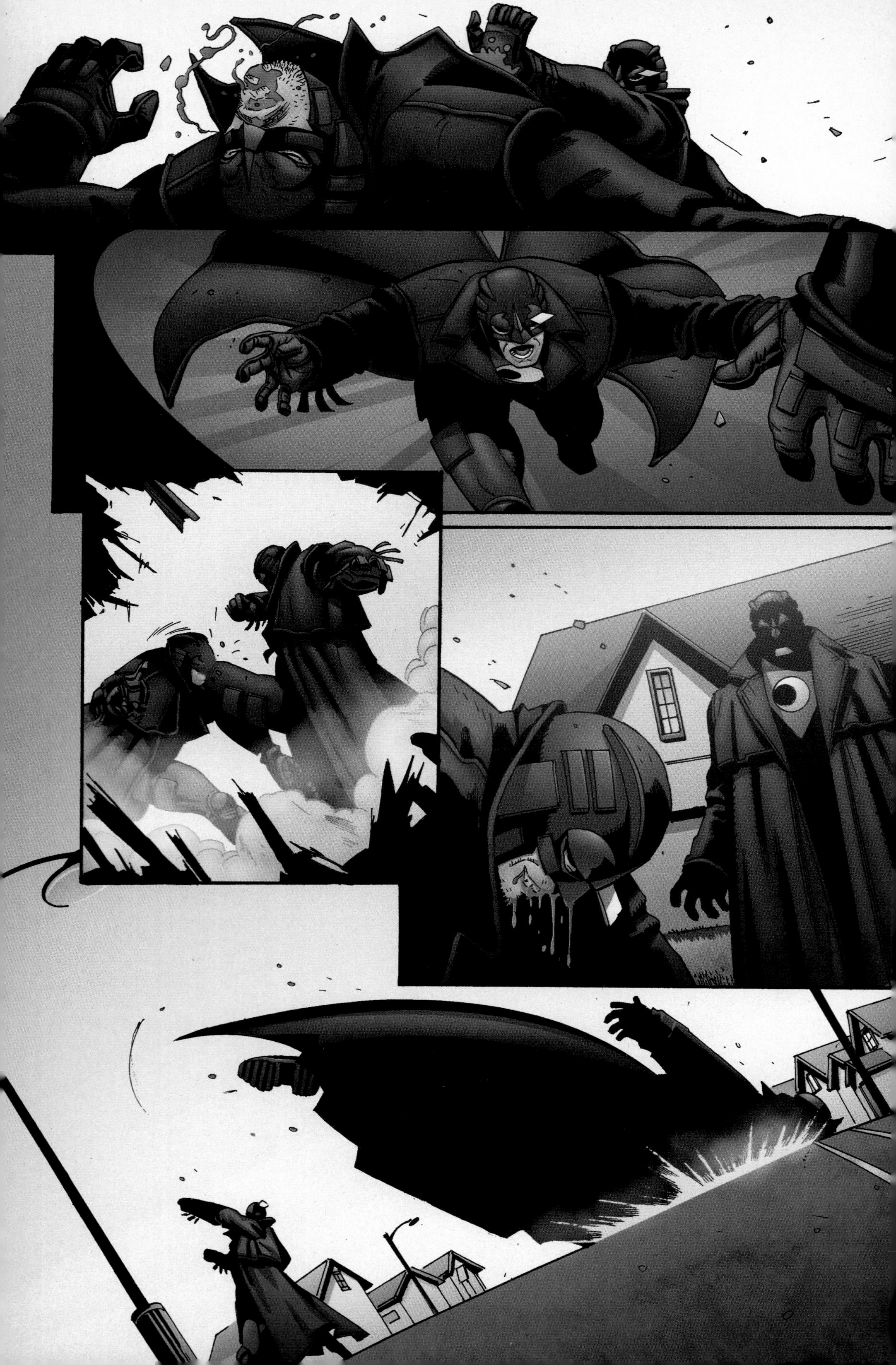

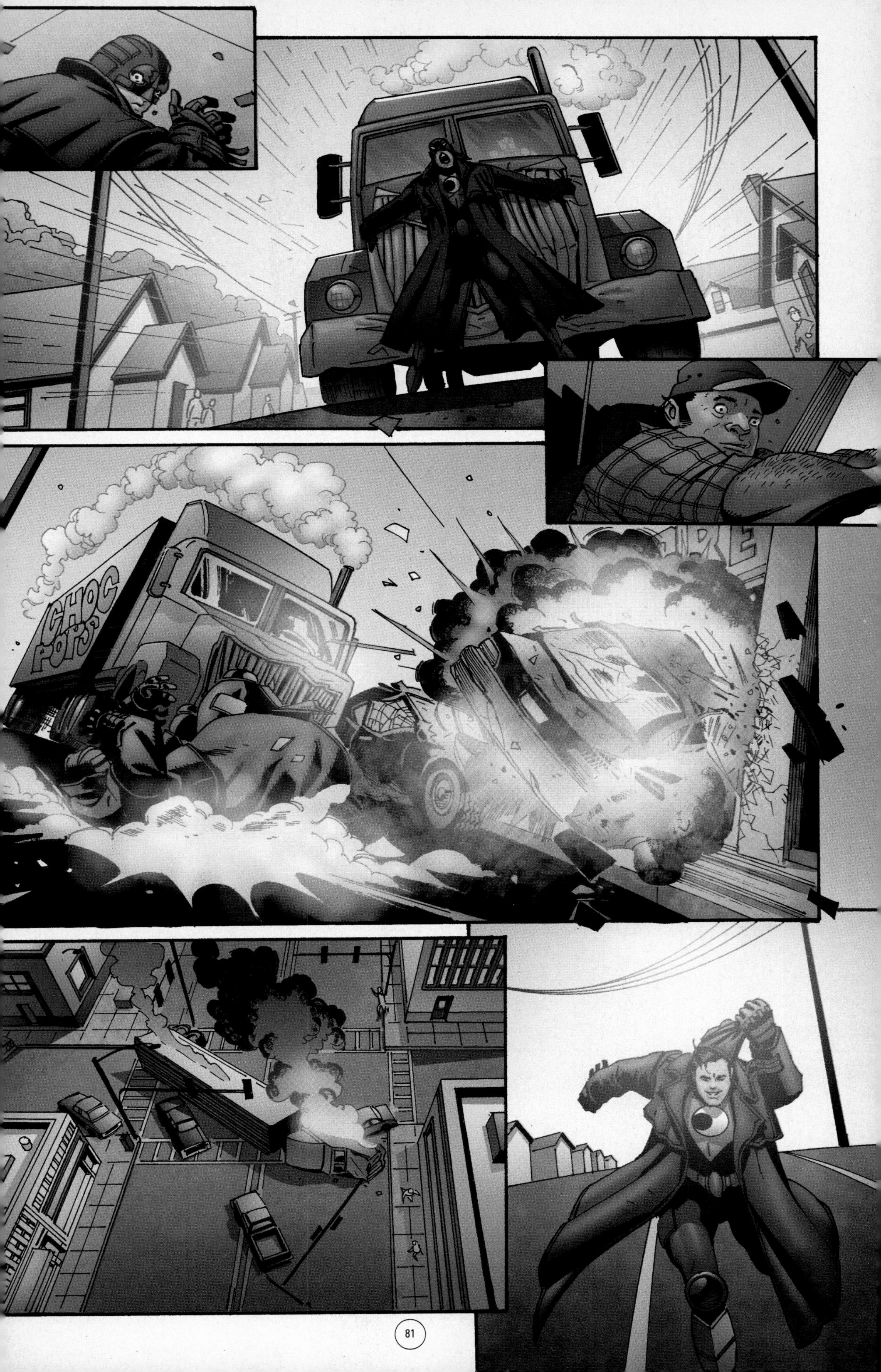
CHOC
POPS

JESUS WEPT!

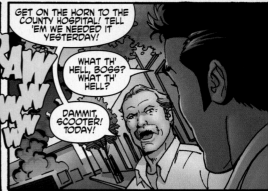

GET ON THE HORN TO THE COUNTY HOSPITAL! TELL 'EM WE NEEDED IT YESTERDAY!

WHAT TH' HELL, BOSS? WHAT TH' HELL?

DAMMIT, SCOOTER! TODAY!

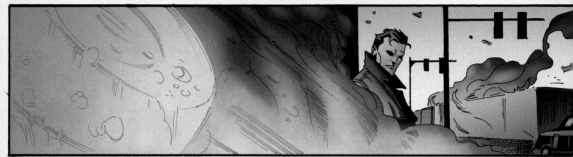

WELL, QUITE THE RESILIENT ONE, AREN'T YOU?

PARTA MY CHARM.

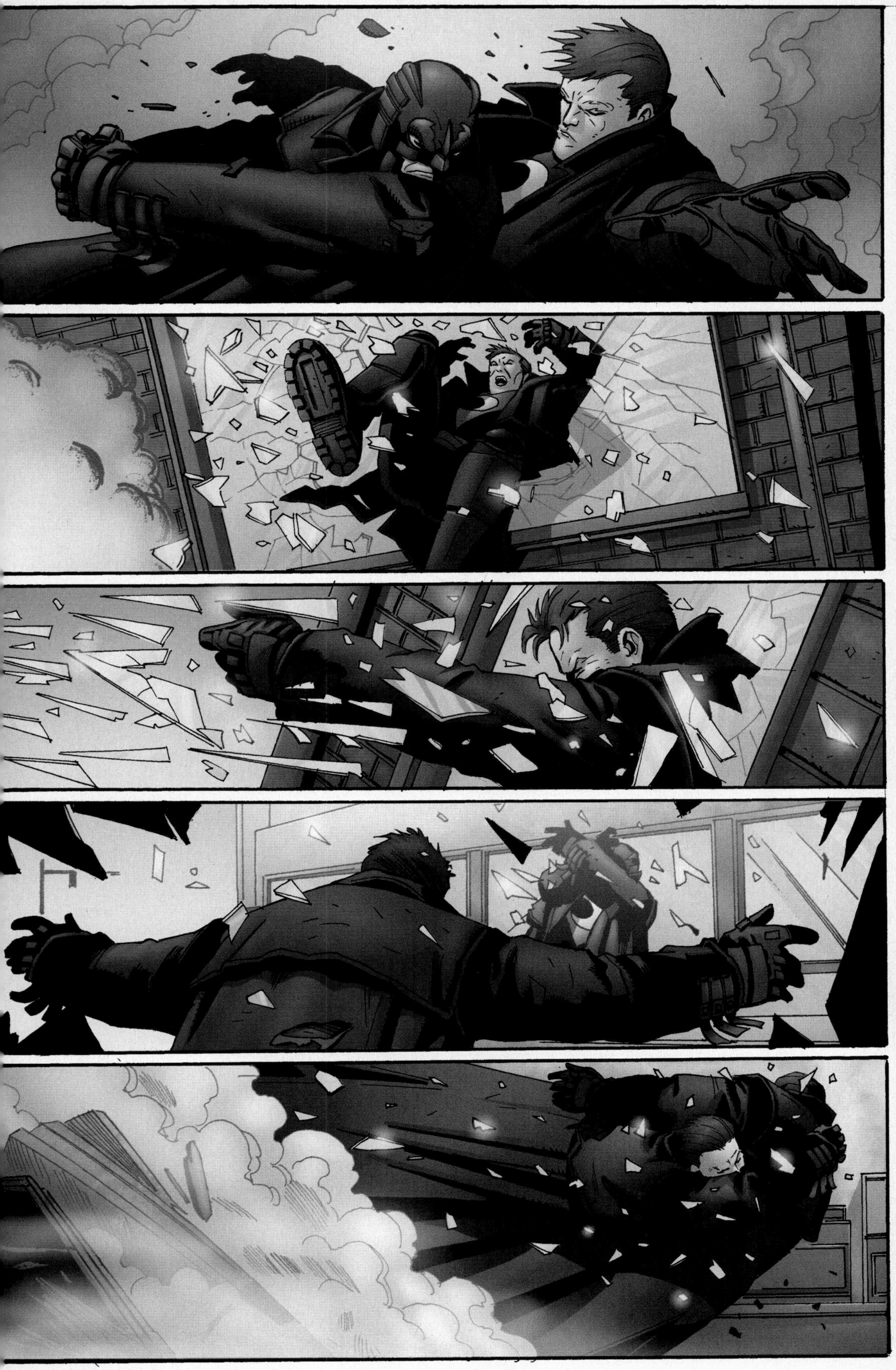

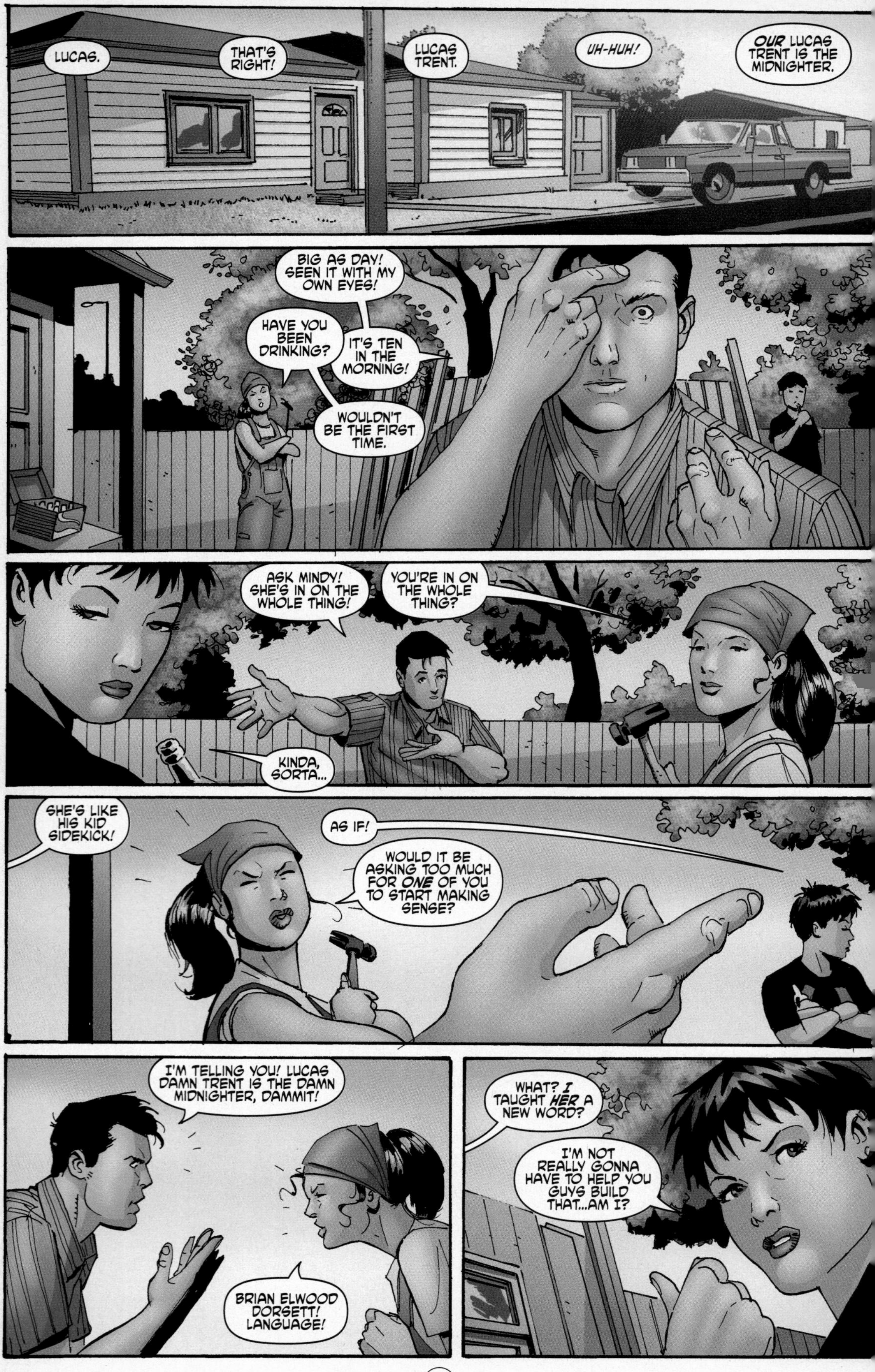
LUCAS.
THAT'S RIGHT!
LUCAS TRENT.
UH-HUH!
OUR LUCAS TRENT IS THE MIDNIGHTER.
BIG AS DAY! SEEN IT WITH MY OWN EYES!
HAVE YOU BEEN DRINKING?
IT'S TEN IN THE MORNING!
WOULDN'T BE THE FIRST TIME.
ASK MINDY! SHE'S IN ON THE WHOLE THING!
YOU'RE IN ON THE WHOLE THING?
KINDA, SORTA...
SHE'S LIKE HIS KID SIDEKICK!
AS IF!
WOULD IT BE ASKING TOO MUCH FOR ONE OF YOU TO START MAKING SENSE?
I'M TELLING YOU! LUCAS DAMN TRENT IS THE DAMN MIDNIGHTER, DAMMIT!
BRIAN ELWOOD DORSETT! LANGUAGE!
WHAT? I TAUGHT HER A NEW WORD?
I'M NOT REALLY GONNA HAVE TO HELP YOU GUYS BUILD THAT...AM I?

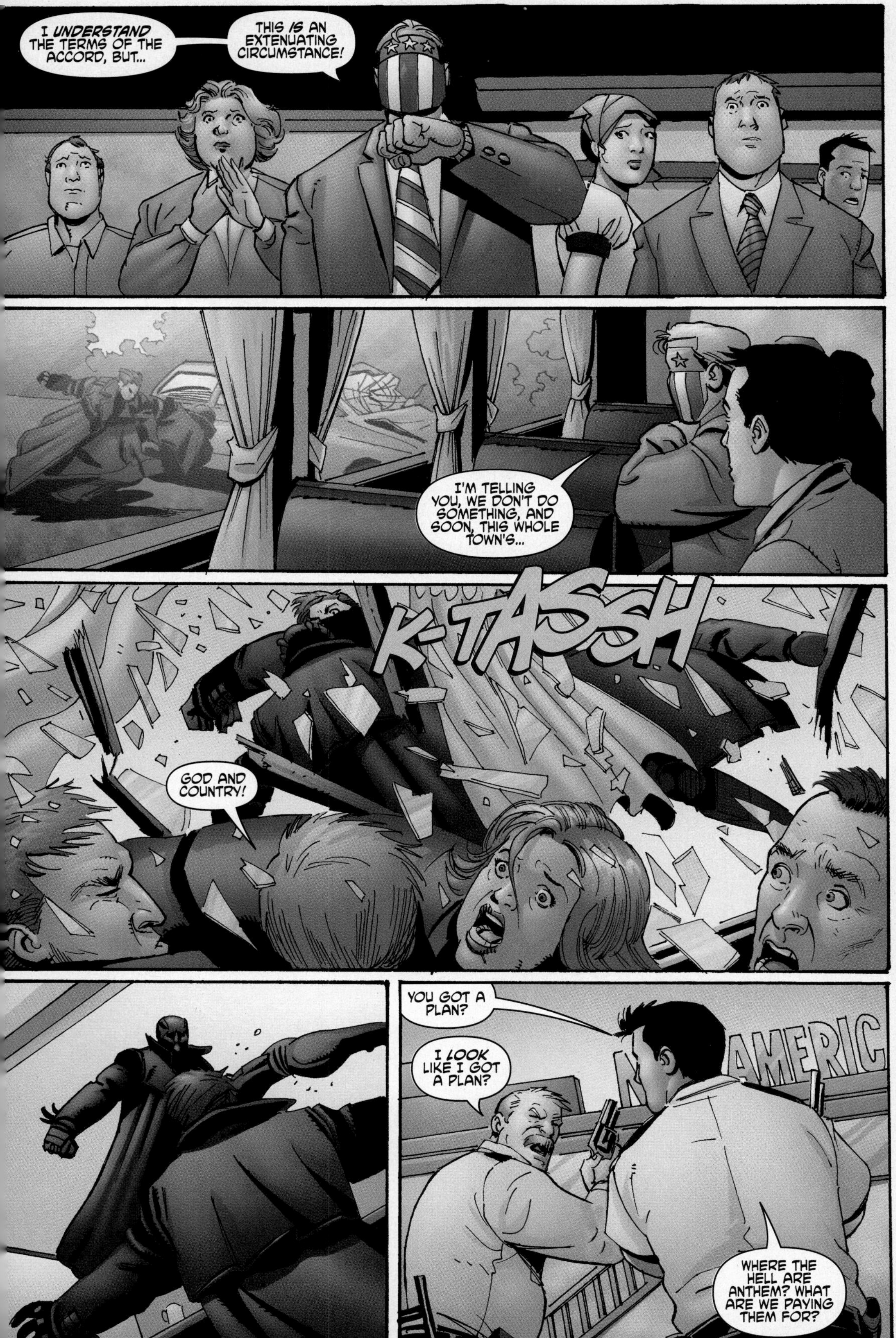
I *UNDERSTAND* THE TERMS OF THE ACCORD, BUT...
THIS *IS* AN EXTENUATING CIRCUMSTANCE!
I'M TELLING YOU, WE DON'T DO SOMETHING, AND SOON, THIS WHOLE TOWN'S...
K-TASSH
GOD AND COUNTRY!
YOU GOT A PLAN?
I *LOOK* LIKE I GOT A PLAN?
AMERIC
WHERE THE HELL ARE ANTHEM? WHAT ARE WE PAYING THEM FOR?

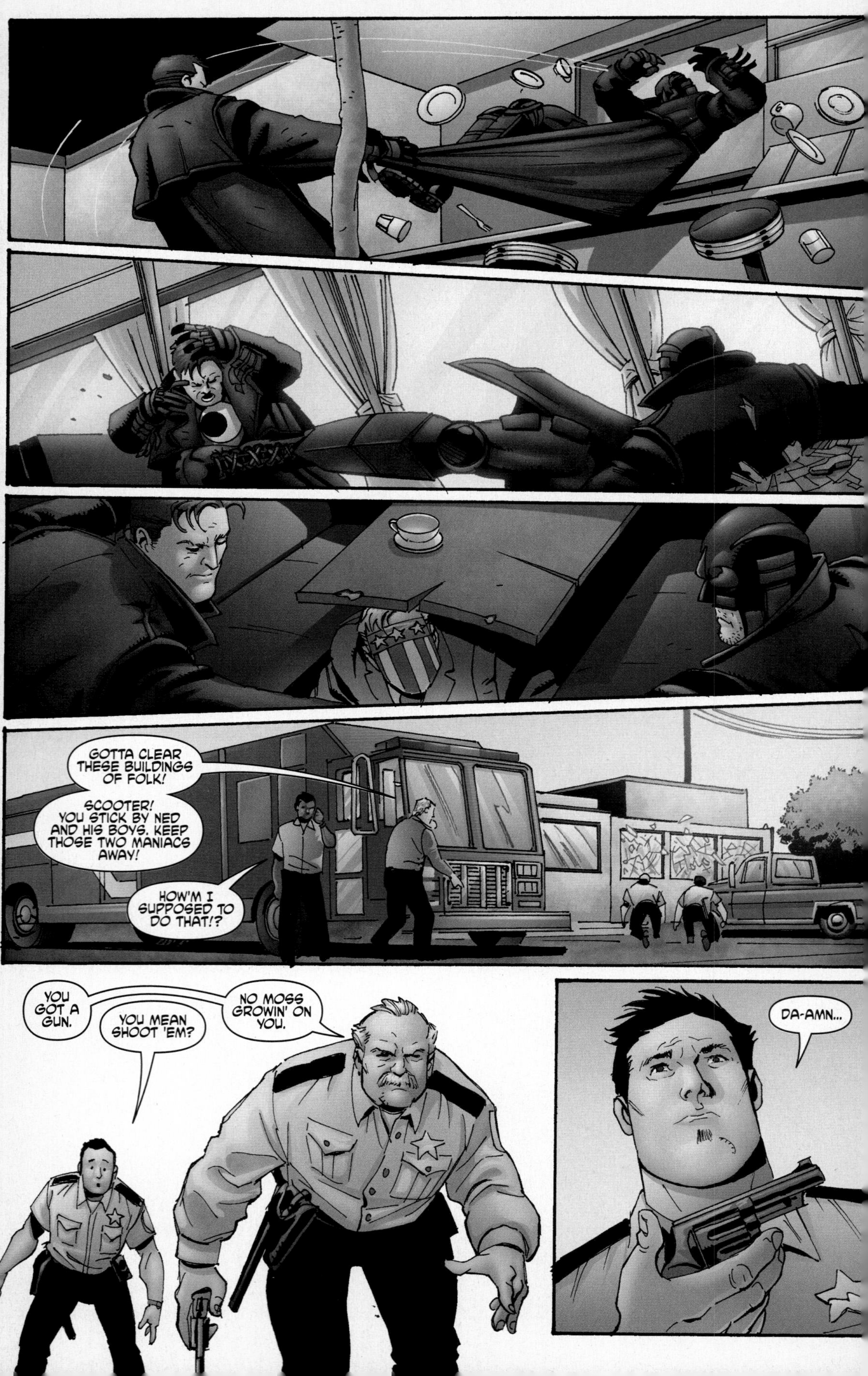
GOTTA CLEAR THESE BUILDINGS OF FOLK!
SCOOTER! YOU STICK BY NED AND HIS BOYS. KEEP THOSE TWO MANIACS AWAY!
HOW'M I SUPPOSED TO DO THAT!?
YOU GOT A GUN.
YOU MEAN SHOOT 'EM?
NO MOSS GROWIN' ON YOU.
DA-AMN...

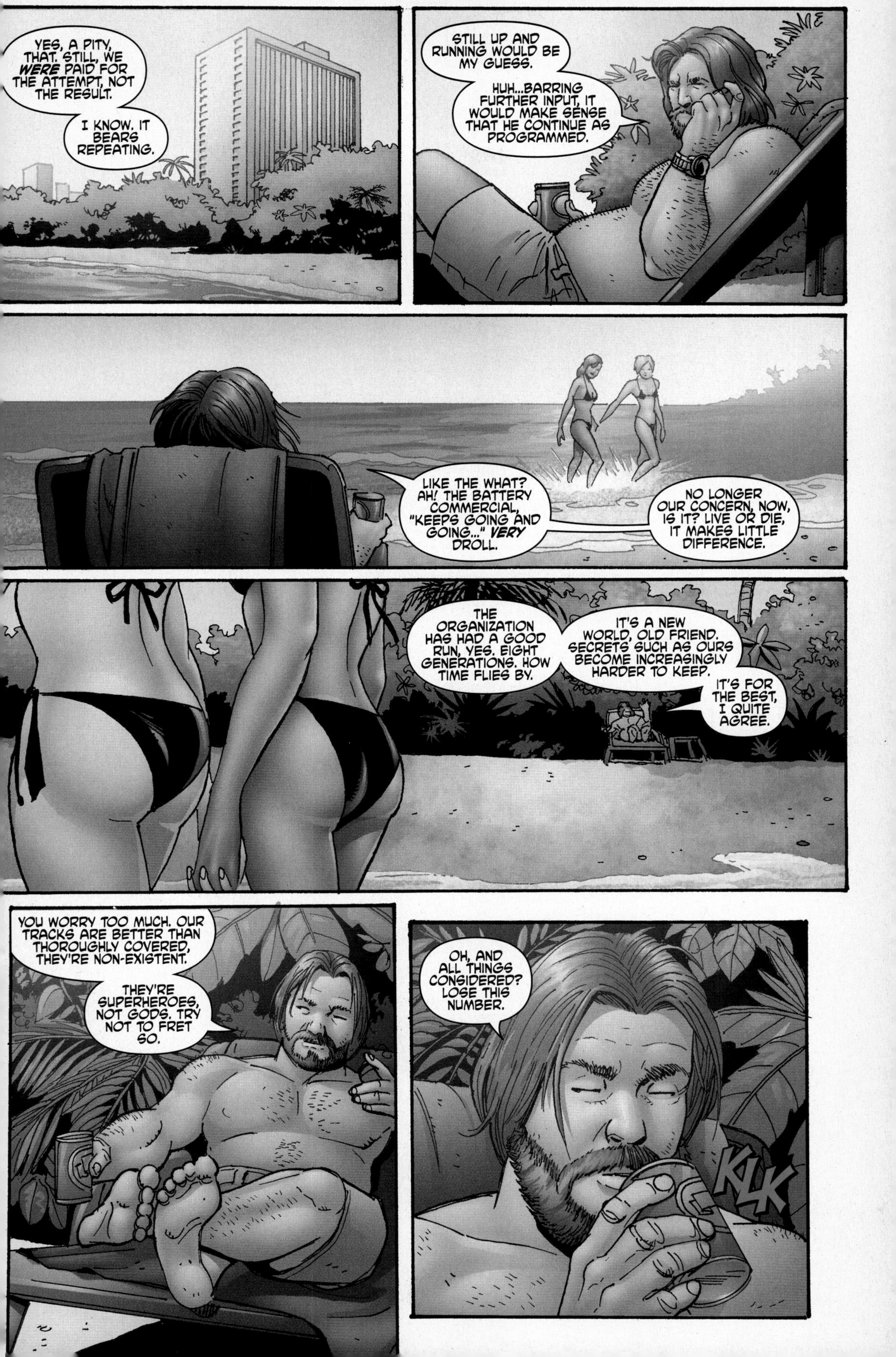
YES, A PITY, THAT. STILL, WE *WERE* PAID FOR THE ATTEMPT, NOT THE RESULT.
I KNOW. IT BEARS REPEATING.
STILL UP AND RUNNING WOULD BE MY GUESS.
HUH...BARRING FURTHER INPUT, IT WOULD MAKE SENSE THAT HE CONTINUE AS PROGRAMMED.
LIKE THE WHAT? AH! THE BATTERY COMMERCIAL, "KEEPS GOING AND GOING..." *VERY* DROLL.
NO LONGER OUR CONCERN, NOW, IS IT? LIVE OR DIE, IT MAKES LITTLE DIFFERENCE.
THE ORGANIZATION HAS HAD A GOOD RUN, YES. EIGHT GENERATIONS. HOW TIME FLIES BY.
IT'S A NEW WORLD, OLD FRIEND. SECRETS SUCH AS OURS BECOME INCREASINGLY HARDER TO KEEP.
IT'S FOR THE BEST, I QUITE AGREE.
YOU WORRY TOO MUCH. OUR TRACKS ARE BETTER THAN THOROUGHLY COVERED, THEY'RE NON-EXISTENT.
THEY'RE SUPERHEROES, NOT GODS. TRY NOT TO FRET SO.
OH, AND ALL THINGS CONSIDERED? LOSE THIS NUMBER.
KLIK

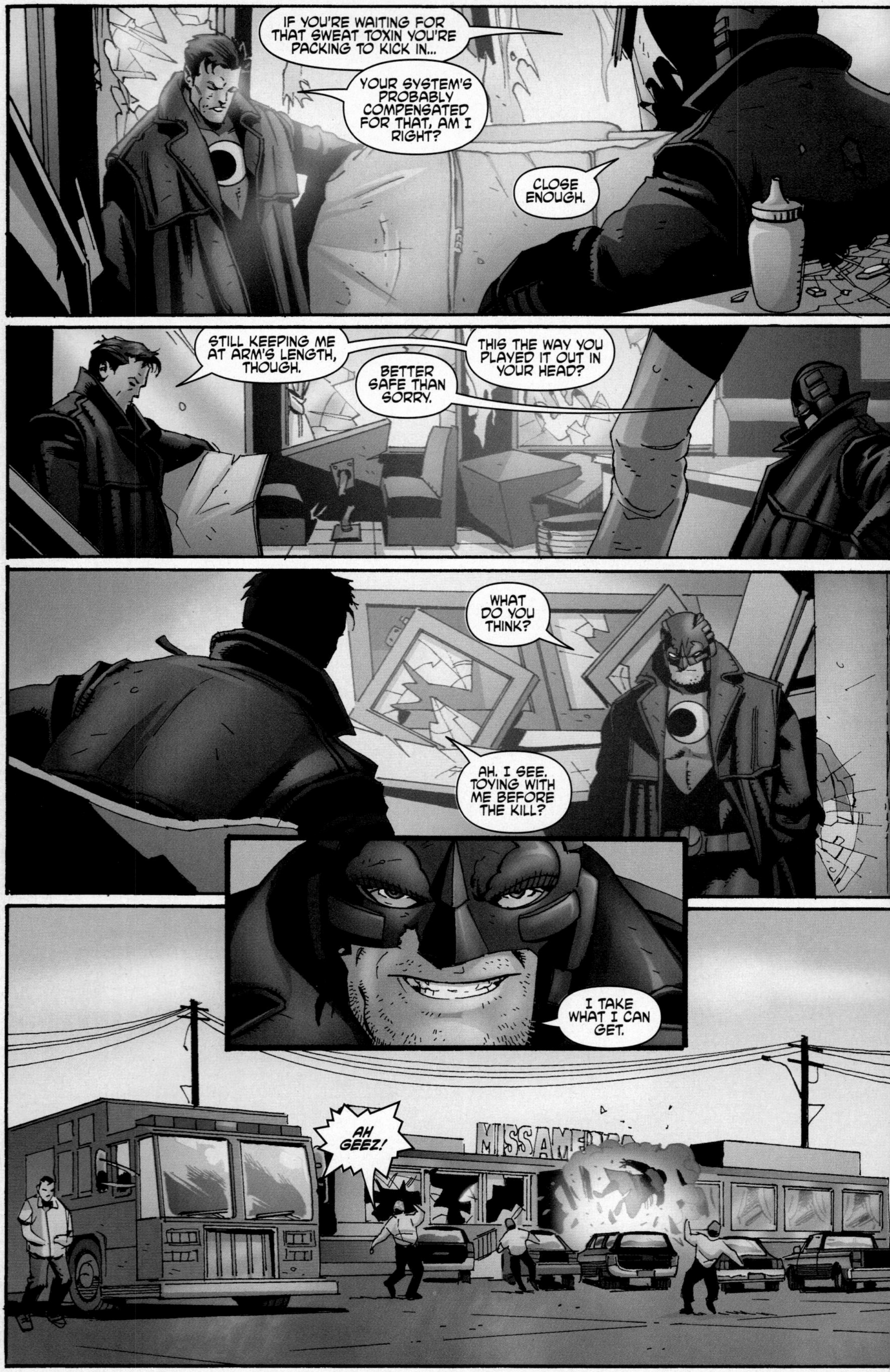
IF YOU'RE WAITING FOR THAT SWEAT TOXIN YOU'RE PACKING TO KICK IN...
YOUR SYSTEM'S PROBABLY COMPENSATED FOR THAT, AM I RIGHT?
CLOSE ENOUGH.
STILL KEEPING ME AT ARM'S LENGTH, THOUGH.
BETTER SAFE THAN SORRY.
THIS THE WAY YOU PLAYED IT OUT IN YOUR HEAD?
WHAT DO YOU THINK?
AH. I SEE. TOYING WITH ME BEFORE THE KILL?
I TAKE WHAT I CAN GET.
AH GEEZ!
MISS AME

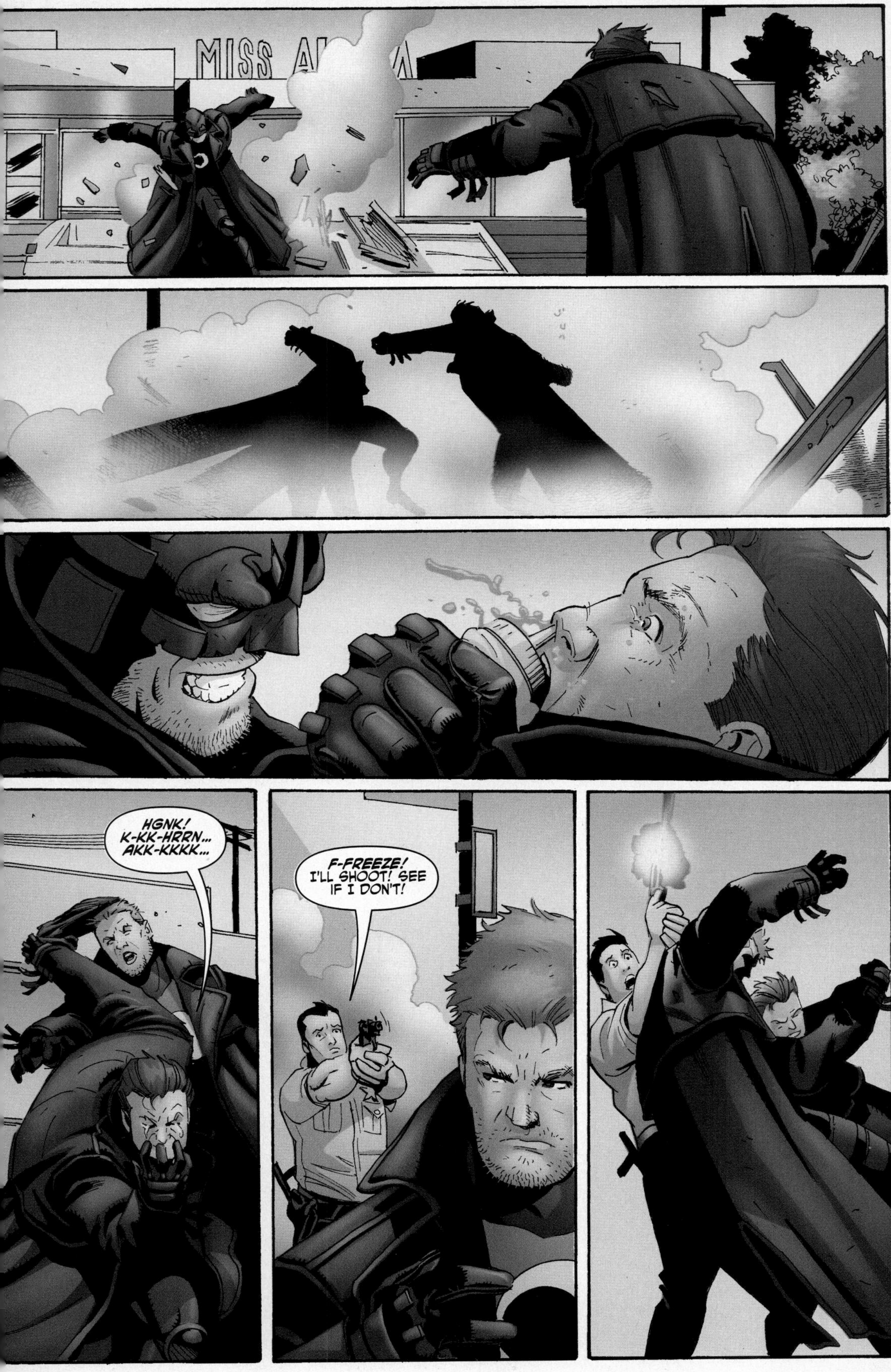
MISS AL
HGNK! K-KK-HRRN... AKK-KKKK...
F-FREEZE! I'LL SHOOT! SEE IF I DON'T!

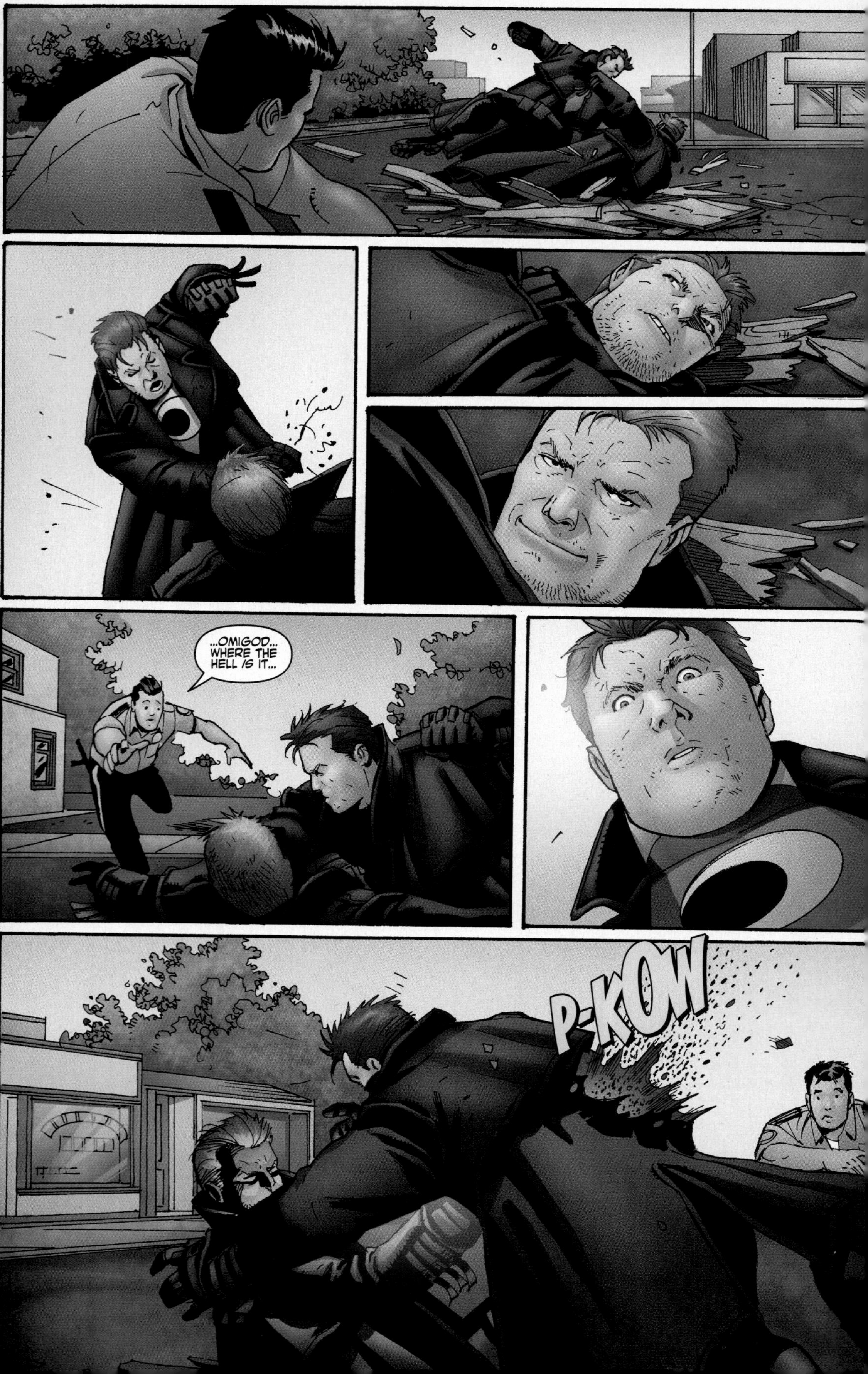
...OMIGOD... WHERE THE HELL IS IT...
P-KOW

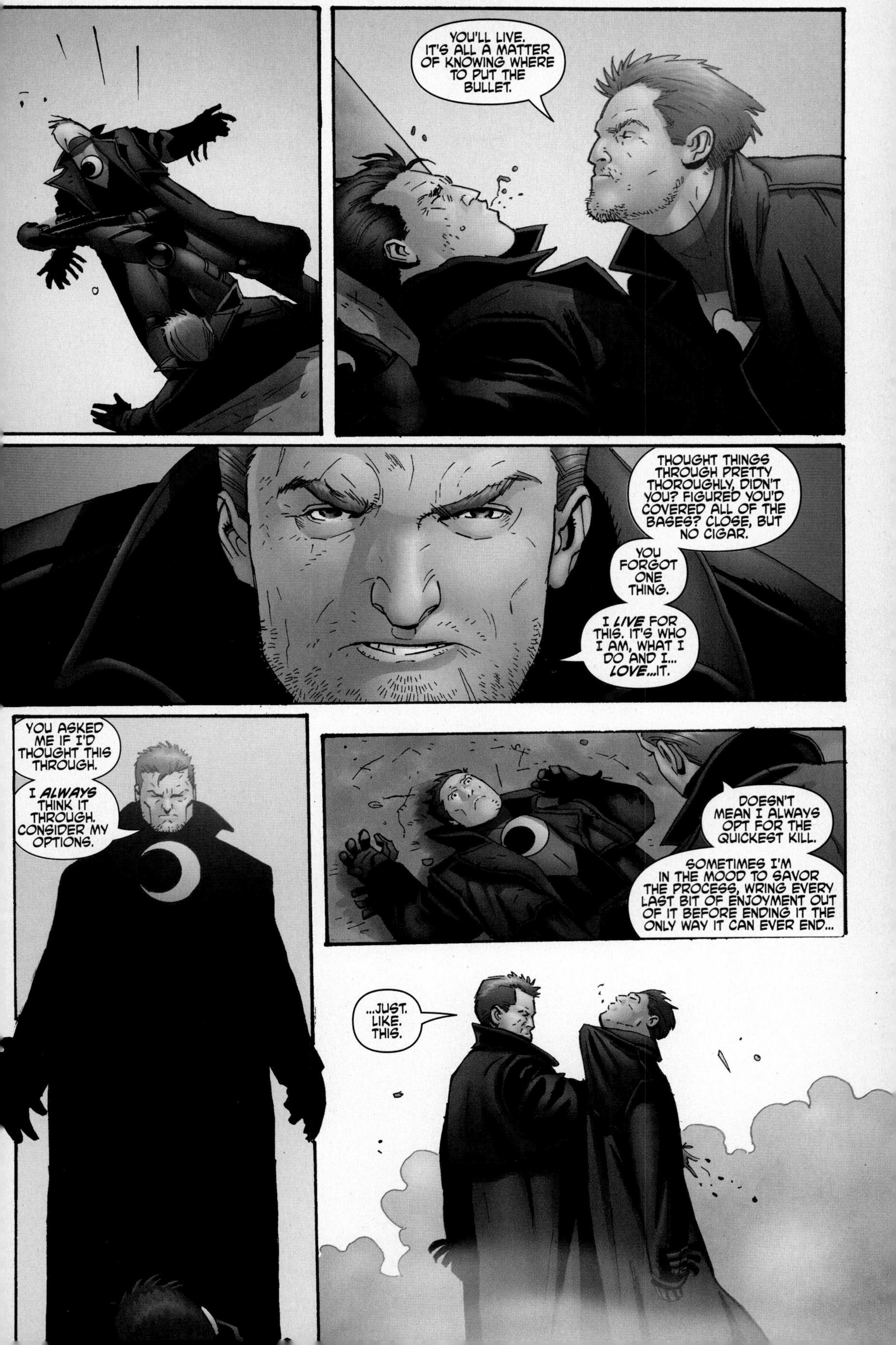
YOU'LL LIVE. IT'S ALL A MATTER OF KNOWING WHERE TO PUT THE BULLET.
THOUGHT THINGS THROUGH PRETTY THOROUGHLY, DIDN'T YOU? FIGURED YOU'D COVERED ALL OF THE BASES? CLOSE, BUT NO CIGAR.
YOU FORGOT ONE THING.
I *LIVE* FOR THIS. IT'S WHO I AM, WHAT I DO AND I... *LOVE*...IT.
YOU ASKED ME IF I'D THOUGHT THIS THROUGH.
I *ALWAYS* THINK IT THROUGH. CONSIDER MY OPTIONS.
DOESN'T MEAN I ALWAYS OPT FOR THE QUICKEST KILL.
SOMETIMES I'M IN THE MOOD TO SAVOR THE PROCESS, WRING EVERY LAST BIT OF ENJOYMENT OUT OF IT BEFORE ENDING IT THE ONLY WAY IT CAN EVER END...
...JUST. LIKE. THIS.

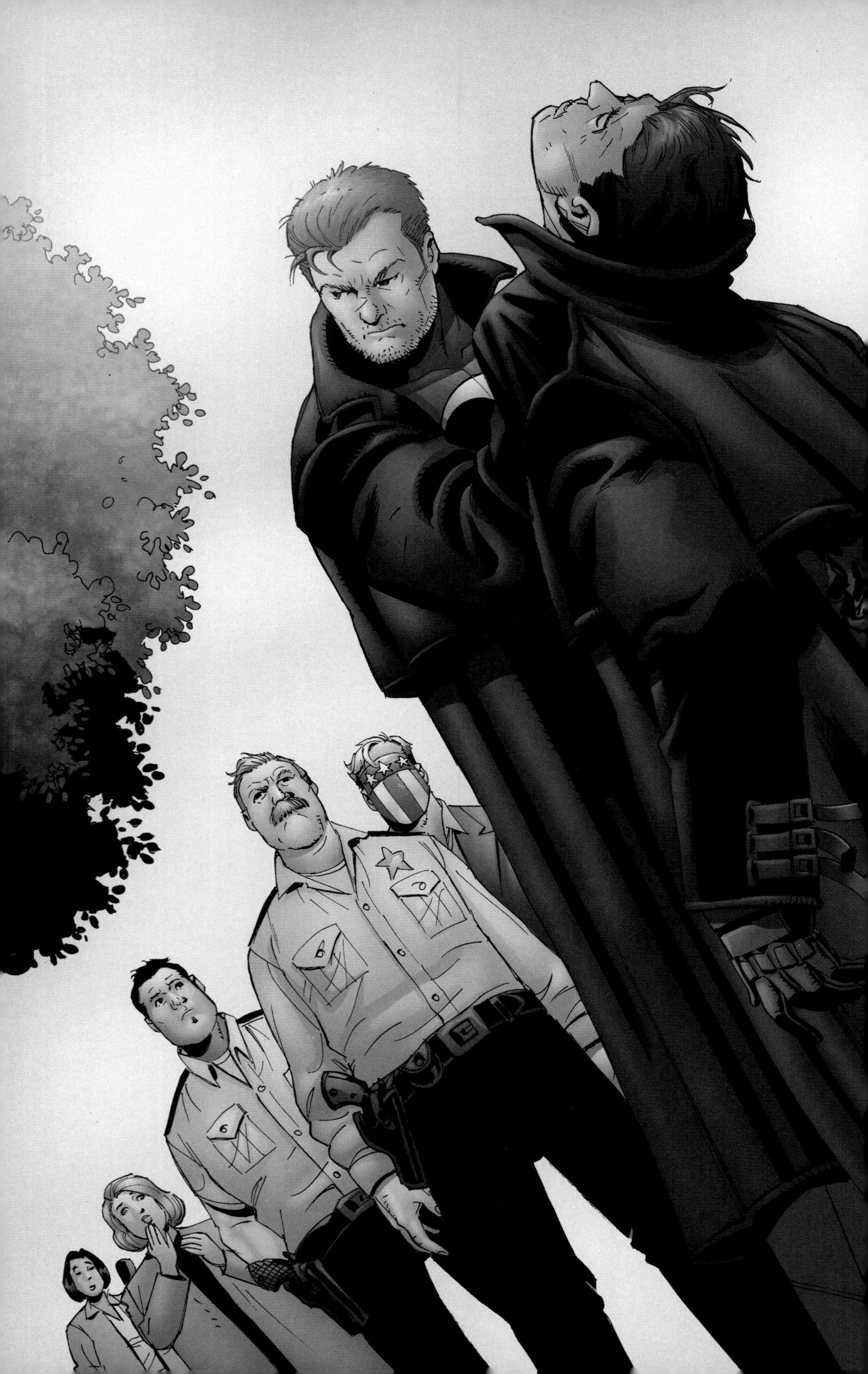

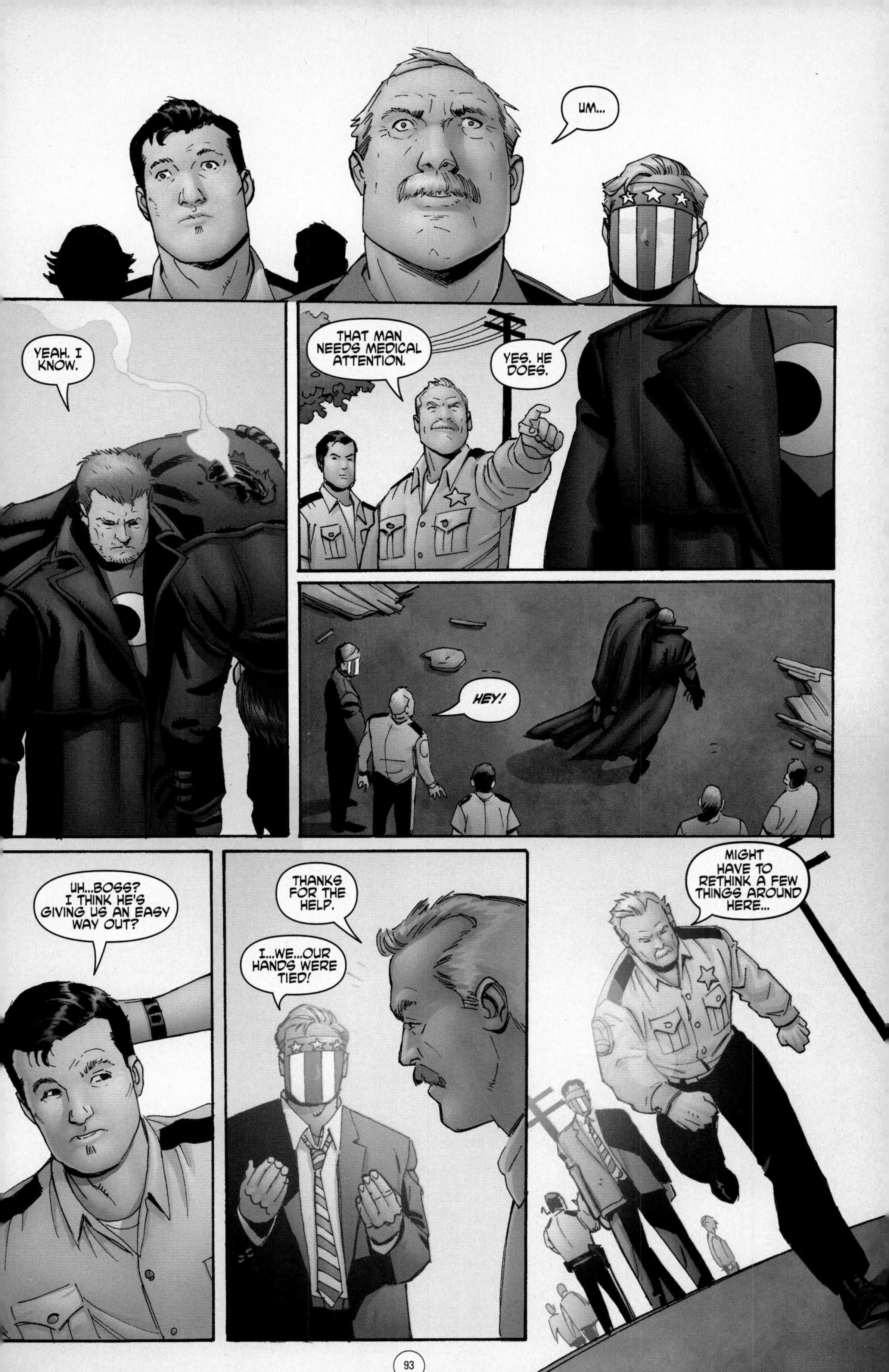
UM...
YEAH. I KNOW.
THAT MAN NEEDS MEDICAL ATTENTION.
YES, HE DOES.
HEY!
UH...BOSS? I THINK HE'S GIVING US AN EASY WAY OUT?
THANKS FOR THE HELP.
I...WE...OUR HANDS WERE TIED!
MIGHT HAVE TO RETHINK A FEW THINGS AROUND HERE...

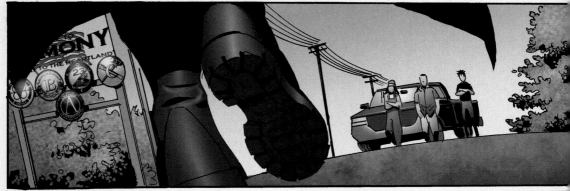

MINDY, SHE *SAID* YOU'D BE MAKING TRACKS.

DID SHE.

GUESS YOU DON'T HAVE MUCH CHOICE, I MEAN, AFTER...UM...

I SAW HIM PRY THAT DOOR THING OUT OF YOU, SO...

YOU ASSUMED I'D BE HOOFING IT.

ASSUMED... YEAH.

WHAT...WHAT GAVE YOU THE RIGHT? BRINGING THIS TO US? WHAT GAVE YOU THE DAMN RIGHT!?

AMANDA! GEEZ!

NO HARM, NO FOUL.

YOU KEEPING HIM?

I'VE GOT QUESTIONS. HE'S GOT ANSWERS. I CAN BE VERY PERSUASIVE.

LUCAS?

NOT MY NAME.

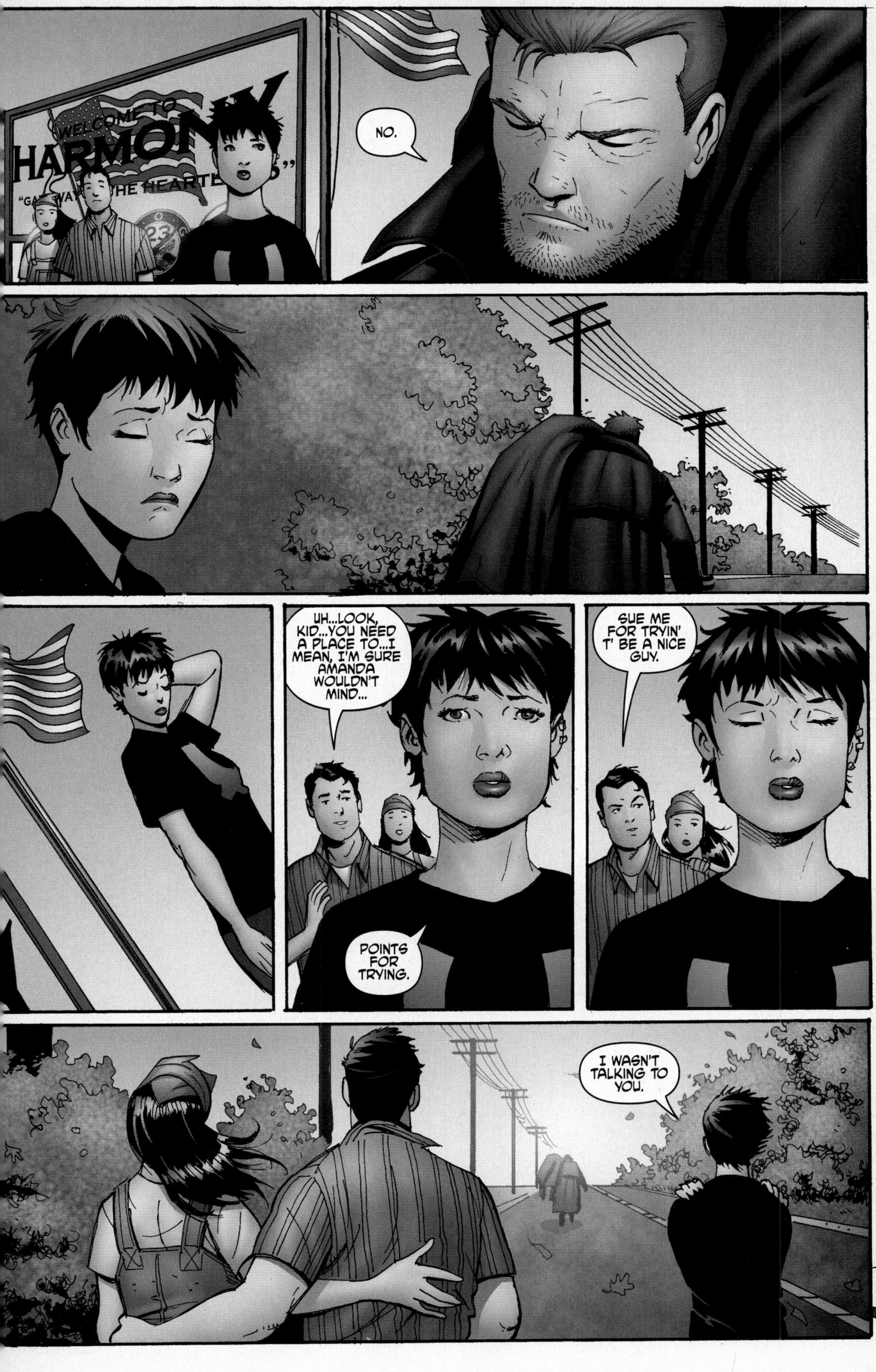
WELCOME TO
HARMONY
"GATEWAY TO THE HEARTE...S"
NO.
UH...LOOK, KID...YOU NEED A PLACE TO...I MEAN, I'M SURE AMANDA WOULDN'T MIND...
POINTS FOR TRYING.
SUE ME FOR TRYIN' T' BE A NICE GUY.
I WASN'T TALKING TO YOU.

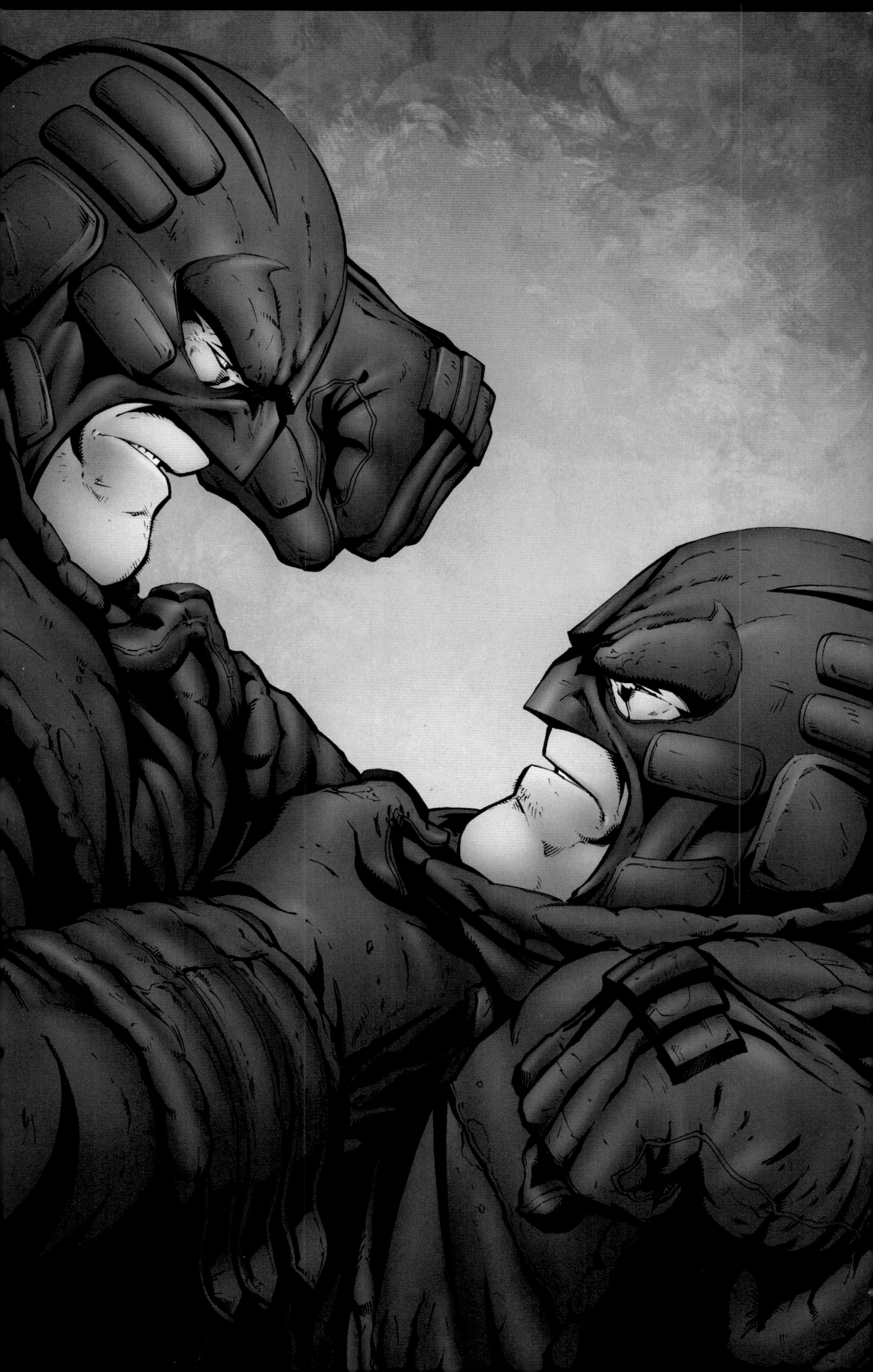

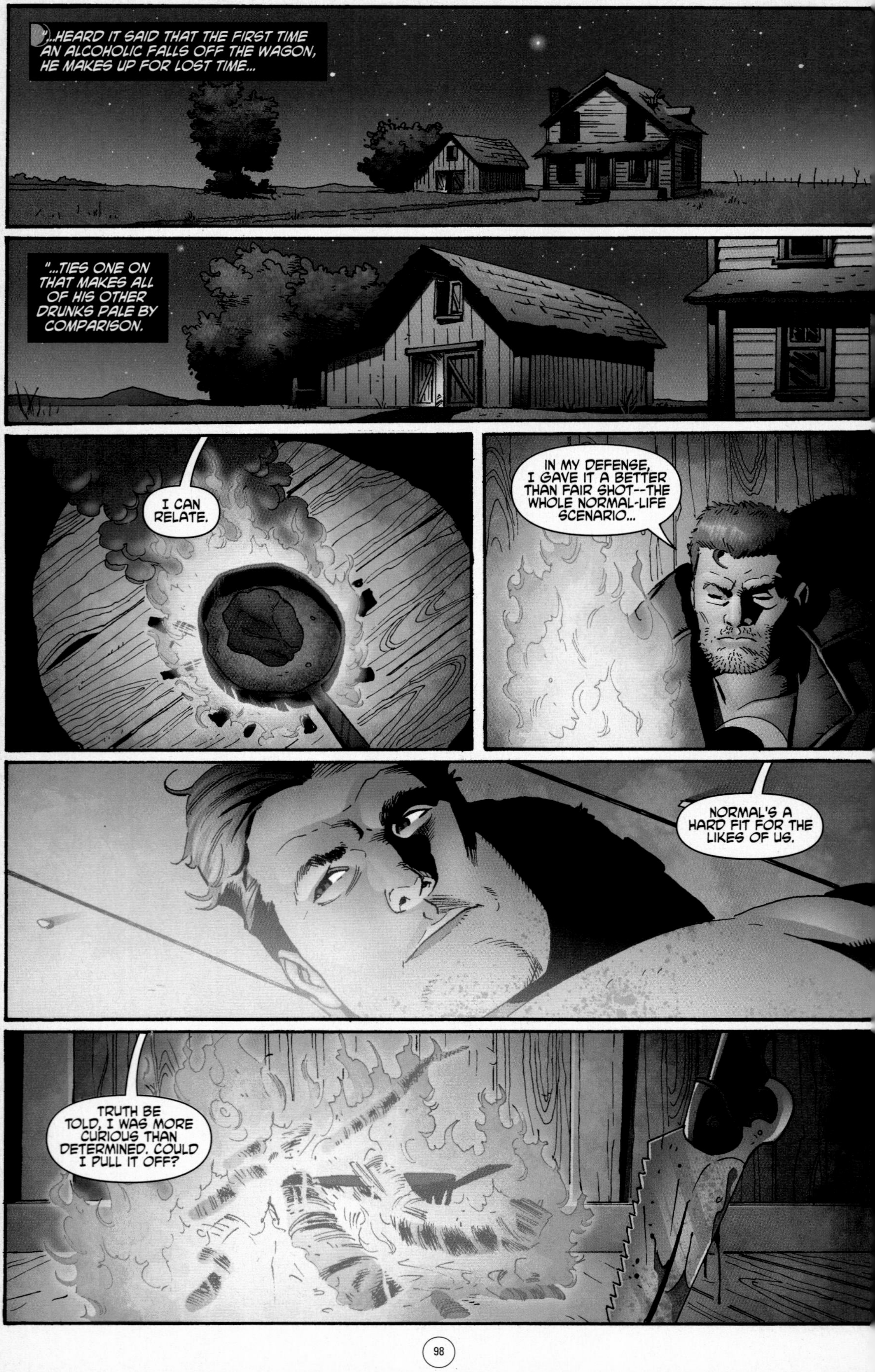
"...HEARD IT SAID THAT THE FIRST TIME AN ALCOHOLIC FALLS OFF THE WAGON, HE MAKES UP FOR LOST TIME...
"...TIES ONE ON THAT MAKES ALL OF HIS OTHER DRUNKS PALE BY COMPARISON.
I CAN RELATE.
IN MY DEFENSE, I GAVE IT A BETTER THAN FAIR SHOT--THE WHOLE NORMAL-LIFE SCENARIO...
NORMAL'S A HARD FIT FOR THE LIKES OF US.
TRUTH BE TOLD, I WAS MORE CURIOUS THAN DETERMINED. COULD I PULL IT OFF?

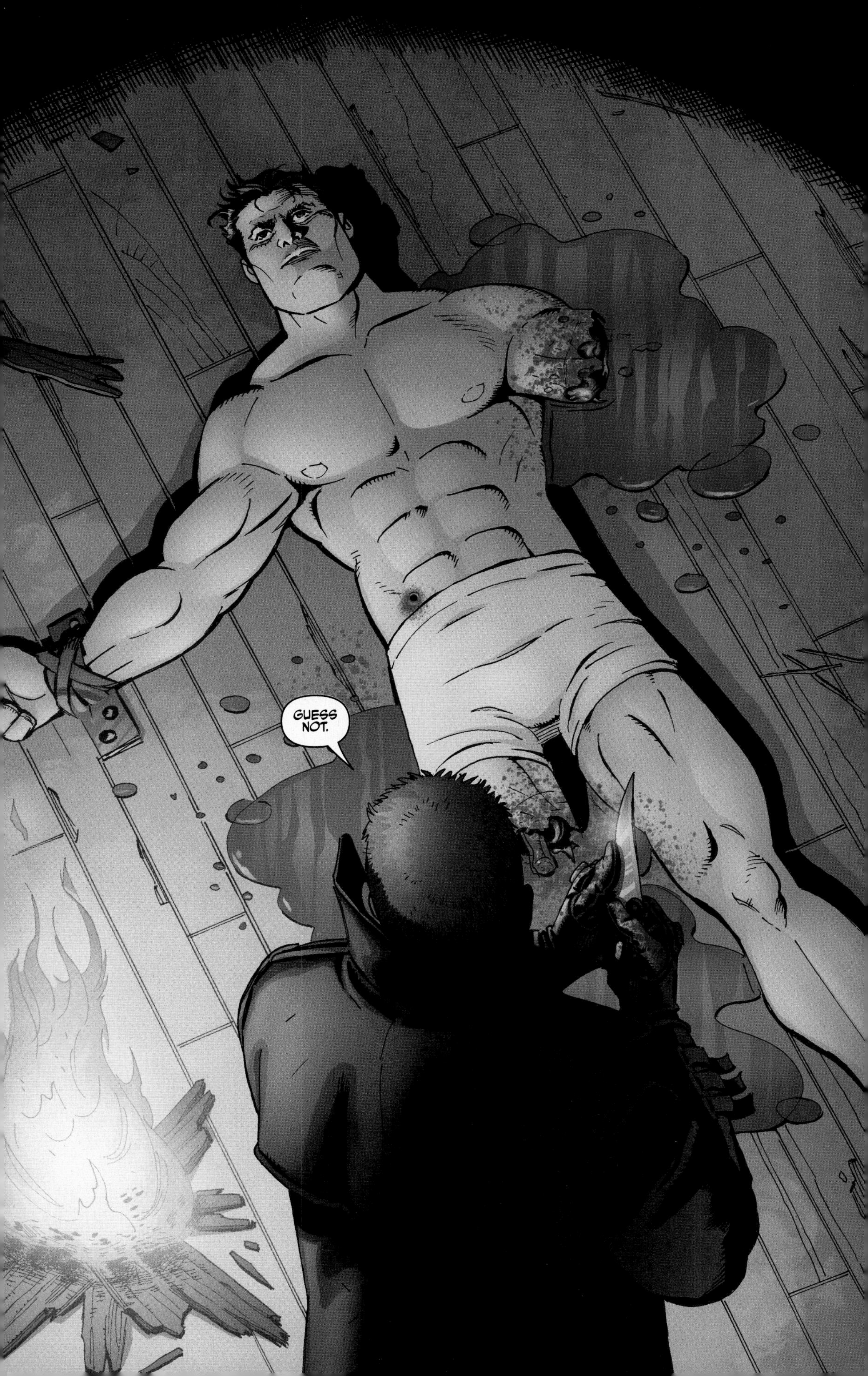
GUESS NOT.

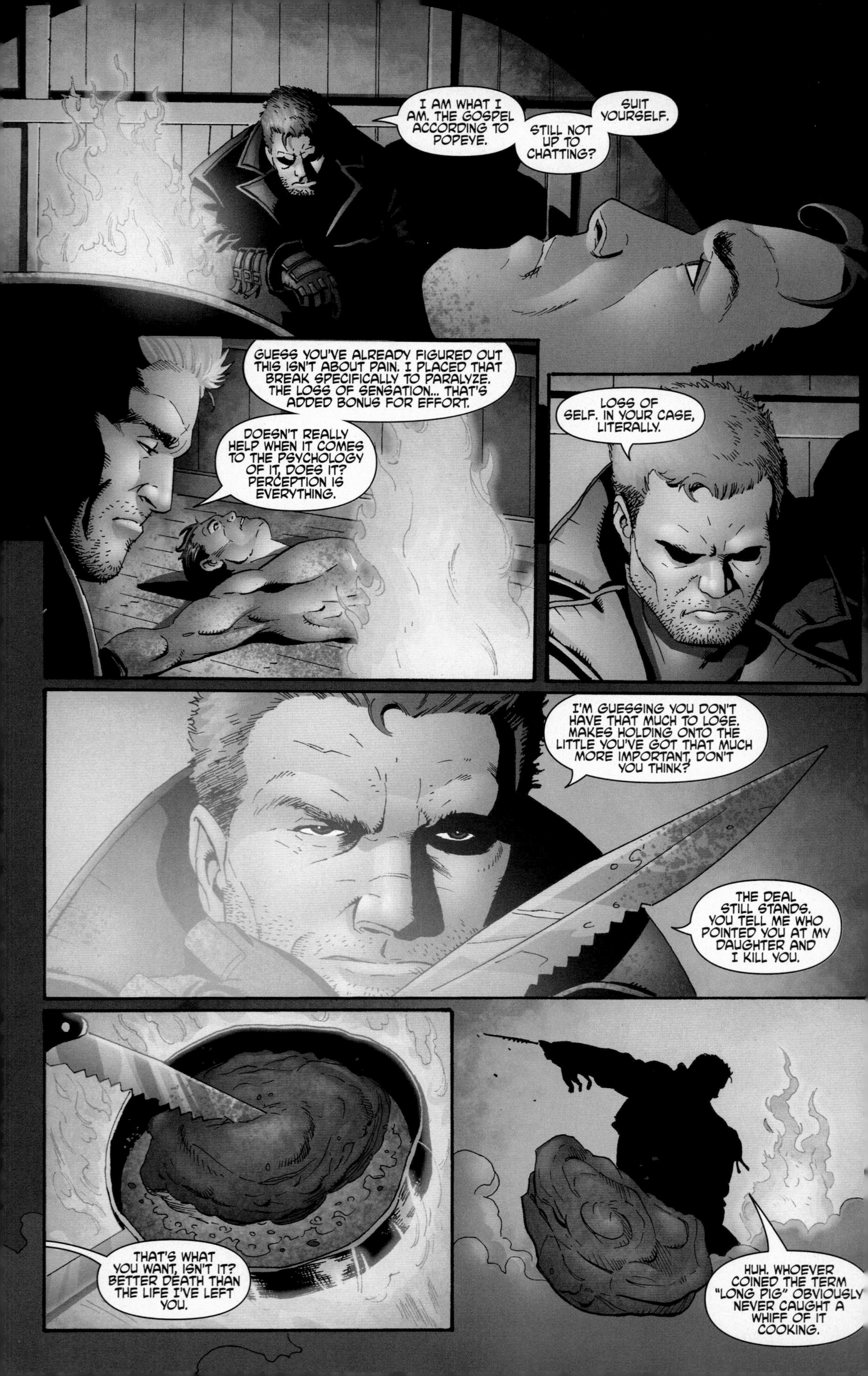
I AM WHAT I AM. THE GOSPEL ACCORDING TO POPEYE.
STILL NOT UP TO CHATTING?
SUIT YOURSELF.
GUESS YOU'VE ALREADY FIGURED OUT THIS ISN'T ABOUT PAIN. I PLACED THAT BREAK SPECIFICALLY TO PARALYZE. THE LOSS OF SENSATION... THAT'S ADDED BONUS FOR EFFORT.
DOESN'T REALLY HELP WHEN IT COMES TO THE PSYCHOLOGY OF IT, DOES IT? PERCEPTION IS EVERYTHING.
LOSS OF SELF. IN YOUR CASE, LITERALLY.
I'M GUESSING YOU DON'T HAVE THAT MUCH TO LOSE. MAKES HOLDING ONTO THE LITTLE YOU'VE GOT THAT MUCH MORE IMPORTANT, DON'T YOU THINK?
THE DEAL STILL STANDS. YOU TELL ME WHO POINTED YOU AT MY DAUGHTER AND I KILL YOU.
THAT'S WHAT YOU WANT, ISN'T IT? BETTER DEATH THAN THE LIFE I'VE LEFT YOU.
HUH. WHOEVER COINED THE TERM "LONG PIG" OBVIOUSLY NEVER CAUGHT A WHIFF OF IT COOKING.

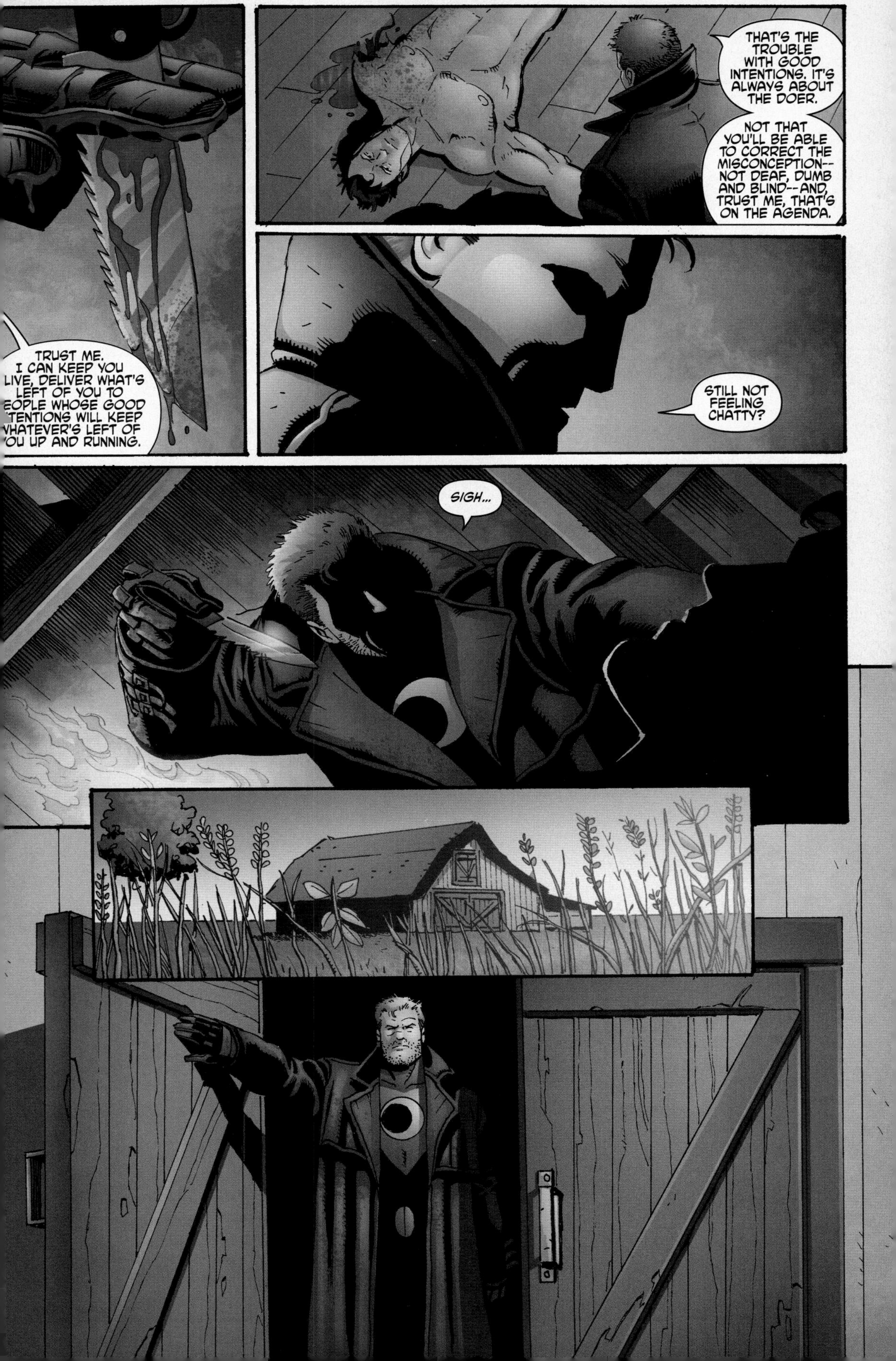
TRUST ME. I CAN KEEP YOU LIVE, DELIVER WHAT'S LEFT OF YOU TO EOPLE WHOSE GOOD TENTIONS WILL KEEP WHATEVER'S LEFT OF YOU UP AND RUNNING.
THAT'S THE TROUBLE WITH GOOD INTENTIONS. IT'S ALWAYS ABOUT THE DOER.
NOT THAT YOU'LL BE ABLE TO CORRECT THE MISCONCEPTION-- NOT DEAF, DUMB AND BLIND--AND, TRUST ME, THAT'S ON THE AGENDA.
STILL NOT FEELING CHATTY?
SIGH...

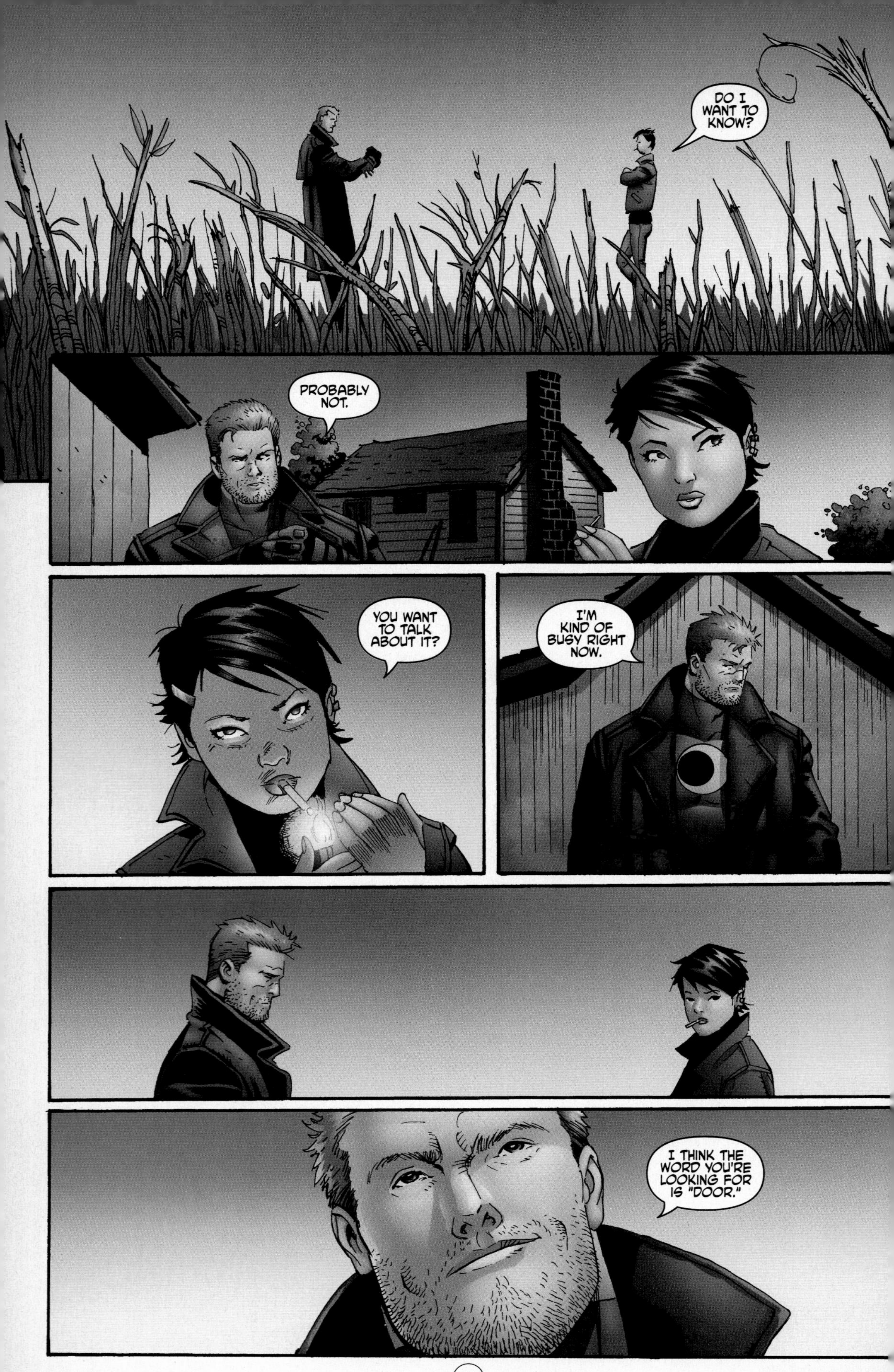
DO I WANT TO KNOW?
PROBABLY NOT.
YOU WANT TO TALK ABOUT IT?
I'M KIND OF BUSY RIGHT NOW.
I THINK THE WORD YOU'RE LOOKING FOR IS "DOOR."

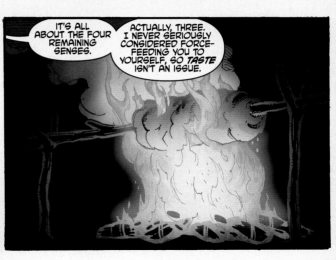

IT'S ALL ABOUT THE FOUR REMAINING SENSES.

ACTUALLY, THREE. I NEVER SERIOUSLY CONSIDERED FORCE-FEEDING YOU TO YOURSELF, SO *TASTE* ISN'T AN ISSUE.

SIGHT'S NOT THE BIG ONE. YOU'D THINK SO, BEING WITNESS TO YOUR OWN...DECONSTRUCTION. ENJOYING THE SHOW?

HEARING'S A BIT MORE THAN LISTENING TO ME RAMBLE ON, ISN'T IT?

THE RASP OF BLADE ON BONE, THE SIZZLE OF THE MEAT, THE HISS OF CAUTERIZATION...HARDER TO BLOCK OUT THAN SIGHT. YOU CAN CLOSE YOUR EYES, BUT YOUR EARS?

IF I HAD TO CHOOSE, I'D PUT SCENT RIGHT UP THERE. SMELL IN HERE'S ENOUGH TO PUT YOU OFF MEAT FOR THE REST OF YOUR LIFE.

FEELING CHATTY YET?

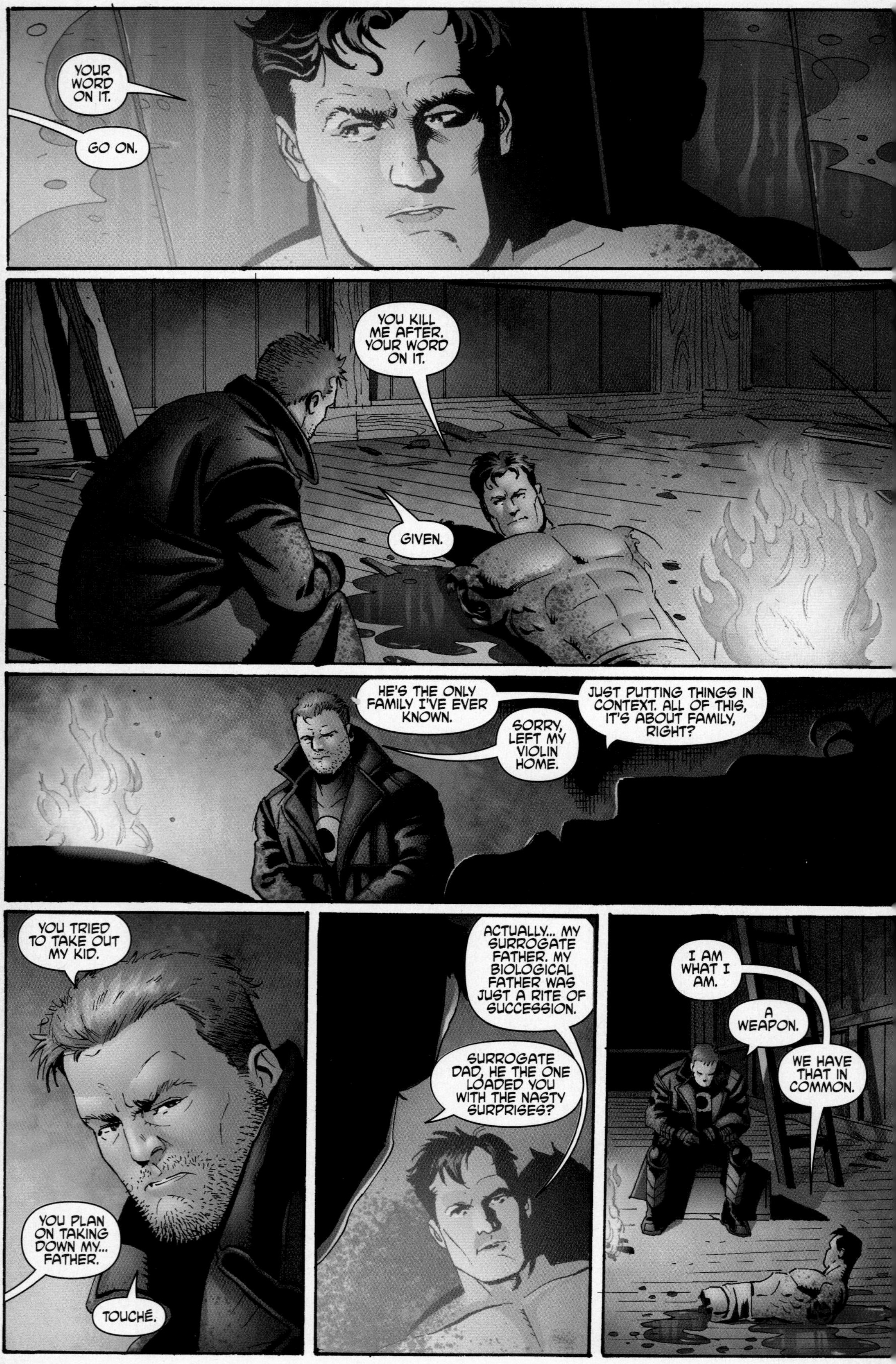
YOUR WORD ON IT.
GO ON.
YOU KILL ME AFTER. YOUR WORD ON IT.
GIVEN.
HE'S THE ONLY FAMILY I'VE EVER KNOWN.
SORRY, LEFT MY VIOLIN HOME.
JUST PUTTING THINGS IN CONTEXT. ALL OF THIS, IT'S ABOUT FAMILY, RIGHT?
YOU TRIED TO TAKE OUT MY KID.
YOU PLAN ON TAKING DOWN MY... FATHER.
TOUCHÉ.
ACTUALLY... MY SURROGATE FATHER. MY BIOLOGICAL FATHER WAS JUST A RITE OF SUCCESSION.
SURROGATE DAD, HE THE ONE LOADED YOU WITH THE NASTY SURPRISES?
I AM WHAT I AM.
A WEAPON.
WE HAVE THAT IN COMMON.

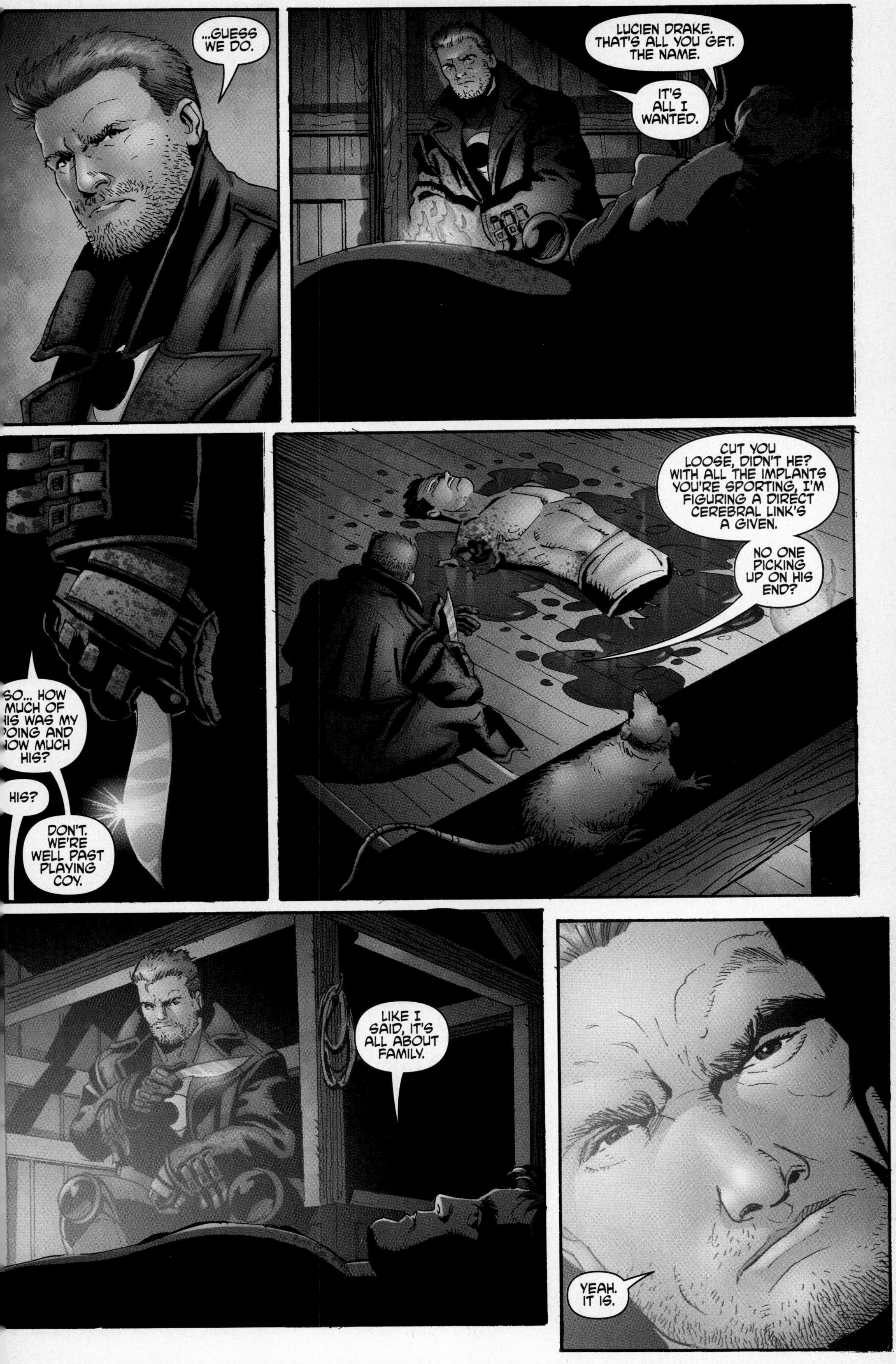
...GUESS WE DO.
LUCIEN DRAKE. THAT'S ALL YOU GET. THE NAME.
IT'S ALL I WANTED.
SO... HOW MUCH OF HIS WAS MY DOING AND HOW MUCH HIS?
HIS?
DON'T. WE'RE WELL PAST PLAYING COY.
CUT YOU LOOSE, DIDN'T HE? WITH ALL THE IMPLANTS YOU'RE SPORTING, I'M FIGURING A DIRECT CEREBRAL LINK'S A GIVEN.
NO ONE PICKING UP ON HIS END?
LIKE I SAID, IT'S ALL ABOUT FAMILY.
YEAH. IT IS.

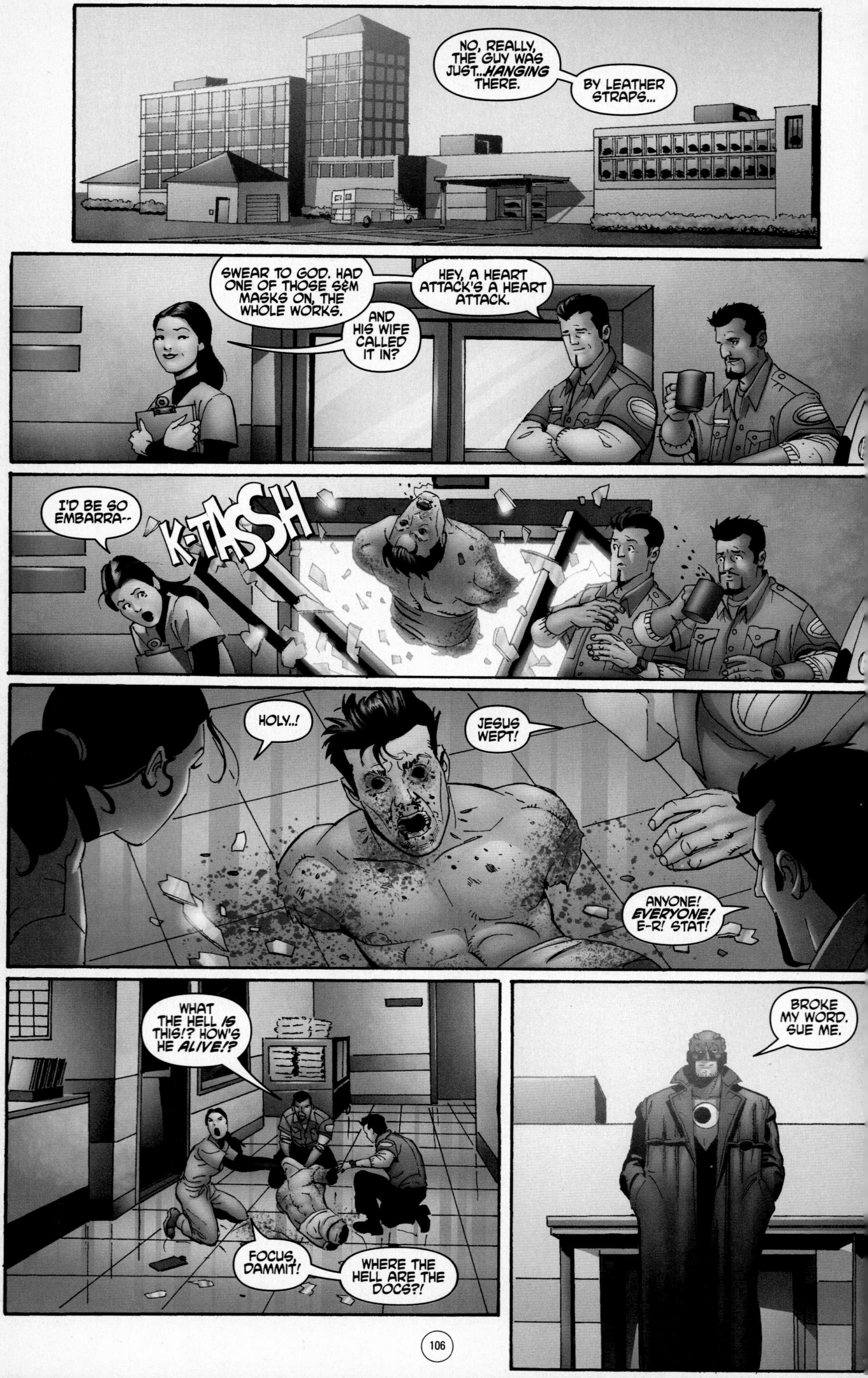
NO, REALLY, THE GUY WAS JUST...HANGING THERE.
BY LEATHER STRAPS...
SWEAR TO GOD. HAD ONE OF THOSE S&M MASKS ON, THE WHOLE WORKS.
HEY, A HEART ATTACK'S A HEART ATTACK.
AND HIS WIFE CALLED IT IN?
I'D BE SO EMBARRA--
K-TASH
HOLY..!
JESUS WEPT!
ANYONE! EVERYONE! E-R! STAT!
WHAT THE HELL IS THIS!? HOW'S HE ALIVE!?
FOCUS, DAMMIT!
WHERE THE HELL ARE THE DOCS?!
BROKE MY WORD. SUE ME.

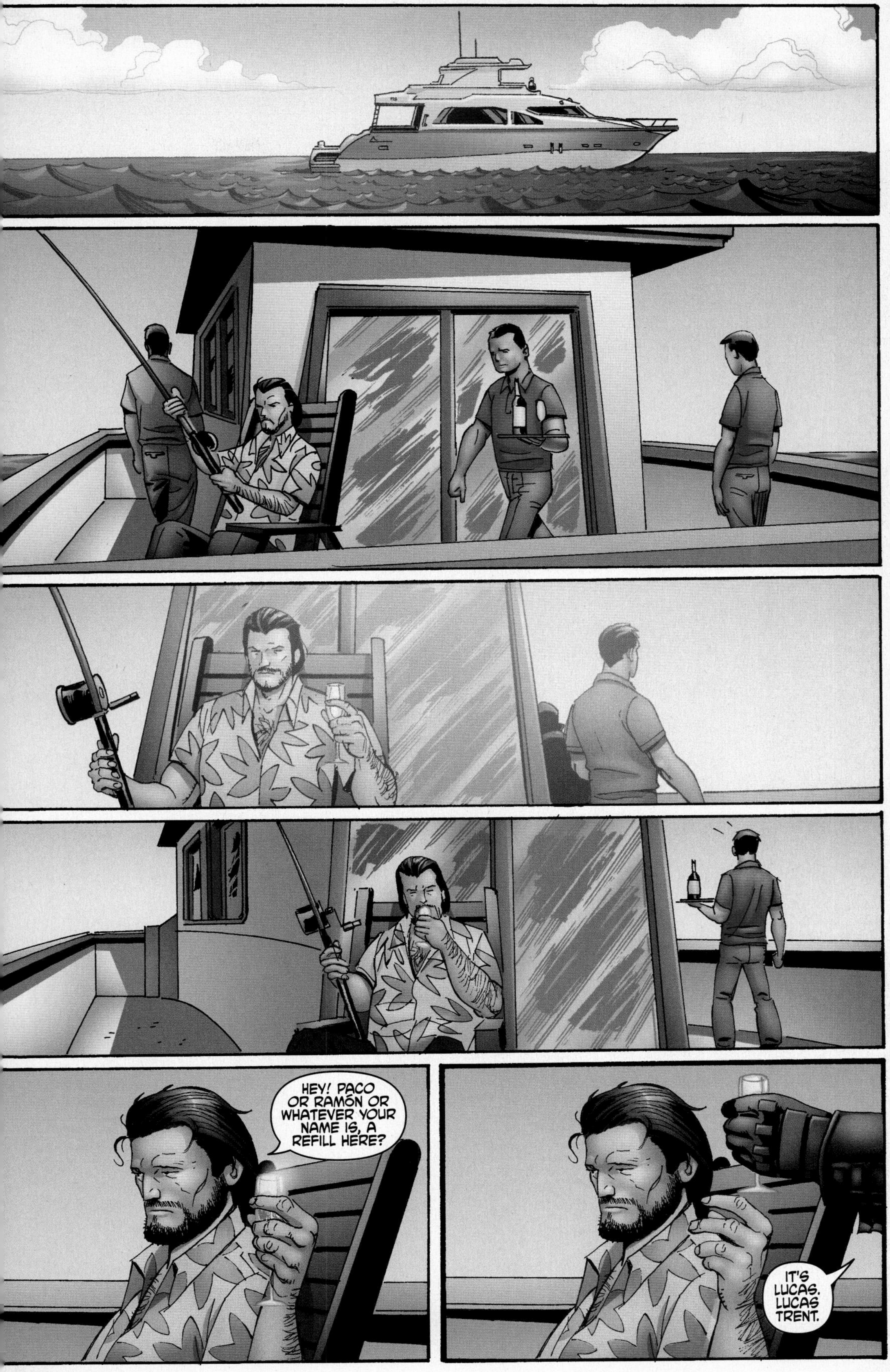
HEY! PACO OR RAMÓN OR WHATEVER YOUR NAME IS, A REFILL HERE?
IT'S LUCAS. LUCAS TRENT.

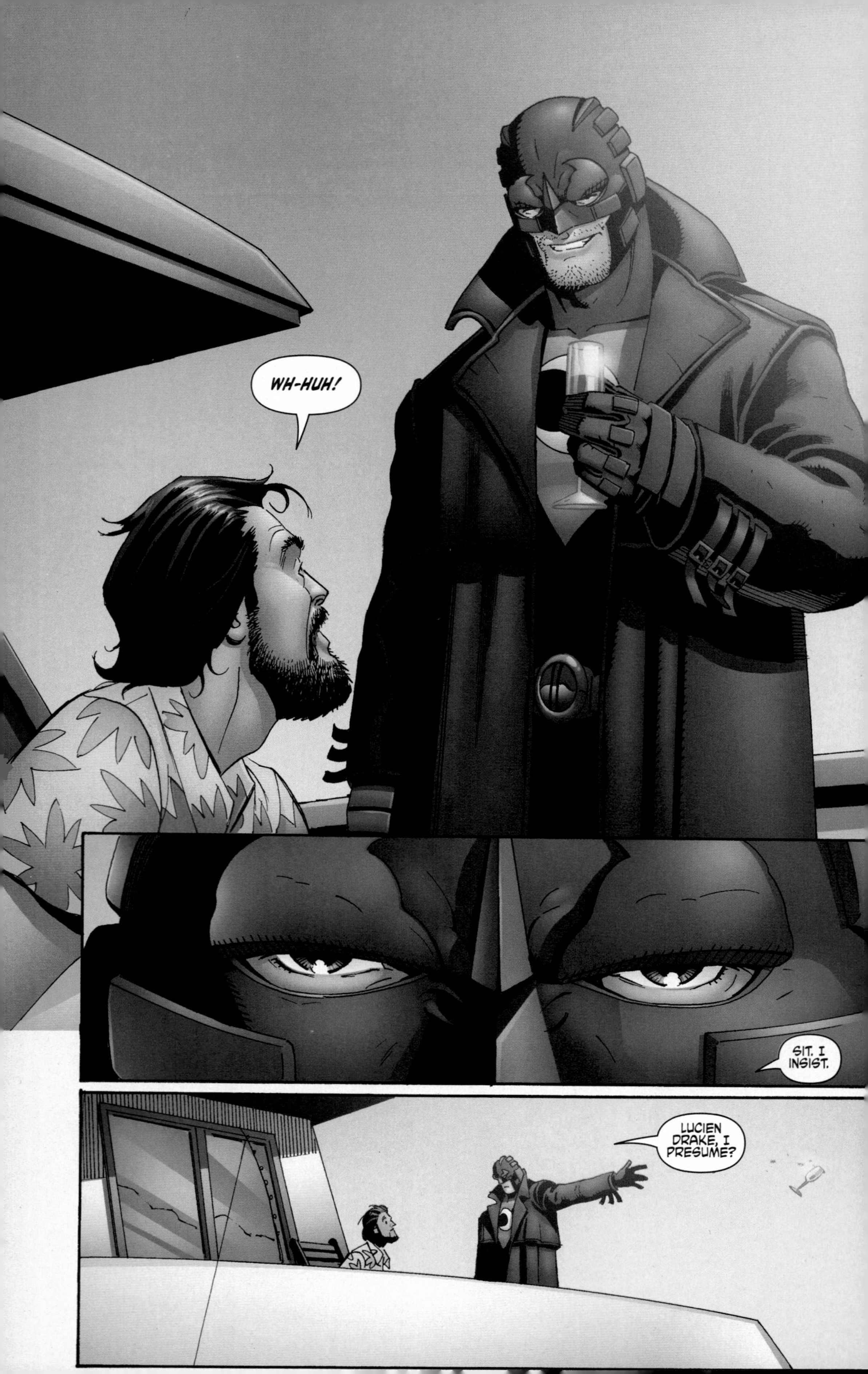
WH-HUH!
SIT. I INSIST.
LUCIEN DRAKE, I PRESUME?

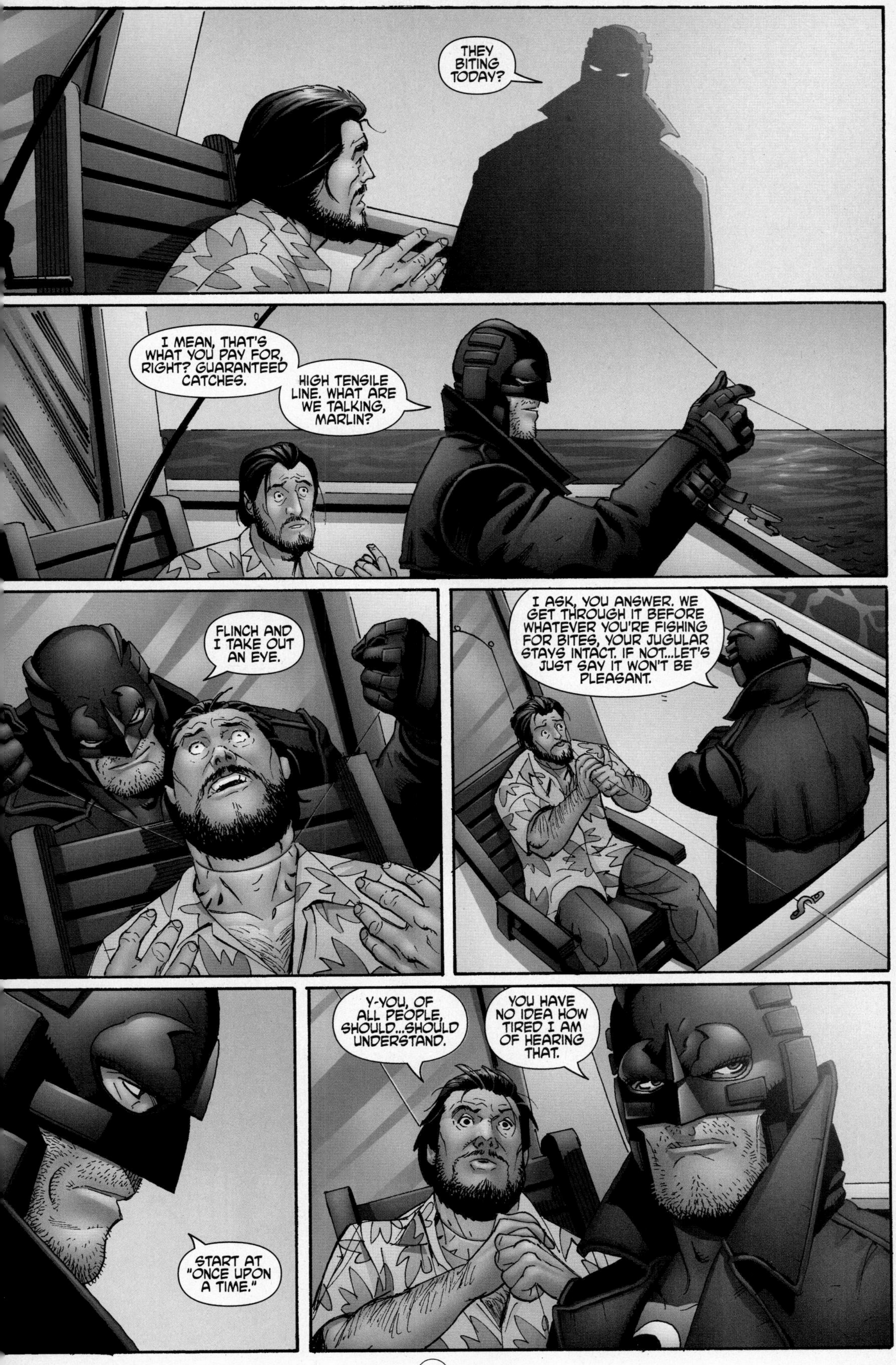
THEY BITING TODAY?
I MEAN, THAT'S WHAT YOU PAY FOR, RIGHT? GUARANTEED CATCHES.
HIGH TENSILE LINE. WHAT ARE WE TALKING, MARLIN?
FLINCH AND I TAKE OUT AN EYE.
I ASK, YOU ANSWER. WE GET THROUGH IT BEFORE WHATEVER YOU'RE FISHING FOR BITES, YOUR JUGULAR STAYS INTACT. IF NOT...LET'S JUST SAY IT WON'T BE PLEASANT.
START AT "ONCE UPON A TIME."
Y-YOU, OF ALL PEOPLE, SHOULD...SHOULD UNDERSTAND.
YOU HAVE NO IDEA HOW TIRED I AM OF HEARING THAT.

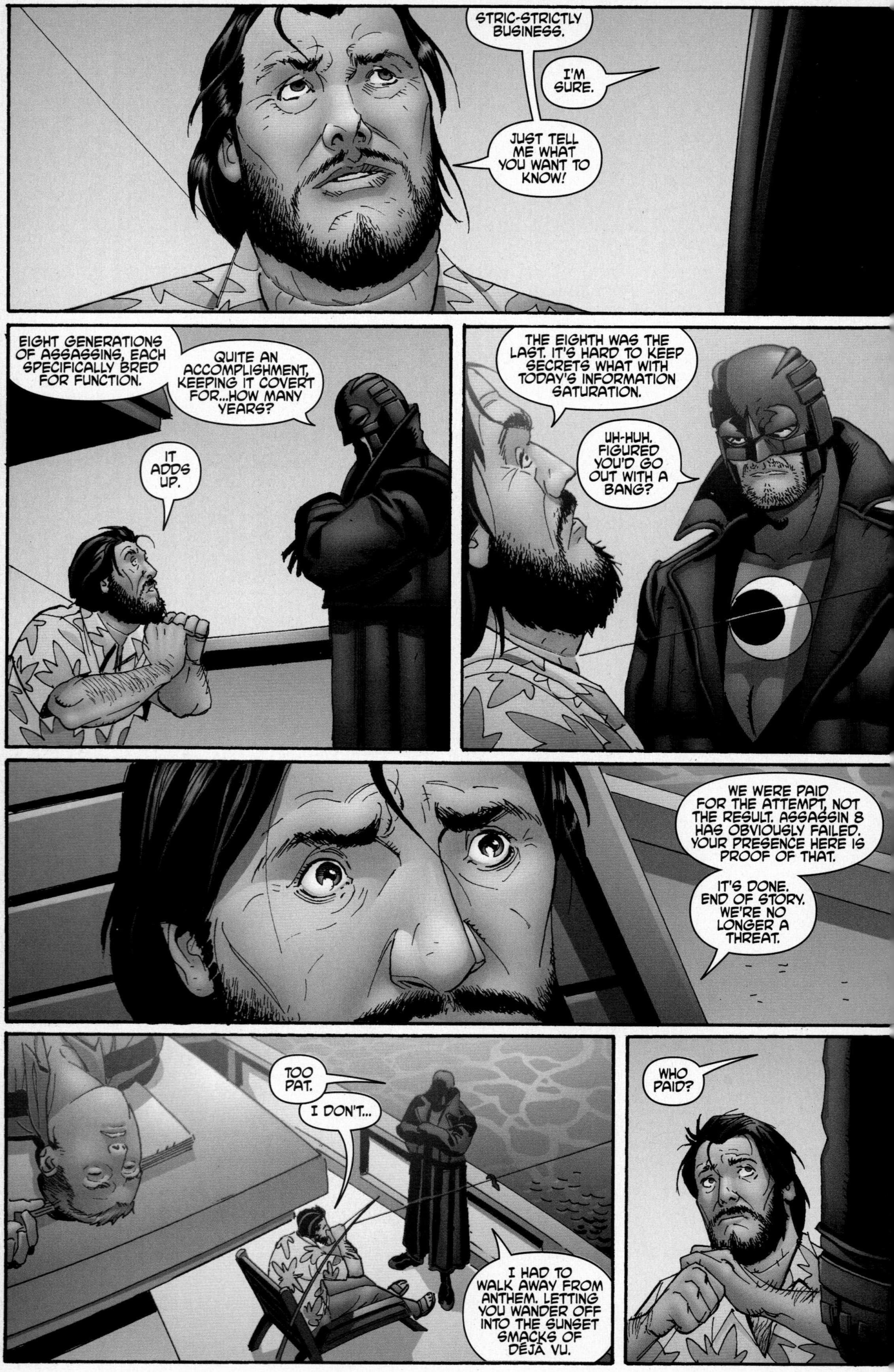
STRIC-STRICTLY BUSINESS.
I'M SURE.
JUST TELL ME WHAT YOU WANT TO KNOW!
EIGHT GENERATIONS OF ASSASSINS, EACH SPECIFICALLY BRED FOR FUNCTION.
QUITE AN ACCOMPLISHMENT, KEEPING IT COVERT FOR...HOW MANY YEARS?
IT ADDS UP.
THE EIGHTH WAS THE LAST. IT'S HARD TO KEEP SECRETS WHAT WITH TODAY'S INFORMATION SATURATION.
UH-HUH. FIGURED YOU'D GO OUT WITH A BANG?
WE WERE PAID FOR THE ATTEMPT, NOT THE RESULT. ASSASSIN 8 HAS OBVIOUSLY FAILED. YOUR PRESENCE HERE IS PROOF OF THAT.
IT'S DONE. END OF STORY. WE'RE NO LONGER A THREAT.
TOO PAT.
I DON'T...
I HAD TO WALK AWAY FROM ANTHEM. LETTING YOU WANDER OFF INTO THE SUNSET SMACKS OF DÉJÀ VU.
WHO PAID?

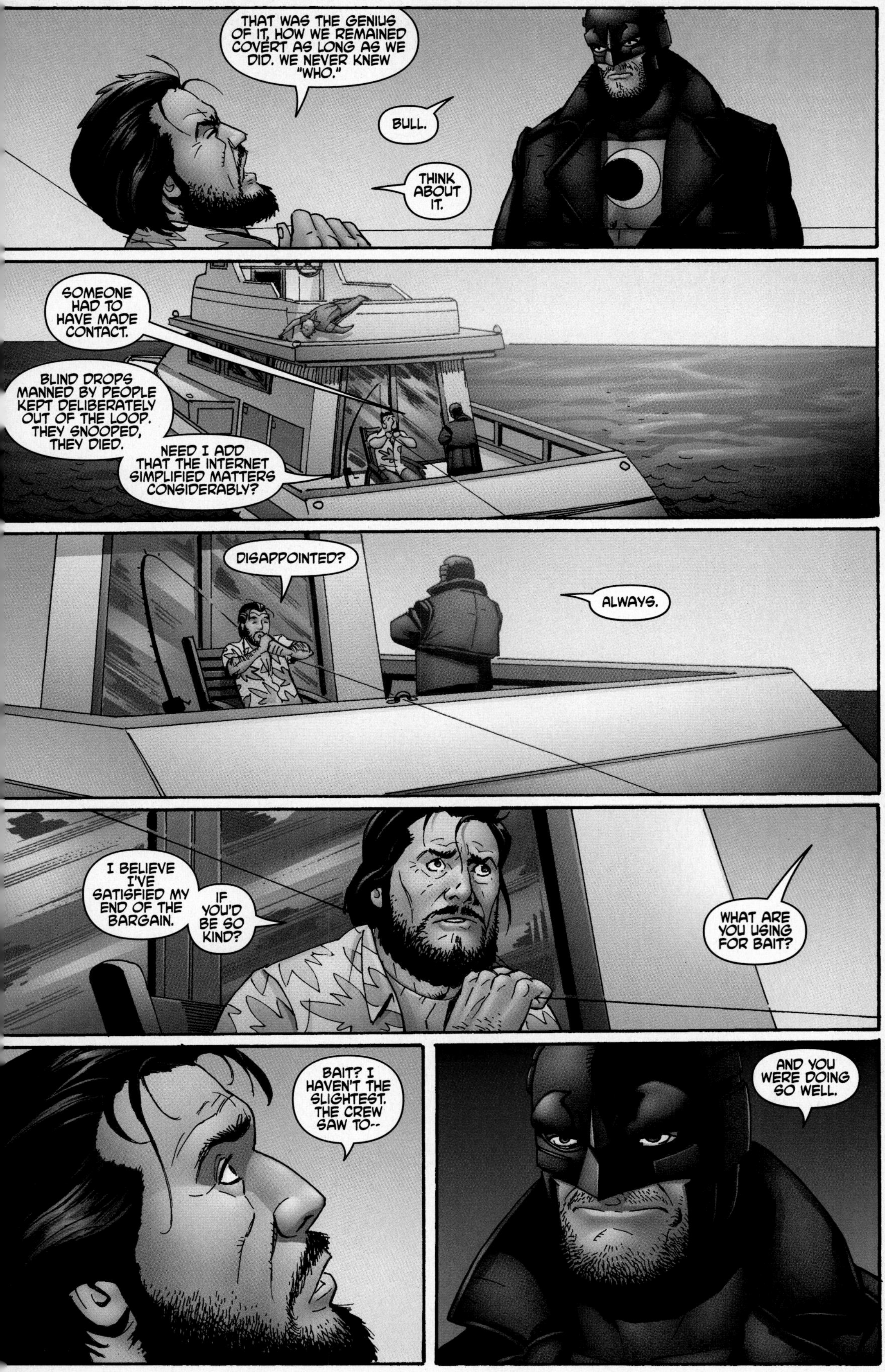
THAT WAS THE GENIUS OF IT, HOW WE REMAINED COVERT AS LONG AS WE DID. WE NEVER KNEW "WHO."
BULL.
THINK ABOUT IT.
SOMEONE HAD TO HAVE MADE CONTACT.
BLIND DROPS MANNED BY PEOPLE KEPT DELIBERATELY OUT OF THE LOOP. THEY SNOOPED, THEY DIED.
NEED I ADD THAT THE INTERNET SIMPLIFIED MATTERS CONSIDERABLY?
DISAPPOINTED?
ALWAYS.
I BELIEVE I'VE SATISFIED MY END OF THE BARGAIN.
IF YOU'D BE SO KIND?
WHAT ARE YOU USING FOR BAIT?
BAIT? I HAVEN'T THE SLIGHTEST. THE CREW SAW TO--
AND YOU WERE DOING SO WELL.

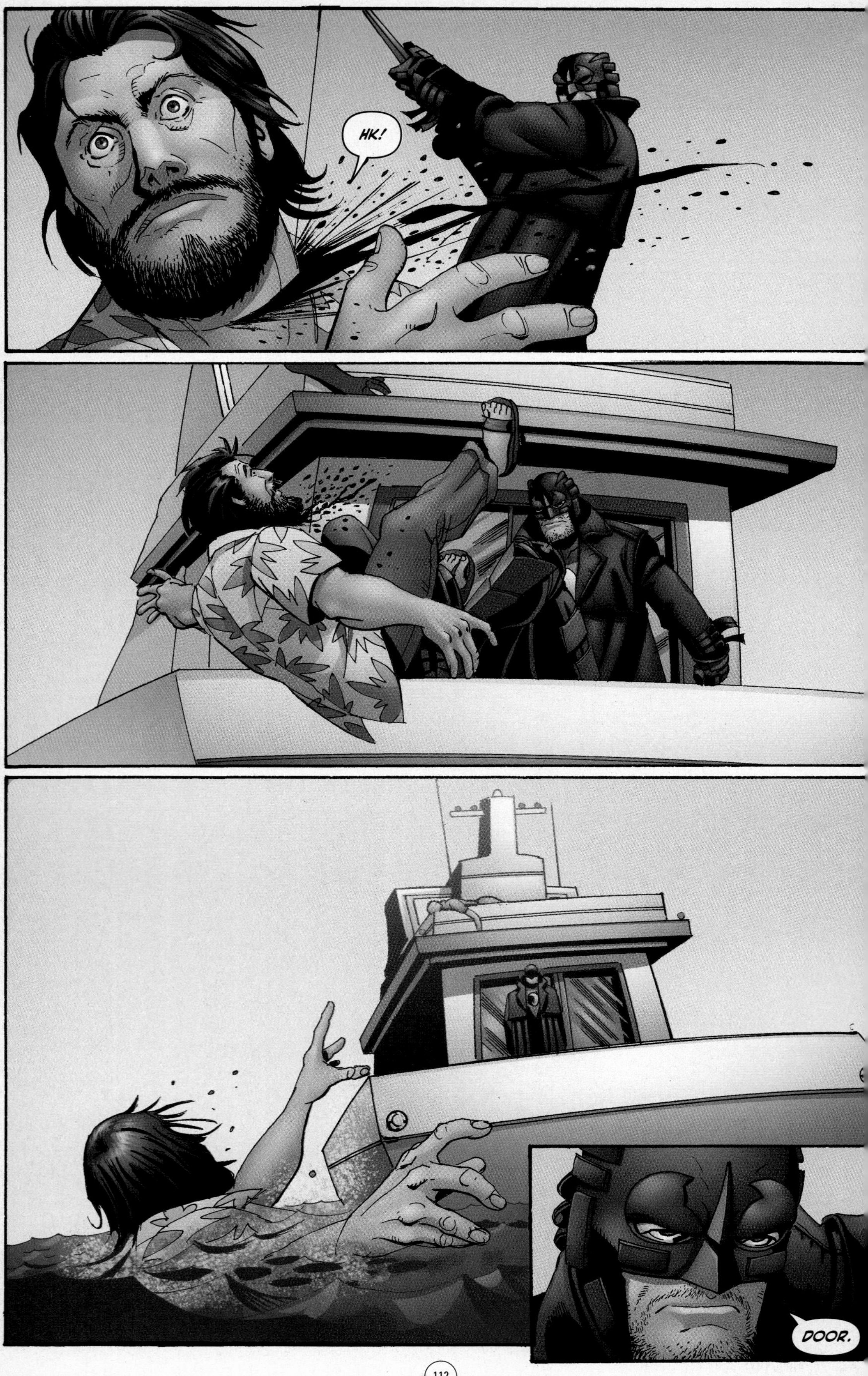
HK!
DOOR.

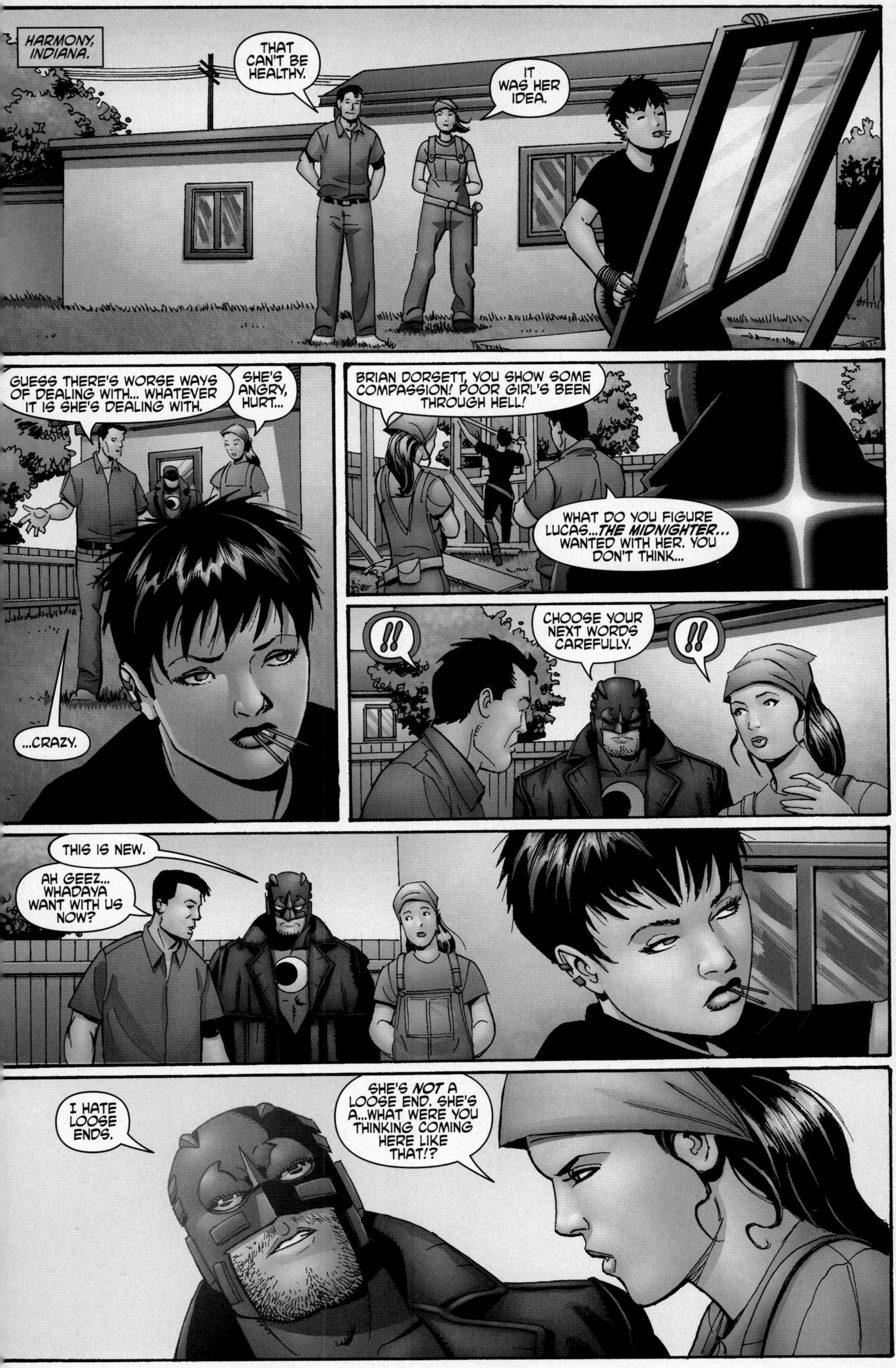
HARMONY, INDIANA.
THAT CAN'T BE HEALTHY.
IT WAS HER IDEA.
GUESS THERE'S WORSE WAYS OF DEALING WITH... WHATEVER IT IS SHE'S DEALING WITH.
SHE'S ANGRY, HURT...
...CRAZY.
BRIAN DORSETT, YOU SHOW SOME COMPASSION! POOR GIRL'S BEEN THROUGH HELL!
WHAT DO YOU FIGURE LUCAS...THE MIDNIGHTER... WANTED WITH HER. YOU DON'T THINK...
!!
CHOOSE YOUR NEXT WORDS CAREFULLY.
!!
THIS IS NEW.
AH GEEZ... WHADAYA WANT WITH US NOW?
I HATE LOOSE ENDS.
SHE'S NOT A LOOSE END. SHE'S A...WHAT WERE YOU THINKING COMING HERE LIKE THAT!?

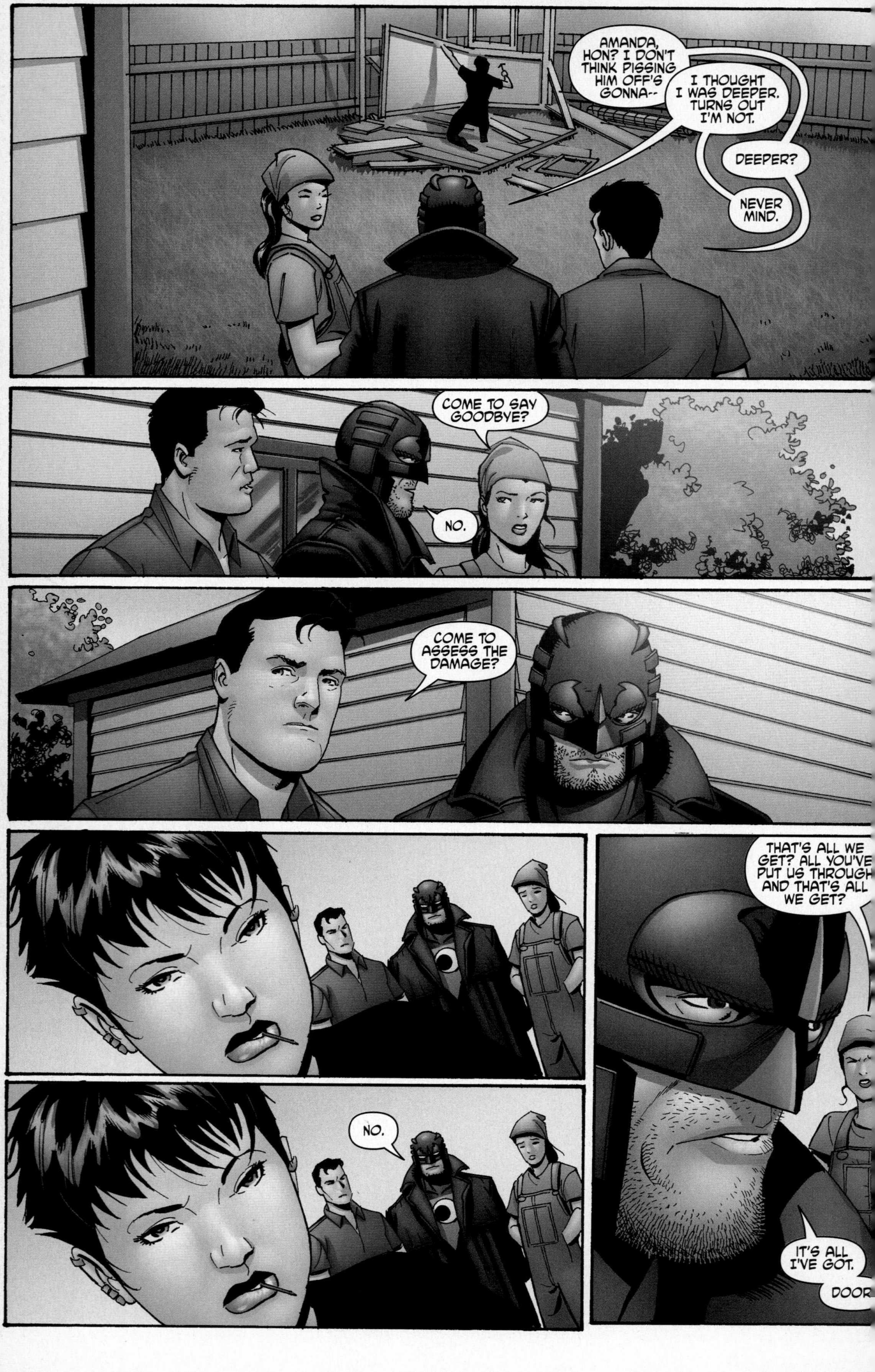
AMANDA, HON? I DON'T THINK PISSING HIM OFF'S GONNA--
I THOUGHT I WAS DEEPER. TURNS OUT I'M NOT.
DEEPER?
NEVER MIND.
COME TO SAY GOODBYE?
NO.
COME TO ASSESS THE DAMAGE?
NO.
THAT'S ALL WE GET? ALL YOU'VE PUT US THROUGH AND THAT'S ALL WE GET?
IT'S ALL I'VE GOT.
DOOR

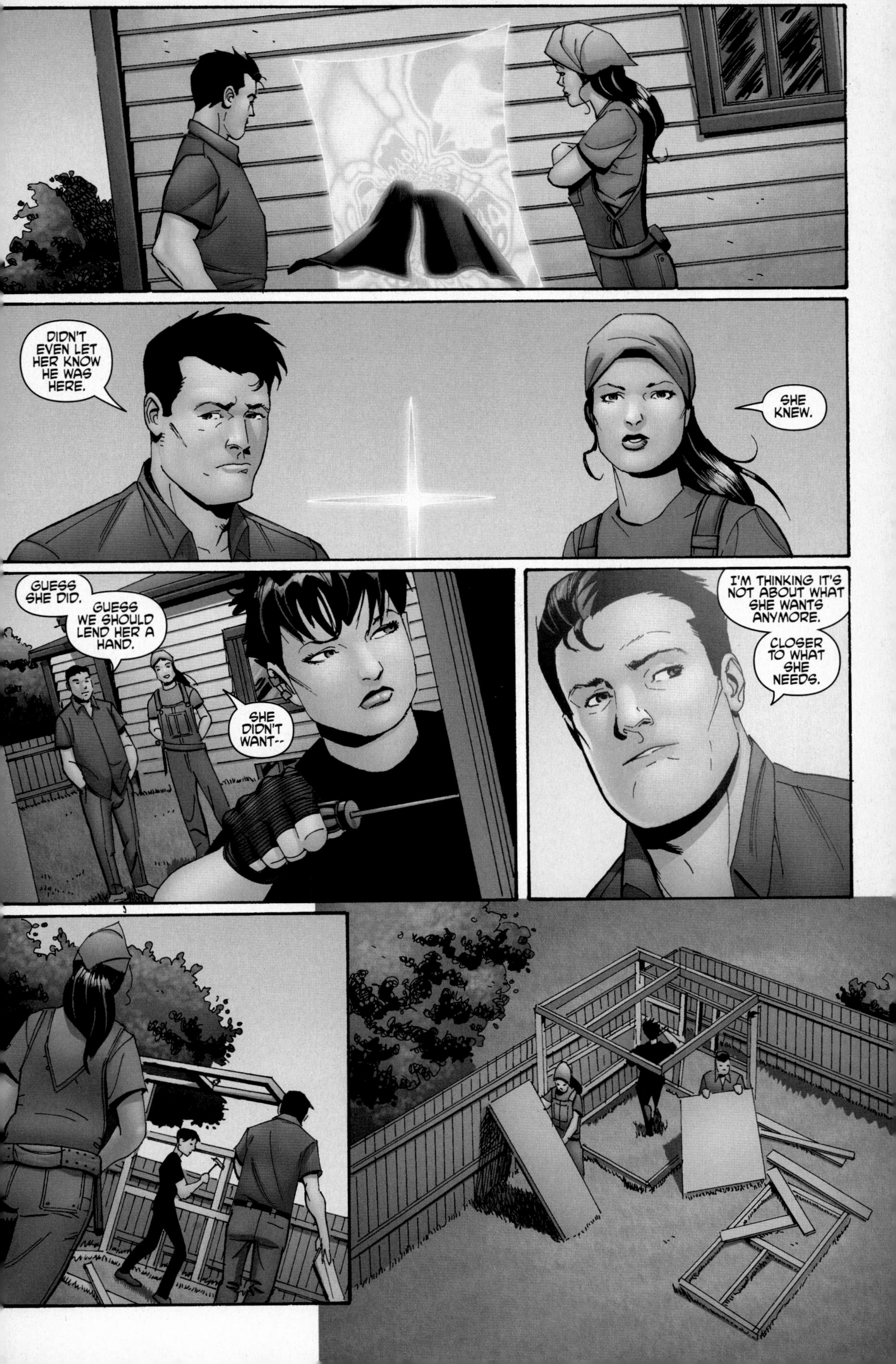
DIDN'T EVEN LET HER KNOW HE WAS HERE.
SHE KNEW.
GUESS SHE DID.
GUESS WE SHOULD LEND HER A HAND.
SHE DIDN'T WANT--
I'M THINKING IT'S NOT ABOUT WHAT SHE WANTS ANYMORE.
CLOSER TO WHAT SHE NEEDS.

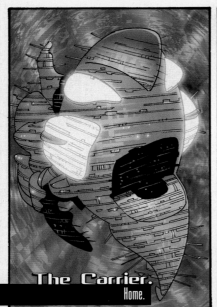

The Carrier.
Home.

GOT IT
OUT OF YOUR
SYSTEM?

YOU KNOW
WHERE TO
FIND ME.

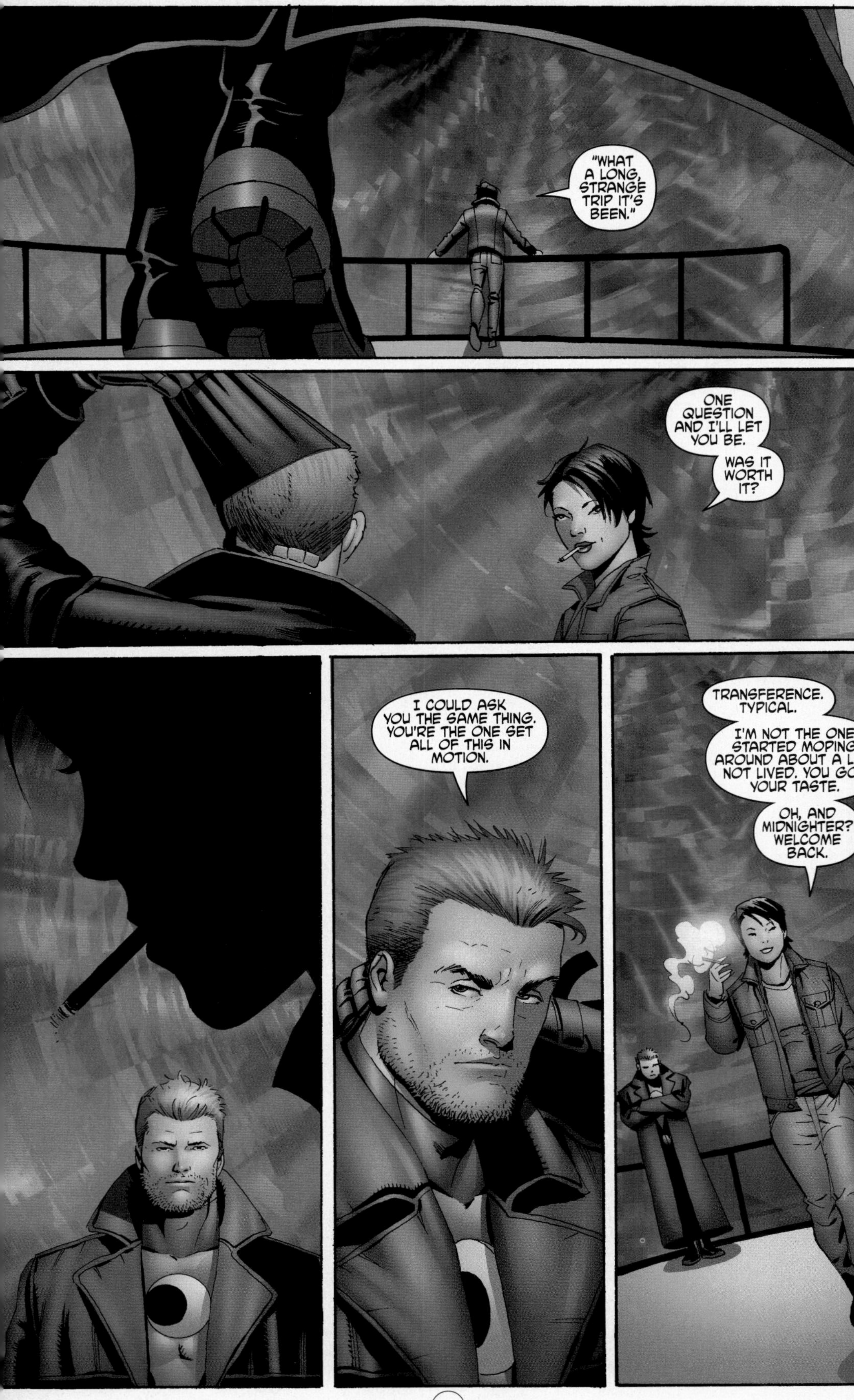
"WHAT A LONG, STRANGE TRIP IT'S BEEN."
ONE QUESTION AND I'LL LET YOU BE.
WAS IT WORTH IT?
I COULD ASK YOU THE SAME THING. YOU'RE THE ONE SET ALL OF THIS IN MOTION.
TRANSFERENCE. TYPICAL.
I'M NOT THE ONE STARTED MOPING AROUND ABOUT A LIFE NOT LIVED. YOU GOT YOUR TASTE.
OH, AND MIDNIGHTER? WELCOME BACK.

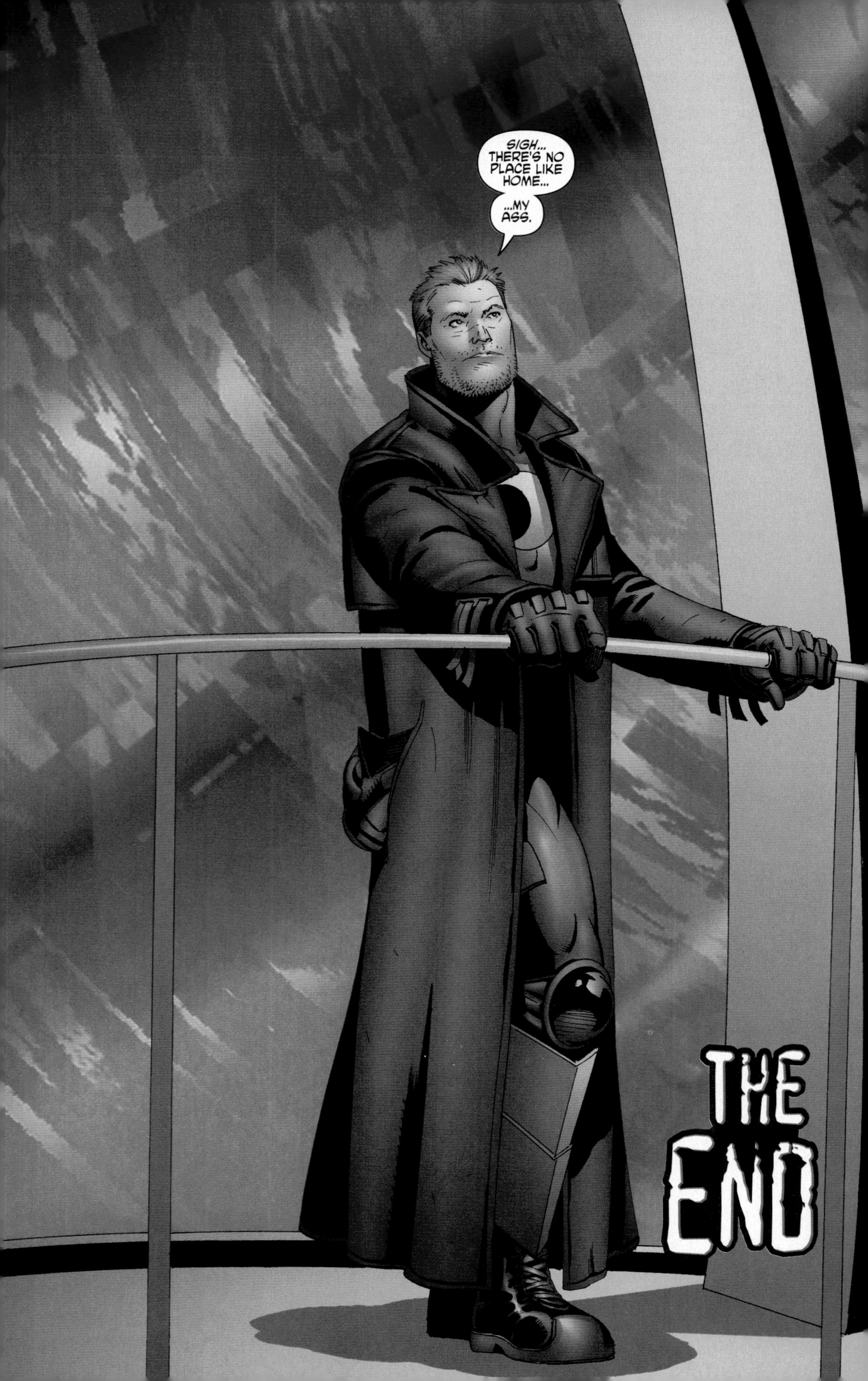
SIGH... THERE'S NO PLACE LIKE HOME...
...MY ASS.
THE END

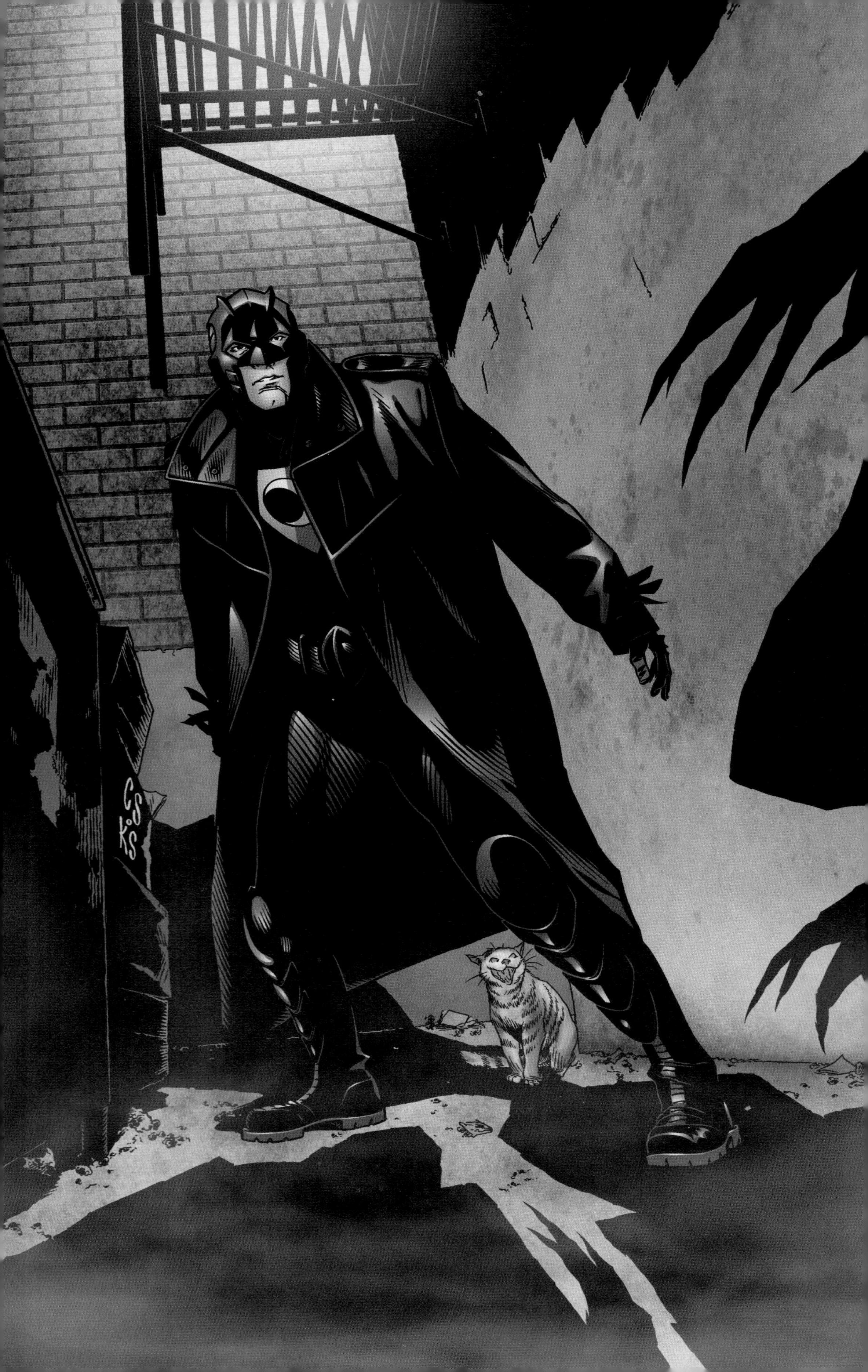

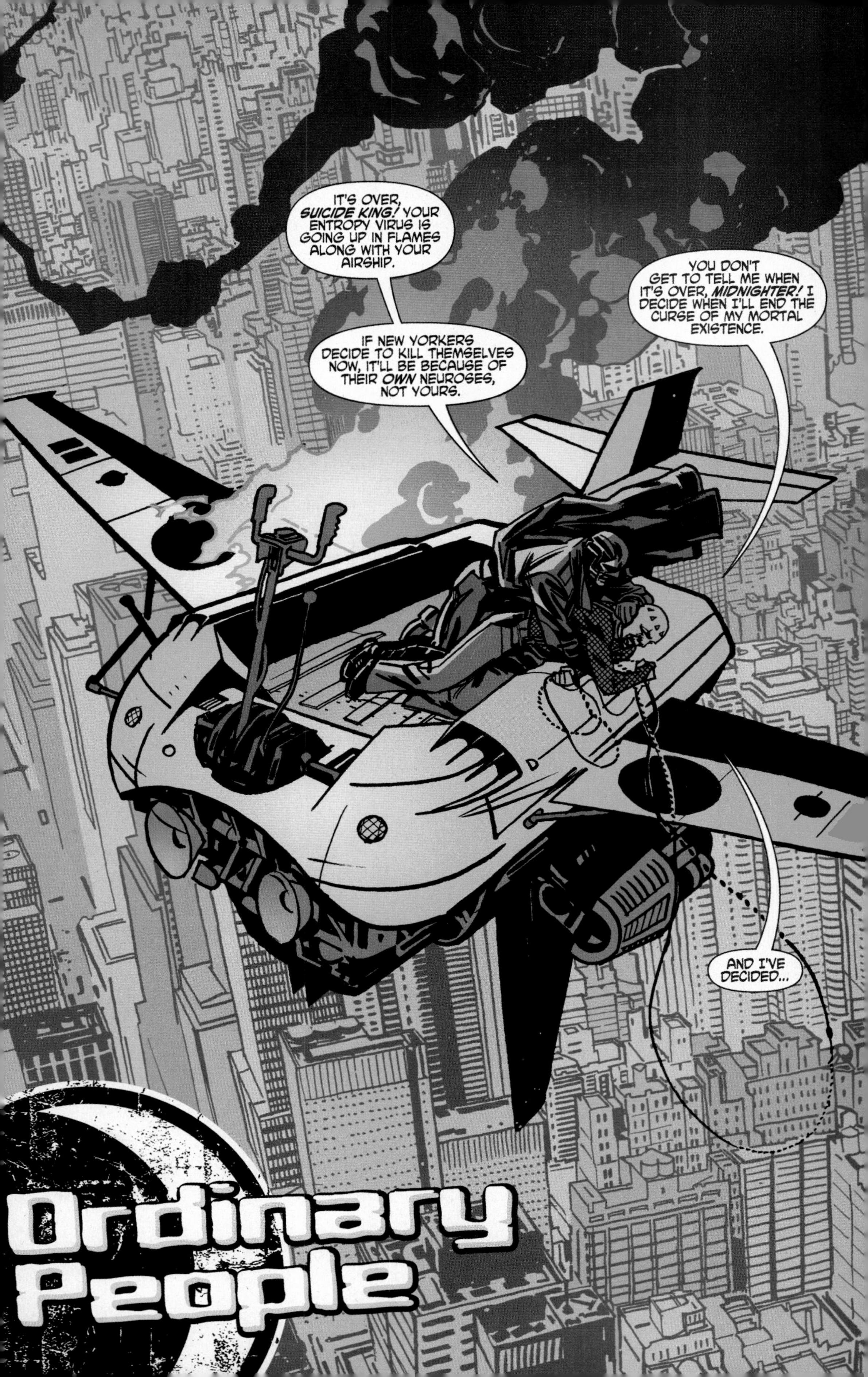

IT'S OVER, SUICIDE KING! YOUR ENTROPY VIRUS IS GOING UP IN FLAMES ALONG WITH YOUR AIRSHIP.
IF NEW YORKERS DECIDE TO KILL THEMSELVES NOW, IT'LL BE BECAUSE OF THEIR OWN NEUROSES, NOT YOURS.
YOU DON'T GET TO TELL ME WHEN IT'S OVER, MIDNIGHTER! I DECIDE WHEN I'LL END THE CURSE OF MY MORTAL EXISTENCE.
AND I'VE DECIDED...
Ordinary People

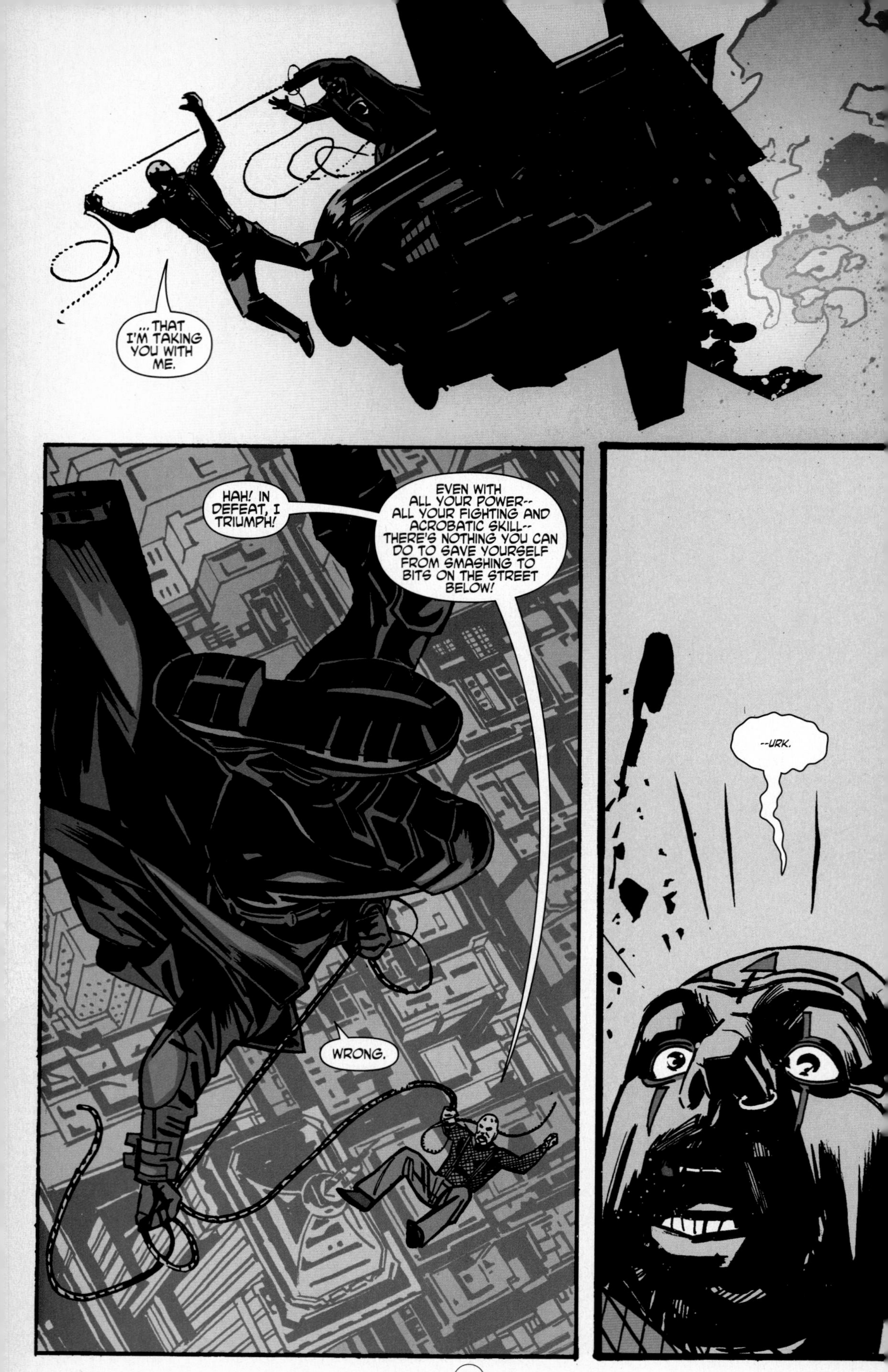
...THAT I'M TAKING YOU WITH ME.
HAH! IN DEFEAT, I TRIUMPH!
EVEN WITH ALL YOUR POWER-- ALL YOUR FIGHTING AND ACROBATIC SKILL-- THERE'S NOTHING YOU CAN DO TO SAVE YOURSELF FROM SMASHING TO BITS ON THE STREET BELOW!
WRONG.
--URK.

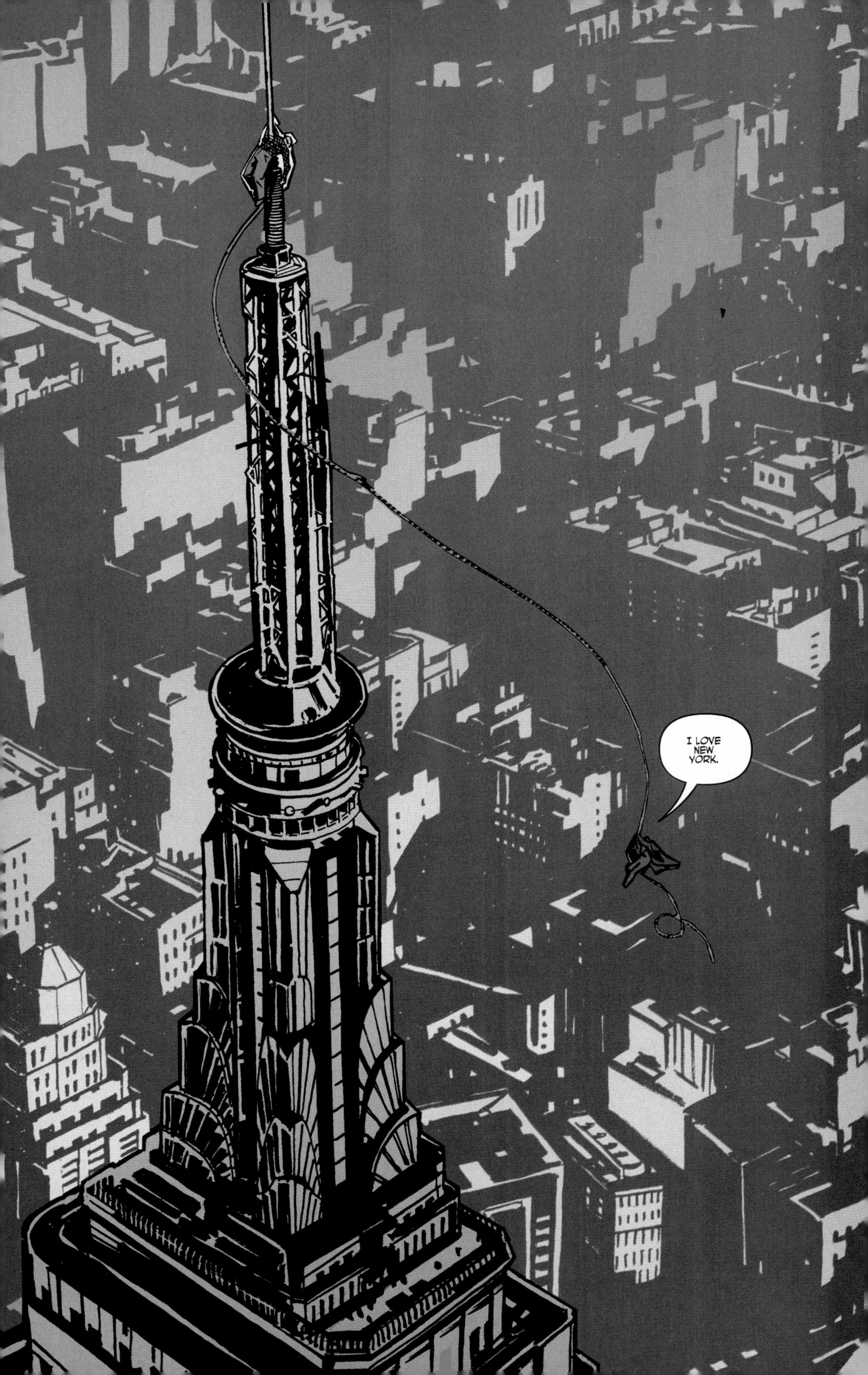
I LOVE NEW YORK.

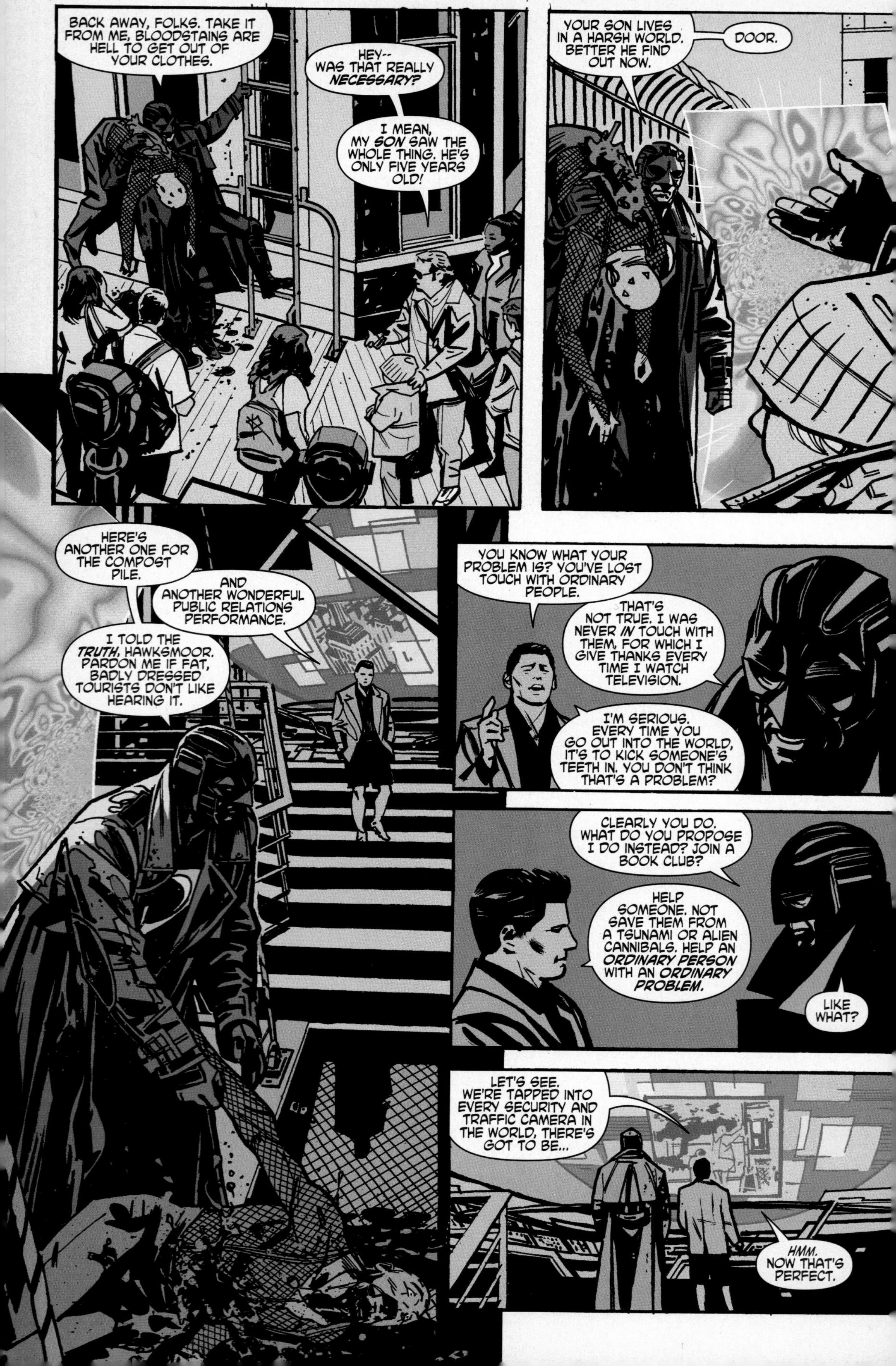
BACK AWAY, FOLKS. TAKE IT FROM ME, BLOODSTAINS ARE HELL TO GET OUT OF YOUR CLOTHES.
HEY-- WAS THAT REALLY NECESSARY?
I MEAN, MY SON SAW THE WHOLE THING. HE'S ONLY FIVE YEARS OLD!
YOUR SON LIVES IN A HARSH WORLD. BETTER HE FIND OUT NOW.
DOOR.
HERE'S ANOTHER ONE FOR THE COMPOST PILE.
AND ANOTHER WONDERFUL PUBLIC RELATIONS PERFORMANCE.
I TOLD THE TRUTH, HAWKSMOOR. PARDON ME IF FAT, BADLY DRESSED TOURISTS DON'T LIKE HEARING IT.
YOU KNOW WHAT YOUR PROBLEM IS? YOU'VE LOST TOUCH WITH ORDINARY PEOPLE.
THAT'S NOT TRUE. I WAS NEVER IN TOUCH WITH THEM, FOR WHICH I GIVE THANKS EVERY TIME I WATCH TELEVISION.
I'M SERIOUS. EVERY TIME YOU GO OUT INTO THE WORLD, IT'S TO KICK SOMEONE'S TEETH IN. YOU DON'T THINK THAT'S A PROBLEM?
CLEARLY YOU DO. WHAT DO YOU PROPOSE I DO INSTEAD? JOIN A BOOK CLUB?
HELP SOMEONE. NOT SAVE THEM FROM A TSUNAMI OR ALIEN CANNIBALS. HELP AN ORDINARY PERSON WITH AN ORDINARY PROBLEM.
LIKE WHAT?
LET'S SEE. WE'RE TAPPED INTO EVERY SECURITY AND TRAFFIC CAMERA IN THE WORLD, THERE'S GOT TO BE...
HMM. NOW THAT'S PERFECT.

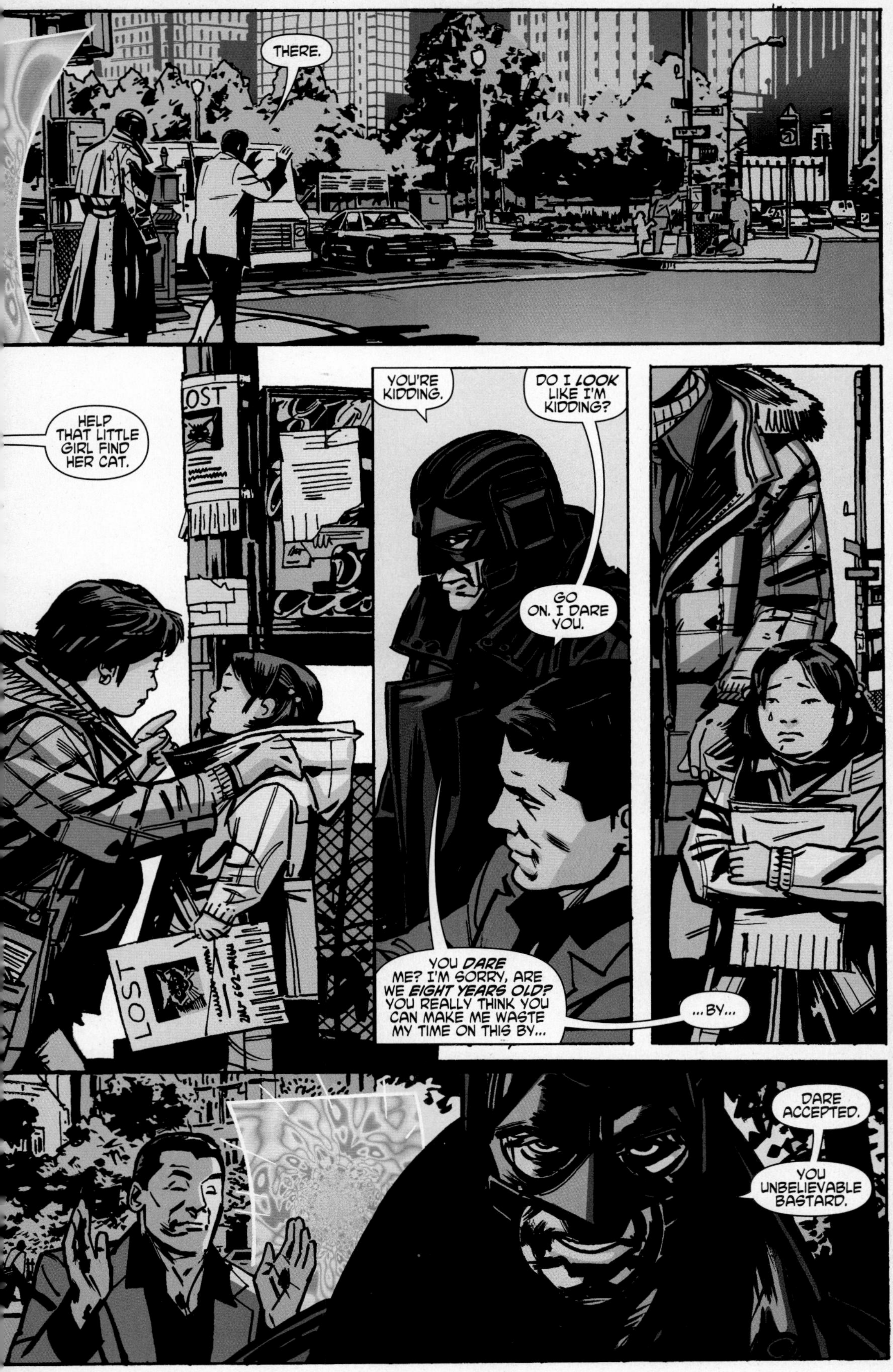
THERE.
HELP THAT LITTLE GIRL FIND HER CAT.
LOST
YOU'RE KIDDING.
DO I LOOK LIKE I'M KIDDING?
GO ON. I DARE YOU.
YOU DARE ME? I'M SORRY, ARE WE EIGHT YEARS OLD? YOU REALLY THINK YOU CAN MAKE ME WASTE MY TIME ON THIS BY...
...BY...
LOST
DARE ACCEPTED.
YOU UNBELIEVABLE BASTARD.

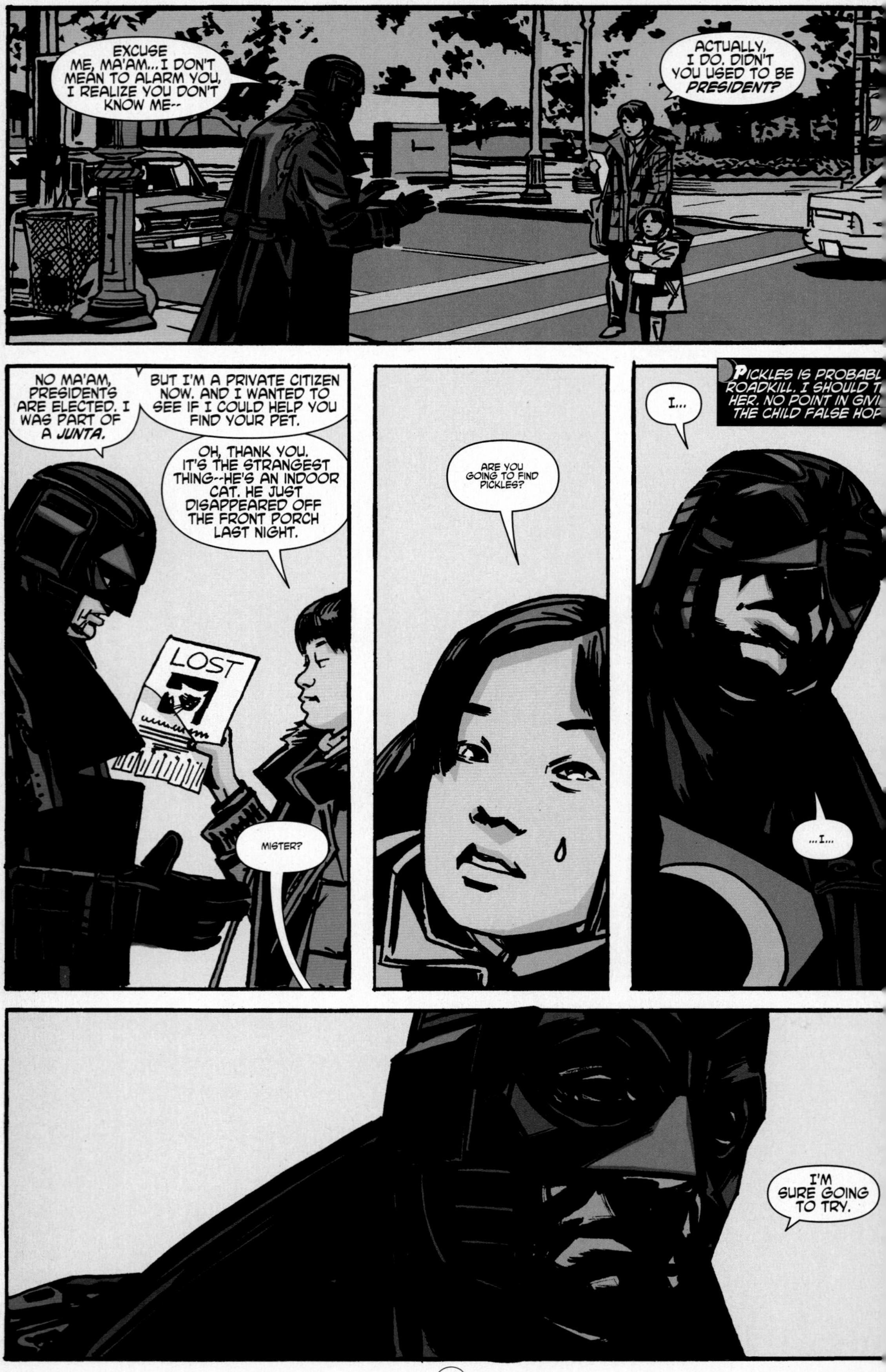
EXCUSE ME, MA'AM...I DON'T MEAN TO ALARM YOU, I REALIZE YOU DON'T KNOW ME--
ACTUALLY, I DO. DIDN'T YOU USED TO BE *PRESIDENT?*
NO MA'AM, PRESIDENTS ARE ELECTED. I WAS PART OF A *JUNTA.*
BUT I'M A PRIVATE CITIZEN NOW. AND I WANTED TO SEE IF I COULD HELP YOU FIND YOUR PET.
OH, THANK YOU. IT'S THE STRANGEST THING--HE'S AN INDOOR CAT. HE JUST DISAPPEARED OFF THE FRONT PORCH LAST NIGHT.
LOST
MISTER?
ARE YOU GOING TO FIND PICKLES?
I...
PICKLES IS PROBABL
ROADKILL. I SHOULD T
HER. NO POINT IN GIVI
THE CHILD FALSE HOP
...I...
I'M SURE GOING TO TRY.

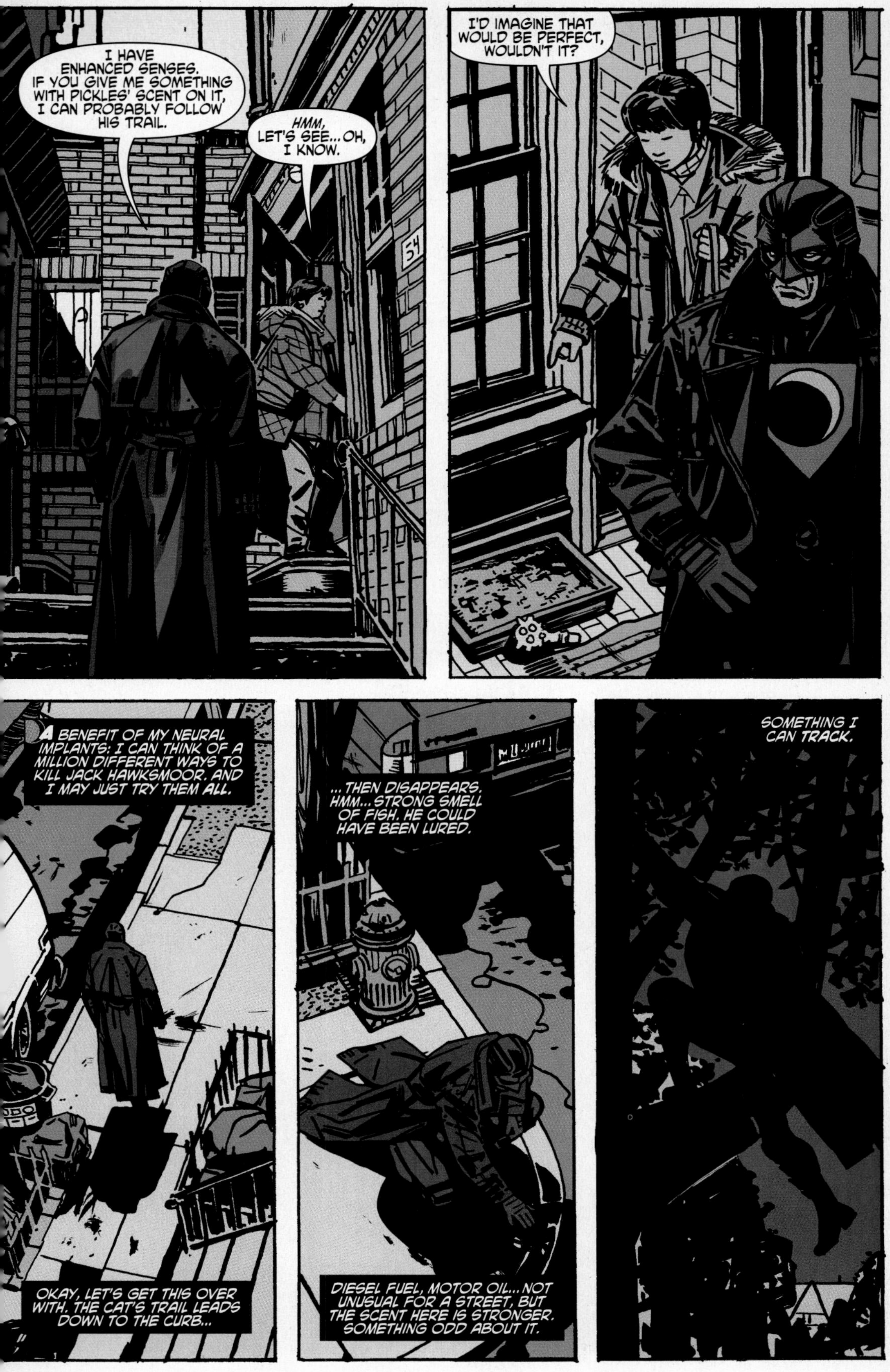
I HAVE ENHANCED SENSES. IF YOU GIVE ME SOMETHING WITH PICKLES' SCENT ON IT, I CAN PROBABLY FOLLOW HIS TRAIL.
HMM, LET'S SEE...OH, I KNOW.
54
I'D IMAGINE THAT WOULD BE PERFECT, WOULDN'T IT?
A BENEFIT OF MY NEURAL IMPLANTS: I CAN THINK OF A MILLION DIFFERENT WAYS TO KILL JACK HAWKSMOOR. AND I MAY JUST TRY THEM ALL.
OKAY, LET'S GET THIS OVER WITH. THE CAT'S TRAIL LEADS DOWN TO THE CURB...
...THEN DISAPPEARS. HMM...STRONG SMELL OF FISH. HE COULD HAVE BEEN LURED.
DIESEL FUEL, MOTOR OIL...NOT UNUSUAL FOR A STREET, BUT THE SCENT HERE IS STRONGER. SOMETHING ODD ABOUT IT.
SOMETHING I CAN TRACK.

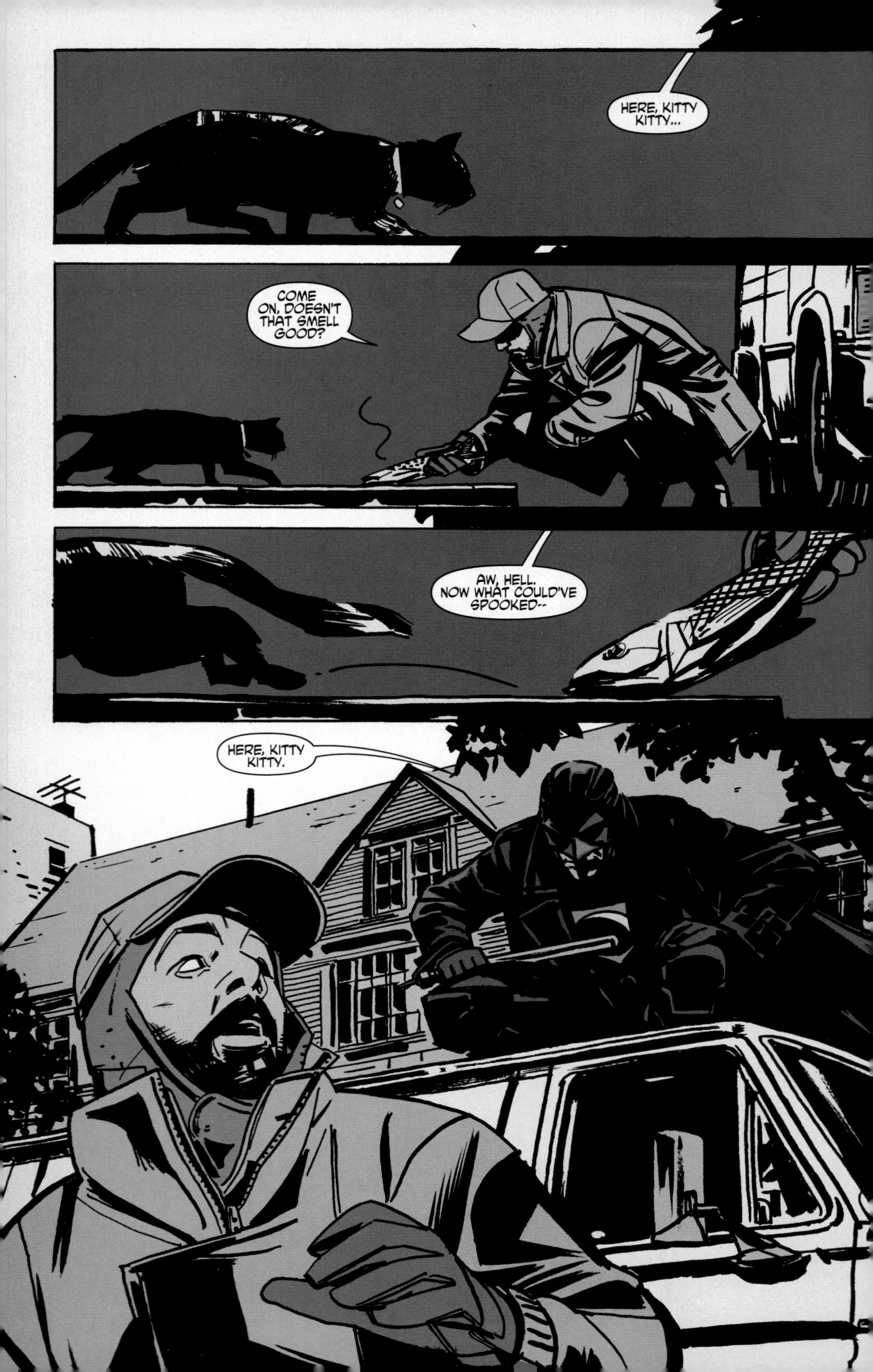
HERE, KITTY KITTY...
COME ON, DOESN'T THAT SMELL GOOD?
AW, HELL. NOW WHAT COULD'VE SPOOKED--
HERE, KITTY KITTY.

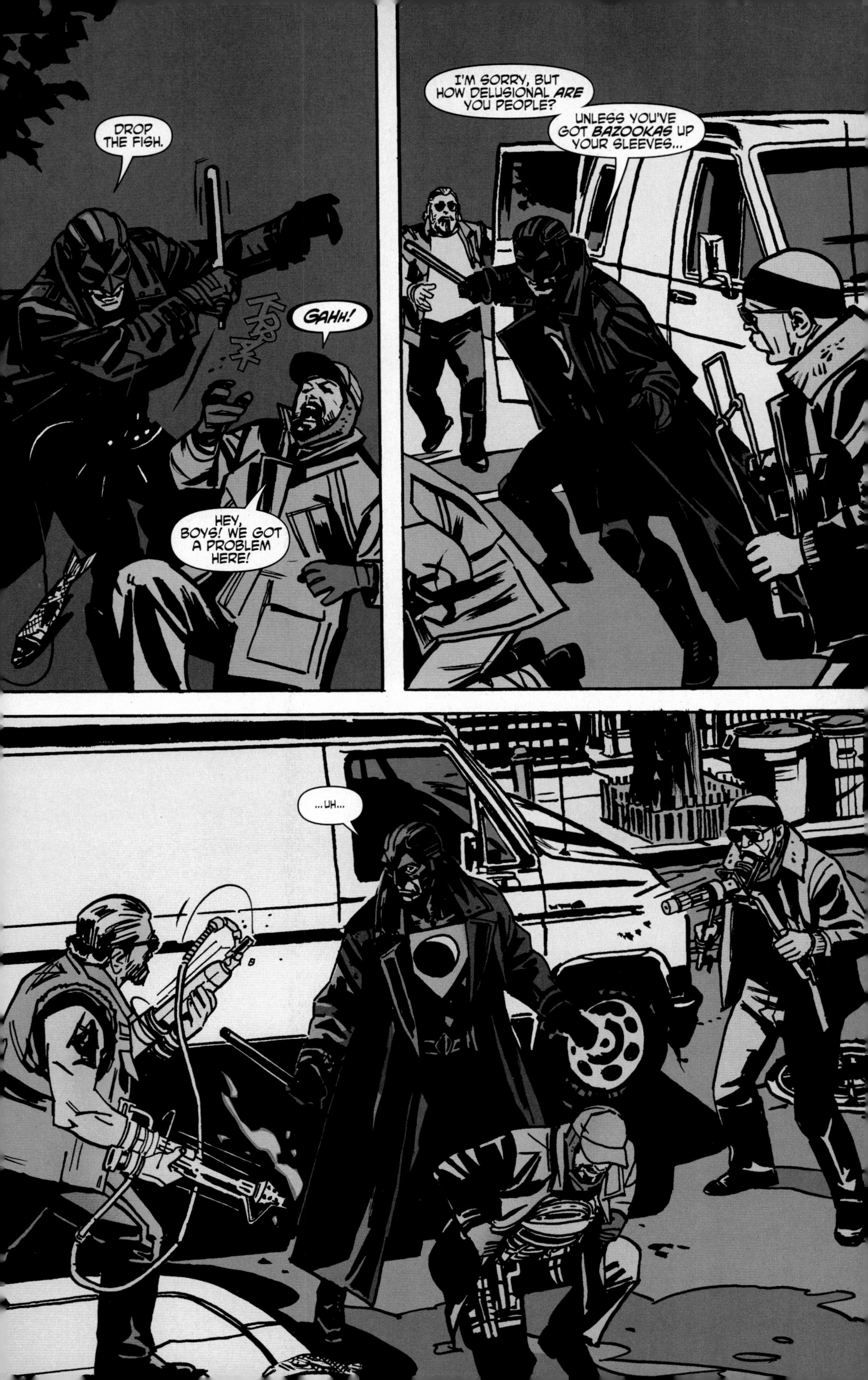
DROP THE FISH.
KRAK
GAHH!
HEY, BOYS! WE GOT A PROBLEM HERE!
I'M SORRY, BUT HOW DELUSIONAL *ARE* YOU PEOPLE?
UNLESS YOU'VE GOT *BAZOOKAS* UP YOUR SLEEVES...
...UH...

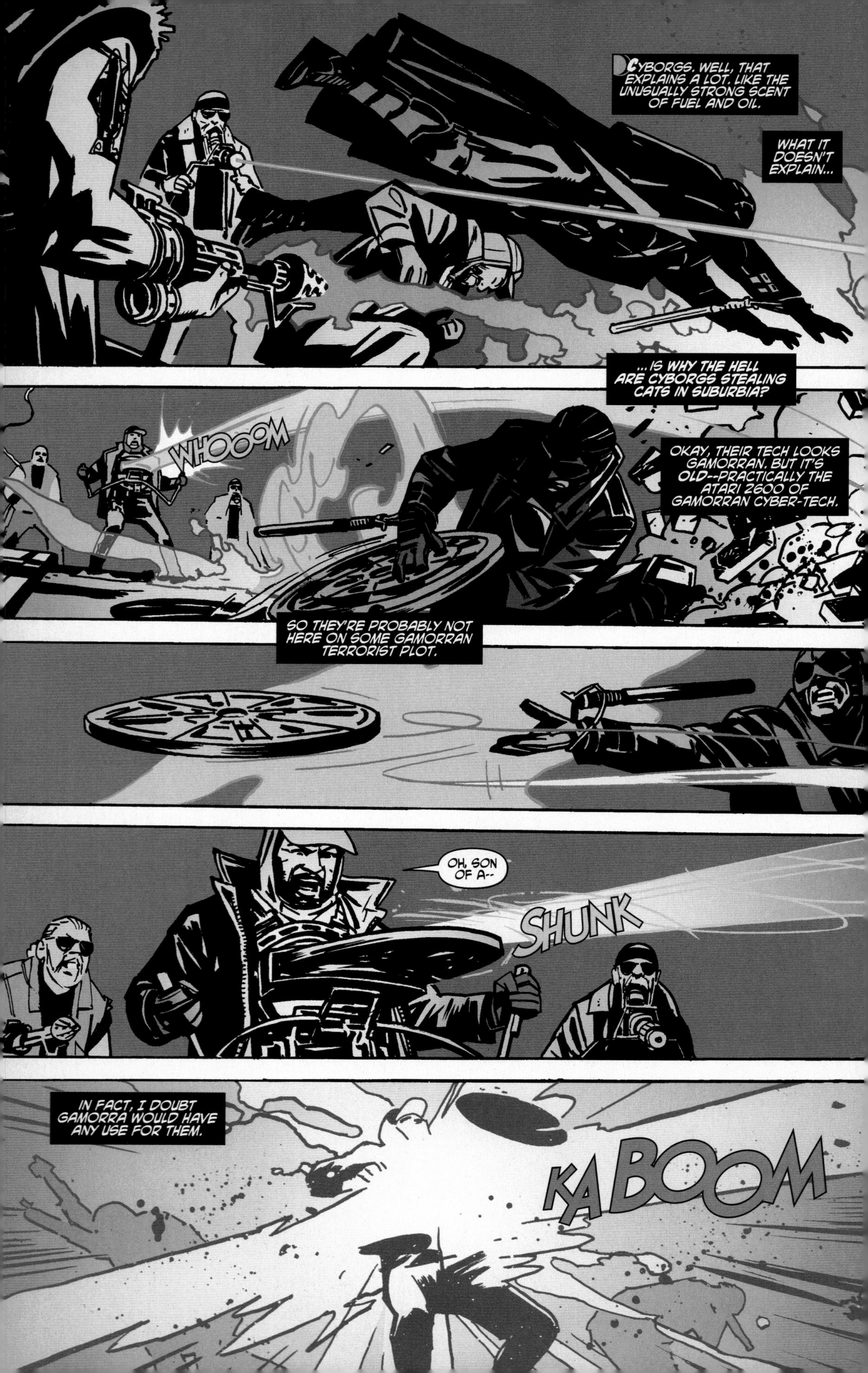
CYBORGS. WELL, THAT EXPLAINS A LOT. LIKE THE UNUSUALLY STRONG SCENT OF FUEL AND OIL.
WHAT IT DOESN'T EXPLAIN...
...IS WHY THE HELL ARE CYBORGS STEALING CATS IN SUBURBIA?
WHOOOM
OKAY, THEIR TECH LOOKS GAMORRAN. BUT IT'S OLD--PRACTICALLY THE ATARI 2600 OF GAMORRAN CYBER-TECH.
SO THEY'RE PROBABLY NOT HERE ON SOME GAMORRAN TERRORIST PLOT.
OH, SON OF A--
SHUNK
IN FACT, I DOUBT GAMORRA WOULD HAVE ANY USE FOR THEM.
KABOOM

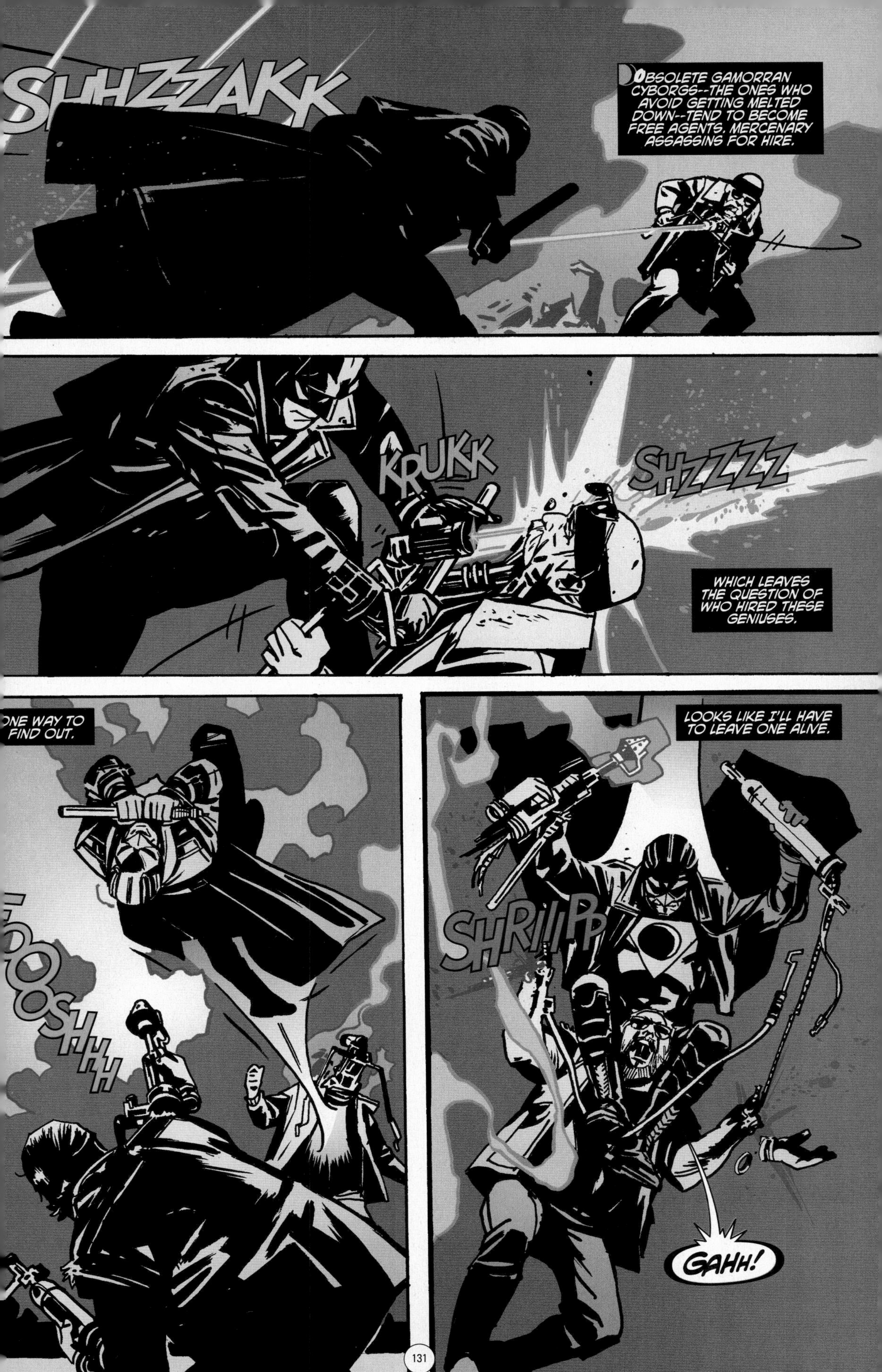
SHHZZAKK
OBSOLETE GAMORRAN CYBORGS--THE ONES WHO AVOID GETTING MELTED DOWN--TEND TO BECOME FREE AGENTS. MERCENARY ASSASSINS FOR HIRE.
KRUKK
SHZZZZ
WHICH LEAVES THE QUESTION OF WHO HIRED THESE GENIUSES.
ONE WAY TO FIND OUT.
FOOOSHHH
LOOKS LIKE I'LL HAVE TO LEAVE ONE ALIVE.
SHRIIIPP
GAHH!

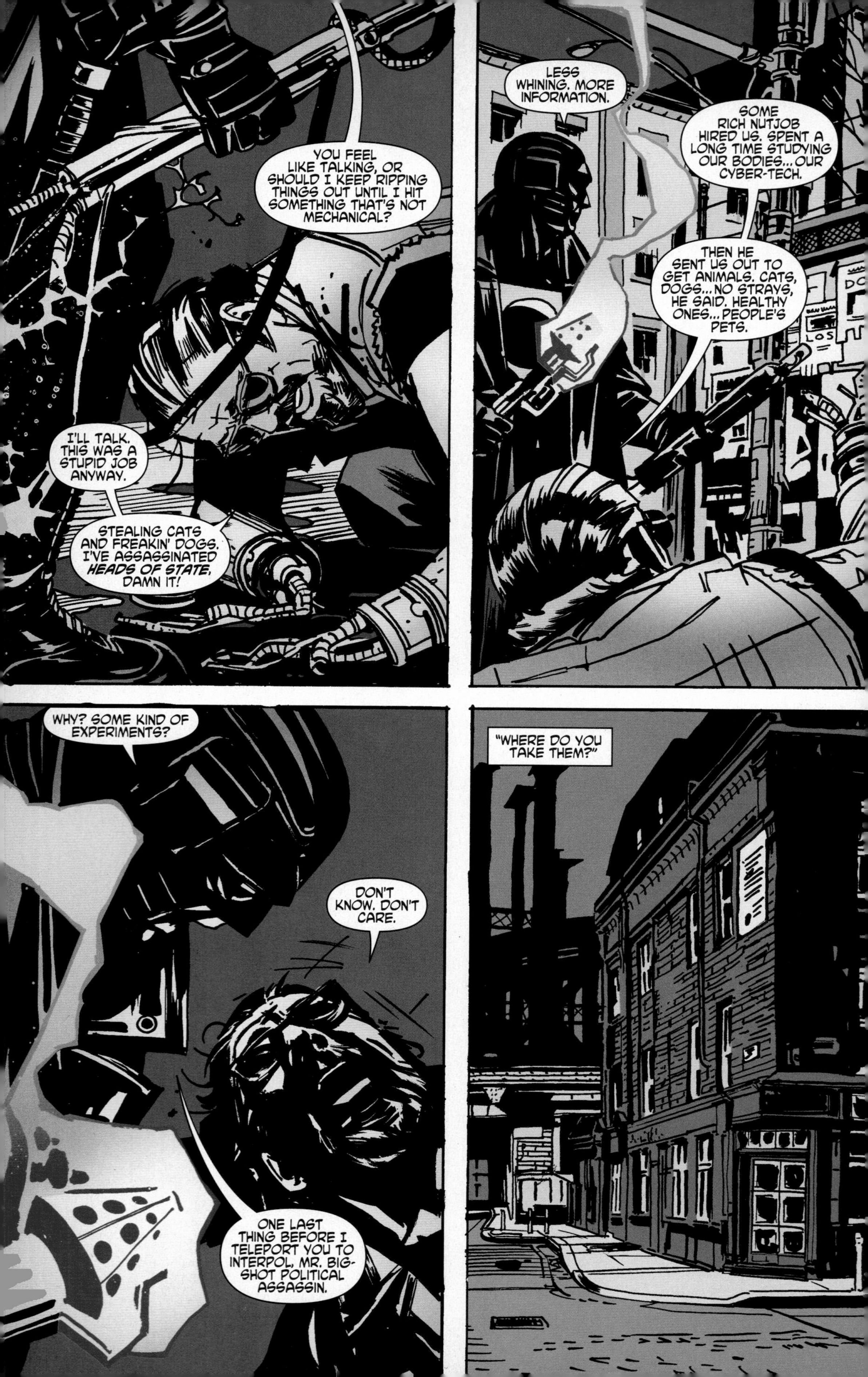
YOU FEEL LIKE TALKING, OR SHOULD I KEEP RIPPING THINGS OUT UNTIL I HIT SOMETHING THAT'S NOT MECHANICAL?
I'LL TALK. THIS WAS A STUPID JOB ANYWAY.
STEALING CATS AND FREAKIN' DOGS. I'VE ASSASSINATED *HEADS OF STATE*, DAMN IT!
LESS WHINING. MORE INFORMATION.
SOME RICH NUTJOB HIRED US. SPENT A LONG TIME STUDYING OUR BODIES... OUR CYBER-TECH.
THEN HE SENT US OUT TO GET ANIMALS. CATS, DOGS... NO STRAYS, HE SAID. HEALTHY ONES... PEOPLE'S PETS.
WHY? SOME KIND OF EXPERIMENTS?
DON'T KNOW. DON'T CARE.
ONE LAST THING BEFORE I TELEPORT YOU TO INTERPOL, MR. BIG-SHOT POLITICAL ASSASSIN.
"WHERE DO YOU TAKE THEM?"

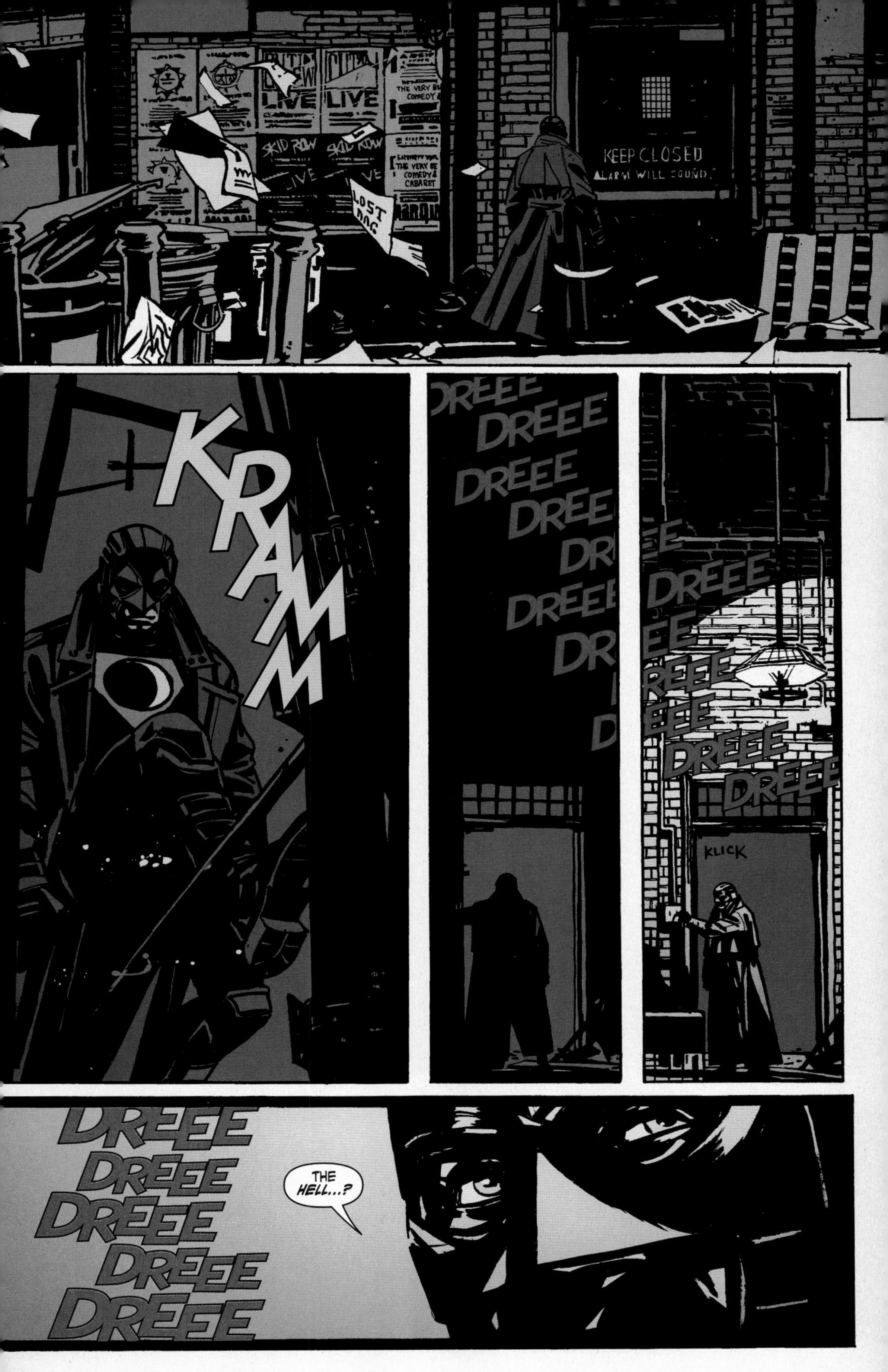
LIVE
LIVE
THE VERY BEST COMEDY
SKID ROW
SKID ROW
THE VERY BEST COMEDY & CABARET
LOST DOG
KEEP CLOSED
ALARM WILL SOUND.
KRAMM
DREEE DREEE DREEE DREEE DREEE DREEE DREEE DREEE DREEE DREEE DREEE DREEE DREEE
KLICK
DREEE DREEE DREEE DREEE DREEE
THE HELL...?

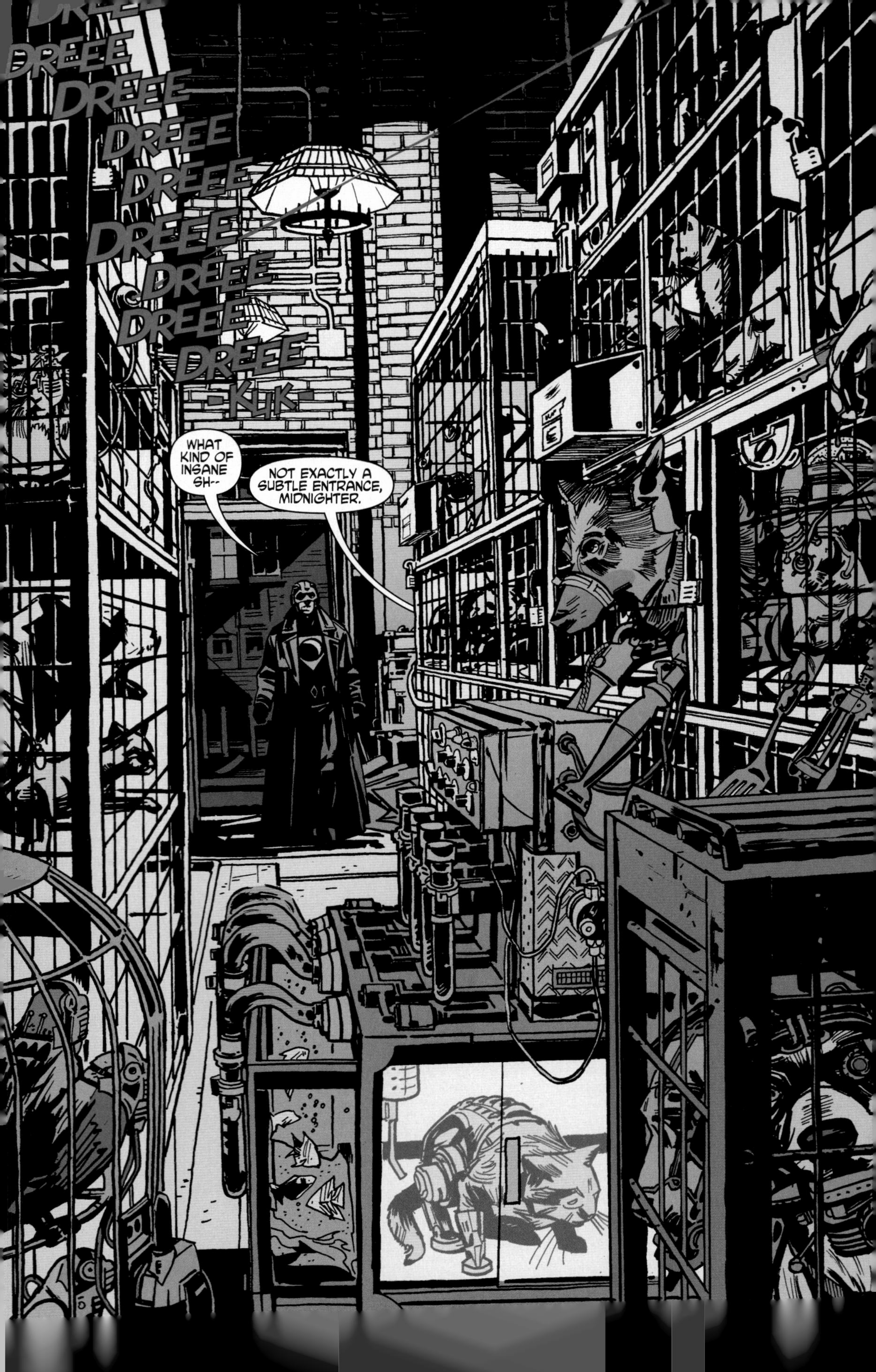
DREEE
DREEE
DREEE
DREEE
DREEE
DREEE
DREEE
DREEE
-KLIK-
WHAT KIND OF INSANE SH--
NOT EXACTLY A SUBTLE ENTRANCE, MIDNIGHTER.

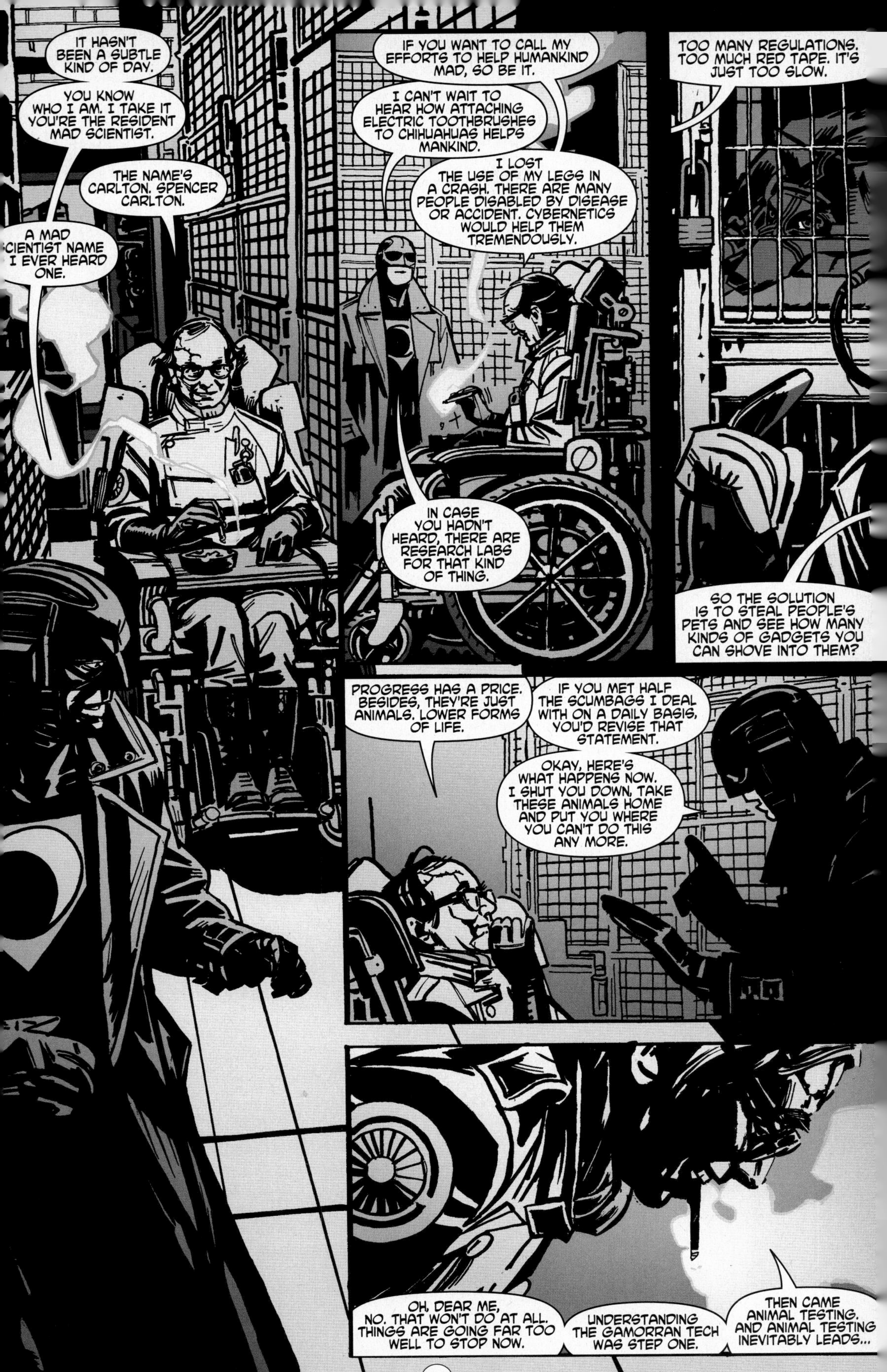
IT HASN'T BEEN A SUBTLE KIND OF DAY.
YOU KNOW WHO I AM. I TAKE IT YOU'RE THE RESIDENT MAD SCIENTIST.
THE NAME'S CARLTON. SPENCER CARLTON.
A MAD SCIENTIST NAME I EVER HEARD ONE.
IF YOU WANT TO CALL MY EFFORTS TO HELP HUMANKIND MAD, SO BE IT.
I CAN'T WAIT TO HEAR HOW ATTACHING ELECTRIC TOOTHBRUSHES TO CHIHUAHUAS HELPS MANKIND.
I LOST THE USE OF MY LEGS IN A CRASH. THERE ARE MANY PEOPLE DISABLED BY DISEASE OR ACCIDENT. CYBERNETICS WOULD HELP THEM TREMENDOUSLY.
IN CASE YOU HADN'T HEARD, THERE ARE RESEARCH LABS FOR THAT KIND OF THING.
TOO MANY REGULATIONS. TOO MUCH RED TAPE. IT'S JUST TOO SLOW.
SO THE SOLUTION IS TO STEAL PEOPLE'S PETS AND SEE HOW MANY KINDS OF GADGETS YOU CAN SHOVE INTO THEM?
PROGRESS HAS A PRICE. BESIDES, THEY'RE JUST ANIMALS. LOWER FORMS OF LIFE.
IF YOU MET HALF THE SCUMBAGS I DEAL WITH ON A DAILY BASIS, YOU'D REVISE THAT STATEMENT.
OKAY, HERE'S WHAT HAPPENS NOW. I SHUT YOU DOWN, TAKE THESE ANIMALS HOME AND PUT YOU WHERE YOU CAN'T DO THIS ANY MORE.
OH, DEAR ME, NO. THAT WON'T DO AT ALL. THINGS ARE GOING FAR TOO WELL TO STOP NOW.
UNDERSTANDING THE GAMORRAN TECH WAS STEP ONE.
THEN CAME ANIMAL TESTING. AND ANIMAL TESTING INEVITABLY LEADS...

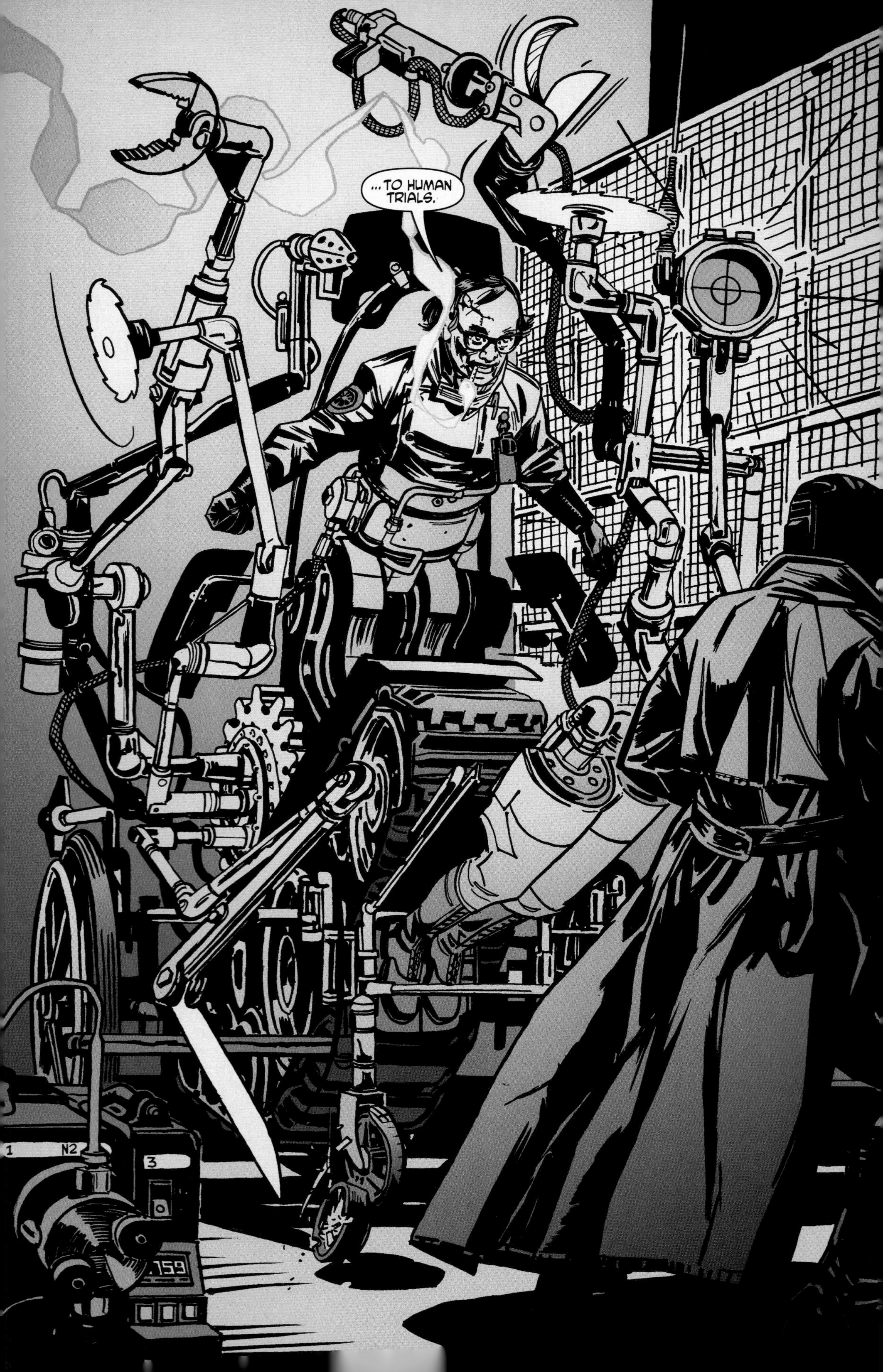
...TO HUMAN TRIALS.
1
N2
3
159

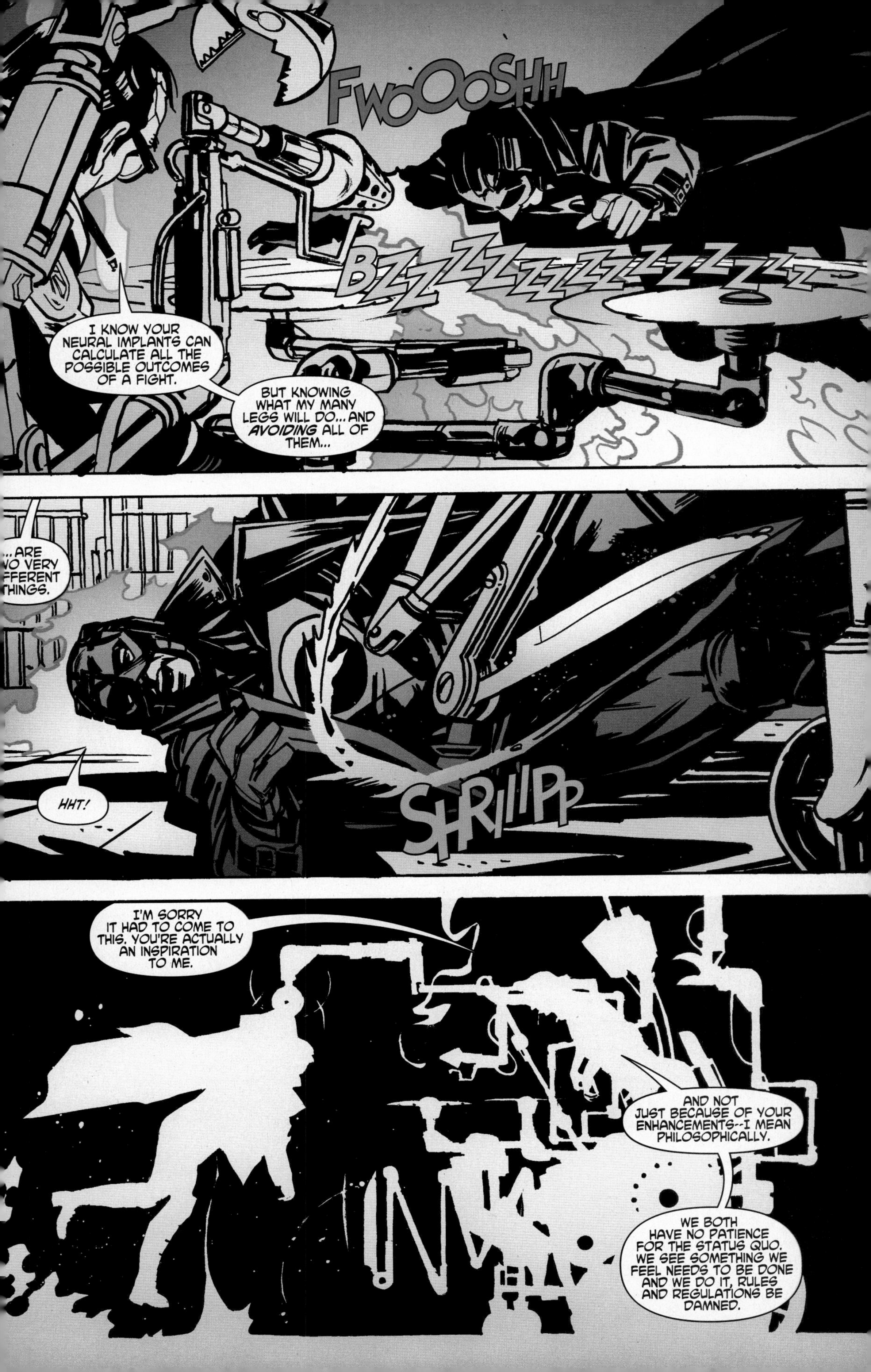
FWOOOOSHH
BZZZZZZZZZZZZZZZZ
I KNOW YOUR NEURAL IMPLANTS CAN CALCULATE ALL THE POSSIBLE OUTCOMES OF A FIGHT.
BUT KNOWING WHAT MY MANY LEGS WILL DO... AND *AVOIDING* ALL OF THEM...
...ARE WO VERY FFERENT THINGS.
HHT!
SHRIIIPP
I'M SORRY IT HAD TO COME TO THIS. YOU'RE ACTUALLY AN INSPIRATION TO ME.
AND NOT JUST BECAUSE OF YOUR ENHANCEMENTS--I MEAN PHILOSOPHICALLY.
WE BOTH HAVE NO PATIENCE FOR THE STATUS QUO. WE SEE SOMETHING WE FEEL NEEDS TO BE DONE AND WE DO IT, RULES AND REGULATIONS BE DAMNED.

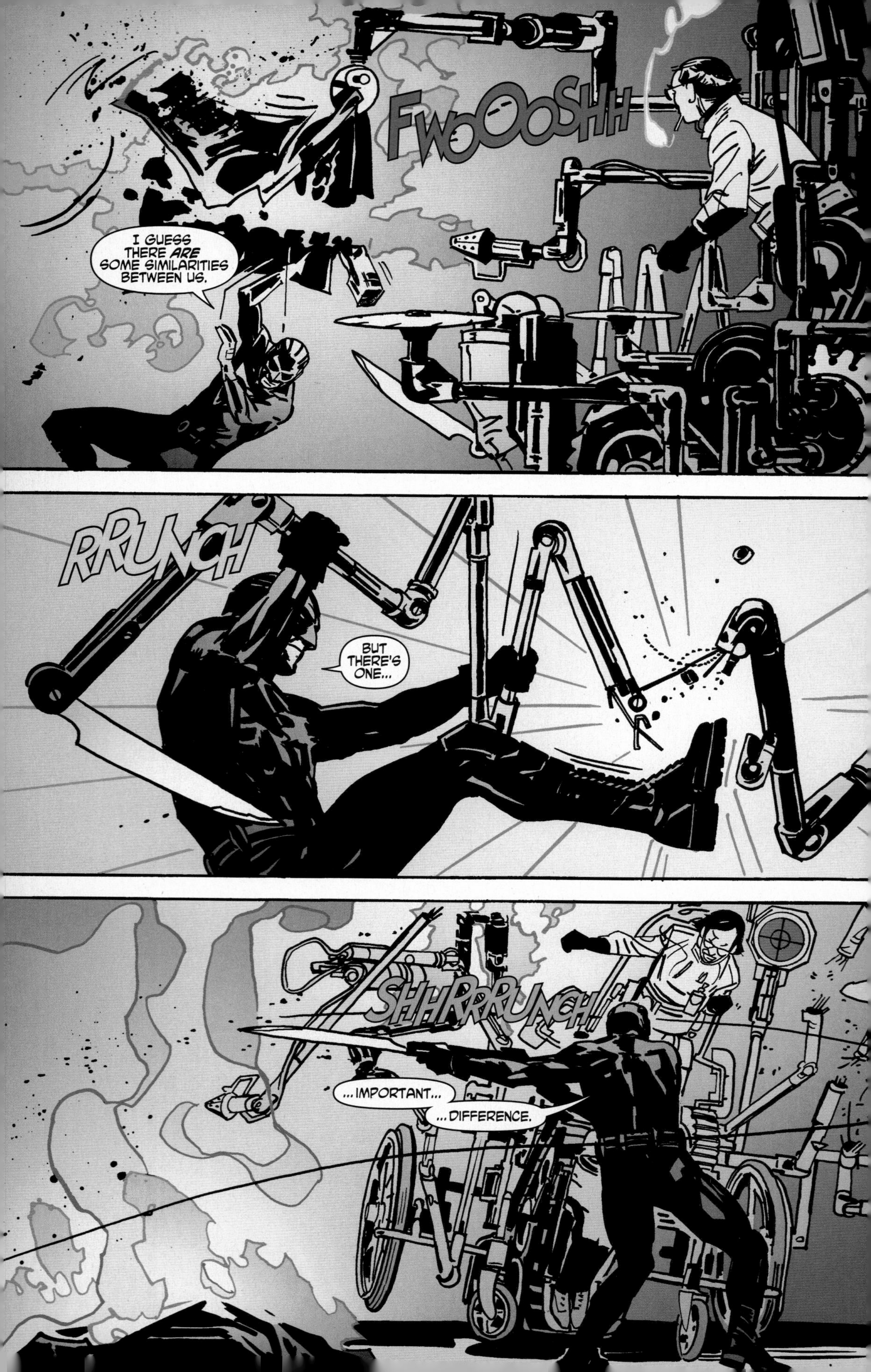
FWOOOOSHH
I GUESS THERE ARE SOME SIMILARITIES BETWEEN US.
RRUNCH
BUT THERE'S ONE...
SHHRRRUNCH
...IMPORTANT...
...DIFFERENCE.

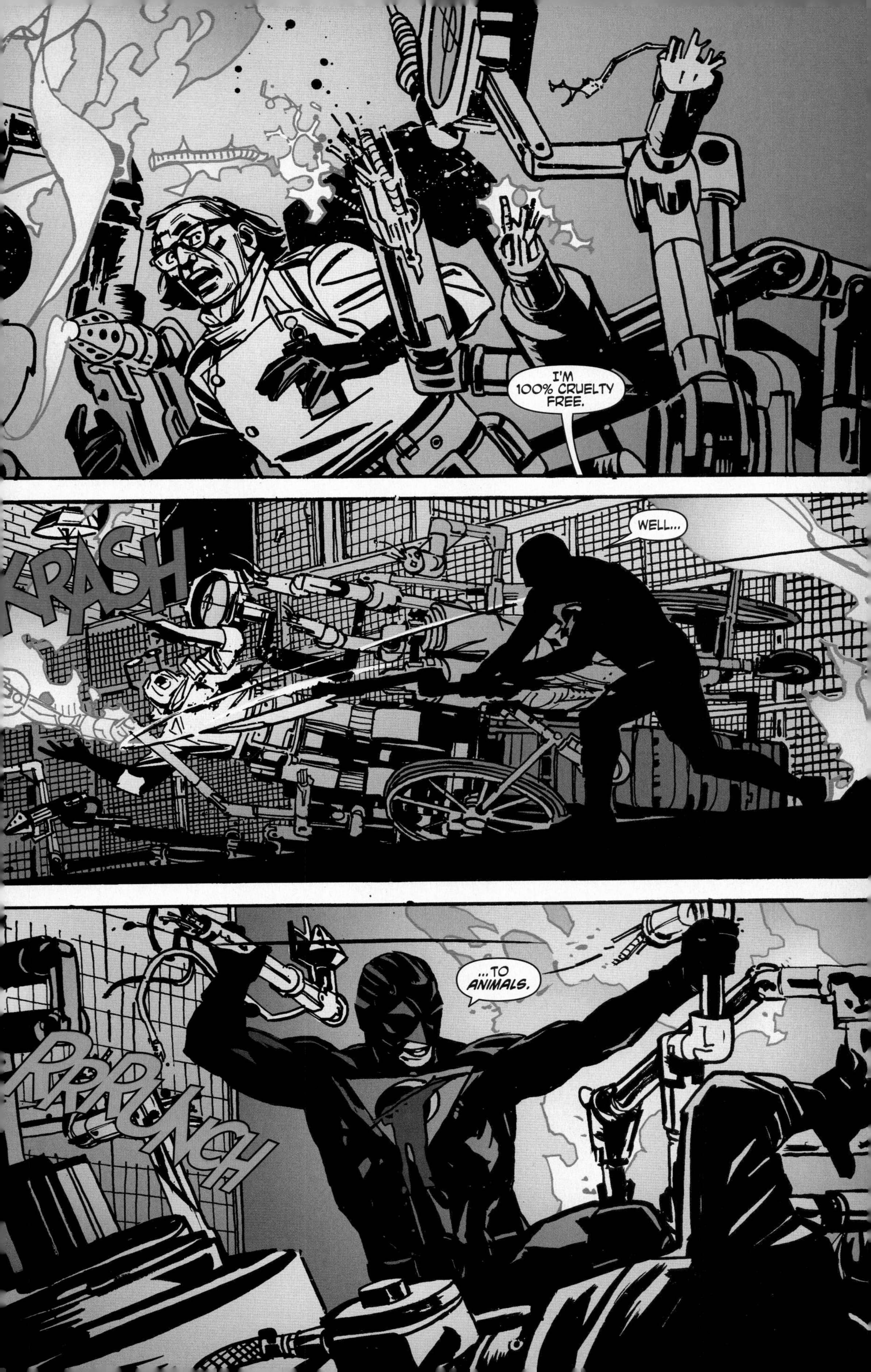
I'M 100% CRUELTY FREE.
KRASH
WELL...
...TO ANIMALS.
RRRUNCH

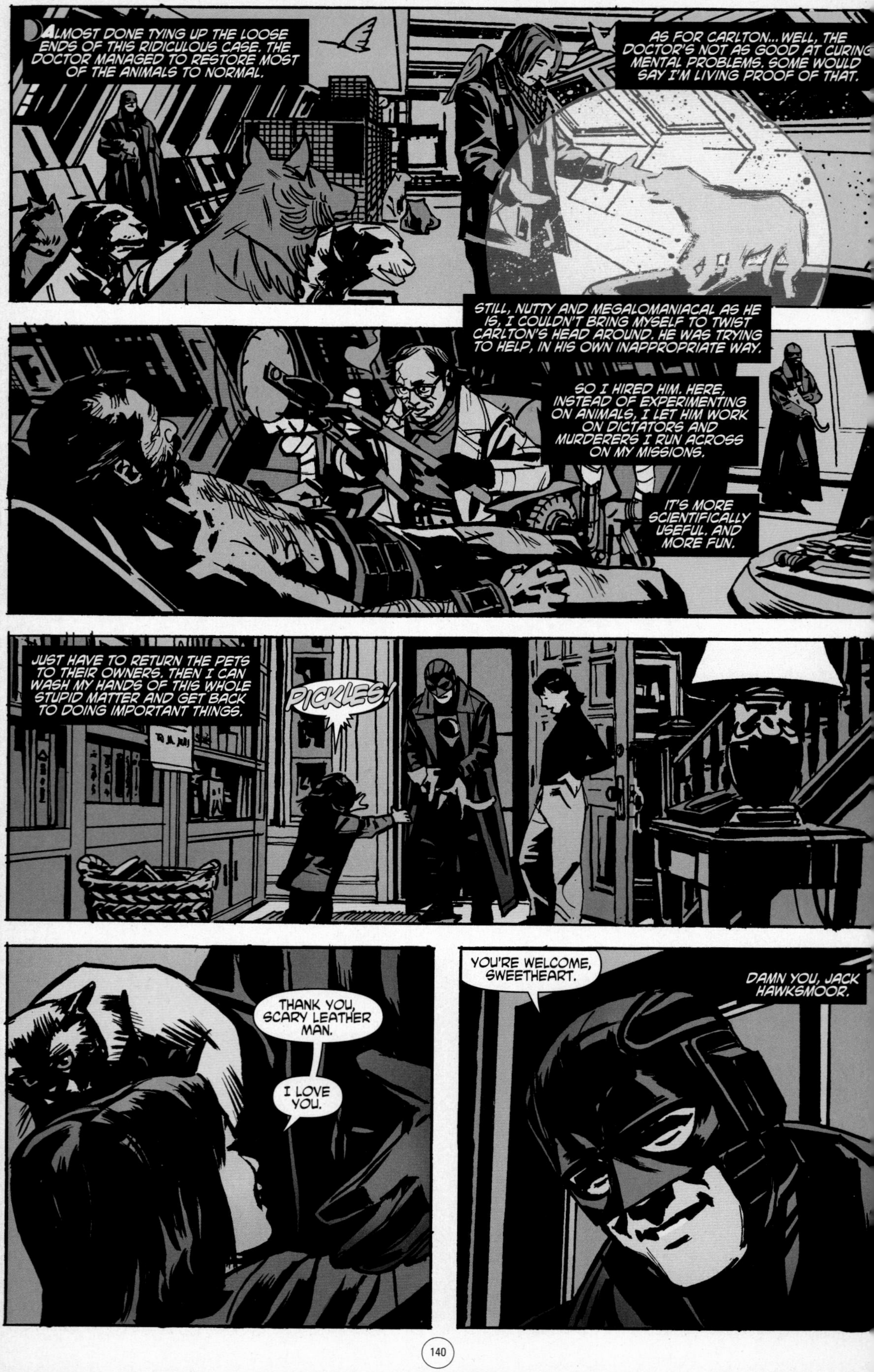
ALMOST DONE TYING UP THE LOOSE ENDS OF THIS RIDICULOUS CASE. THE DOCTOR MANAGED TO RESTORE MOST OF THE ANIMALS TO NORMAL.
AS FOR CARLTON... WELL, THE DOCTOR'S NOT AS GOOD AT CURING MENTAL PROBLEMS. SOME WOULD SAY I'M LIVING PROOF OF THAT.
STILL, NUTTY AND MEGALOMANIACAL AS HE IS, I COULDN'T BRING MYSELF TO TWIST CARLTON'S HEAD AROUND. HE WAS TRYING TO HELP, IN HIS OWN INAPPROPRIATE WAY.
SO I HIRED HIM. HERE, INSTEAD OF EXPERIMENTING ON ANIMALS, I LET HIM WORK ON DICTATORS AND MURDERERS I RUN ACROSS ON MY MISSIONS.
IT'S MORE SCIENTIFICALLY USEFUL. AND MORE FUN.
JUST HAVE TO RETURN THE PETS TO THEIR OWNERS. THEN I CAN WASH MY HANDS OF THIS WHOLE STUPID MATTER AND GET BACK TO DOING IMPORTANT THINGS.
PICKLES!
THANK YOU, SCARY LEATHER MAN.
I LOVE YOU.
YOU'RE WELCOME, SWEETHEART.
DAMN YOU, JACK HAWKSMOOR.

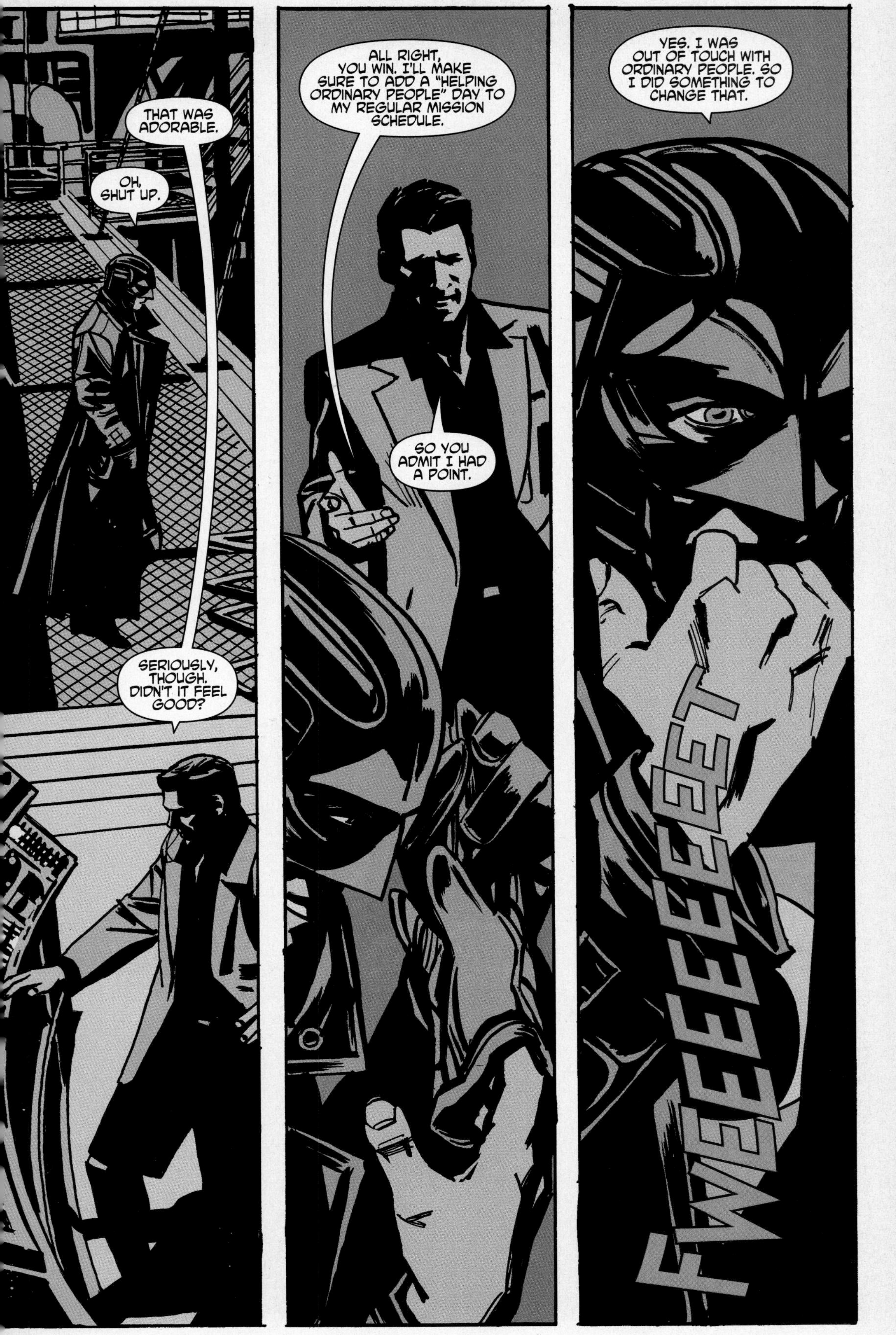
THAT WAS ADORABLE.
OH, SHUT UP.
SERIOUSLY, THOUGH. DIDN'T IT FEEL GOOD?
ALL RIGHT, YOU WIN. I'LL MAKE SURE TO ADD A "HELPING ORDINARY PEOPLE" DAY TO MY REGULAR MISSION SCHEDULE.
SO YOU ADMIT I HAD A POINT.
YES. I WAS OUT OF TOUCH WITH ORDINARY PEOPLE. SO I DID SOMETHING TO CHANGE THAT.
FWEEEEEEEET

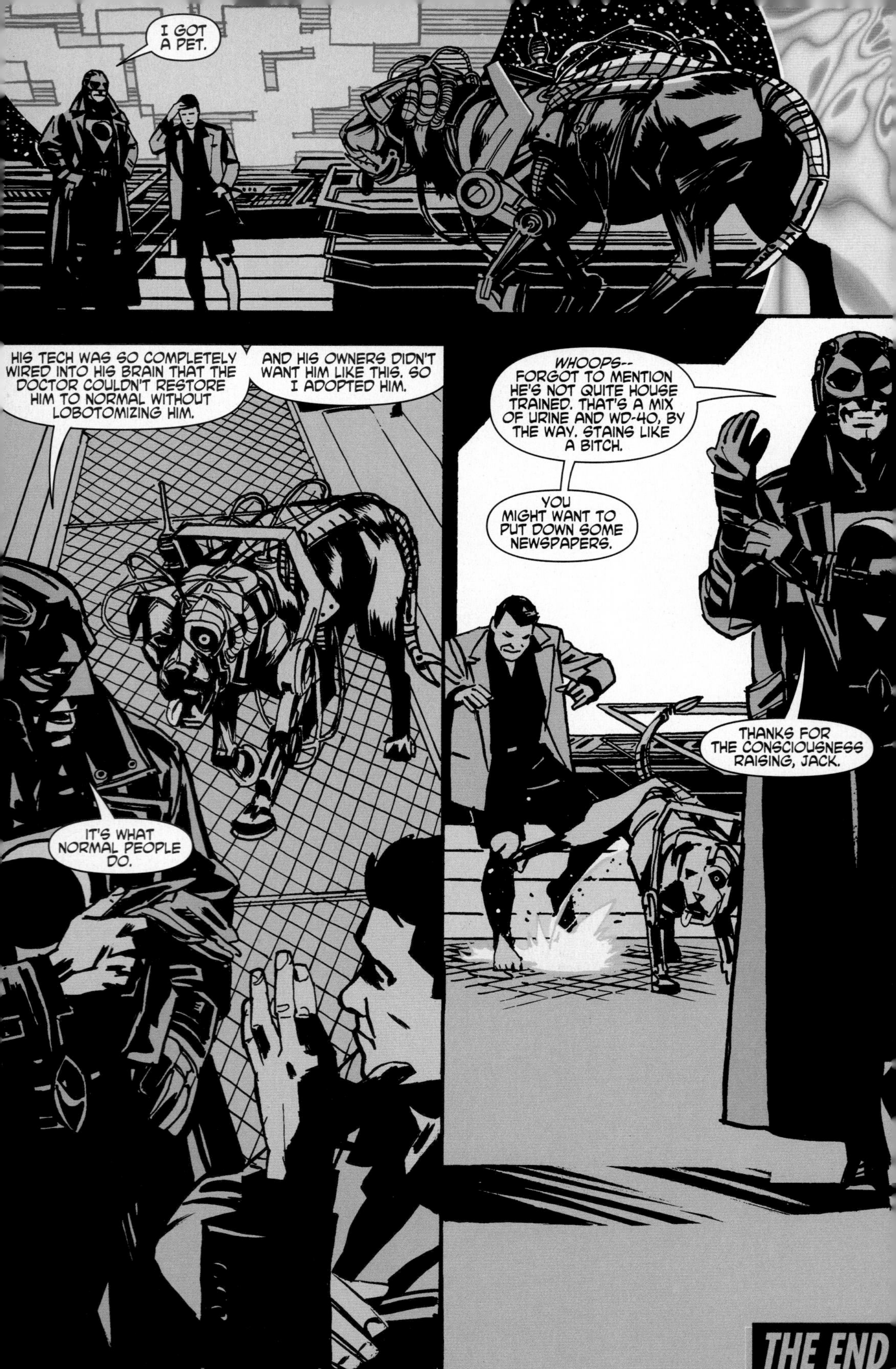
I GOT A PET.
HIS TECH WAS SO COMPLETELY WIRED INTO HIS BRAIN THAT THE DOCTOR COULDN'T RESTORE HIM TO NORMAL WITHOUT LOBOTOMIZING HIM.
AND HIS OWNERS DIDN'T WANT HIM LIKE THIS. SO I ADOPTED HIM.
IT'S WHAT NORMAL PEOPLE DO.
WHOOPS-- FORGOT TO MENTION HE'S NOT QUITE HOUSE TRAINED. THAT'S A MIX OF URINE AND WD-40, BY THE WAY. STAINS LIKE A BITCH.
YOU MIGHT WANT TO PUT DOWN SOME NEWSPAPERS.
THANKS FOR THE CONSCIOUSNESS RAISING, JACK.
THE END

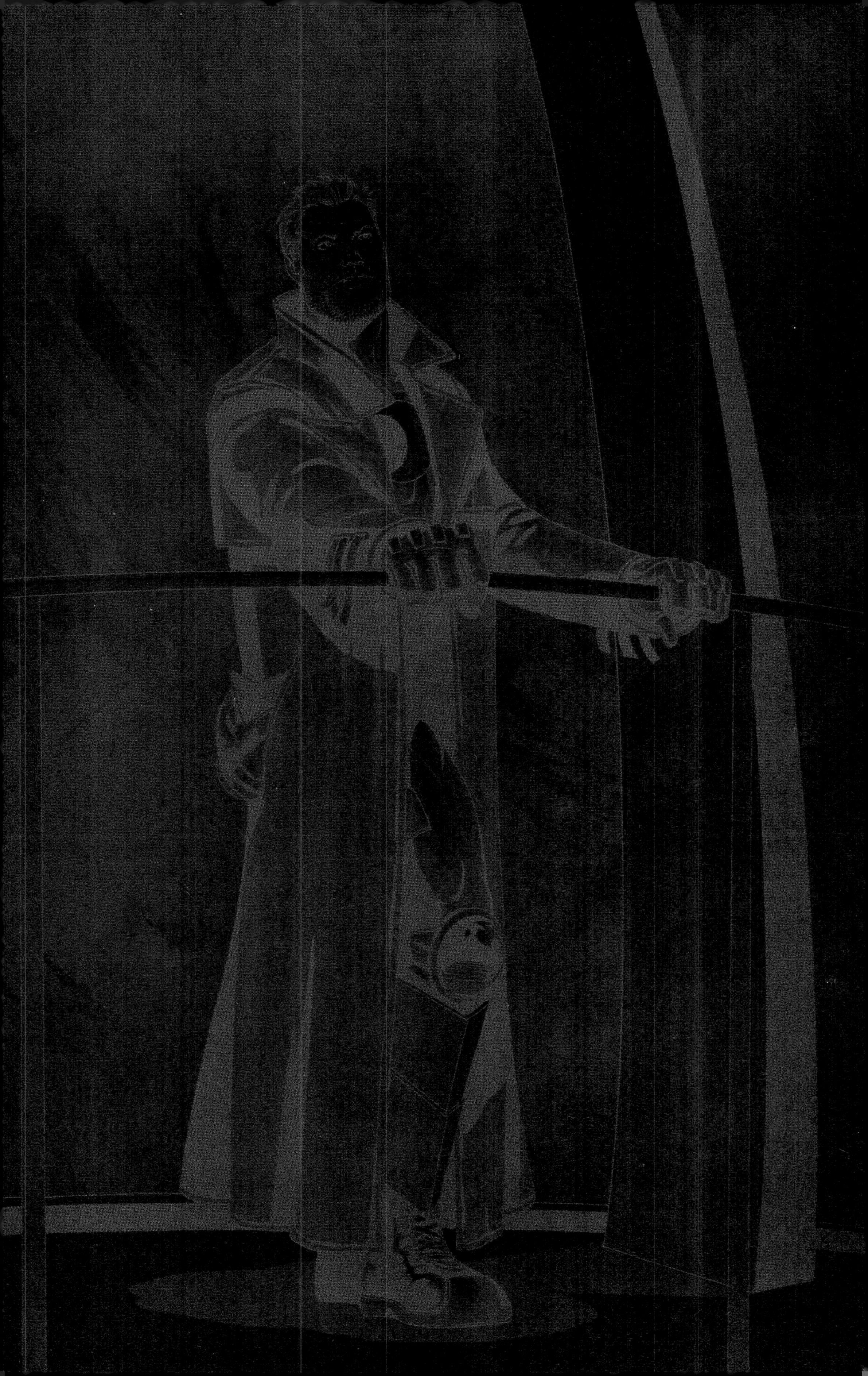

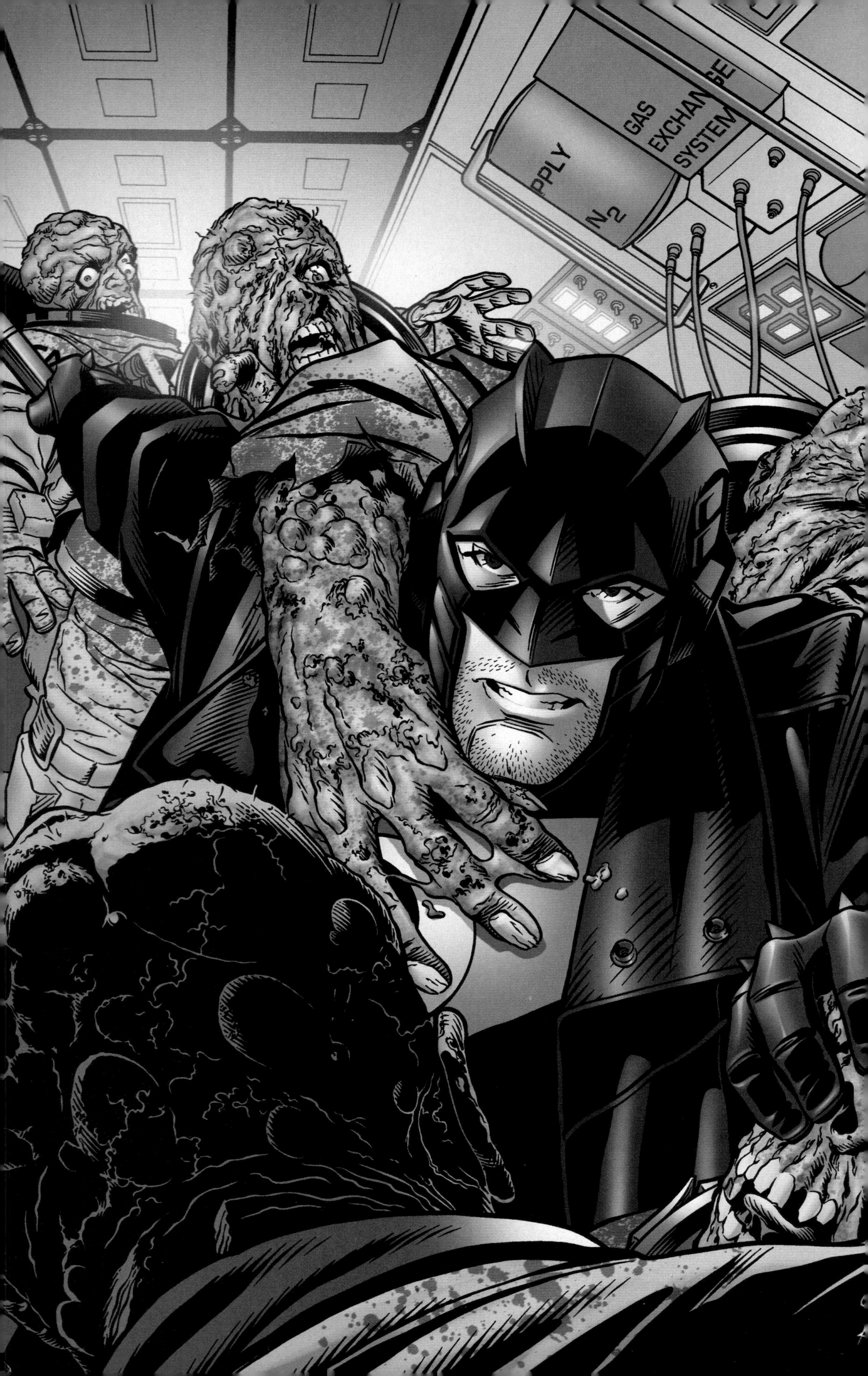
GAS
SYSTEM
$N_2$

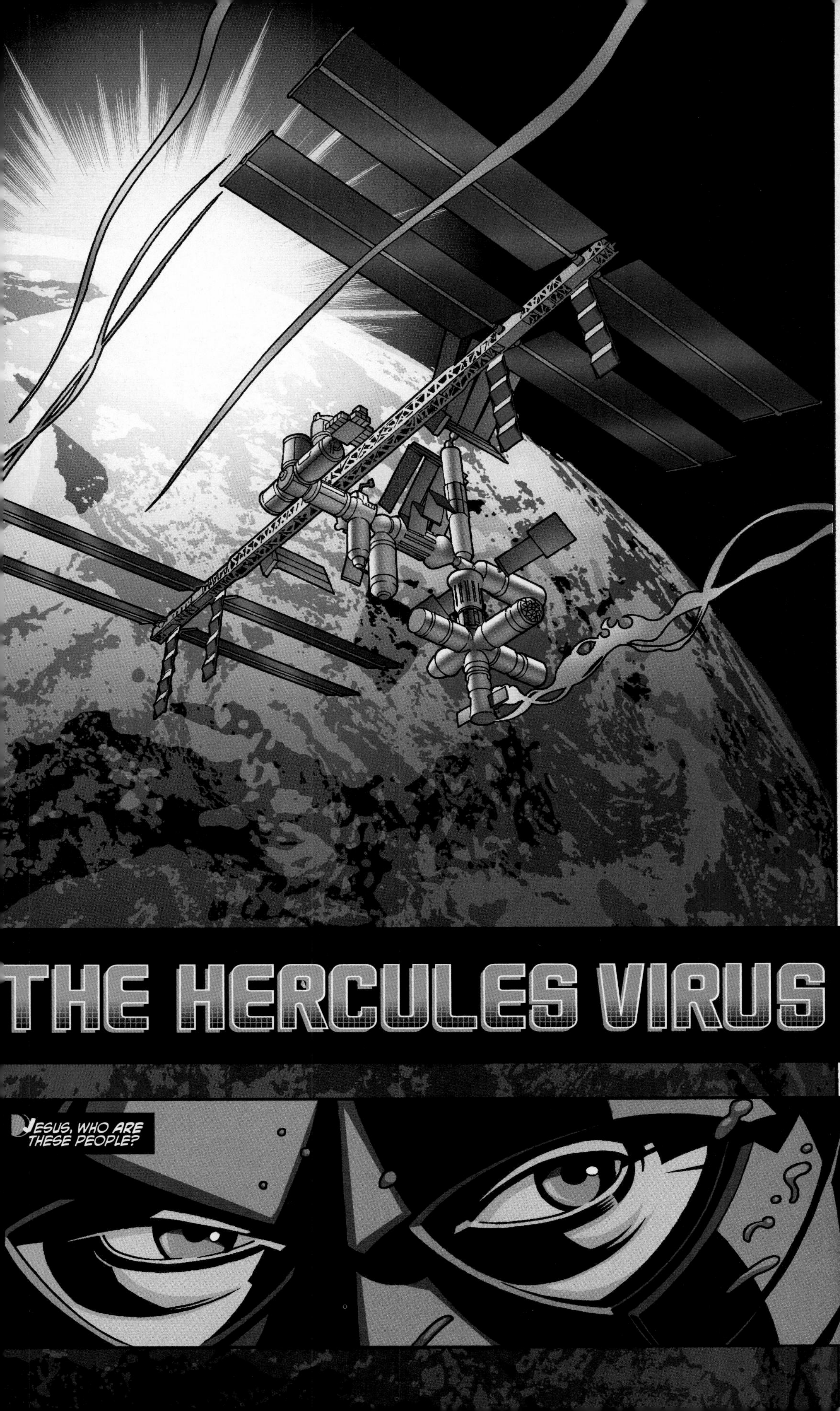
THE HERCULES VIRUS
JESUS, WHO ARE THESE PEOPLE?

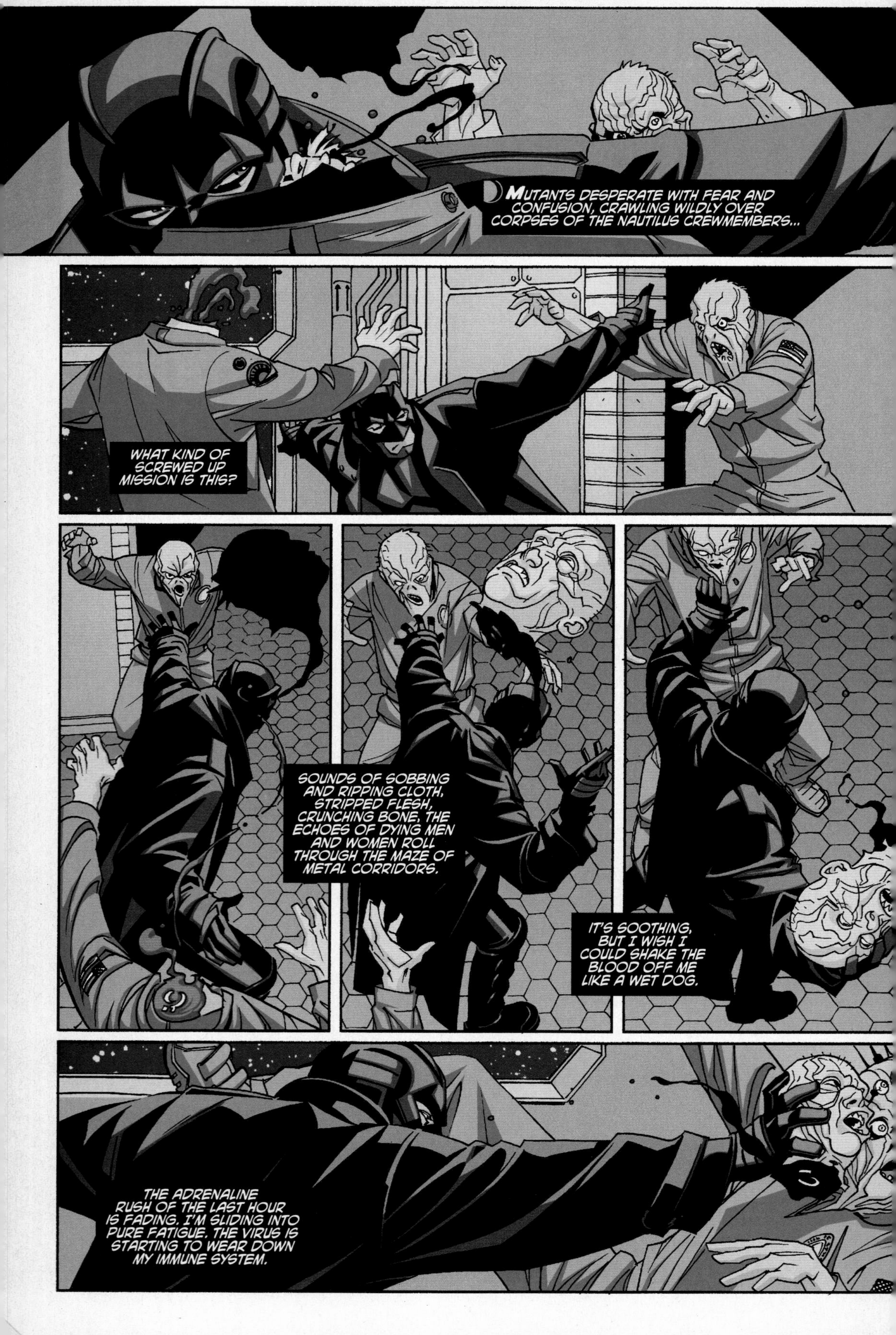
MUTANTS DESPERATE WITH FEAR AND CONFUSION, CRAWLING WILDLY OVER CORPSES OF THE NAUTILUS CREWMEMBERS...
WHAT KIND OF SCREWED UP MISSION IS THIS?
SOUNDS OF SOBBING AND RIPPING CLOTH, STRIPPED FLESH, CRUNCHING BONE, THE ECHOES OF DYING MEN AND WOMEN ROLL THROUGH THE MAZE OF METAL CORRIDORS.
IT'S SOOTHING, BUT I WISH I COULD SHAKE THE BLOOD OFF ME LIKE A WET DOG.
THE ADRENALINE RUSH OF THE LAST HOUR IS FADING. I'M SLIDING INTO PURE FATIGUE. THE VIRUS IS STARTING TO WEAR DOWN MY IMMUNE SYSTEM.

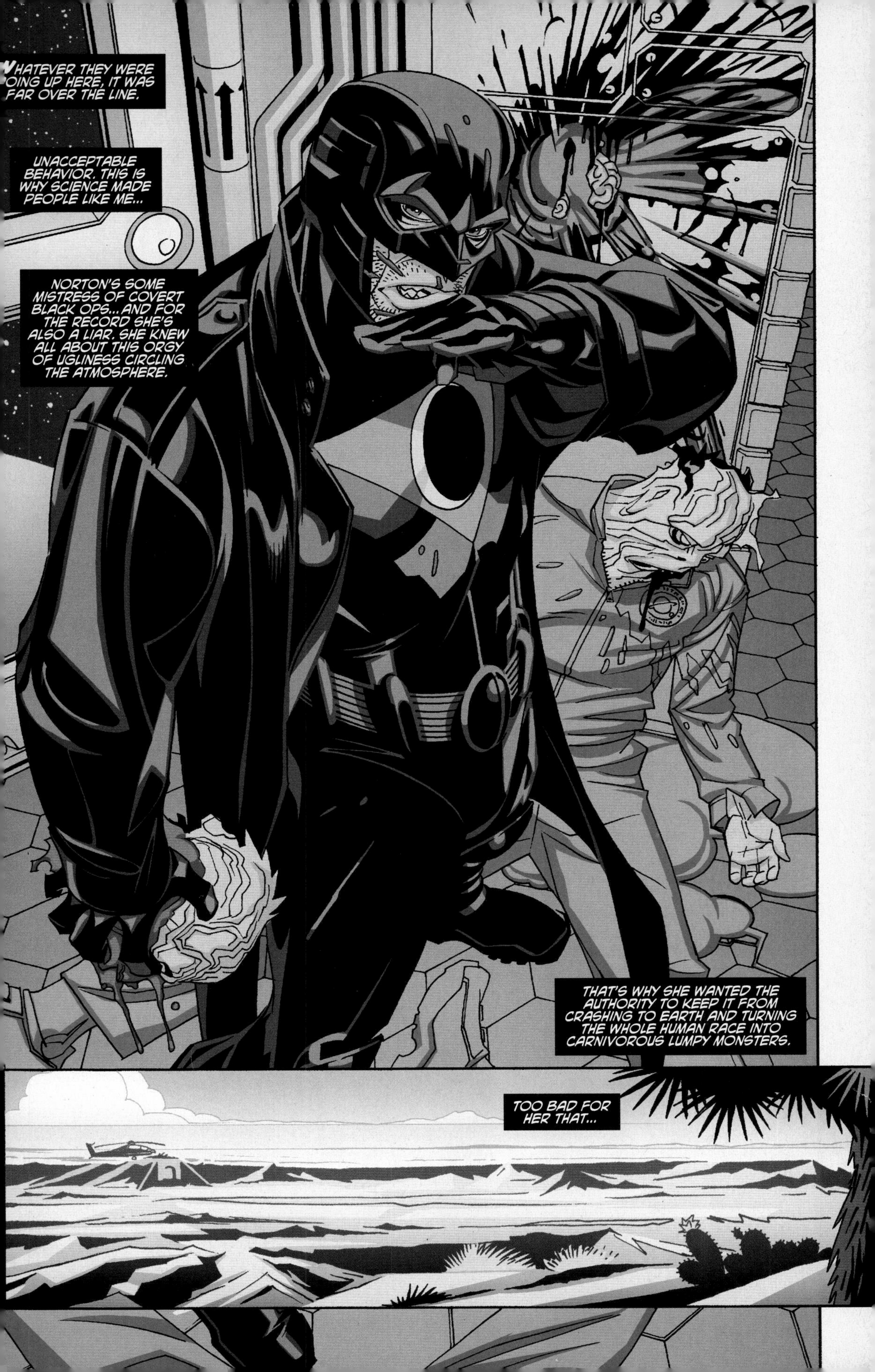
WHATEVER THEY WERE OING UP HERE, IT WAS FAR OVER THE LINE.
UNACCEPTABLE BEHAVIOR. THIS IS WHY SCIENCE MADE PEOPLE LIKE ME...
NORTON'S SOME MISTRESS OF COVERT BLACK OPS...AND FOR THE RECORD SHE'S ALSO A LIAR. SHE KNEW ALL ABOUT THIS ORGY OF UGLINESS CIRCLING THE ATMOSPHERE.
THAT'S WHY SHE WANTED THE AUTHORITY TO KEEP IT FROM CRASHING TO EARTH AND TURNING THE WHOLE HUMAN RACE INTO CARNIVOROUS LUMPY MONSTERS.
TOO BAD FOR HER THAT...

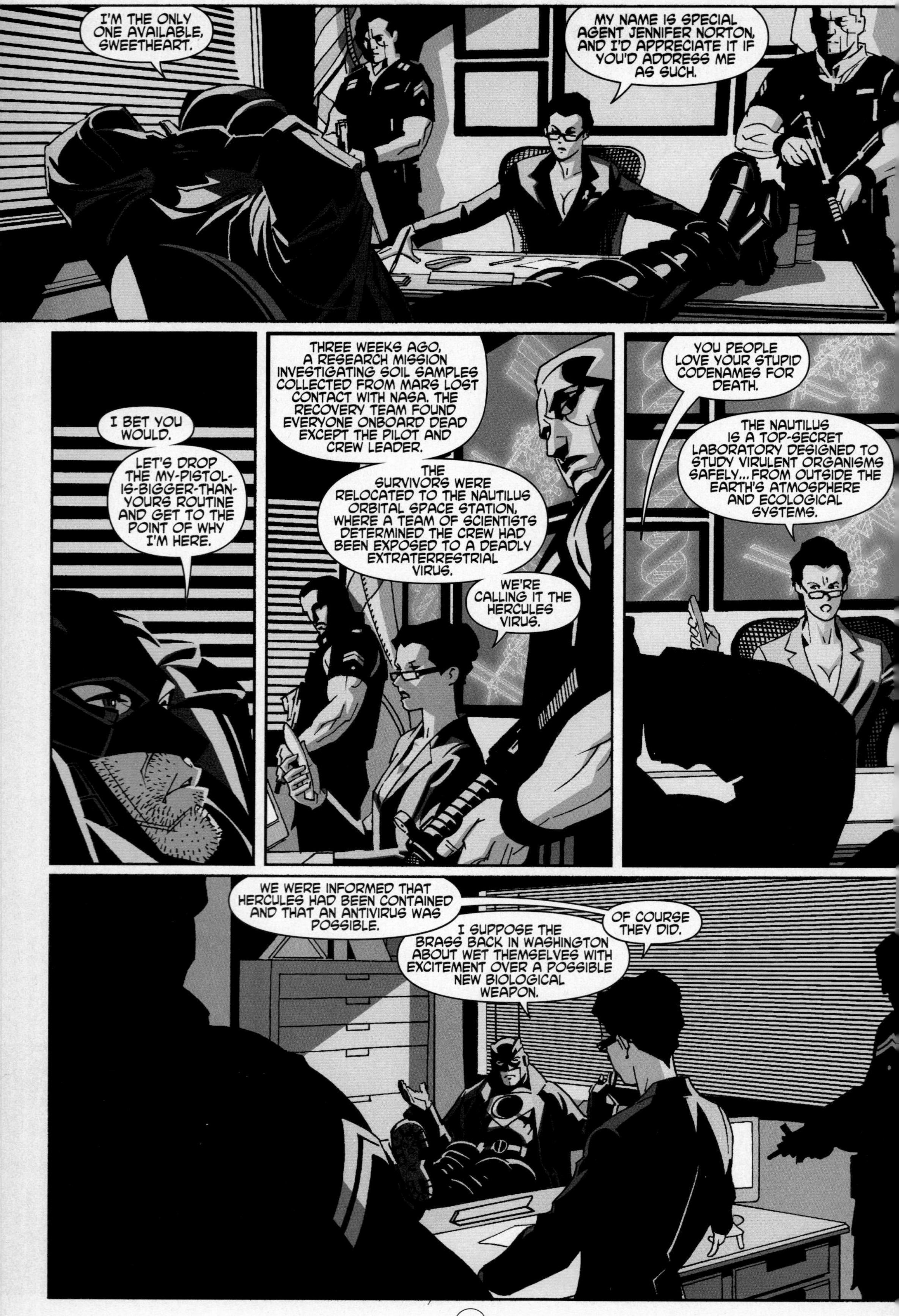
I'M THE ONLY ONE AVAILABLE, SWEETHEART.
MY NAME IS SPECIAL AGENT JENNIFER NORTON, AND I'D APPRECIATE IT IF YOU'D ADDRESS ME AS SUCH.
I BET YOU WOULD.
LET'S DROP THE MY-PISTOL-IS-BIGGER-THAN-YOURS ROUTINE AND GET TO THE POINT OF WHY I'M HERE.
THREE WEEKS AGO, A RESEARCH MISSION INVESTIGATING SOIL SAMPLES COLLECTED FROM MARS LOST CONTACT WITH NASA. THE RECOVERY TEAM FOUND EVERYONE ONBOARD DEAD EXCEPT THE PILOT AND CREW LEADER.
THE SURVIVORS WERE RELOCATED TO THE NAUTILUS ORBITAL SPACE STATION, WHERE A TEAM OF SCIENTISTS DETERMINED THE CREW HAD BEEN EXPOSED TO A DEADLY EXTRATERRESTRIAL VIRUS.
WE'RE CALLING IT THE HERCULES VIRUS.
YOU PEOPLE LOVE YOUR STUPID CODENAMES FOR DEATH.
THE NAUTILUS IS A TOP-SECRET LABORATORY DESIGNED TO STUDY VIRULENT ORGANISMS SAFELY... FROM OUTSIDE THE EARTH'S ATMOSPHERE AND ECOLOGICAL SYSTEMS.
WE WERE INFORMED THAT HERCULES HAD BEEN CONTAINED AND THAT AN ANTIVIRUS WAS POSSIBLE.
OF COURSE THEY DID.
I SUPPOSE THE BRASS BACK IN WASHINGTON ABOUT WET THEMSELVES WITH EXCITEMENT OVER A POSSIBLE NEW BIOLOGICAL WEAPON.

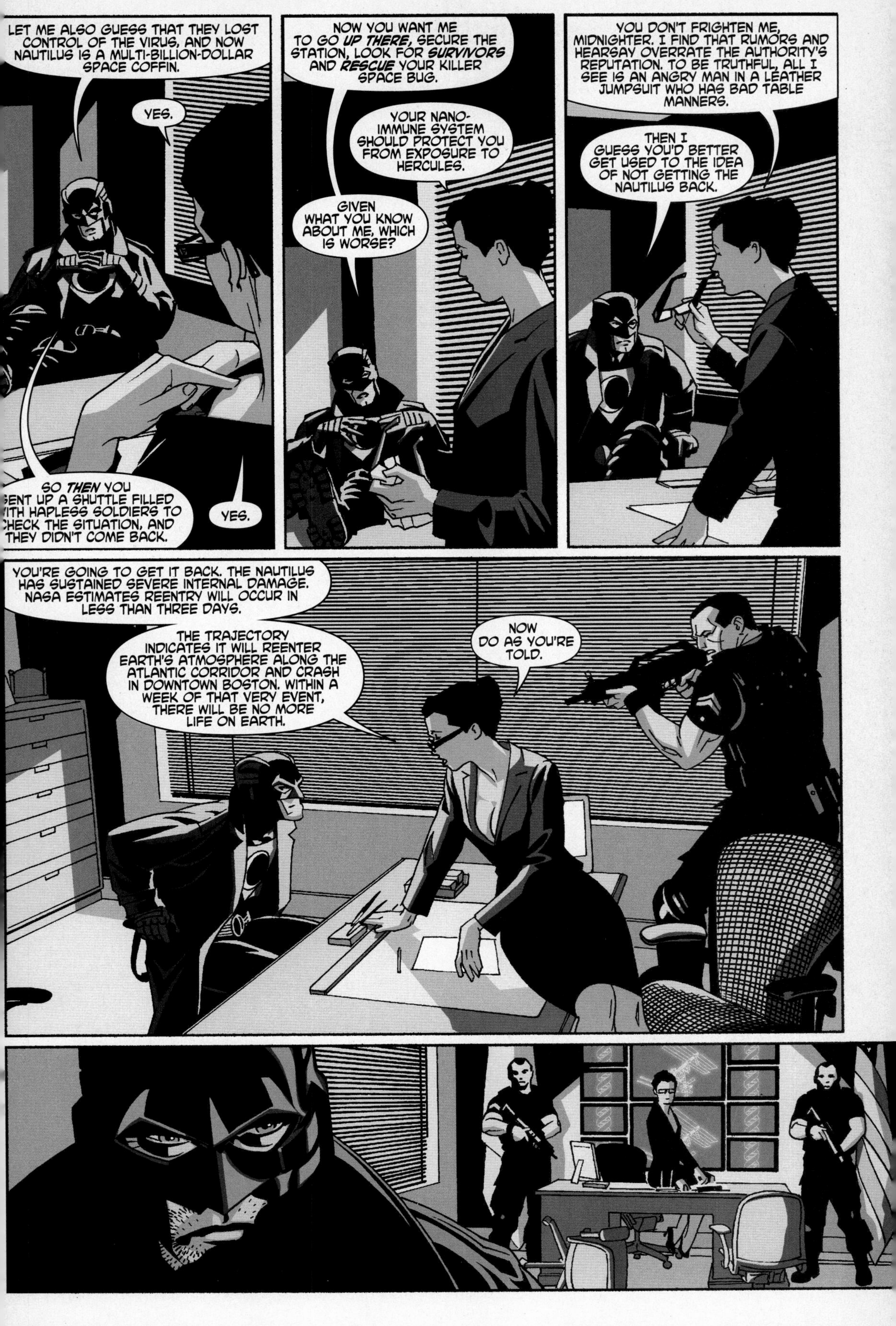
LET ME ALSO GUESS THAT THEY LOST CONTROL OF THE VIRUS, AND NOW NAUTILUS IS A MULTI-BILLION-DOLLAR SPACE COFFIN.
YES.
SO THEN YOU SENT UP A SHUTTLE FILLED WITH HAPLESS SOLDIERS TO CHECK THE SITUATION, AND THEY DIDN'T COME BACK.
YES.
NOW YOU WANT ME TO GO UP THERE, SECURE THE STATION, LOOK FOR SURVIVORS AND RESCUE YOUR KILLER SPACE BUG.
YOUR NANO-IMMUNE SYSTEM SHOULD PROTECT YOU FROM EXPOSURE TO HERCULES.
GIVEN WHAT YOU KNOW ABOUT ME, WHICH IS WORSE?
YOU DON'T FRIGHTEN ME, MIDNIGHTER. I FIND THAT RUMORS AND HEARSAY OVERRATE THE AUTHORITY'S REPUTATION. TO BE TRUTHFUL, ALL I SEE IS AN ANGRY MAN IN A LEATHER JUMPSUIT WHO HAS BAD TABLE MANNERS.
THEN I GUESS YOU'D BETTER GET USED TO THE IDEA OF NOT GETTING THE NAUTILUS BACK.
YOU'RE GOING TO GET IT BACK. THE NAUTILUS HAS SUSTAINED SEVERE INTERNAL DAMAGE. NASA ESTIMATES REENTRY WILL OCCUR IN LESS THAN THREE DAYS.
THE TRAJECTORY INDICATES IT WILL REENTER EARTH'S ATMOSPHERE ALONG THE ATLANTIC CORRIDOR AND CRASH IN DOWNTOWN BOSTON. WITHIN A WEEK OF THAT VERY EVENT, THERE WILL BE NO MORE LIFE ON EARTH.
NOW DO AS YOU'RE TOLD.

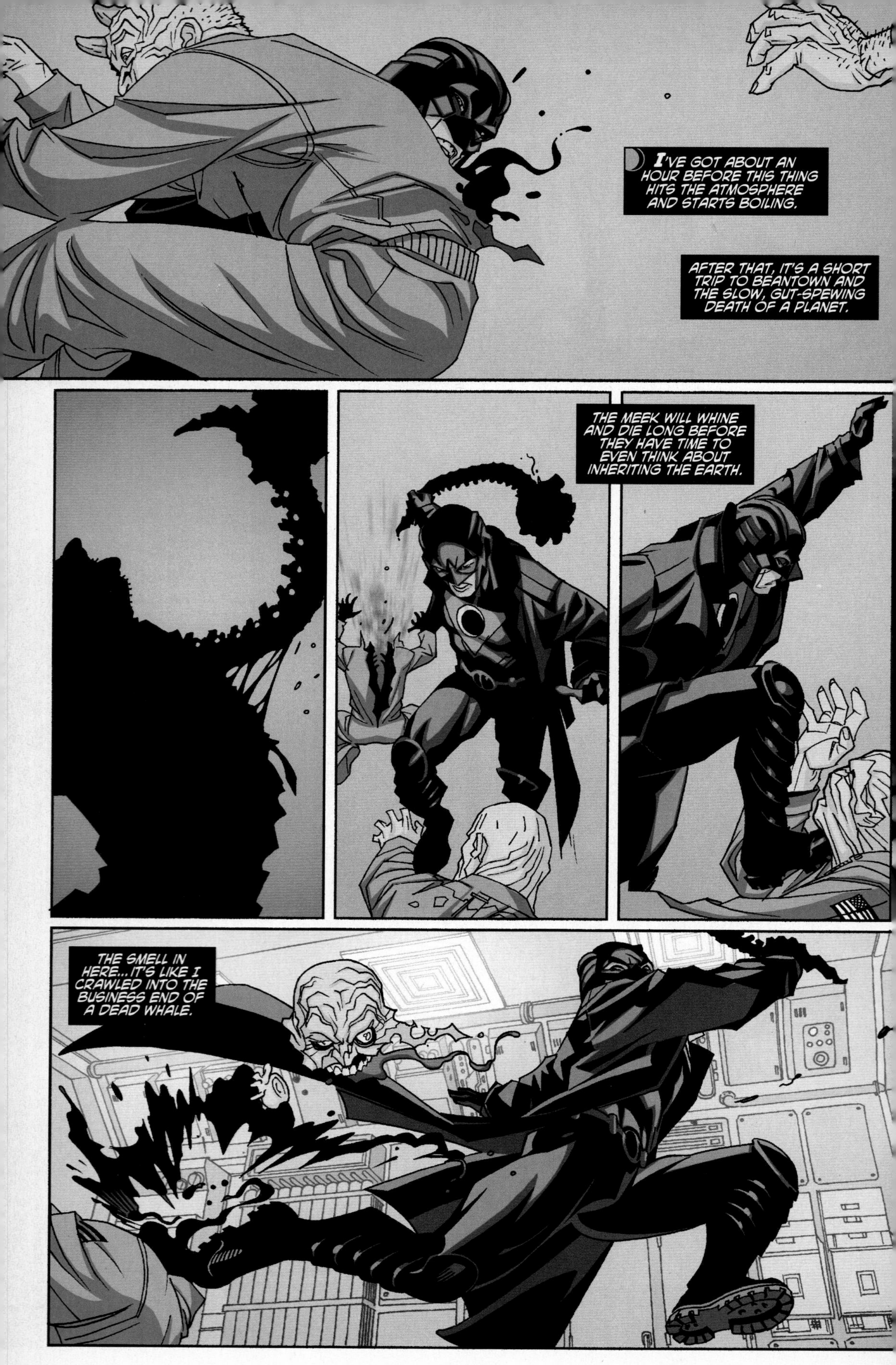
I'VE GOT ABOUT AN HOUR BEFORE THIS THING HITS THE ATMOSPHERE AND STARTS BOILING.
AFTER THAT, IT'S A SHORT TRIP TO BEANTOWN AND THE SLOW, GUT-SPEWING DEATH OF A PLANET.
THE MEEK WILL WHINE AND DIE LONG BEFORE THEY HAVE TIME TO EVEN THINK ABOUT INHERITING THE EARTH.
THE SMELL IN HERE...IT'S LIKE I CRAWLED INTO THE BUSINESS END OF A DEAD WHALE.

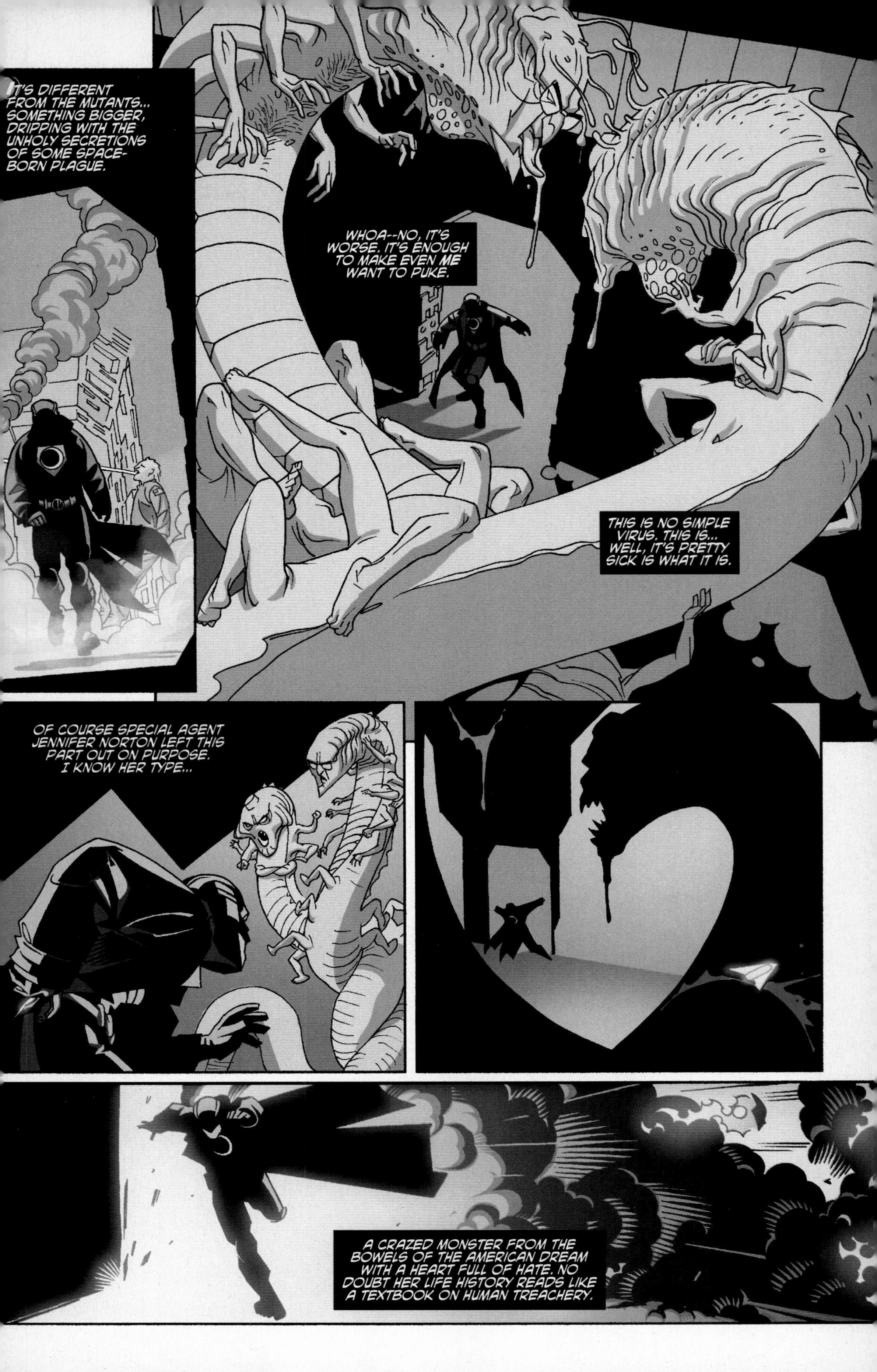
IT'S DIFFERENT FROM THE MUTANTS... SOMETHING BIGGER, DRIPPING WITH THE UNHOLY SECRETIONS OF SOME SPACE-BORN PLAGUE.
WHOA--NO, IT'S WORSE. IT'S ENOUGH TO MAKE EVEN ME WANT TO PUKE.
THIS IS NO SIMPLE VIRUS. THIS IS... WELL, IT'S PRETTY SICK IS WHAT IT IS.
OF COURSE SPECIAL AGENT JENNIFER NORTON LEFT THIS PART OUT ON PURPOSE. I KNOW HER TYPE...
A CRAZED MONSTER FROM THE BOWELS OF THE AMERICAN DREAM WITH A HEART FULL OF HATE. NO DOUBT HER LIFE HISTORY READS LIKE A TEXTBOOK ON HUMAN TREACHERY.

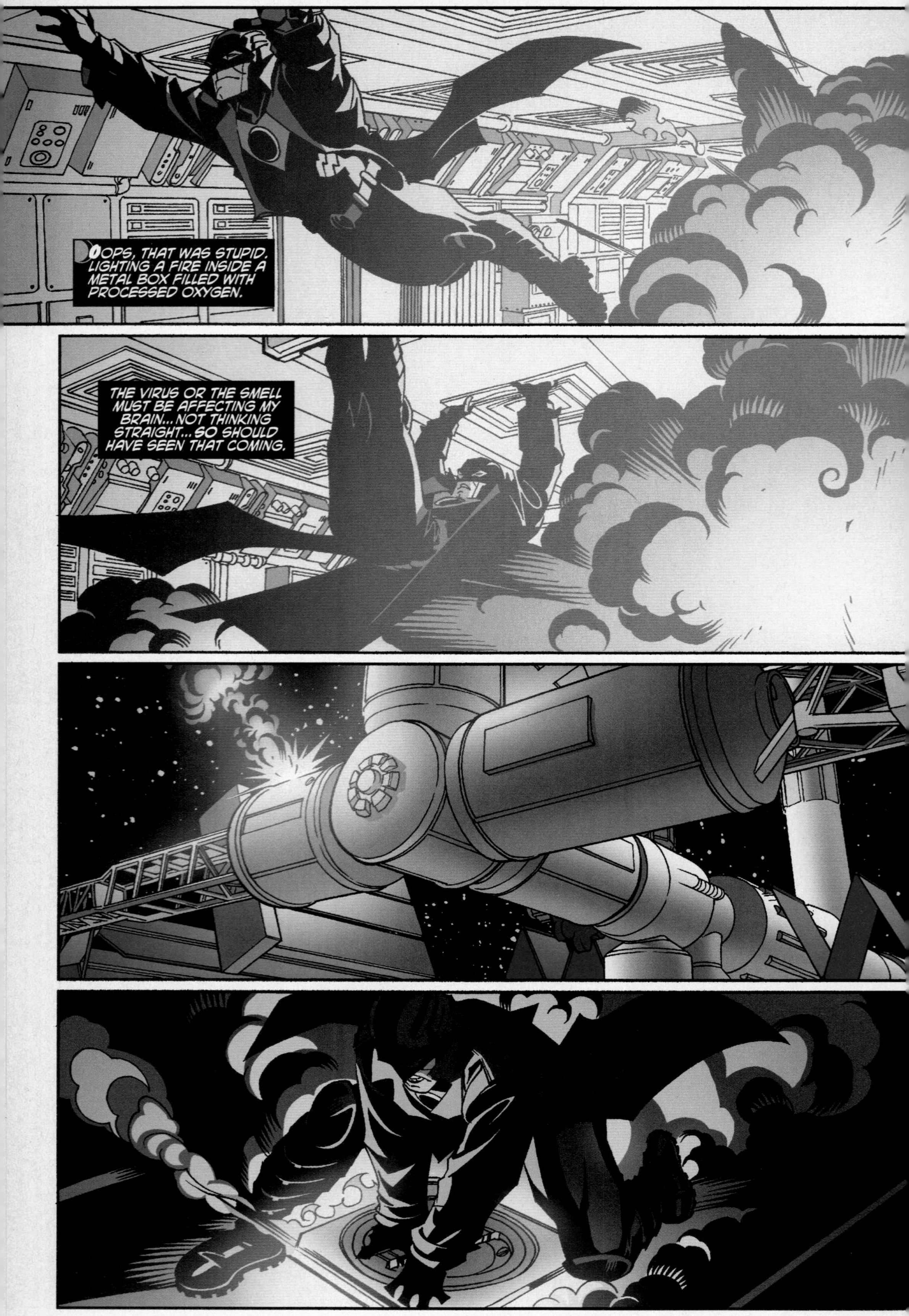
OOPS, THAT WAS STUPID. LIGHTING A FIRE INSIDE A METAL BOX FILLED WITH PROCESSED OXYGEN.
THE VIRUS OR THE SMELL MUST BE AFFECTING MY BRAIN...NOT THINKING STRAIGHT...SO SHOULD HAVE SEEN THAT COMING.

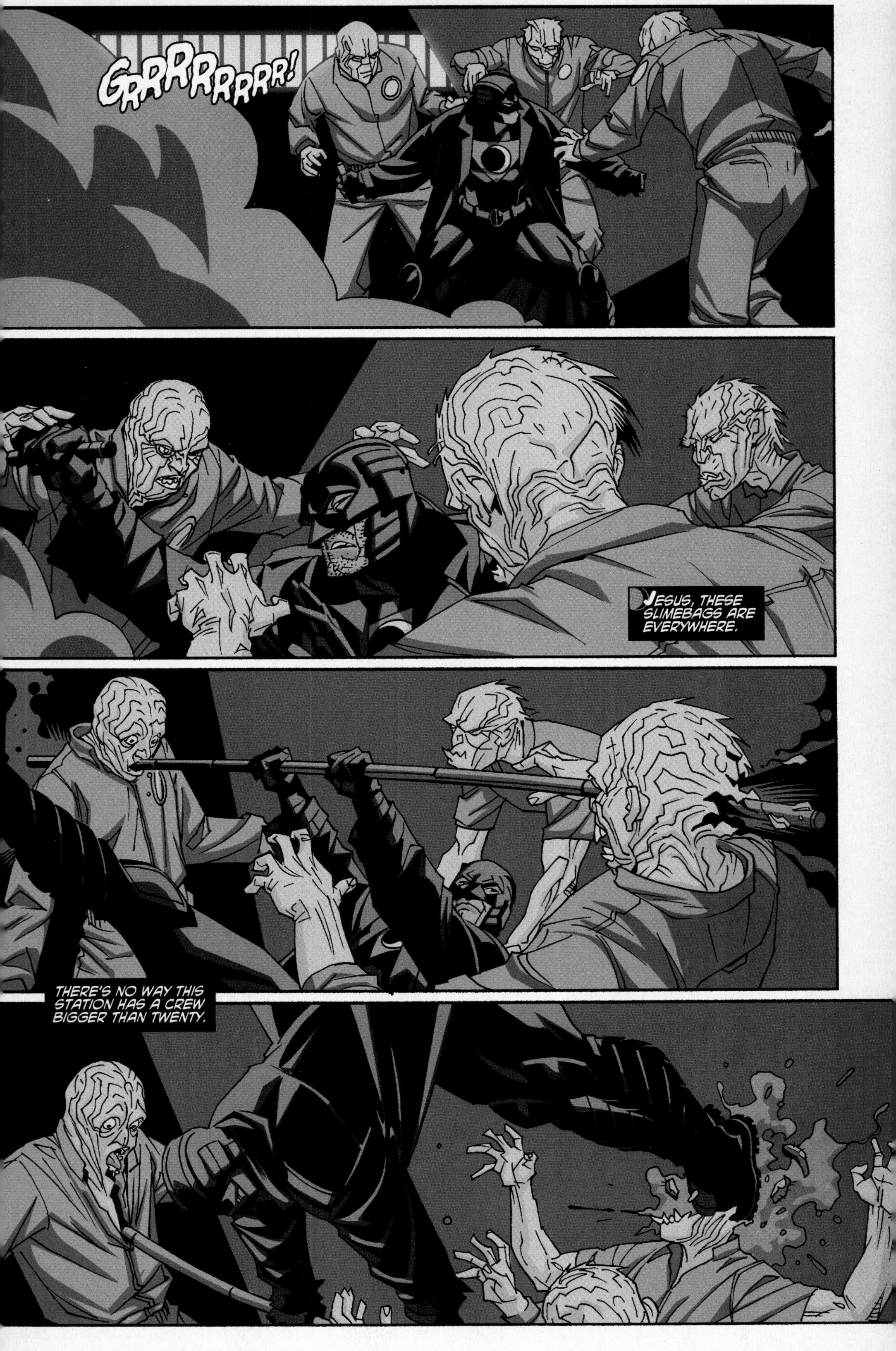
GRRRRRRRR!
JESUS, THESE SLIMEBAGS ARE EVERYWHERE.
THERE'S NO WAY THIS STATION HAS A CREW BIGGER THAN TWENTY.

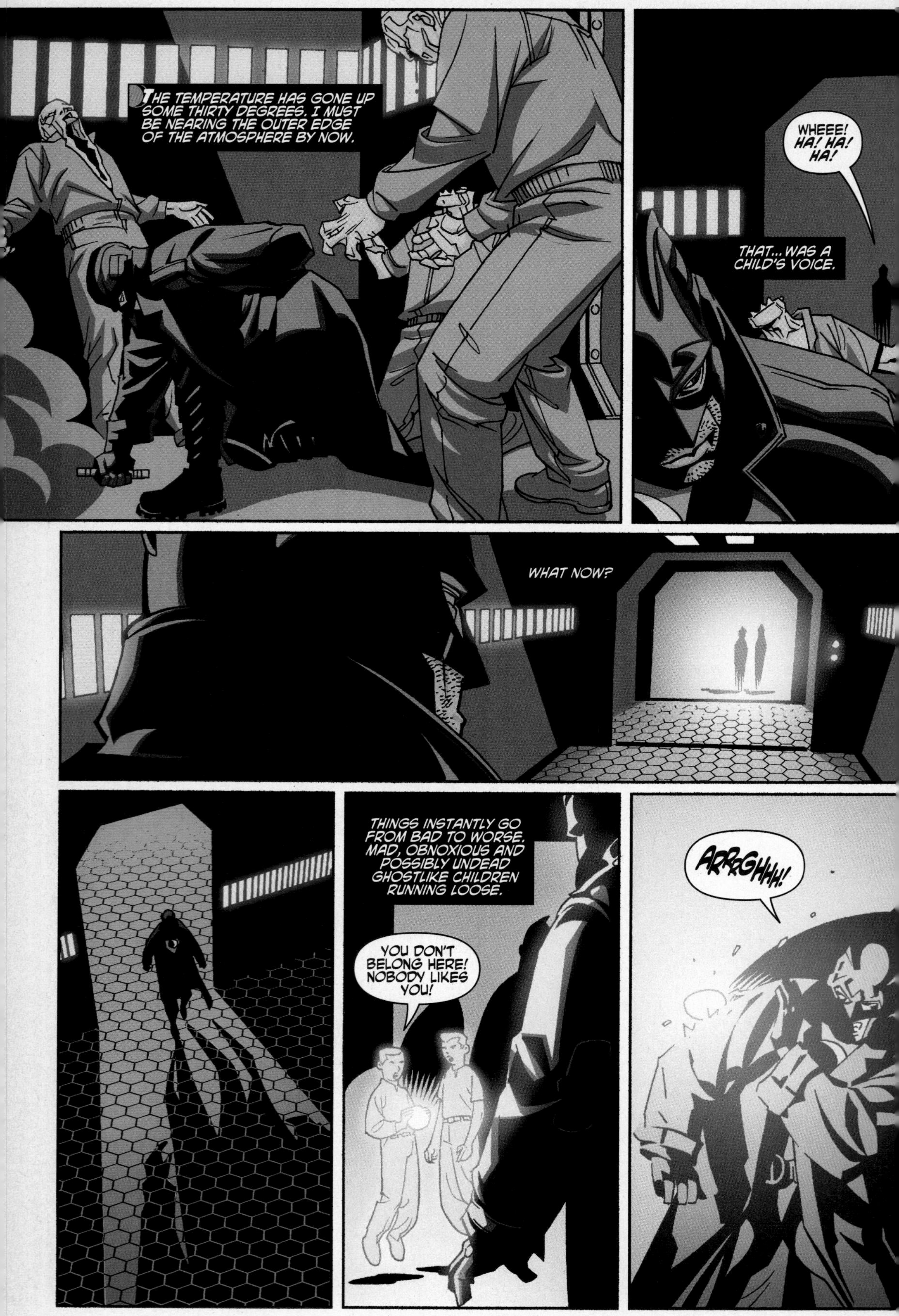
THE TEMPERATURE HAS GONE UP SOME THIRTY DEGREES. I MUST BE NEARING THE OUTER EDGE OF THE ATMOSPHERE BY NOW.
WHEEE! HA! HA! HA!
THAT... WAS A CHILD'S VOICE.
WHAT NOW?
THINGS INSTANTLY GO FROM BAD TO WORSE. MAD, OBNOXIOUS AND POSSIBLY UNDEAD GHOSTLIKE CHILDREN RUNNING LOOSE.
YOU DON'T BELONG HERE! NOBODY LIKES YOU!
ARRRGHHH!

I'M RUNNING OUT OF NEGATIVE THINGS TO SAY ABOUT THIS PLACE. I HATE IT AND I WANT OUT.

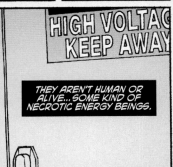

HIGH VOLTAGE KEEP AWAY

THEY AREN'T HUMAN OR ALIVE...SOME KIND OF NECROTIC ENERGY BEINGS.

THERE'S NO TELLING WHAT ELSE IS UP HERE.

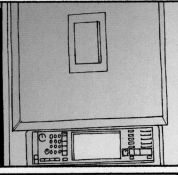

THE LIGHT CUTS RIGHT THROUGH MY PAIN DAMPENERS. THAT'S NOT SUPPOSED TO HAPPEN.

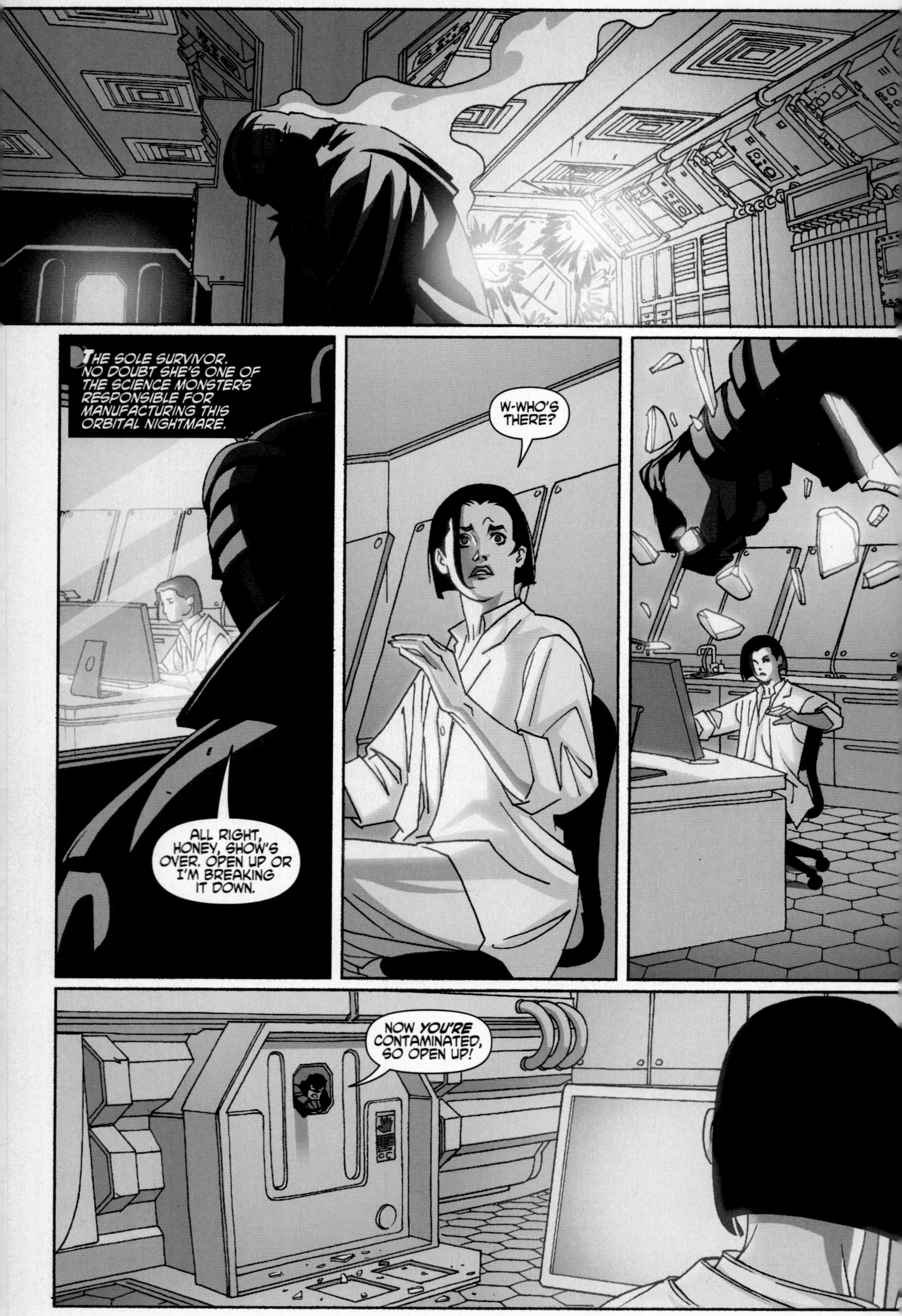
THE SOLE SURVIVOR. NO DOUBT SHE'S ONE OF THE SCIENCE MONSTERS RESPONSIBLE FOR MANUFACTURING THIS ORBITAL NIGHTMARE.
ALL RIGHT, HONEY, SHOW'S OVER. OPEN UP OR I'M BREAKING IT DOWN.
W-WHO'S THERE?
NOW *YOU'RE* CONTAMINATED, SO OPEN UP!

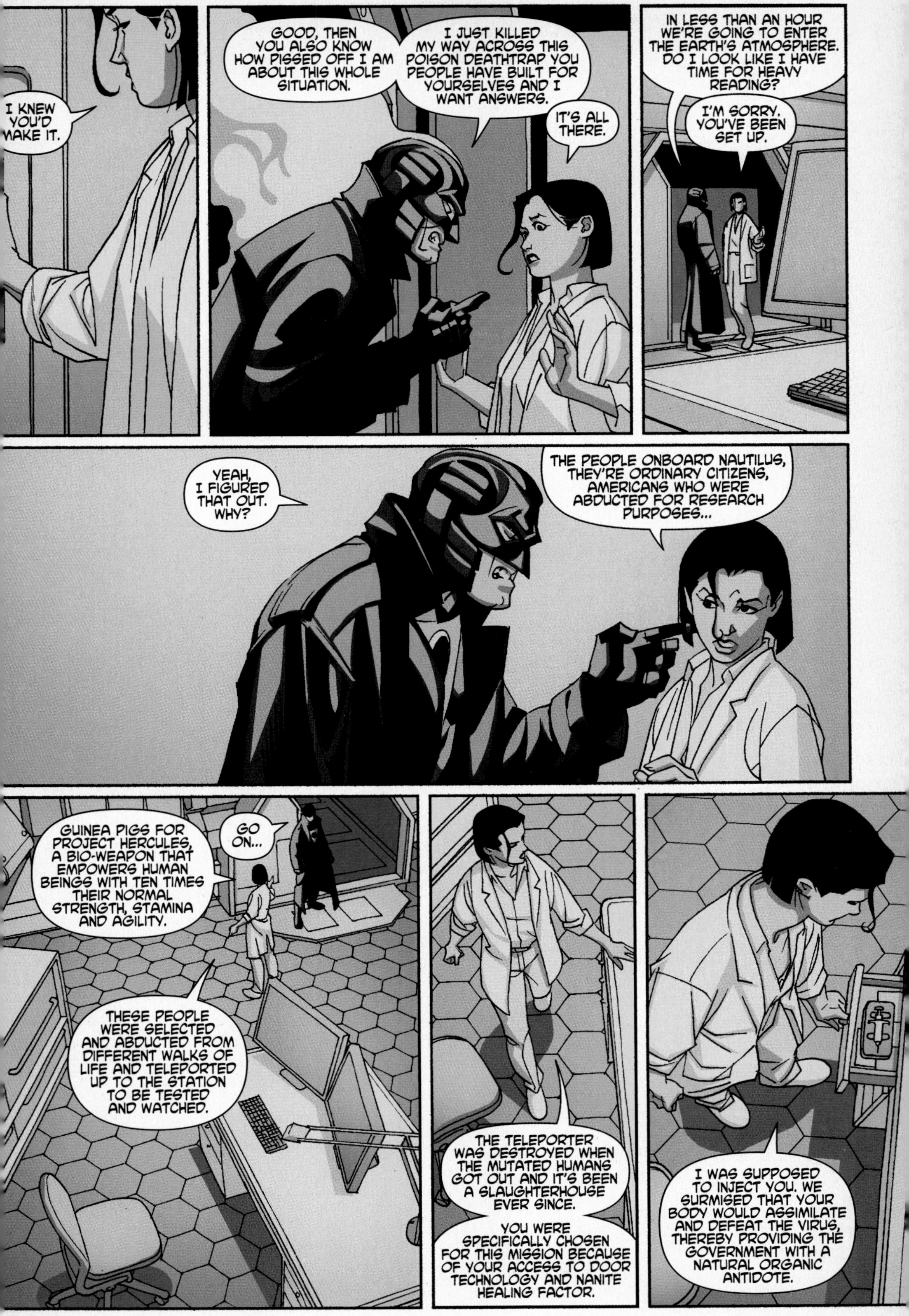
I KNEW YOU'D MAKE IT.
GOOD, THEN YOU ALSO KNOW HOW PISSED OFF I AM ABOUT THIS WHOLE SITUATION.
I JUST KILLED MY WAY ACROSS THIS POISON DEATHTRAP YOU PEOPLE HAVE BUILT FOR YOURSELVES AND I WANT ANSWERS.
IT'S ALL THERE.
IN LESS THAN AN HOUR WE'RE GOING TO ENTER THE EARTH'S ATMOSPHERE. DO I LOOK LIKE I HAVE TIME FOR HEAVY READING?
I'M SORRY. YOU'VE BEEN SET UP.
YEAH, I FIGURED THAT OUT. WHY?
THE PEOPLE ONBOARD NAUTILUS, THEY'RE ORDINARY CITIZENS, AMERICANS WHO WERE ABDUCTED FOR RESEARCH PURPOSES...
GUINEA PIGS FOR PROJECT HERCULES, A BIO-WEAPON THAT EMPOWERS HUMAN BEINGS WITH TEN TIMES THEIR NORMAL STRENGTH, STAMINA AND AGILITY.
GO ON...
THESE PEOPLE WERE SELECTED AND ABDUCTED FROM DIFFERENT WALKS OF LIFE AND TELEPORTED UP TO THE STATION TO BE TESTED AND WATCHED.
THE TELEPORTER WAS DESTROYED WHEN THE MUTATED HUMANS GOT OUT AND IT'S BEEN A SLAUGHTERHOUSE EVER SINCE.
YOU WERE SPECIFICALLY CHOSEN FOR THIS MISSION BECAUSE OF YOUR ACCESS TO DOOR TECHNOLOGY AND NANITE HEALING FACTOR.
I WAS SUPPOSED TO INJECT YOU. WE SURMISED THAT YOUR BODY WOULD ASSIMILATE AND DEFEAT THE VIRUS, THEREBY PROVIDING THE GOVERNMENT WITH A NATURAL ORGANIC ANTIDOTE.

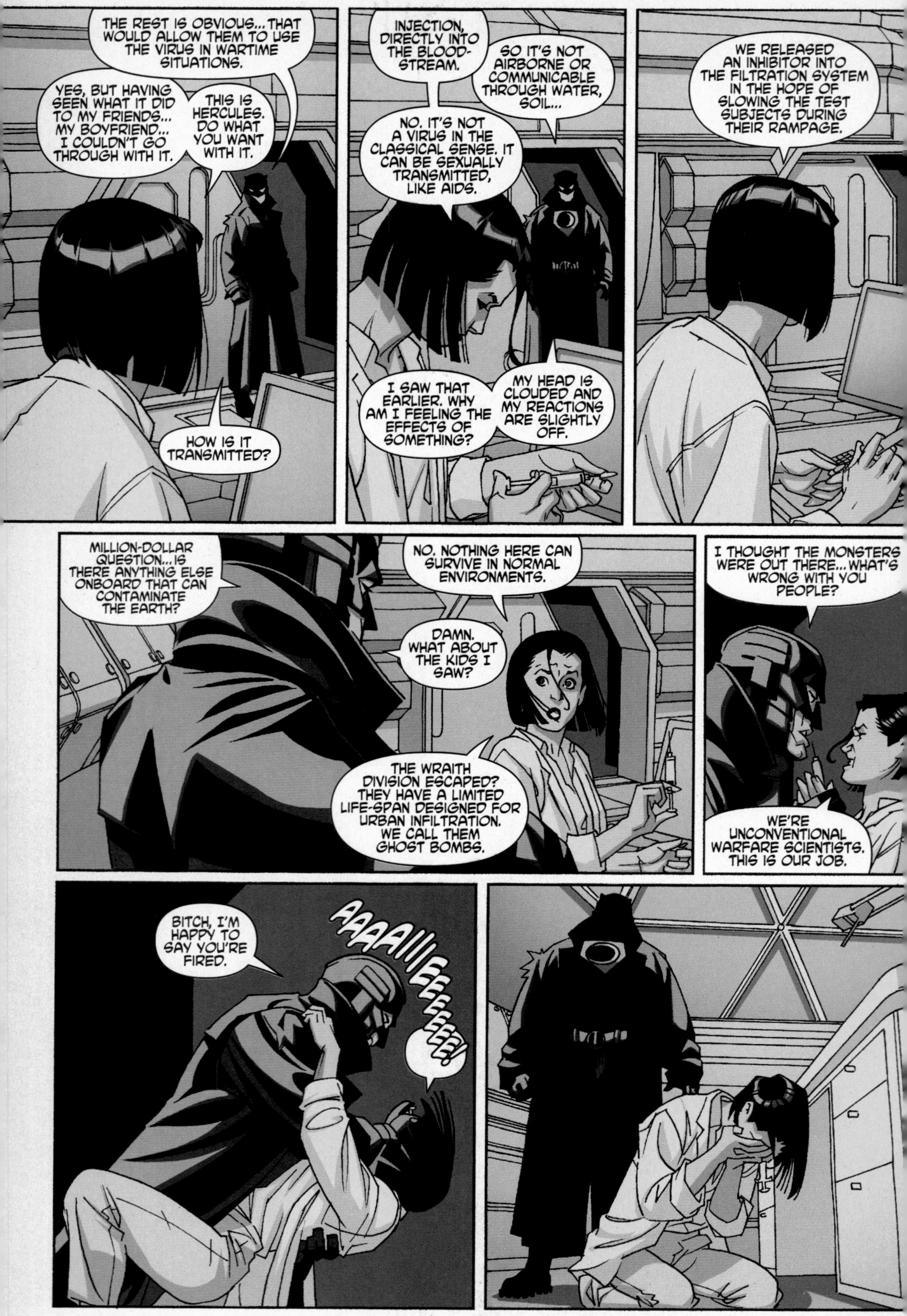
THE REST IS OBVIOUS... THAT WOULD ALLOW THEM TO USE THE VIRUS IN WARTIME SITUATIONS.
YES, BUT HAVING SEEN WHAT IT DID TO MY FRIENDS... MY BOYFRIEND... I COULDN'T GO THROUGH WITH IT.
THIS IS HERCULES. DO WHAT YOU WANT WITH IT.
HOW IS IT TRANSMITTED?
INJECTION, DIRECTLY INTO THE BLOOD-STREAM.
SO IT'S NOT AIRBORNE OR COMMUNICABLE THROUGH WATER, SOIL...
NO. IT'S NOT A VIRUS IN THE CLASSICAL SENSE. IT CAN BE SEXUALLY TRANSMITTED, LIKE AIDS.
I SAW THAT EARLIER. WHY AM I FEELING THE EFFECTS OF SOMETHING?
MY HEAD IS CLOUDED AND MY REACTIONS ARE SLIGHTLY OFF.
WE RELEASED AN INHIBITOR INTO THE FILTRATION SYSTEM IN THE HOPE OF SLOWING THE TEST SUBJECTS DURING THEIR RAMPAGE.
MILLION-DOLLAR QUESTION... IS THERE ANYTHING ELSE ONBOARD THAT CAN CONTAMINATE THE EARTH?
NO. NOTHING HERE CAN SURVIVE IN NORMAL ENVIRONMENTS.
DAMN. WHAT ABOUT THE KIDS I SAW?
THE WRAITH DIVISION ESCAPED? THEY HAVE A LIMITED LIFE-SPAN DESIGNED FOR URBAN INFILTRATION. WE CALL THEM GHOST BOMBS.
I THOUGHT THE MONSTERS WERE OUT THERE... WHAT'S WRONG WITH YOU PEOPLE?
WE'RE UNCONVENTIONAL WARFARE SCIENTISTS. THIS IS OUR JOB.
BITCH, I'M HAPPY TO SAY YOU'RE FIRED.
AAAAIIIEEEEEEEE!

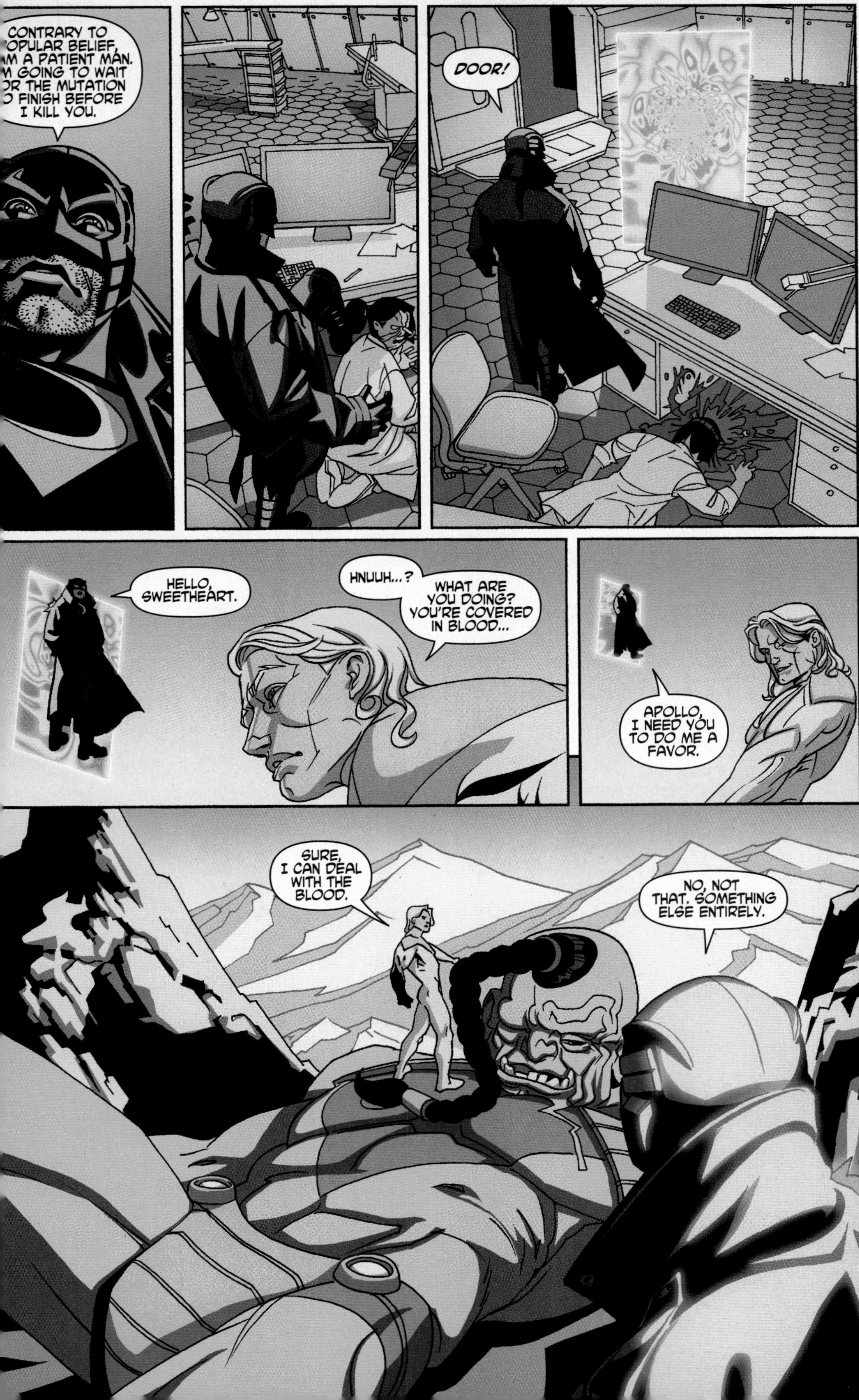
CONTRARY TO
POPULAR BELIEF,
AM A PATIENT MAN.
M GOING TO WAIT
OR THE MUTATION
O FINISH BEFORE
I KILL YOU.
DOOR!
HELLO, SWEETHEART.
HNUUH...?
WHAT ARE YOU DOING? YOU'RE COVERED IN BLOOD...
APOLLO, I NEED YOU TO DO ME A FAVOR.
SURE, I CAN DEAL WITH THE BLOOD.
NO, NOT THAT. SOMETHING ELSE ENTIRELY.

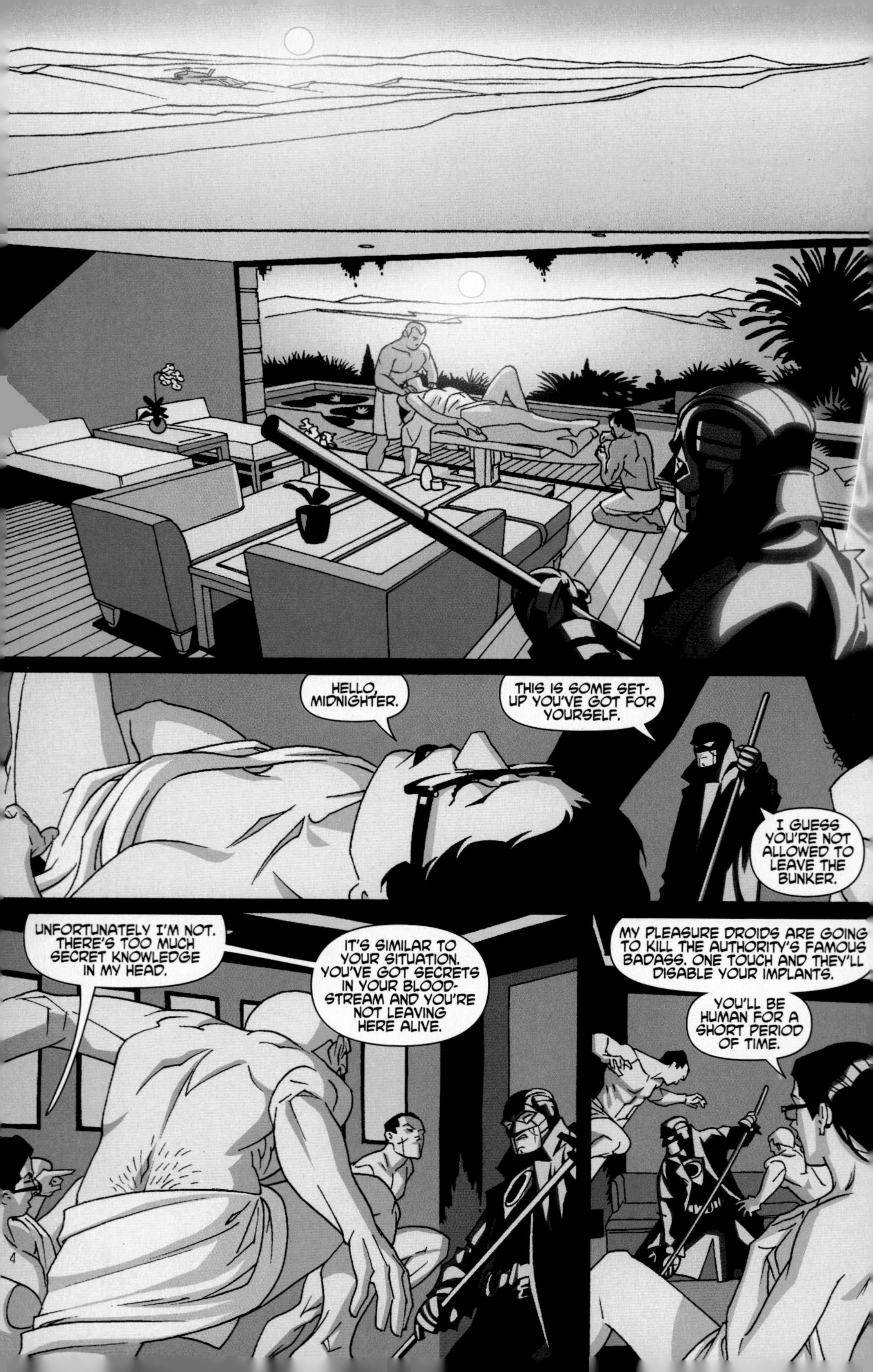
HELLO, MIDNIGHTER.
THIS IS SOME SET-UP YOU'VE GOT FOR YOURSELF.
I GUESS YOU'RE NOT ALLOWED TO LEAVE THE BUNKER.
UNFORTUNATELY I'M NOT. THERE'S TOO MUCH SECRET KNOWLEDGE IN MY HEAD.
IT'S SIMILAR TO YOUR SITUATION. YOU'VE GOT SECRETS IN YOUR BLOOD-STREAM AND YOU'RE NOT LEAVING HERE ALIVE.
MY PLEASURE DROIDS ARE GOING TO KILL THE AUTHORITY'S FAMOUS BADASS. ONE TOUCH AND THEY'LL DISABLE YOUR IMPLANTS.
YOU'LL BE HUMAN FOR A SHORT PERIOD OF TIME.

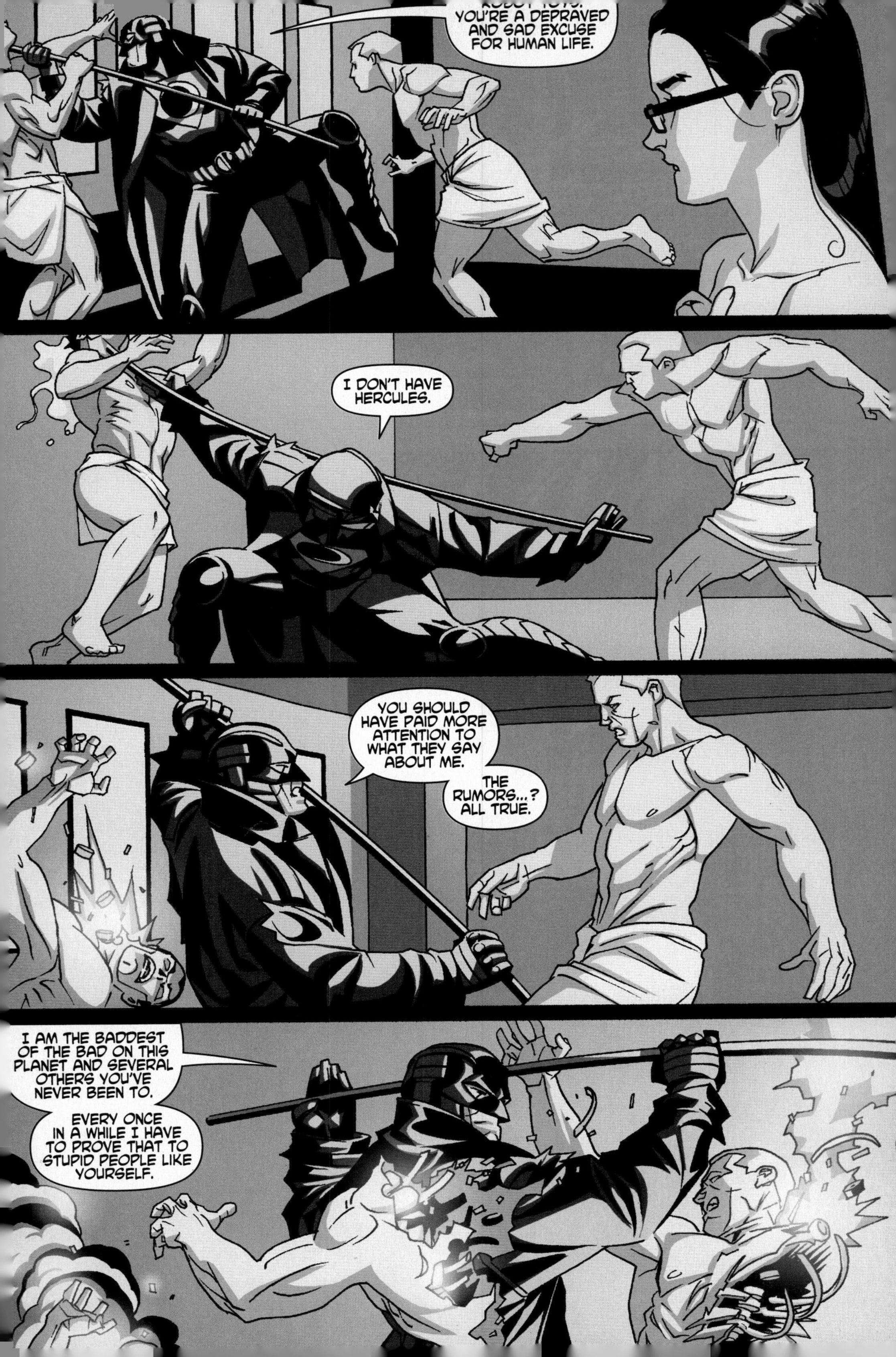
YOU'RE A DEPRAVED AND SAD EXCUSE FOR HUMAN LIFE.
I DON'T HAVE HERCULES.
YOU SHOULD HAVE PAID MORE ATTENTION TO WHAT THEY SAY ABOUT ME.
THE RUMORS...? ALL TRUE.
I AM THE BADDEST OF THE BAD ON THIS PLANET AND SEVERAL OTHERS YOU'VE NEVER BEEN TO.
EVERY ONCE IN A WHILE I HAVE TO PROVE THAT TO STUPID PEOPLE LIKE YOURSELF.

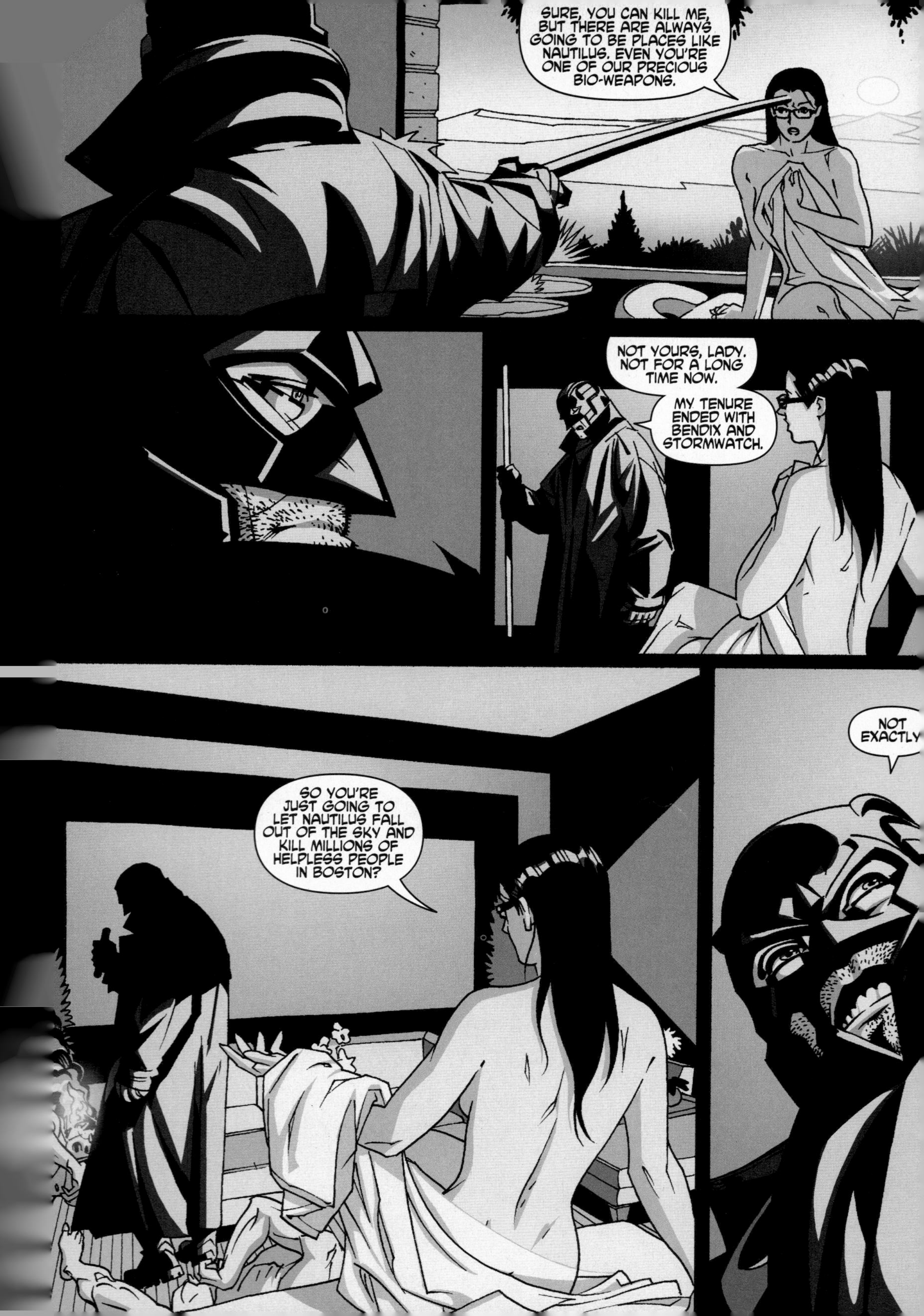
SURE, YOU CAN KILL ME, BUT THERE ARE ALWAYS GOING TO BE PLACES LIKE NAUTILUS. EVEN YOU'RE ONE OF OUR PRECIOUS BIO-WEAPONS.
NOT YOURS, LADY. NOT FOR A LONG TIME NOW.
MY TENURE ENDED WITH BENDIX AND STORMWATCH.
SO YOU'RE JUST GOING TO LET NAUTILUS FALL OUT OF THE SKY AND KILL MILLIONS OF HELPLESS PEOPLE IN BOSTON?
NOT EXACTLY

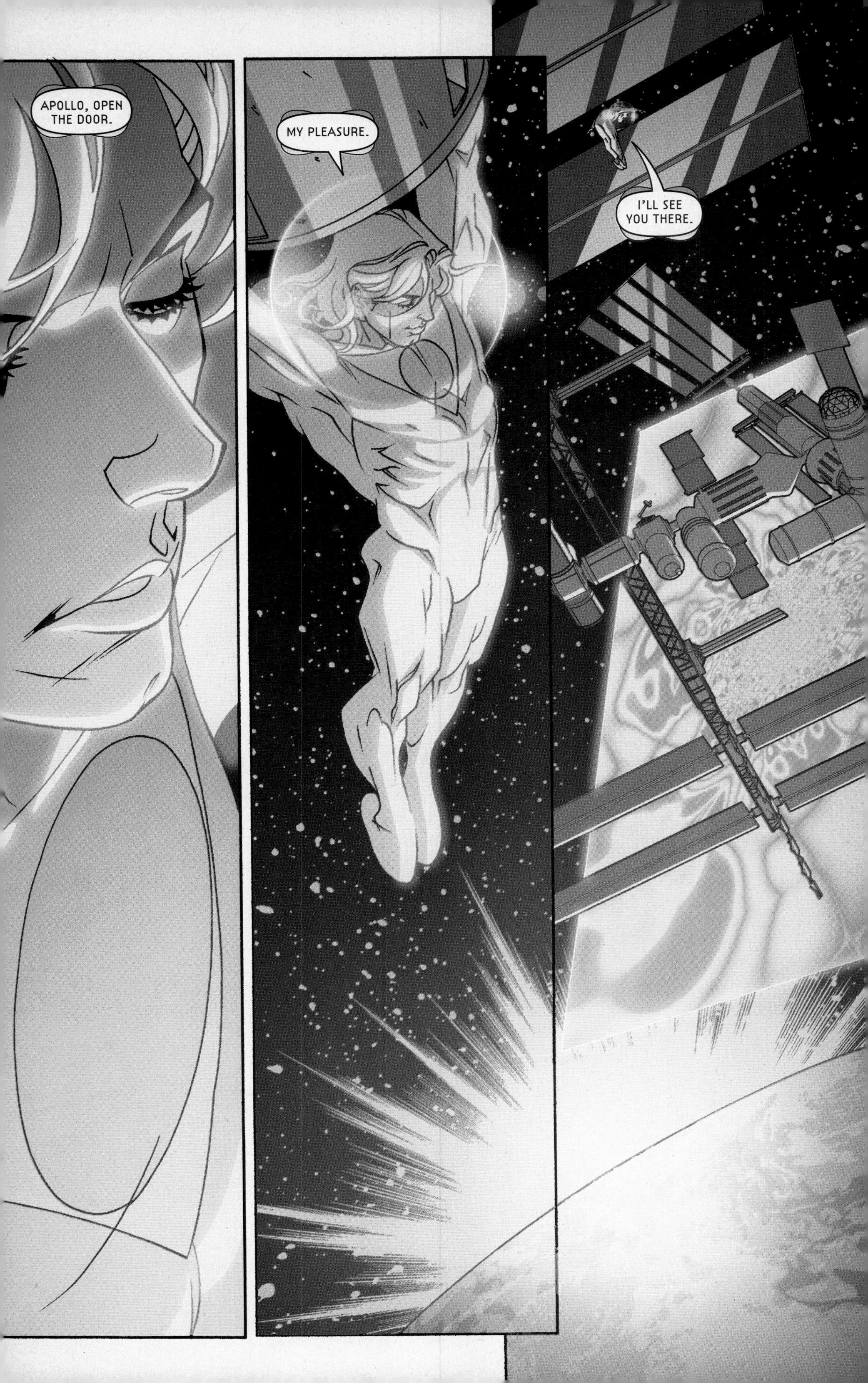
APOLLO, OPEN THE DOOR.
MY PLEASURE.
I'LL SEE YOU THERE.

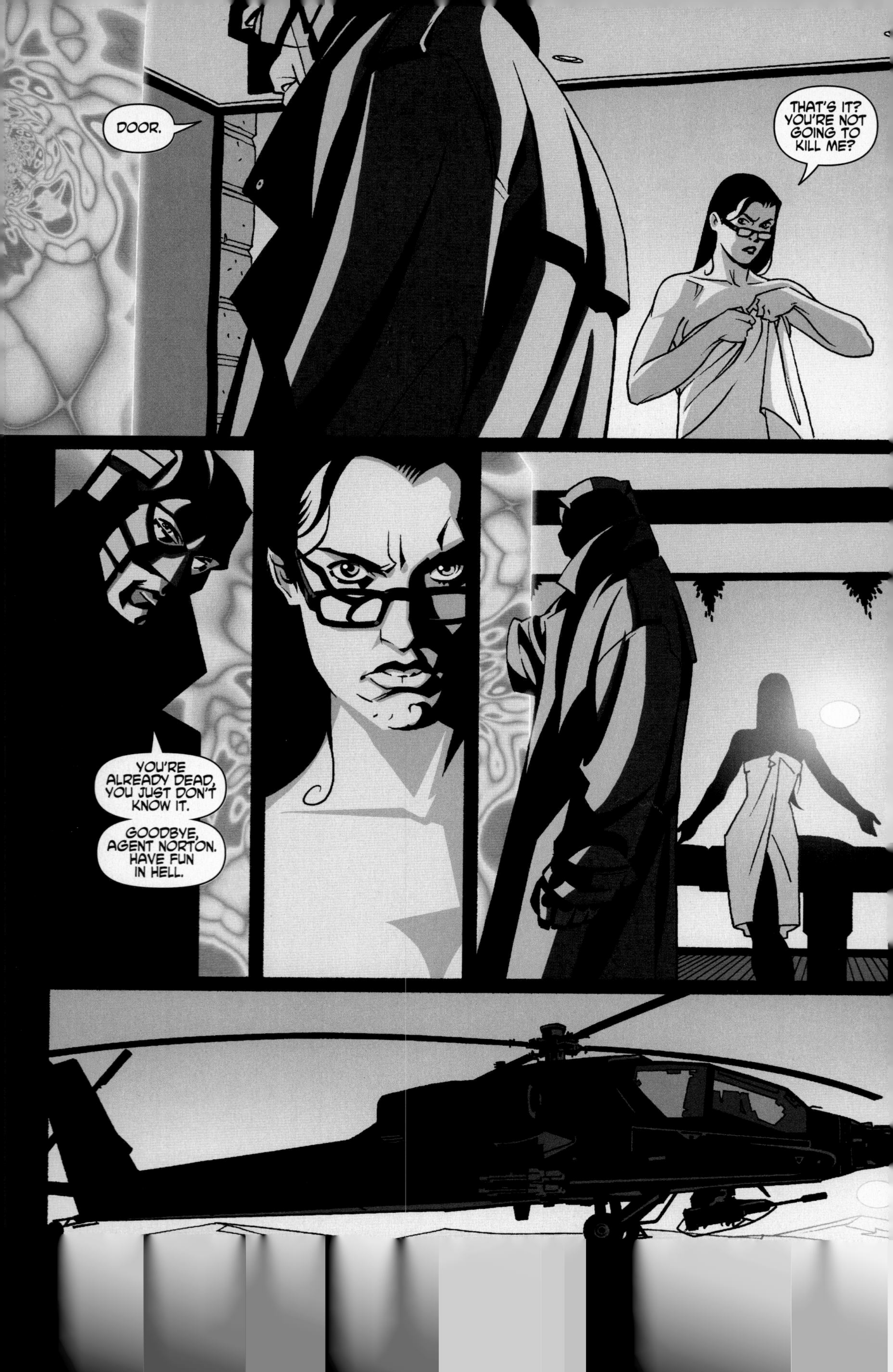
DOOR.
THAT'S IT? YOU'RE NOT GOING TO KILL ME?
YOU'RE ALREADY DEAD, YOU JUST DON'T KNOW IT.
GOODBYE, AGENT NORTON. HAVE FUN IN HELL.

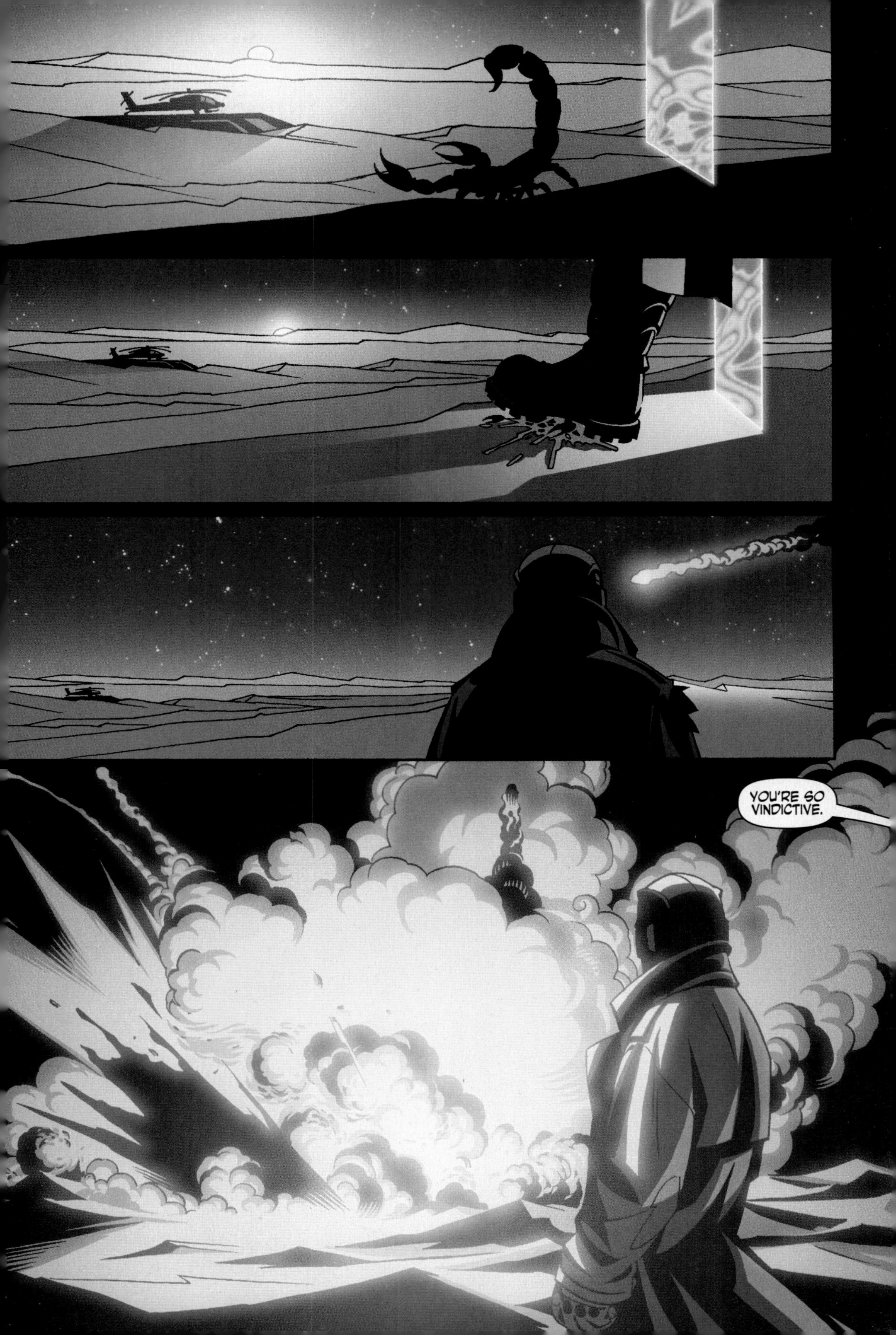
YOU'RE SO VINDICTIVE.

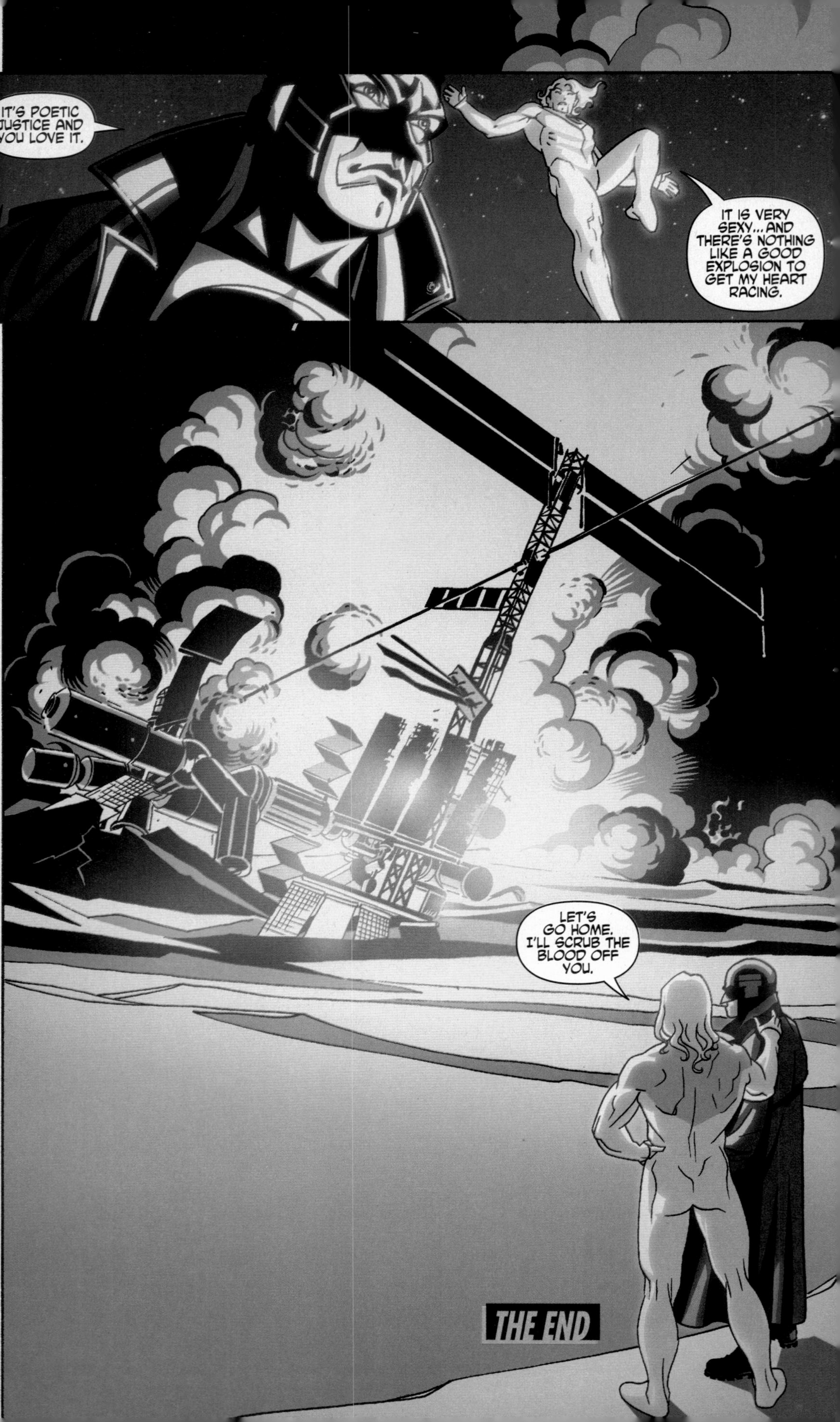
IT'S POETIC JUSTICE AND YOU LOVE IT.
IT IS VERY SEXY... AND THERE'S NOTHING LIKE A GOOD EXPLOSION TO GET MY HEART RACING.
LET'S GO HOME. I'LL SCRUB THE BLOOD OFF YOU.
THE END